THE
SUPREME COURT
AND
AMERICAN
DEMOCRACY

David G. Barnum
DePaul University

ST. MARTIN'S PRESS
New York

Senior editor: Don Reisman
Managing editor: Patricia Mansfield-Phelan
Project editor: Amy Horowitz
Production supervisor: Alan Fischer
Art director: Sheree Goodman
Photo research: Inge King
Cover design: Jeanette Jacobs Design
Cover photo: The Image Bank © Pamela J. Zilly

Manufactured in the United States of America.
76543
fedcba

For information, write:
St. Martin's Press, Inc.
175 Fifth Avenue
New York, NY 10010

ISBN: 0-312-06106-4 (paperback)
       0-312-08686-5 (hardcover)

Library of Congress Cataloging-in-Publication Data

Barnum, David G.
   The Supreme Court and American democracy / by David G. Barnum.
       p. cm.
   Includes bibliographical references and index.
   ISBN 0-312-08686-5 (cl.)—ISBN 0-312-06106-4 (pbk.)
   1. United States. Supreme Court. 2. Political questions and judicial power—United States. 3. Judicial review—United States.
   I. Title.
   KF8742.B334   1993
   347.73′26—dc20
   [347.30735]   92-50012
                                                       CIP

For
Anne Ridings Barnum
and
Robert A. Horn

Preface

In the 1830s a French administrative official named Alexis de Tocqueville toured the United States. The purpose of his visit was to evaluate the American prison system, but the lasting and celebrated outcome of his travels was the publication in Paris in 1835 and 1840 of his classic study *Democracy in America*.[1] Among the many famous insights contained in Tocqueville's book was his observation that, in the United States, "[s]carcely any political question arises . . . that is not resolved, sooner or later, into a judicial question."[2]

Tocqueville's reference to the close relationship between law and politics has become a mainstay of commentary on American society. Tocqueville was the first of many to note that, in the United States, law and politics are inseparable, and that one manifestation of this inseparability is the frequency with which political and social issues are translated into legal questions to be decided by the courts.

In 1907 Charles Evans Hughes reminded an audience to which he was speaking that law and politics are inseparable. In the process, he added new layers of meaning to Tocqueville's insight. At the time of his address, Hughes was governor of New York, and he went on to serve as an associate justice of the Supreme Court (1910–1916) and later as chief justice of the United States (1930–1941). "We are under a Constitution," Hughes said, "but the Constitution is what the judges say it is."[3]

Hughes's statement is important because it highlights the disturbing but inevitable fact that a written document such as the U.S. Constitution gains meaning through interpretation and that those who interpret the Constitution are fallible human beings. The point Hughes was making — that judges participate in making as well as applying law — was reiterated with even greater punch by Jeremiah Smith. Smith taught law at the Harvard Law School after a career on the New Hampshire Supreme Court. "Do judges make law?" Smith asked. "Course they do. Made some myself."[4]

The insights embodied in these three quotes — that law and politics are inseparable, that judges make law by virtue of their power to interpret written materials such as statutes and constitutional provisions, and that judicial decisions have policy implications — were at one time quite shocking. In the early part of the nineteenth century, or even in the early part of this century, most Americans probably believed that the sole job of judges was — and should be — to apply the law, and that politics and law were — and should remain — distinct.

We are no longer so naive. We have come to accept the notions that judges are fallible human beings, that courts make public policy, and that politics play a pervasive role in both the selection of judges and the formulation of judicial answers to legal questions. Courts are *judicial* institutions, and the judges who staff them are responsive to a distinctive set of norms with roots in the *legal culture* of the United States. At the same time, few, if any, decision-making institutions in any real society can escape the influence of politics. In the United States, courts and judges are no exception to this rule.[5]

The fact that most Americans would no longer be shocked to learn that an intimate relationship exists between law and politics does not mean, however, that the relationship itself is no longer significant or interesting. On the contrary, it is more important than ever for Americans to understand how law and politics relate to one another. In addition, it is more important than ever for Americans to develop their views on the normative dimensions of the problem: that is, to confront the question of what the relationship between law and politics *should be*, as well as the question of what that relationship *is*.

The Supreme Court and American Democracy seeks to address some of the key factual and normative questions that arise from the interaction of law and politics in the United States. The book is about the Supreme Court and its place in the American system of democratic self-government, and it has three specific purposes: (1) to provide accurate and up-to-date information about the Supreme Court as an institution and about the judicial and political system of which it is a part; (2) to convey the flavor of the process of constitutional litigation in the United States; and (3) to explore the critical normative question of the Court's role in American democracy.

The three parts of the book correspond to these three purposes. In *Part I*, we examine the American judicial system and the various courts of which it consists. We also examine the appellate process in American law — that is, the process by which cases move from the lower courts up to the U.S. Supreme Court. Finally, we look at the Supreme Court's internal operation and at patterns and trends in the Court's decision making.

Part II focuses on the process of constitutional litigation in the United States. We examine seven prominent Supreme Court cases, each of which we trace from its origins in society to its eventual resolution by the Supreme Court. The purpose of this part is to convey a sense of the excitement and complexity of the process of constitutional litigation. An additional purpose is to bring the material in Part I down to earth by providing concrete examples of how cases arise, how they move upward through the judicial system, and how the Supreme Court deals with them.

Part III focuses directly on the question of the Supreme Court's role in American democracy. The Court occupies a curious place in our constitutional order. On the one hand, it formulates public policy on a number of important issues that affect many aspects of our lives. On the other hand, none of its nine members is elected or is in any other way directly accountable to the American people. The Supreme Court is therefore exempt from one of the key "rules of the game" of democratic politics — the rule that governmental decision makers should be accountable to the people. The purpose of Part III is to explore the question of whether and how the power of the Supreme Court can be reconciled with the fundamental principles of democratic self-government.

The book begins with a chapter that sets the stage for the material that follows. In Chapter 1, we explore the origins of the Supreme Court's power of judicial review of legislation. We then turn to a discussion of the fundamental principles of democratic politics. We conclude by asking whether the Supreme Court's exercise of the power of judicial review is compatible with the fundamental principles of American democracy.

Throughout the book, the reader will find extensive references to additional sources of information about the Supreme Court and its decisions. These references include books and articles by legal scholars on issues of constitutional law and constitutional theory, as well as empirical studies by political scientists (and others) on Supreme Court decision making and the relationship between the Supreme Court and its political environment. These references are meant to provide students with a solid foundation for further research on the various issues raised in the text.

Acknowledgments

I welcome the opportunity to express my gratitude to a number of people who have helped in the preparation of this book. Michael Perry provided valuable feedback on several portions of the book and in particular helped me to sharpen my views on the normative issues discussed in Chapter 14. Ira Carmen was a stimulating, encouraging, and irreverent companion on those all-too-rare occasions when we could discuss our mutual interest in the Supreme Court and its work. Several colleagues at DePaul — including Michael Mezey, Larry Bennett, Patrick Callahan, and Harry Wray — provided intellectual and moral support during the long gestation of the book. Various grants and leaves provided by the College of Liberal Arts and Sciences and the University Research Council helped to expedite completion of the book. On several occasions I sought assistance from staff and students at DePaul —

including Lisa Milam, Mata Binteris, Eric Emad, Joe Baker, Lynn Horowitz, and Michelle Byczek—and in every instance the people to whom I turned were helpful, courteous, professional, and prompt. Don Reisman of St. Martin's Press made numerous sound suggestions about the content and organization of the book and supervised its development with consummate skill and patience.

Finally, I received a host of excellent suggestions from several reviewers: Elizabeth Bussiere, University of Massachusetts, Boston; Robert A. Carp, University of Houston; John Culver, California Polytechnic State University; Carl E. Meacham, State University of New York, College at Oneonta; John K. Price, Louisiana Tech University; Joseph Ripple, Missouri Western State College; Elliot E. Slotnick, Ohio State University; and Frank Way, University of California, Riverside. To the extent I was able to implement these suggestions, the book is clearly better than it would otherwise have been. For any remaining errors and ambiguities, I accept full responsibility.

DAVID G. BARNUM

Notes

1. Alexis de Tocqueville, *Democracy in America*, 2 vols. (New York: Vintage Books, 1960).
2. Id. at Vol. 1, p. 290.
3. *Addresses and Papers of Charles Evans Hughes* (1908), p. 139.
4. Quoted in Paul Freund, *On Understanding the Supreme Court* (1951), p. 3.
5. For examinations of the American legal system that emphasize the connections between law and politics, see Louis Fisher, *Constitutional Dialogues: Interpretation as Political Process* (1988); Herbert Jacob, *Law and Politics in the United States* (1986); and Walter F. Murphy and C. Herman Pritchett (eds.), *Courts, Judges, and Politics*, 4th ed., (1986). See also Richard Hodder-Williams, "Six Notions of 'Political' and the United States Supreme Court," 22 *Brit. J. Pol. Sci.* 1 (1992).

Contents

THE
SUPREME COURT
AND
AMERICAN DEMOCRACY

CHAPTER 1

Introduction:
The Supreme Court
in the Constitutional Order

T he U.S. Supreme Court, like the other institutions of American government, is a product of the Constitution. When the fifty-five delegates to the Constitutional Convention assembled in Philadelphia in the summer of 1787, one of their tasks was to define the basic contours of a judicial system to serve the new nation. The framers' conclusions were eventually embodied in Article III of the Constitution. "The judicial Power of the United States," they wrote, "shall be vested in one supreme Court, and in such inferior Courts as the Congress may from time to time ordain and establish."[1]

An overriding concern of the framers of the new Constitution was to establish a government that would be powerful enough to govern but not so powerful as to threaten the rights of the people. Thus, the framers focused repeatedly on the question of how much power to allocate to each of the three branches of government. Of the three branches of government, the available evidence suggests that the framers were least concerned about the power of the "one supreme Court" established by Article III.

Alexander Hamilton was one of the principal framers of the Constitution, and he argued that the Supreme Court would be the weakest of the three branches of government (or "departments of power," as they were sometimes called). Hamilton's views, along with those of James Madison and John Jay, were embodied in a series of essays known as the *Federalist Papers*.[2] In "Federalist No. 78," Hamilton wrote that

> Whoever attentively considers the different departments of power must perceive that . . . the judiciary, from the nature of its functions, will always be the least dangerous to the political rights of the Constitution. . . . The executive not only dispenses the honors, but holds the sword of the community. The legislature not only commands the purse, but prescribes the rules by which the rights and duties of every citizen are to be regulated. The judiciary, on the contrary, has no influence over either the sword or the purse. . . . It may truly be said to have neither FORCE nor WILL, but merely judgment; and must ultimately depend upon the aid of the executive arm even for the efficacy of its judgments.[3]

1

For several years after the Constitution was ratified, Hamilton's predictions about the relative weakness of the Supreme Court proved to be rather accurate. Congress specified by law that the Court would consist of six justices, and on September 24, 1789, President Washington made his initial nominations. One of Washington's nominees declined to serve, however, and another resigned within two years. During the next few years, additional nominees declined to serve, and several justices were regularly absent from the Court because they were involved in the pursuit of other responsibilities.

The Court's initial meeting as one of the three co-equal branches of American government was particularly inauspicious. When the Court assembled for the first time, on February 1, 1790, only three justices were present. The lack of a quorum was not a serious problem, however, because the Court had no cases to decide. In fact, it had no cases to decide during the first three years of its existence. All in all, the early Supreme Court did not give much hint that it was destined for future greatness—or even that it had much future at all.

It has now been more than two hundred years since the Supreme Court assembled for the first time. In stature and power, the modern Court has come a long way from the rather forlorn institution that could not muster a quorum on its first day of operation in 1790. The Court's emergence as a major player in the political process was noted by constitutional scholar Alexander Bickel, who wrote, in 1962, that "[t]he least dangerous branch of the American government is the most extraordinarily powerful court of law the world has ever known."[4] The modern Supreme Court has become a truly co-equal branch of the American government and enjoys a worldwide reputation for independence and activism.[5]

Today few would dispute that the Supreme Court has become an "extraordinarily powerful court of law." One hallmark of American democracy, however, is a certain skepticism about the idea of governmental power. When any institution of American government becomes extremely powerful, serious questions are going to be raised—and should be raised—about the scope and legitimacy of its decision-making activities. The Supreme Court is no exception. The power of the Supreme Court, like the power of Congress and the president, does not and should not escape scrutiny.

In the case of the Supreme Court, however, there is an added dimension to the debate. The Supreme Court wields great power. At the same time, certain features of the Court set it apart from most other institutions of American government, including both Congress and the presidency. The purpose of this chapter is to highlight those features and to frame the important questions that consequently arise about the Court's role in American democracy.

The chapter is divided into two sections. In the first section, we examine the origins of the Court's power of judicial review. Judicial review is among the recognized powers of the Supreme Court, but its exercise raises serious questions about the role of the Supreme Court in American democracy. The

second section examines the meaning of the word *democracy*. We \
what qualities make the Supreme Court "different" from other institutic
American government and why this difference has led to persistent allegat.
that the Supreme Court's decision making is an undemocratic component
the political process.

The Origin and Development
of Judicial Review

The U.S. Supreme Court exercises what is known as the power of judicial
review, which may be defined as the Court's power to overturn or invalidate
acts of Congress, and other legislative acts, on the ground that they conflict
with the U.S. Constitution. Judicial review is among the most important
powers exercised by the Supreme Court. At the same time, this power has
provoked the most serious concerns about the Court's role in American
democracy.

The events that culminated in the Supreme Court's assumption of the
power of judicial review make a fascinating story. They occurred relatively
early in our political history, and they came about as a direct consequence of
the United States' adoption of a written Constitution.

Judicial Review and a Written Constitution

The American political system is based on a written Constitution. The Constitution identifies the three branches of government, describes the powers
they possess, and stipulates what procedures must be followed in passing laws
and accomplishing other governmental objectives. The American Constitution, though brief, is a blueprint for our entire governmental system.

At the time the United States was founded in 1787, written constitutions
were a rarity. Few other societies were based on a single, written document.
Especially conspicuous among the countries that had no written constitution
was England, the country to which the framers traced their origins. The
framers resolved to break with tradition, however, and to embody their
designs for a new government in a written document.[6]

One of the principal purposes of a written constitution is to place limits
on government. The theory of a written constitution is that no governmental
institution—and certainly no individual public official—is all powerful.
Under a written constitution, the power of governmental officials and governmental institutions flows *from* the constitution and is subject to limitations
prescribed *in* the constitution.

The framers of the U.S. Constitution were emphatic in their belief that
the United States should be governed by a written constitution and that
everyone should understand the implications of this fact. Toward the end of
the Constitution—in Article VI—they included a provision that is known as

the Supremacy Clause, namely, "This Constitution, and the Laws of the United States which shall be made in Pursuance thereof . . . shall be the supreme Law of the Land; and the Judges in every State shall be bound thereby, any Thing in the Constitution or Laws of any State to the Contrary notwithstanding."

The Supremacy Clause and Its Implications

The wording of the Supremacy Clause makes it clear that one of the framers' primary concerns was to establish the supremacy of the new national government over the existing state governments. Thus, they stipulated that both the Constitution and "the Laws of the United States" — that is, laws passed by Congress, or what we usually call federal laws — shall be the "supreme Law of the Land."

It is also clear from the Supremacy Clause — although not as clear as it might be — that the framers regarded the relationship between the Constitution and federal law to be an unequal one. The framers apparently assumed that it was possible for a federal law to fail to satisfy the requirements of the Constitution. Thus, in the Supremacy Clause they asserted that federal laws, in order to join the Constitution in the category described as the "supreme Law of the Land," must be made "in Pursuance" of the Constitution.

If this interpretation of the Supremacy Clause is correct, it means that anytime there is a conflict between the Constitution and federal law, or between the Constitution and state law, the Constitution must prevail. Most people would concede that this is an inescapable implication of living in a society that is governed by a written Constitution. More importantly, the framers were trying to achieve precisely this goal when they adopted a written constitution in the first place.

If this is what the framers intended to achieve, however, obviously they neglected to address one very important issue. The Constitution is a document — a piece of paper — and it cannot enforce itself. However, if the Constitution is superior to ordinary law, someone or something will need to decide when there is a conflict between the Constitution and ordinary law and what to do about it. A real society governed by a written constitution requires a mechanism to enforce the supremacy of that constitution. Otherwise that supremacy will be purely hypothetical and will have no practical significance in the everyday affairs of the society.

Somewhat surprisingly, the Constitution itself is completely silent on this critical issue. No language anywhere in the Constitution stipulates what person or what institution will be empowered to resolve alleged conflicts between the Constitution and ordinary law. This glaring omission created a classic political vacuum. Ready to fill that vacuum, as it happened, was the Supreme Court under the leadership of John Marshall.

John Marshall and the Origins of Judicial Review

The man who is credited with establishing the practice of judicial review in the United States is John Marshall, the fourth chief justice of the Supreme Court. Later in this book we will discuss the Marshall Court's various contributions to the development of American constitutional law. For now, however, our concern is with the origins of judicial review. At the time John Marshall became chief justice, it was unclear which of the institutions of American government, if any, would have the power to enforce the supremacy of the Constitution. Marshall found a way to claim that power for the Supreme Court.

The case that established the Supreme Court's power of judicial review was *Marbury* v. *Madison*, decided in 1803. In order to understand the case itself, however, we must first know something about the politics of the founding period of American history.

Politics in the Founding Period

America's first Constitution, the Articles of Confederation, went into effect in 1781. The national government under the Articles of Confederation was extremely weak, however, and during the 1780s an assortment of political leaders called for the creation of a stronger government under a new Constitution. Their efforts led to the Philadelphia Convention of 1787 and to the drafting of a new Constitution. A principal purpose of the new document, in the view of the framers, was to substantially strengthen the national government.

In the months that followed the Philadelphia Convention, the question of whether to ratify the new Constitution was debated in each of the existing thirteen states. In the debates over ratification, the proponents of the new Constitution adopted the name "Federalists." Their opponents were forced to settle, reluctantly, for the name "Anti-Federalists." In Chapter 2, we explore the political divisions between the Federalists and the Anti-Federalists in more detail. Those divisions had a profound impact on the whole process by which the American judicial system was formed. One particular consequence of the rivalry between them was that it dictated the timing and circumstances of the establishment of judicial review.

John Adams, the second president of the United States, was a Federalist. When he ran for reelection in 1800, he faced Thomas Jefferson, leader of the newly emergent Republican party. Jefferson defeated Adams, and Adams's defeat brought to a close a lengthy era of Federalist domination of American politics.

The Federalists, however, were not about to completely disappear from the political scene. Although they were forced to leave the White House, they resolved to perpetuate themselves in power in other ways. Thus, before he left the presidency, in 1801, Adams appointed a number of staunch Federalists to lifetime judicial positions. One of those appointments was Adams's choice of John Marshall (who had been Adams's secretary of state) to become chief justice of the United States.

Marbury v. Madison (1803)

Marbury v. *Madison* was among the first cases the Supreme Court decided under Marshall's leadership. The plaintiff in the *Marbury* case, William Marbury, was, like Marshall and Adams, a Federalist. He had been appointed to a low-level judgeship by Adams as part of the Federalists' last-ditch effort to retain some of their former political power. Through an oversight, however, Marbury had not actually received his commission by the time Adams left office, and the newly elected president, Thomas Jefferson, refused to deliver it. The case arose when Marbury sued James Madison (Jefferson's secretary of state) to obtain the commission.

Marbury chose to invoke the "original jurisdiction" of the Supreme Court, that is, to file his case directly in the Supreme Court, without going first to a lower court. Marbury based his decision on a provision of federal law — Section 13 of the Judiciary Act of 1789 — which indicated, in Marbury's opinion, that his case was one of those that Congress had assigned to the original jurisdiction of the Supreme Court.

Marbury's suit presented John Marshall with a serious political dilemma. As a fellow Federalist, Marshall undoubtedly believed that Marbury was entitled to his commission. If Marshall decided in Marbury's favor, however, Jefferson would almost certainly ignore the decision and humiliate the Court. Thus, while Marshall wanted to rule in Marbury's favor, it seemed that he could not do so without jeopardizing the power and dignity of the Supreme Court.

Marshall's solution to this predicament was to rule *against* Marbury but in the process to claim for the Court the power of judicial review of legislation. He held that Marbury was entitled to his commission, but he also held that Section 13 of the Judiciary Act — the provision of federal law on which Marbury had relied to invoke the original jurisdiction of the Supreme Court — was unconstitutional. Thus, according to Marshall, Marbury had improperly brought his case directly to the Supreme Court and was not entitled to judicial relief.

The Political and Constitutional Significance of *Marbury* v. *Madison*

The principal significance of Chief Justice Marshall's decision in *Marbury* v. *Madison*, of course, is that it established that the Supreme Court was entitled, through the exercise of its power of judicial review of legislation, to enforce the supremacy of the Constitution. The decision has acquired an especially romantic aura, however, because it represented a classic example of "snatch-ing victory from the jaws of defeat." In the words of one commentator, the decision was "a masterwork of indirection, a brilliant example of Marshall's capacity to sidestep danger while seeming to court it, to advance in one direction while his opponents are looking in another."[7]

Later in this book, in Chapter 14, we look at the specific argument that John Marshall crafted to justify his conclusion that the Supreme Court should exercise the power of judicial review. In brief, Marshall relied heavily on the fact that the United States is governed by a written Constitution. He argued that "all those who have framed written constitutions contemplate them as forming the fundamental and paramount law of the nation, and consequently, the theory of every such government must be, that an act of the legislature repugnant to the constitution is void. This theory is essentially attached to a written constitution, and is, consequently, to be considered, by this court, as one of the fundamental principles of our society."[8] Marshall purported to find an incompatibility between (1) the definition of the Supreme Court's original jurisdiction contained in Article III of the Constitution and (2) the scope of the Court's original jurisdiction as authorized by Section 13 of the Judiciary Act of 1789. He concluded that the discovery of this incompatibility left the Supreme Court no choice — under our written Constitution — but to strike down the offending provision of federal law.

There is an unending debate among legal scholars about the soundness of Marshall's opinion in *Marbury* v. *Madison*.[9] The consequences of the deci-sion, however, are beyond dispute. From *Marbury* onward, the Supreme Court has exercised the power of judicial review of legislation, that is, the authority to determine the meaning of the Constitution and to enforce the supremacy of the Constitution in cases of alleged conflict between the Con-stitution and ordinary law.[10]

Judicial Review in American History

Marbury v. *Madison* was the Supreme Court's first exercise of its power of judicial review. The Court in *Marbury* held that a provision of federal law — Section 13 of the Judiciary Act of 1789 — was unconstitutional. A few years later, in *United States* v. *Peters* (1809) and *Fletcher* v. *Peck* (1810), the Court handed down its first decisions overturning state statutes.

Since these early decisions, the Court has exercised its power of judicial review on many occasions. According to one compilation, the Court had overturned 130 acts of Congress (in whole or in part) by the end of its 1987 term. In that same period, the Court had declared unconstitutional 1,058 state statutes.[11]

Clearly, the Supreme Court's exercise of judicial review is significant in purely quantitative terms. In attempting to assess the significance of this power, however, it is also important to note some of the specific cases in which the Court has overturned a state or federal law. The Supreme Court's decision in *Brown* v. *Board of Education* (1954), which overturned state statutes requiring racial segregation of public schools, is widely regarded as the Court's most important decision in this century. A few years later, in the "school prayer decisions," *Engel* v. *Vitale* (1962) and *School District of Abington Township* v. *Schempp* (1963), the Court ruled that prayer in public schools violated the constitutional separation of church and state. In 1973, in *Roe* v. *Wade*, the Court held that the Constitution protects a woman's right to choose to have an abortion.

The 1980s produced additional controversial examples of the Court's exercise of its power of judicial review. In a case called *Immigration and Naturalization Service* v. *Chadha* (1983), the Court held that a technique used extensively by Congress to control the executive branch — the "legislative veto" — was not compatible with the constitutional doctrine of separation of powers.[12] Three years later, in *Bowsher* v. *Synar*, the Court overturned a key portion of the Gramm-Rudman Act — the attempt by Congress to curb the phenomenal growth of the federal budget — concluding that Congress in passing the law had again violated the constitutional doctrine of separation of powers.[13] In *Texas* v. *Johnson* (1989) and *United States* v. *Eichman* (1990), the Court invalidated state and federal statutes that prohibited burning the flag as an act of protest.

We will explore some of these cases in detail later in this book. For now we will simply note that Supreme Court decisions may and do affect the lives of millions of people. From this perspective, the Supreme Court is clearly a major player in the American political process.

The question to which we must turn is whether it is entirely appropriate for the Supreme Court to have the power, in the American democracy, to make such sweeping decisions. The fact that the United States is a democracy means that its political system is based on certain basic principles. The Supreme Court appears to violate some of those principles. The Court's failure to conform to some of the basic principles of democracy, in turn, raises serious questions about the legitimacy of its power of judicial review.

Judicial Review and American Democracy

What is a democracy and why are democracies different from other kinds of political systems? Political theorists and practicing politicians have been wrestling with these questions for centuries, and of course, there are no easy answers. It is possible, however, to identify some of the fundamental principles that have emerged from the long debate over the meaning of democracy. Our goal in this section is to identify those principles, after which we apply them to the Supreme Court to make a preliminary assessment of the Court's role in American democracy.[14]

Fundamental Principles of Democracy

The starting point of most theories of democracy is the concept of *popular sovereignty*. In this view, what is distinctive about democracy is that the exercise of decision-making power by governmental leaders rests on "the consent of the governed." In other political systems, political power may be passed from generation to generation within families or may be acquired or retained by brute force or deception. By contrast, in a democracy, citizens retain the right to choose for themselves the persons who will exercise decision-making power in their behalf. No aspiring political leader is entitled to exercise governmental power without first seeking the authority to do so from the people, and no incumbent public official is entitled to continue in office unless he or she is willing to return to the voters for renewed authorization to govern.

In practice, a political system that depends on the consent of the governed usually takes the form of a *representative democracy*. For a variety of reasons, it is not practical for all the people to be directly involved in every policy decision. Thus, popular control of governmental decisions is implemented through a system of representation. Elections are held at periodic intervals, prospective leaders present themselves as candidates for office, and citizens express their preference for particular candidates by the act of voting. The candidates who win gain the right to represent the people for a specified period of time—usually two, four, or six years—at which time the office-holder must return to the voters to seek approval for a further term.

Political theorists often go on to argue that a political system cannot qualify as a genuine representative democracy unless certain specific conditions are met. Elections, for instance, must be held at reasonably frequent intervals. Virtually all adult citizens must be eligible to vote, and every citizen's vote must be weighted equally. The electoral process must not be contaminated by coercion or corruption, and voting itself must take place by means of a secret ballot. Aspiring candidates must be free to form political organizations and to campaign openly for the office they seek. Freedom of speech and press must be protected, and voters must have access to various sources of information—not just information supplied, for instance, by the government itself—so they can make an informed choice among candidates. Political theorists are in broad agreement that a political system cannot be considered a democracy unless the foregoing conditions—often subsumed under the headings *political equality* and *political liberty*—have been met.

The most common basis for making decisions in a democracy is majority rule. It is here that serious disagreements may arise among political theorists, but ordinarily what is in dispute is whether *all* decisions in a democracy *should* be made by majority rule, not whether *most* decisions in a democracy *are* made by majority rule. In most democracies most of the time, majority rule determines the outcome of disputes. Moreover, it governs the outcome of disputes that lie at the very heart of the democratic process. Majority rule determines the winner in contested elections between two candidates for legislative office, and it also determines which of the many proposals that are introduced in a legislative body will be enacted into law.

In sum, a political system qualifies as a democracy if it has succeeded in making governmental decision makers politically accountable to the people. The most common mechanism for achieving this goal is the periodic election. Moreover, both the electoral process and the legislative process must be governed by principles of political equality, political freedom, and majority rule. Political theorist H. B. Mayo has synthesized these principles into the following working definition of democracy. A democratic political system, Mayo says, "is one in which public policies are made, on a majority basis, by representatives subject to effective popular control at periodic elections which are conducted on the principle of political equality and under conditions of political freedom."[15]

The Supreme Court and Democratic Principles

How well does the U.S. Supreme Court conform to the foregoing criteria by which the democratic character of a political system is judged? The answer, many allege, is "Not very." In several respects, the Supreme Court violates key principles that distinguish a democracy from other types of political systems.

Consider, first, the way in which Supreme Court justices are chosen. They are appointed by the president and confirmed (by a majority vote) by the Senate. We will discuss the appointment process in more detail in Chapter 13. Here it is sufficient to note that the process fails to conform to the bedrock principle that political leaders in a democracy must be directly accountable to the public through periodic elections. The public has indirect influence over the appointment process through the president and members of the Senate. Clearly, however, vacancies on the Supreme Court are not filled by contested elections involving two or more candidates, nor is any American citizen ever allowed to cast a personal vote for or against a particular nominee. The appointment process therefore differs significantly from the basic mechanism —the contested election—by which leaders in a democratic system are ordinarily chosen.

Consider, second, the extraordinary job security of Supreme Court justices. According to Article III of the Constitution, Supreme Court justices "shall hold their Offices during good Behaviour." The framers did not define what they meant by *good Behaviour.* In practice, however, it means that Supreme Court justices—and in fact all federal judges—are appointed "for life." Again, we will have occasion to discuss the job security of Supreme Court justices in more detail later (in Chapter 12). Clearly, however, to a politician who must run for office every two, four, or six years, the life tenure enjoyed by Supreme Court justices must seem like a very sweet arrangement indeed!

Consider, third, the way in which Supreme Court justices are removed from office. To say that justices enjoy life tenure is not quite accurate, because the Constitution provides a mechanism for removing justices from office involuntarily. The mechanism is impeachment, and, according to Article II of the Constitution, it applies to the president, the vice president, and "all civil Officers of the United States." As we will see, however, impeachment is a difficult process to implement—it requires a majority vote in the House and a two-thirds vote in the Senate—and for these and other reasons it is rarely used. Once again, we can see that a major difference exists between elected officials—who face the risk of being removed from office at the next election—and Supreme Court justices—who only have to worry about the unlikely possibility of being impeached.

Finally, consider the unusual finality of the Supreme Court's interpretations of the meaning of the Constitution. Most policy decisions in the United States can be changed by an ordinary exercise of the legislative process, that is, by a majority vote of Congress or the legislature of a particular state. Reversal of a constitutional decision of the Supreme Court, however, is not so easy. If the Supreme Court decides that the Constitution has a particular meaning— for instance, that it protects a woman's right to obtain an abortion or a person's right to burn the flag as an act of protest—the Court's decision can be reversed only by amending the Constitution itself. According to Article V, amendment requires a two-thirds vote in both houses of Congress, plus ratification by three-fourths of the state legislatures. Clearly, amending the Constitution is far more difficult than enacting ordinary legislation. In this sense, the Supreme Court is able to frustrate the democratic process, and once again it becomes clear that its power is not entirely compatible with the basic principles of democratic self-government.

Is the Supreme Court Undemocratic?

These special features of the Supreme Court have led several observers to allege that the Supreme Court's exercise of the power of judicial review is countermajoritarian, that is, that it violates the fundamental democratic principle of majority rule by elected representatives. Other observers have argued, simply, that judicial review is undemocratic. Many critics level both charges simultaneously.

A prominent reference to the undemocratic character of judicial review is contained, for instance, in Justice Felix Frankfurter's dissent in *West Virginia State Board of Education* v. *Barnette* in 1943. We will explore the Court's decision in *Barnette*, the so-called flag salute case, in Chapter 5. The case involved two children who were Jehovah's Witnesses and who, on the basis of their religious beliefs, declined to take part in flag salute ceremonies at their school. They were expelled from school for their disobedience. In the Supreme Court, they argued that expulsion violated their constitutional right to freedom of religion, and a majority of the Supreme Court agreed. Justice

Frankfurter filed a dissenting opinion, however, in which he alluded to the tension between judicial review and democratic self-government. "The reason why from the beginning even the narrow judicial authority to nullify legislation has been viewed with a jealous eye," he wrote, "is that it serves to prevent the full play of the democratic process. The fact that it may be an undemocratic aspect of our scheme of government does not call for its rejection or its disuse. But it is the best of reasons . . . for the greatest caution in its use."[16]

The allegation that Supreme Court decision making violates fundamental principles of democracy was repeated in *Roe* v. *Wade* in 1973. *Roe* is an extremely controversial decision, and we will examine the case itself in Chapter 10. In his dissenting opinion in *Roe*, Justice Byron White argued that the Supreme Court was wrong to hold that states were prevented by the Constitution from passing laws against abortion. The issue of abortion, he said, "should be left with the people and to the political processes the people have devised to govern their affairs."[17]

Members of the Supreme Court have also taken the opportunity to question the democratic character of judicial review in off-the-court remarks. A particularly emphatic assertion of the Court's dubious role in a political democracy was included in a 1976 law school address by then-Associate Justice William Rehnquist. "[T]hose who have pondered the matter," Rehnquist said, "have always recognized that the ideal of judicial review has basically antidemocratic and antimajoritarian facets that require some justification in this Nation, which prides itself on being a self-governing representative democracy."[18]

Finally, as recently as 1990, Justice Anthony Kennedy repeated the charge that policy making by unelected judges is not necessarily consistent with fundamental principles of democratic self-government. His remarks were included in his concurring opinion in a complicated Supreme Court decision involving the power of the lower federal courts to order school districts to levy taxes to pay for school desegregation. Kennedy questioned the propriety of allowing the federal courts to interfere with local control of tax levels. "Today's casual embrace of taxation imposed by the unelected, life-tenured federal judiciary," he wrote, "disregards fundamental precepts for the democratic control of public institutions."[19]

Scholarly Criticism of Supreme Court Decision Making

Criticism of judicial review has not been confined to the justices themselves. Supreme Court scholars have also expressed concern about its undemocratic character. One of the best known examples of such concern appears in Alexander Bickel's 1962 book, *The Least Dangerous Branch*. "The root difficulty," Bickel wrote, "is that judicial review is a counter-majoritarian force in our system. . . . [W]hen the Supreme Court declares unconstitutional a legislative act or the action of an elected executive, it thwarts the will of representatives of the actual people of the here and now; it exercises control, not in behalf of the prevailing majority, but against it. That . . . is the reason the charge can be made that judicial review is undemocratic."[20]

In developing his argument that, as he puts it, judicial review is "a deviant institution in the American democracy,"[21] Bickel reaches back to the fundamental principles of democracy which we outlined in our earlier discussion. In democratic theory and practice, he writes, "nothing can finally depreciate the central function that is assigned . . . to the electoral process; nor can it be denied that the policy-making power of representative institutions, born of the electoral process, is the distinguishing characteristic of the system. Judicial review works counter to this characteristic."[22]

Clearly, many thoughtful people have expressed skepticism about the wisdom of conferring upon unelected, life-tenured judges the power to overturn the decisions of duly elected legislative representatives. Supreme Court decisions that overturn legislation are examples of countermajoritarian judicial decision making in a political system that is otherwise based on principles of electoral accountability and majority rule. It follows, for some, that judicial review is an undemocratic feature of the American political system.

The Undemocratic Character of Judicial Review: One Response

One response to the accusation that judicial review is undemocratic, of course, is to note that judicial review may not be the only countermajoritarian feature of American politics. That being the case, it is sometimes argued, it is unfair to single out judicial review for condemnation.

In fact, observers have been able to find a wealth of evidence to support the conclusion that American politics is hardly a pristine example of majoritarian democracy in action.[23] The Constitution itself contains several features that may frustrate the majoritarian political process. The electoral college, for instance, is a constitutionally prescribed institution that permits a presidential candidate to be elected even though he or she has received less than a majority (or even a plurality) of the popular vote. The Constitution also stipulates that every state, regardless of population, is entitled to have two representatives in the Senate. Under this arrangement, it is theoretically possible that a majority of fifty-one Senators could be assembled — and could pass legislation — even though they represented only about 15 percent of the American population. Finally, the Constitution prescribes that the president may veto legislation and that a presidential veto may be overridden only by a two-thirds majority of both houses of Congress. In the wake of a presidential veto, therefore, a minority of legislators — consisting of 33 percent plus one of the members of either house of Congress — can frustrate the passage of legislation.

Several features of the electoral process offer even clearer evidence that American democracy does not operate purely on majoritarian principles. In recent elections, for instance, the turnout of voters has rarely exceeded 50 percent of those who are eligible to vote. In addition, many voters are quite poorly informed, and almost no voter will be completely familiar with the policy positions of every candidate on every issue. Finally, the influence of money or the advantages enjoyed by incumbent candidates may distort the outcome of elections. For these and many other reasons, the electoral process is not necessarily an ideal mechanism for translating popular preferences into policy outcomes.

The strength of the linkage between the electoral process and the legislative process is also unclear. Within Congress, committees and committee chairmen have disproportionate power and may be able to block the passage or even the consideration of legislation that enjoys majoritarian support. In addition, pressure from special interests and lobbying groups may succeed in producing countermajoritarian policy outcomes. Moreover, on some issues some of the time, legislators may feel it is simply inappropriate to follow public preferences. Finally, even when they would like to follow the will of the majority, legislators may find it impossible to do so, because some public preferences are unknown. Opinion polls are conducted on only a handful of especially prominent issues. On most issues, therefore, politicians will be ignorant of the distribution of opinion among the American people as a whole or among their constituents. For a host of reasons, therefore, there is no guarantee that the legislative process will produce policy outcomes that mirror the preferences of a majority of the American people.[24]

Our Imperfect Democracy: Implications for Judicial Review

Clearly, the political process as it actually operates in the United States is not a perfect example of majoritarian democracy. This fact has potential implications for the debate over the legitimacy of judicial review. Judicial review, it appears, is only one of several countermajoritarian features of the American political system. That being the case, perhaps it does not require any special justification.

Although this position holds some merit, there are at least two compelling reasons to reject it. First, if we accept the idea that political accountability and majority rule are key attributes of a democratic political system, then to defend judicial review as being only one among many countermajoritarian features of American democracy is to argue, in effect, that two wrongs make a right. Bickel is among those who have pointed this out. He concedes that neither the electoral process nor the legislative process is guaranteed to produce outcomes that accurately reflect the will of a popular majority. Nevertheless, he argues, "impurities and imperfections . . . in one part of the system are no argument for total departure from the desired norm in another part."[25]

The second reason why it is unavailing to defend judicial review on the ground that it is only one of many countermajoritarian features of American government is that this defense of judicial review ignores a key element in the argument against judicial review. Judicial review is alleged to be a problematic component of American democracy not only because it may produce countermajoritarian policy outcomes, but also because the public officials who exercise the power of judicial review—Supreme Court justices and other federal judges—are insulated from the electoral process. Unlike other public officials, their performance is not examined by the public at periodic intervals, and they are not subject to removal from office by an ordinary majority of voters. From the point of view of democratic theory, this "defect" in the Supreme Court—the fact that its members are not politically accountable—is not cured by arguing, even successfully, that those branches of government that *are* politically accountable are also capable of producing countermajoritarian policy outcomes.

Conclusion

In short, it appears that the allegation that judicial review is an undemocratic component of the political process has substantial validity. It also appears that the allegation cannot be successfully refuted by arguing that judicial review is only one of several countermajoritarian features of American democracy. Both the Supreme Court as an institution and judicial review as a practice appear to violate fundamental principles that distinguish a democratic political system from other kinds of political systems.

As we embark on our discussion of the Supreme Court and its decisions, we must, therefore, keep in mind that the Court is an unusual institution in American democracy and that judicial review is a practice sorely in need of justification. In Part II of the book, we examine specific examples of the Court's exercise of its power of judicial review, and we will be able to judge for ourselves whether the Court has acted properly and reached correct decisions. In Part III, we examine various arguments designed to reconcile judicial review with majoritarian democracy, and we will be able to judge whether any of these arguments weakens or refutes the persistent allegation that judicial review is an undemocratic feature of the political process.

Before broaching these complex and controversial issues, however, it is important to learn about the Supreme Court as an institution and its place in the American judicial system. We turn now to this matter.

Notes

1. The text of the Constitution is reprinted in many places. Two common locations are textbooks on American government and casebooks on constitutional law.

2. Supporters of the new Constitution had adopted the name of "Federalists." During the battle for ratification of the Constitution, they presented their views in

various forums. The *Federalist Papers* were a series of eighty-five essays that appeared in New York newspapers between October 1787 and April 1788. Their purpose was to convince citizens of New York to vote to ratify the new Constitution. At the time, readers were informed only that the *Federalist Papers* were authored by someone identified as "Publius." The actual authors, however, were Alexander Hamilton, James Madison, and John Jay, and historians have been able to connect most of the essays with one or another of these individuals. There are many published collections of the *Federalist Papers*. Quotations that appear in this book are taken from Roy P. Fairfield (ed.), *The Federalist Papers* (1961).

    3. Alexander Hamilton, "Federalist No. 78," in Fairfield (ed.), *The Federalist Papers*, p. 227.

    4. Alexander M. Bickel, *The Least Dangerous Branch: The Supreme Court at the Bar of Politics* (1962), p. 1.

    5. For a collection of essays presenting overseas perspectives on the Supreme Court, see Louis Henkin and Albert J. Rosenthal (eds.), *Constitutionalism and Rights: The Influence of the United States Constitution Abroad* (1990).

    6. The body of historical scholarship focusing on the founding period is enormous. See, for example, Daniel A. Farber and Suzanna Sherry, *A History of the American Constitution* (1990); J. Jackson Barlow, Leonard W. Levy, and Ken Masugi (eds.), *The American Founding* (1988); Leonard W. Levy and Dennis J. Mahoney (eds.), *The Framing and Ratification of the Constitution* (1987); Leonard W. Levy (ed.), *Essay on the Making of the Constitution* (1987); Bernard Bailyn, *The Ideological Origins of the American Revolution* (1969); and Gordon Wood, *The Creation of the American Republic* (1969).

    7. Robert G. McCloskey, *The American Supreme Court* (1960), p. 40.

    8. *Marbury v. Madison*, 5 U.S. (1 Cranch) 137, 177 (1803).

    9. See, for example, James M. O'Fallon, "Marbury," 44 *Stan. L. Rev.* 219 (1992); and William W. Van Alstyne, "A Critical Guide to Marbury v. Madison," 1969 *Duke L. J.* 1 (1969).

    10. Recent discussions of *Marbury* v. *Madison* and the origins of judicial review include Sylvia Snowiss, *Judicial Review and the Law of the Constitution* (1990); J. M. Sosin, *The Aristocracy of the Long Robe: The Origins of Judicial Review in America* (1989); and Robert Lowry Clinton, *Marbury* v. *Madison and Judicial Review* (1989).

    11. Congressional Research Service, *The Constitution of the United States of America: Analysis and Interpretation* (1987); *1988 Supplement*.

    12. Barbara Hinkson Craig, *Chadha: The Story of an Epic Constitutional Struggle* (1988).

    13. Louis Fisher and Neal Devins, *Political Dynamics of Constitutional Law* (1992), Ch. 4.

    14. The following discussion draws upon H. B. Mayo, *An Introduction to Democratic Theory* (1960). Other excellent discussions of the theory and practice of democracy include J. Roland Pennock, *Democratic Political Theory* (1979); J. Roland Pennock and John W. Chapman (eds.), *Liberal Democracy* (1983); David Held, *Models of Democracy* (1987); Mattei Dogan (ed.), *Comparing Pluralist Democracies: Strains on Legitimacy* (1988); and Robert A. Dahl, *Democracy and Its Critics* (1989).

    15. Mayo, *An Introduction to Democratic Theory*, p. 70.

    16. *West Virginia State Board of Education* v. *Barnette*, 319 U.S. 624, 650 (1943) (Frankfurter, J., dissenting).

    17. *Roe* v. *Wade*, 410 U.S. 113, 222 (1973) (White, J., dissenting).

18. William H. Rehnquist, "The Notion of a Living Constitution," 54 *Tex. L Rev.* 693, 695–96 (1976).

19. *Missouri* v. *Jenkins*, 110 S.Ct. 1651, 1667 (1990) (Kennedy, J., concurring in part).

20. Bickel, *The Least Dangerous Branch*, pp. 16–17.

21. Id. at 18.

22. Id. at 19.

23. For discussions of the many countermajoritarian features of American democracy, see Jesse H. Choper, *Judicial Review and the National Political Process* (1980), Ch. 2; and William R. Bishin, "Judicial Review in Democratic Theory," 50 *S. Cal. L. Rev.* 1099 (1977).

24. For discussions of the complex linkage between public opinion and public policy, see Norman R. Luttbeg (ed.), *Public Opinion and Public Policy* (1981); and Robert Weissberg, *Public Opinion and Popular Government* (1976).

25. Bickel, *The Least Dangerous Branch*, p. 18.

PART I

The Supreme Court in the American Judicial System

W E SAW IN CHAPTER 1 that the Supreme Court exercises the power of judicial review of legislation. Judicial review is among the established powers of the Supreme Court, and in fact the Court overturns local, state, and federal laws with some frequency. As we also noted in Chapter 1, however, many observers have alleged that judicial review constitutes an undemocratic feature of American government. Unlike almost all other officials of American government, Supreme Court justices are not elected, and they cannot be removed from office except by impeachment. The exceptional job security of Supreme Court justices distinguishes them from other governmental decision makers and raises serious questions about the role of the Supreme Court in American democracy.

The overall purpose of this book is to allow students to explore these questions and to resolve, in their own minds, whether the Supreme Court plays an appropriate role in American democracy. The place to begin, however, is with the Court itself. Part I is therefore devoted to explaining how the Supreme Court operates and how it fits into the American judicial system.

Chapter 2 examines the organization and jurisdiction of American courts, focusing specifically on the history of the American judicial system and the origin and development of the federal courts. We also describe the contemporary jurisdiction of the federal courts and the place of the Supreme Court in the overall system of American courts.

Chapter 3 examines the appellate process. Almost all cases that are eventually decided by the Supreme Court were originally decided by one of the lower courts in the American judicial system. This chapter examines the way in which cases move from the lower courts to the Supreme Court and how the Supreme Court selects the cases it will hear and decide.

Chapter 4 focuses on Supreme Court decision making. We explore the internal operation of the Court, the history of the Court's involvement in the political process, and patterns and trends in its decision making.

CHAPTER 2

The Organization and
Jurisdiction of American Courts

The Supreme Court stands at the pinnacle of a large and somewhat complicated judicial system. The system consists of thousands of individual courts in which, in any given year, millions of cases are commenced. Most of the parties to these cases no doubt believe that their case will go "all the way to the Supreme Court." In fact, as we will see, the Supreme Court is very selective about the cases it decides. The pool of cases from which it selects, however, is comprised of cases initially decided by one or another of the lower courts in the American judicial system. These lower courts, together with the cases they decide, are the subject of this chapter.

The chapter is divided into four sections. Section I outlines the basic organization of the American judicial system. Section II focuses on the constitutional politics of the founding period of American history. Section III examines the documents—the Constitution and the Judiciary Act of 1789— that established the federal courts. Finally, Section IV outlines the contemporary jurisdiction of the federal courts.[1]

Organization of the American Judicial System

The American political system is based on the principle of *federalism*. The essence of federalism is the division of governmental power between the states, on the one hand, and the federal or national government, on the other. The organization of the American judicial system is a direct reflection of the federalist principles that animated the framers of the Constitution.[2]

When the Republic was being founded, each state already had its own system of courts. The framers of the Constitution were concerned, however, that state courts—or rather the judges who staffed those courts—would be prejudiced in favor of state and local interests at the expense of the national interest. Thus, the framers established a separate set of federal courts. Today the American judicial system consists of two parallel sets of courts—state courts and federal courts.

The creation of a bifurcated system of courts was a deliberate decision on the part of the framers to extend the concept of federalism into the judicial arena. It was also a political decision, that is, one motivated by the fear that state court judges would be prejudiced against the federal government. As we noted in the Preface, today almost everyone accepts the Supreme Court and other courts as an integral part of the political system and recognizes that Supreme Court decision making does not occur in a political vacuum but in a complex and ever-changing political environment. The subject matter of this chapter serves to remind us that interactions between the Supreme Court and its political environment began as early as the formation of the American judicial system.

Judicial Organization and Political Controversy

The overall organization of the American judicial system is pictured in Figure 2.1. The judicial system as a whole consists of two sets of courts—state courts and federal courts—and each set of courts, in turn, is organized in a hierarchical fashion.

The bottom tier of courts in each system consists of *trial courts*—the courts in which legal disputes, both civil and criminal, will first be heard. The federal judicial system and most state judicial systems also include an intermediate tier of courts, known as *appellate courts* or *courts of appeal*. These are the courts to which a case will be appealed—assuming at least one of the parties to the case chooses to appeal—after the trial court has reached its decision. Finally, each system has a final or highest appellate court, the *supreme court* of the judicial hierarchy.

What makes the American judicial system complicated (and incidentally produces political controversy) is the fact that the lower federal courts are physically located in the states and often share jurisdiction with state courts. There may be a preliminary battle among the lawyers over which court has jurisdiction, that is, which court is entitled to decide the case. In addition, some issues affecting the states are clearly assigned to the jurisdiction of the federal courts, and state citizens may resent the fact that a legal dispute affecting their interests cannot be decided by their "own" state courts and must instead be decided by a federal court. For a variety of reasons, therefore, the way in which American courts are organized makes controversy inevitable.

The Federal Courts: Then and Now

The federal judicial system has been in place since the earliest days of the Republic. The creation of the federal judicial system, however, was a two-stage process. The process began with the drafting and ratification of the

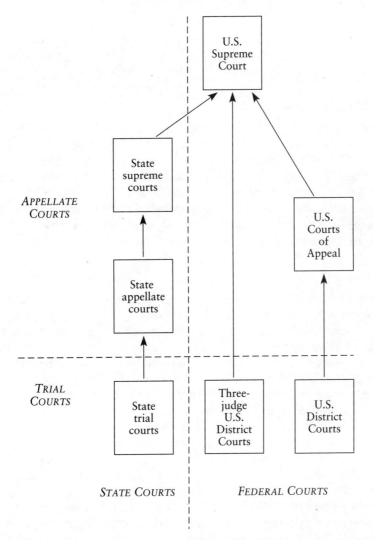

FIGURE 2.1 Courts and Routes of Appeal in the American Judicial System

Constitution in 1787–1788. It was completed with congressional passage of the Judiciary Act of 1789.[3]

The first mention of the federal judicial system appears in Article III of the Constitution. This article specifies that "the judicial Power of the United States"—that is, the federal power to resolve legal disputes—"shall be vested in one supreme Court, and in such inferior Courts as the Congress may from time to time ordain and establish." The text of Article III contains a hint of the political controversy that surrounded the establishment of the federal judicial system. The institution known as the Supreme Court was created by the Constitution itself, and it came into being the moment the Constitution was ratified. The framers of the Constitution were unable to reach a consensus, however, on the shape of the remainder of the federal judicial system. The task of creating that system was delegated to Congress.

The Judiciary Act of 1789

In 1789 the First Congress as its first legislative action passed the Judiciary Act of 1789. The act established thirteen federal district courts (precursors of the modern U.S. District Courts) and three federal circuit courts (precursors of the modern U.S. Courts of Appeal). At the pinnacle of the federal judicial system stood the constitutionally prescribed "one supreme Court."

After two hundred years of development, the federal judicial system has grown tremendously in size and complexity. In its basic organization, however, it closely resembles the system that was put in place in 1789.[4]

U.S. District Courts

The present distribution of federal courts is pictured in Figure 2.2. The federal government is represented in each of the states by at least one U.S. District Court. Some states contain a single district court, while other states — including California, New York, and Texas — contain as many as four. In all, there are ninety-four district courts throughout the country. These ninety-four courts are staffed by about 576 district judges. When a case is being heard by a district court, a single judge presides. In major urban centers, therefore, several cases may be underway simultaneously in the various courtrooms of a single district court. Juries are used in some cases, while in others — known as bench trials — the judge alone presides.

The U.S. District Courts are the "trial courts" of the federal judicial system, that is, the courts in which all cases that fall within the jurisdiction of the federal courts will initially be heard. Such cases may involve a criminal prosecution (for instance, a U.S. government prosecution of drug smugglers or tax evaders) or a civil dispute (for instance, a contractual dispute between two companies). The concept of jurisdiction is explored below. For the moment, we need only note that any case that satisfies the requirements for federal jurisdiction will make its first appearance in a U.S. District Court before a U.S. District judge.[5]

U.S. Courts of Appeal

The U.S. Courts of Appeal comprise the middle tier of the shrinking pyramid of the federal courts. As illustrated in Figure 2.2, eleven courts of appeal hear cases coming from district courts located in states that are divided, for appellate purposes, into the First through Eleventh Circuits. The Court of Appeals for the Seventh Circuit, for instance, is located in Chicago and is responsible for hearing appeals from district courts in Wisconsin, Illinois, and

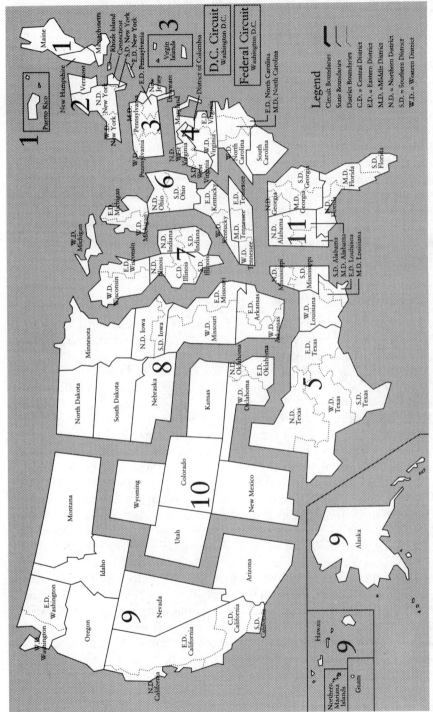

FIGURE 2.2 Geographical Boundaries of U.S. Courts of Appeal and U.S. District Courts (*SOURCE:* The Federal Judicial Center)

Indiana. A twelfth court of appeals serves the District of Columbia Circuit and hears appeals from the U.S. District Court for the District of Columbia (Washington, D.C.). A thirteenth court of appeals — the Court of Appeals for the Federal Circuit, established in 1982 — decides appeals in specialized cases involving customs, patents, and contractual claims against the U.S. government.

The courts of appeal — like the Supreme Court, but unlike the district courts — are *collegial courts*. (A collegial court is one that consists of several judges, rather than a single judge, when hearing a case.) About 168 judges staff the thirteen courts of appeals, and they sit in "panels" of three (and occasionally in larger panels) when deciding cases. There is no jury, and there are no witnesses or first-hand testimony in a case in the court of appeals. The panel of judges makes its decision after reading written briefs submitted by lawyers for the opposing parties and after hearing the lawyers present their oral argument.[6]

Three-Judge U.S. District Courts

We have not yet mentioned one of the courts that is pictured in Figure 2.1 — the so-called three-judge district court. In 1910 Congress enacted legislation that placed certain kinds of federal cases in a class by themselves. The legislation stipulated that if a lawsuit in federal court had two characteristics — e.g., (1) the plaintiff was alleging that a state statute was unconstitutional and (2) the plaintiff was seeking to enjoin enforcement of the statute — the case would have to be heard by an ad hoc district court consisting of *three* judges (including at least one court of appeals judge), and not, as would ordinarily be the case, by a *single* district judge. In addition, as Figure 2.1 indicates, Congress stipulated that cases decided by three-judge district courts could be appealed directly to the U.S. Supreme Court.

Three-judge district courts have played a major role in contemporary American constitutional politics. In fact, of the seven cases we explore in Part II, four began in a three-judge district court. *West Virginia State Board of Education* v. *Barnette* (1943) was a challenge brought by Jehovah's Witnesses to a state statute requiring schoolchildren to salute the flag. *Brown* v. *Board of Education* (1954) was a challenge to state laws requiring or permitting racial segregation of schools. *School District of Abington Township* v. *Schempp* (1963) challenged a Pennsylvania law requiring prayer in public schools. Finally, *Roe* v. *Wade* (1973) (see Chapter 10) challenged a Texas law that outlawed abortion except to save the life of the mother. Each of these cases began in a three-judge district court because (1) it was a challenge to the constitutional validity of a state statute and (2) the plaintiffs in the case — the persons bringing the challenge — were requesting that the court issue an injunction against further enforcement of the challenged statute.

In 1976 Congress severely restricted the jurisdiction of three-judge district courts. As a result, they are no longer as important as they once were. In the two decades between the mid-1950s and the mid-1970s, however, three-judge courts were used by litigants seeking judicial resolution of a wide variety of critical issues of public policy.

Conclusion

One of the most significant features of the American judicial system is its bifurcated structure. Unlike other countries, the United States does not have an integrated set of national courts. Instead, each state has a judicial system of its own, while the nation as a whole is served by a second set of federal courts.

The federal judicial system consists of three levels of courts. The trial courts of the federal system are the district courts. They include both one-judge and three-judge district courts. In 1976 Congress decided to shrink the jurisdiction of three-judge courts, and as a result, such courts are relatively rare today. The intermediate courts of the federal system are the courts of appeal. The U.S. Supreme Court is part of the federal judicial system but stands at the pinnacle of both the state and federal courts.

Throughout American history, the coexistence within individual states of both state and federal courts has been the source of recurrent political and legal tensions. Some view those tensions as one of the chief creative features of the American federal system. Others have a less charitable view of the competition between the state and federal courts — and, more particularly, the tendency of federal courts to "usurp" the jurisdiction of state courts. The rivalry between state and federal courts, and the resulting political tensions, originated in the founding period of American history.

The Political History of the Federal Courts

The creation of a bifurcated system of courts was a deliberate policy decision. At the time the Constitution was being drafted, the only courts in operation were those that had been established by the separate states. The framers of the Constitution were uneasy with the idea that judicial disputes would be decided exclusively by state courts. At the same time, they were acutely aware of the dangers of creating an all-powerful set of federal courts. In the end, they resolved to complement the state courts with a system of federal courts, but they also took pains to circumscribe the power of those courts.

As we might expect, the question of whether to establish a separate system of federal courts was one of the most hotly debated political issues of the time. The reason is clear: The decision to create a federal court system was part of a larger debate over the wisdom of creating a unified political system with a strong central government. Many individuals believed that further unification of the country was essential, and they supported any proposal — including the establishment of a federal court system — that would contribute to this goal. Others in the society, however, were convinced that the new national government was a threat to their local autonomy and their personal liberties. They saw the creation of federal courts as one more step in the dangerous and objectionable process of national centralization.

Federalists and Anti-Federalists

The principal antagonists in the struggle to establish the federal judiciary were known as the Federalists and the Anti-Federalists. The Federalists were proponents of a strong national government. They believed it was essential to establish a full-fledged system of federal courts with as much jurisdiction as possible. The Anti-Federalists, on the other hand, were opposed to creating a strong national government and hoped to prevent the establishment of a separate system of federal courts. As a fallback position, they sought to confine the jurisdiction of federal courts within very narrow limits.

People became deeply exercised by these issues because whoever served as judges in the courts of the new nation would be deciding some very sensitive issues. In particular, those judges would be determining (1) the meaning of congressional statutes, (2) the meaning of state statutes, (3) the meaning of the Constitution, and (4) questions of whether congressional and state statutes were compatible with the Constitution. Judges were human beings, with normal human emotions and biases, and it was unavoidable that those human tendencies—weaknesses, if you will—would play a role in the way in which particular cases were decided. Under the circumstances, a great deal was riding on the question of whether all or most judicial disputes would be decided by federal judges presiding over federal courts or by state judges presiding over state courts.

The Views of the Federalists

The Federalists believed that establishment of a system of federal courts was imperative. Without such courts, all judicial disputes would be decided by state court judges, and the results, in their opinion, would be disastrous. The Federalists had three particular concerns about what would happen if federal courts were not established.

First, state court judges would be solely responsible for determining the meaning of congressional statutes and for enforcing those statutes in particular disputes. The Federalists feared that state court judges would seriously distort and perhaps even nullify the will of Congress in their local areas.

A second fear was based on the possibility that judicial review would become an established practice. If federal courts were not created, state court judges would be able to invalidate federal laws which, in their view, conflicted with the U.S. Constitution or with the constitution of an individual state.

Finally, the Federalists realized that, unless federal courts were created, state court judges, by default, would retain the power to decide whether the laws of their own state did or did not conflict with the U.S. Constitution. The Federalists were convinced that state court judges would rarely bring themselves to decide that a law of their own state violated the U.S. Constitution. The result, in the view of the Federalists, was that conflicts between the Constitution and state laws would almost invariably be resolved in favor of the validity of state laws, and the Constitution, which was supposed to be the supreme law of the land, would become a nullity.

In sum, the Federalists believed that the new Union could not survive unless it was served by a system of federal courts staffed by federal judges. Needless to say, the Anti-Federalists — the opponents of a strong central government — did not agree.

The Views of the Anti-Federalists

The Anti-Federalists believed that the establishment of a system of federal courts would be an unmitigated disaster. No federal judge, they felt, could possibly take an objective view of the meaning of congressional statutes or of conflicts between congressional statutes and state laws. Such judges, the Anti-Federalists believed, would instinctively give an expansive interpretation to federal law and would invariably choose federal law over state law when a conflict arose between the two.

An additional fear of the Anti-Federalists grew out of their realization that judges would be called upon to resolve alleged conflicts between congressional statutes and the Constitution. Constitutional challenges to the validity of congressional laws would often be based on the theory that Congress had improperly interfered with the prerogatives of state governments or the rights of state citizens. If the power to resolve such disputes resided exclusively with federal judges, the outcome of most cases, in the view of the Anti-Federalists, would be a foregone conclusion: Federal judges would rarely conclude that a challenged congressional statute was unconstitutional.

Finally, the Anti-Federalists believed that federal judges would be deeply biased in deciding cases involving a conflict between the U.S. Constitution and the law of a state. The Anti-Federalists were convinced that federal judges would almost automatically rule in favor of constitutional challenges to the validity of state laws and that state laws would be struck down in large numbers.

Obviously, the deepest possible mistrust prevailed between the Federalists and the Anti-Federalists. Each faction dreaded the consequences of conceding victory to the other. At the same time, the two factions were rather evenly matched. As a result, the process of establishing the federal courts took the form of a series of political compromises.

The compromises that emerged from the founding period of American history are readily apparent in the Constitution itself and in early legislation affecting the organization of the judiciary. In particular, the outcome of the political struggle between the Federalists and the Anti-Federalists is embodied in the text of Article III of the Constitution and the text of the Judiciary Act of 1789.

The Constitution and the Law:
Origins of the Federal Judicial System

Article III of the Constitution stipulates that "The judicial Power of the United States, shall be vested in one supreme Court, and in such inferior Courts as the Congress may from time to time ordain and establish." The language of Article III, as we have already seen, is a prime illustration of the delicate balance of political forces at the time. The framers of the Constitution established the Supreme Court, but they deliberately refrained from establishing the lower federal courts. That task — a superb example of what today would be known as a political "hot potato" — was left to members of the First Congress.

Broadly speaking, the members of the First Congress faced four important issues: First, they had to decide whether to establish a system of federal courts at all. Second, assuming such courts were established, they had to decide how they would be staffed, that is, who would be chosen to serve as federal judges and how those choices would be made. Third, the early politicians had to resolve the all-important question of how much jurisdiction the federal courts would possess. Finally, they faced the complicated task of defining the relationship between the state and federal courts.[7]

Creating the Federal Courts

The preeminent question facing the First Congress was whether to establish a system of federal courts at all. Court systems were already in place in each state. In addition, Article III, as drafted, stated that Congress "may" establish inferior courts, not that Congress "must" do so. Thus, Congress had the option of declining to establish a system of lower federal courts.

In fact, as we have seen, Congress decided to complement the existing state court systems with a set of federal courts. The Judiciary Act of 1789 created thirteen district courts and three circuit courts. These courts — along with the Supreme Court, which already existed by virtue of the language of Article III — became the fledgling federal judicial system.

Staffing the Federal Courts

Obviously, the Anti-Federalists had been defeated on what for them was the crucial issue. However, the answers that Congress provided to the second question with which it was faced — the question of staffing the federal courts — represented a concession to the preferences of the Anti-Federalists. The Judiciary Act prescribed that all district courts would be contiguous with state lines, that is, that no district court would straddle the boundary between two states. In addition, the act provided that the president would nominate district judges only from among persons residing in the local area served by a particular district court. Finally, it was decided that before they ascended to the bench, presidential nominees, like Supreme Court justices, would have to be approved by a majority vote of the Senate.

The Judiciary Act of 1789 thus established a system of federal courts but embedded such courts in the political culture of local areas. These concessions to local autonomy were important, because the Constitution prescribes (in Article III, Section 1) that lower federal court judges, like Supreme Court justices, "shall hold their Offices during good Behavior." What this meant, as we have seen, is that federal judges would enjoy life tenure in their jobs and would be subject to removal from office only by the process of impeachment. Given the extraordinary job security of federal judges, the Anti-Federalists were determined to see that judgeships in the federal system were filled by individuals who were familiar with local conditions and were responsive to local preferences.[8]

The decisions reached by the First Congress about creating and staffing the federal courts were important. However, they did not begin to resolve all the disagreements between the Federalists and the Anti-Federalists. Still outstanding were questions of the jurisdiction of the federal courts and the relationship between state courts and federal courts.

Defining the Jurisdiction of the Federal Courts

A court's jurisdiction is the power it is given — or in some cases the power it has seized for itself — to decide particular kinds of cases. Perhaps the clearest example of the concept of jurisdiction is found in the various courts of limited jurisdiction that exist in both the state and federal judicial systems. In a typical state judicial system, for instance, traffic court is empowered to decide only certain kinds of cases — for example, parking violations and speeding offenses. Its jurisdiction does not include cases of robbery or murder, or even cases of personal injury or manslaughter arising from automobile accidents. These cases fall within the jurisdiction of other courts, probably trial courts of general jurisdiction (which in most states are known as district courts or circuit courts). These courts, in turn, ordinarily serve particular geographical areas — typically counties — and cannot decide any cases arising wholly outside their geographical jurisdiction.[9]

Questions of jurisdiction may seem technical to those who are not trained in the law. In fact, such questions often go to the heart of a legal case, and certainly they are intimately related to the politics of the adjudicative process. Often, considerable jockeying takes place among litigants concerning the identity of the court that will decide the case. Almost invariably, this preliminary struggle over jurisdiction arises because the litigants and their lawyers are convinced — rightly or wrongly — that the outcome of the case will be affected by the identity of the court that decides it.

The jurisdiction of the federal courts was a key political issue in 1789. The issue was important because any power that the federal courts possessed would be at the direct expense of the power of the state courts. As we have seen, many people were convinced that federal courts would decide particular cases very differently from state courts. For such people, the scope of the jurisdiction of the federal courts was not a technical issue. What was at stake was not only *who* would decide particular cases but also *how* they would be decided.

The Constitution, Congress, and Federal Jurisdiction

The contemporary jurisdiction of the federal courts derives from two sources: (1) Article III of the Constitution and (2) statutes passed over the years by Congress. Before we examine the scope of that jurisdiction, however, it is important to understand that an "unwritten assumption" governs the relationship between these two sources of federal court jurisdiction.

As a general proposition, of course, the Constitution is "the supreme law of the land." Moreover, Article III contains a rather detailed description of the jurisdiction of the federal courts. This suggests that Article III should be regarded as the definitive source of the jurisdiction of the federal courts. From the earliest days of American history, however, constitutional lawyers have taken the view that the language of Article III is not "self-executing." What this means is that federal courts cannot actually exercise jurisdiction in particular kinds of cases — even cases explicitly mentioned in Article III — until they are empowered to do so by a specific act of Congress. For this reason, it is best to think of the jurisdiction of the federal courts as defined by Article III as the potential rather than the actual jurisdiction of those courts.

The fact that Congress controls the jurisdiction of the federal courts is one of many examples of the theory of "checks and balances" embodied in the U.S. Constitution. The federal courts cannot define their own jurisdiction, nor does Article III in any definitive way prescribe that jurisdiction. Congress by a simple majority vote may enlarge, modify, or eliminate specific categories of federal court jurisdiction. The only exception is the original jurisdiction of the Supreme Court, which cannot be altered except by a constitutional amendment. The remainder of the jurisdiction of the federal courts — including all of the original jurisdiction of the lower courts and all of the appellate jurisdiction of the Supreme Court — is under congressional control.[10]

The task of defining the jurisdiction of the federal courts confronted the framers of the Constitution and the members of the First Congress with two broad issues: (1) how much jurisdiction such courts should have; and (2) what relationship should exist between the federal courts and the state courts. The resolution of these broad issues required the opposing factions — the Federalists and the Anti-Federalists — to forge a further set of political compromises.

Article III and the Original Jurisdiction of the Lower Federal Courts

The phrase used in Article III to describe the original jurisdiction of the federal courts is "the judicial Power of the United States." Section 2 of Article III indicates that "the judicial Power shall extend" to various categories of cases. More particularly, Section 2 contains a list of "Cases" and "Controversies" to which the judicial power of the United States shall extend.

Under Article III, the federal courts are empowered to decide

1. "Cases . . . arising under this Constitution [and] the Laws . . . and Treaties [of the United States];"
2. "Cases affecting Ambassadors, other public Ministers and Consuls;"
3. "Cases of admiralty and maritime Jurisdiction;"
4. "Controversies to which the United States shall be a party;"
5. "Controversies between two or more States;" and
6. "Controversies . . . between Citizens of different States."[11]

This list of Cases and Controversies represents the basic *constitutional* definition of the original jurisdiction of the federal courts. As we have said, however, the list constitutes only the potential jurisdiction of the federal courts and not their actual jurisdiction. Only after Congress has passed specific legislation may the federal courts actually exercise jurisdiction in particular categories of cases.

Article III and the Jurisdiction of the Supreme Court

Article III also addresses the jurisdiction of the Supreme Court. It confers two types of jurisdiction — original and appellate — on the Court. The Court is granted original jurisdiction, that is, the prerogative to function as a trial court, "[i]n all Cases affecting Ambassadors, other public Ministers and Consuls, and those in which a State shall be a Party." Article III then goes on to grant the Supreme Court appellate jurisdiction in "all the other Cases before mentioned," that is, in all cases falling within the basic jurisdiction of the federal courts except those already within the Court's original jurisdiction.

It was the constitutional definition of the Supreme Court's original jurisdiction that led to the establishment of judicial review. Under a strict theory of constitutional supremacy, Congress cannot by ordinary legislation either enlarge or diminish the constitutional (i.e., the Article III) definition of the Court's original jurisdiction. As we saw in Chapter 1, *Marbury* v. *Madison* arose when Marbury tried to invoke the original jurisdiction of the Supreme Court. He argued that in Section 13 of the Judiciary Act of 1789, Congress had empowered the Supreme Court to exercise original jurisdiction in his case. The specific legal issue decided by the Supreme Court in *Marbury* was whether Congress by legislation could enlarge the original jurisdiction of the Supreme Court beyond the limits specified in Article III of the Constitution. For reasons of his own — reasons that were essentially political in nature — John Marshall decided that Section 13 was unconstitutional and therefore that Marbury had improperly filed his suit directly in the Supreme Court.

The constitutional definition of the original jurisdiction of the Supreme Court thus played a key role in establishing judicial review. Since that time, however, it has not had much significance. At most, the Court decides only three or four cases every year in its capacity as a court of original jurisdiction.[12]

The bulk of the Supreme Court's activity involves the exercise of appellate jurisdiction. Article III defines the appellate jurisdiction of the Court in "residual" terms: "In all the other Cases before mentioned [i.e., in all cases not falling within the Court's original jurisdiction] the supreme Court shall have appellate Jurisdiction, both as to Law and Fact, with such Exceptions, and under such Regulations as the Congress shall make."

The language of the Exceptions Clause is a reminder that Article III cannot be viewed as the definitive source of jurisdiction of the federal courts. The appellate jurisdiction of the Supreme Court is defined in Article III as including all cases falling within "the judicial Power of the United States." However, it is also subject to "such Exceptions . . . as the Congress shall make." Thus, the language of Article III implies that Congress may, if it wishes, deprive the Supreme Court of appellate jurisdiction over specific categories of cases. In subsequent chapters, we will see that the *scope* of congressional power to limit the Supreme Court's appellate jurisdiction is a matter of sharp dispute. What is beyond dispute, however, is that Congress possesses a basic, constitutionally prescribed power to make exceptions to the appellate jurisdiction of the Supreme Court.

The fact that Article III defines the potential and not the actual jurisdiction of the federal courts — and that it does so in fairly broad terms — meant that the First Congress had to deal with some complicated and delicate issues. In particular, it had to provide an actual, working definition of the jurisdiction of the new federal courts, and it had to decide what relationship would obtain between the federal courts and the state courts.

The Judiciary Act of 1789 and the Original Jurisdiction of the Lower Federal Courts

We have already noted that the Judiciary Act of 1789 consisted of a bundle of political compromises. It resolved the preeminent issue dividing the Federalists and the Anti-Federalists — whether to establish federal courts at all — in favor of the Federalists. However, it went on to prescribe arrangements for staffing the federal courts which appealed to the Anti-Federalists. The approach the Judiciary Act took to the jurisdiction of the lower federal courts represented an additional victory for the Anti-Federalists.

The principal concession to the Anti-Federalists in the jurisdictional provisions of the Judiciary Act was the deliberate withholding from the federal courts of most of the jurisdiction to which they would be entitled if their jurisdiction were equivalent to the "judicial Power" defined by Article III of the Constitution. In particular, the federal courts were not granted the power to decide cases "arising under" the Constitution and laws of the United States. Jurisdiction over such cases—which are known as *federal question* cases, and which include cases alleging that a state law or the action of a state official violates the U.S. Constitution—was retained by the state courts. It was not until 1875, in the Removal Act of March 3, 1875, that Congress awarded to the federal courts jurisdiction over these important cases.[13]

Thus, in the Judiciary Act of 1789 Congress chose to delegate to state courts initial responsibility for deciding cases involving issues of federal law and constitutional rights. This congressional decision meant that the question of the relationship *between* the state and federal courts acquired special importance. In particular, it was now up to Congress to resolve the difficult question of what relationship would obtain between the state courts, with their original jurisdiction to decide federal question cases, and the Supreme Court, the highest court in the federal system.

The Judiciary Act of 1789 and the Appellate Jurisdiction of the Supreme Court

The policy choice made by Congress represented a victory for the Federalists. Congress decided to define a category of state cases which would be subject to *mandatory review* by the Supreme Court. Section 25 of the Judiciary Act stipulated that the Supreme Court would have appellate jurisdiction over decisions by state courts which

1. *overturned a federal law* or treaty (for whatever reasons) or
2. *upheld a state law* alleged to be repugnant to the Constitution, laws, or treaties of the United States.

Obviously, the decisions identified as falling within the ambit of Section 25 were those which could pose a serious and perhaps fatal threat to the unity of the Republic unless they could be reviewed by a single supreme court of the federal system. Thus, Congress chose to counterbalance the risk to national unity which arose from its decision to give state courts original jurisdiction in federal question cases by subjecting the decisions of state courts in those kinds of cases to mandatory review by the Supreme Court.

Conclusion

The Judiciary Act of 1789 — the initial exercise by Congress of its Article III powers — embodied a complicated set of political compromises designed to satisfy both the Federalists and the Anti-Federalists. The act created the federal courts, but it also tied them closely to the interests of the states. In addition, it withheld from the federal courts the bulk of the "judicial Power" which they were apparently entitled to exercise under the Constitution. In particular, it allowed state courts to retain original jurisdiction over federal question cases, that is, cases arising under the Constitution. At the same time, it stipulated that state court decisions that could threaten national unity would eventually be reviewed on appeal by the U.S. Supreme Court.[14]

The Judiciary Act of 1789 represented the culmination of an intense political struggle. It translated into concrete legislative form the tenuous compromises that had been reached in the political arena between the Federalists and the Anti-Federalists. The tensions implicit in maintaining a bifurcated, overlapping system of state and federal courts persist to the present day. However, the congressional decision to candidly recognize those tensions and to translate them into a series of legislative compromises represented a shrewd political judgment. For the most part, the policy decisions embodied in the Judiciary Act have endured, and today the act is widely regarded as a brilliant and far-sighted response to an exceptionally difficult set of pressures and dilemmas.[15]

The Contemporary Jurisdiction of the Federal Courts

Today, the jurisdiction of the lower federal courts includes a variety of both criminal and civil cases. The U.S. District Courts serve as the trial courts for the prosecution of federal crimes, including, for instance, tax evasion, drug smuggling, embezzlement, fraud, racketeering, interstate theft of an automobile, immigration violations, forgery, counterfeiting, and failure to register with Selective Service. The U.S. District Courts also hear five particularly important (and often overlapping) categories of civil cases:

1. **Diversity of citizenship cases.** Article III extends the judicial power of the United States to controversies "between Citizens of different States." Federal statutes dating back to the Judiciary Act of 1789 have authorized the federal courts to hear such so-called "diversity cases." In recent years, however, Congress has been under considerable pressure to eliminate or curtail the diversity jurisdiction of the federal courts. The original rationale for giving the federal courts jurisdiction over diversity cases was to reduce the possibility of state court bias against out-of-state citizens. However, animosity between the states as geographical entities is no longer as intense as it once

was. Therefore, it is argued, diversity cases represent an unnecessary burden on the federal courts.

2. **Civil actions to which the United States is a party.** In a large number of cases that arise every year, the U.S. government is a party either as plaintiff or defendant. The federal courts have jurisdiction over such cases by virtue of congressional statutes based on the Article III provision extending the judicial power to "all . . . Controversies to which the United States shall be a Party."

3. **Prisoner petitions.** State or federal prisoners who believe they are being confined in violation of their constitutional rights may file a petition in federal court for a writ of habeas corpus. The federal judge who reviews such a petition will do so in the exercise of his or her civil jurisdiction. Petitions filed in federal court by state prisoners often represent a secondary strategy for achieving freedom. After their conviction in state court, criminal defendants may appeal to the highest court of the state and perhaps even to the U.S. Supreme Court. If these avenues of direct appeal are unsuccessful, the next step may be to file a petition for a writ of habeas corpus in federal court. In recent years, the Supreme Court has moved to restrict the availability of the remedy of habeas corpus.[16] However, U.S. District judges still spend a significant proportion of their time responding to habeas corpus petitions.[17]

4. **Civil cases arising under federal statutes.** A broad and ever-growing group of federal statutes authorizes individuals to sue governmental bodies or private parties in civil proceedings in federal court. The purpose of such proceedings is to recover damages or gain other types of "judicial relief," such as reinstatement in a job, health care benefits, nondiscriminatory access to public accommodations, and physical improvements in the workplace. Typical of federal statutes that authorize civil suits are the Black Lung Benefits Act of 1972, the Civil Rights Act of 1964, the Equal Employment Act of 1972, and the Occupational Safety and Health Act of 1970. Civil cases filed under such statutes fall within the Article III category extending the judicial power to cases "arising under . . . the Laws of the United States."

5. **Civil rights cases.** Many lawsuits seeking vindication of federal constitutional rights are filed under federal statutes enacted by Congress in the wake of the Civil War. Most of these statutes went unused for several decades, and some (e.g., the Civil Rights Act of 1875, which was declared unconstitutional by the Supreme Court in a set of cases known as the Civil Rights Cases (1883)) did not survive at all.

Beginning in the 1940s and 1950s, however, the federal government took a renewed interest in protecting civil rights. Many statutes originally passed during the Reconstruction era were revitalized, including 42 U.S.C. #1981 (guaranteeing to all persons equal rights under the law), 42 U.S.C. #1982 (guaranteeing to all citizens equal property rights), and 42 U.S.C. #1985 (authorizing lawsuits to recover damages from persons who conspire to deprive others of the equal protection of the laws). In recent years, these statutes have become a major weapon in the campaign to secure constitutional and legal rights for blacks and other disadvantaged groups.

Of the various statutes that date from Reconstruction, one has become exceptionally popular. The law itself was originally enacted by Congress as the Civil Rights Act of 1871. In 1948 it was re-codified as 42 U.S.C. #1983. Today it is often described simply as "Section 1983."

Section 1983 authorizes lawsuits against "[e]very person who, under color of any statute . . . custom, or usage, of any State . . . subjects . . . any citizen . . . to a deprivation of any rights, privileges or immunities secured by the Constitution and laws [of the United States]." The two basic allegations in a Section 1983 case are (1) that someone has been deprived of his or her constitutional or legal rights and (2) that the deprivation has occurred "under color of state law," that is, pursuant to a state statute or other official state policy. If the allegations are proved, the plaintiff will be entitled to an injunction, money damages, or perhaps some other form of judicial relief. Section 1983 is by far the most common statutory basis for lawsuits in federal court against state officials for allegedly depriving citizens of their federal constitutional or legal rights.[18]

Invoking the Jurisdiction of the Federal Courts

The various provisions of federal law that date from the Civil War, including Section 1983, create what is known as a *right of action* against state officials. They stipulate that any person deprived of his or her constitutional or legal rights by a state official may seek relief (e.g., an injunction or money damages) in a court of law. The Civil War provisions do not, however, explicitly confer jurisdiction in these types of cases on the federal courts. To invoke the jurisdiction of the federal courts, plaintiffs must turn to additional statutory provisions. Civil rights lawyers refer to these additional provisions as the "jurisdictional counterparts" of provisions creating the right of action itself.

Two provisions of federal law are commonly used for the purpose of invoking federal jurisdiction. The first is 28 U.S.C. #1331, which derives from the Removal Act of 1875. Section 1331 is phrased in simple terms. "The district courts," it says, "shall have original jurisdiction of all civil actions arising under the Constitution, laws, or treaties of the United States." Section 1331 allows plaintiffs to invoke the jurisdiction of the federal courts whenever they allege in their lawsuit that they have been deprived by a state official of their constitutional or legal rights.

A second statutory provision that serves to confer jurisdiction on the federal courts in civil rights cases is 28 U.S.C. #1343(3). Section 1343(3) gives U.S. District Courts jurisdiction "to redress the deprivation, under color of any State law . . . of any right, privilege or immunity secured by the Constitution . . . or by any Act of Congress providing for equal rights of citizens." Like Section 1331, Section 1343(3) can be combined with Section 1983 — or other provisions creating a "right of action" against state officials — to invoke the jurisdiction of the federal courts.

The various Civil War statutes frequently refer to "rights secured by the Constitution and laws of the United States" and to deprivations "under color of State law, custom, or usage." The statutes were passed by Congress during the Reconstruction period, and their principal purpose was to secure equal rights for freed slaves. The rights involved were basic constitutional rights, such as the right to vote and the right to receive due process of law in the courts. Southern resistance to extending such rights to blacks was embodied not only in statutes, but also in customs and usages that were deeply entrenched and did not need the support of the law to be observed or enforced. The language of the Civil War statutes reflects the fact that the principal aim of Congress was to curb violations of fundamental constitutional and legal rights by state officials who were responding not only to legislative mandates but also to community pressures and to their own personal antipathy to blacks.

Getting into Three-Judge District Court

Once a plaintiff has succeeded in invoking the jurisdiction of the federal courts, there is a final "wrinkle" to the process of actually getting into federal court. For most plaintiffs, however, the law, as it read up until 1976, represented a welcome opportunity, not an additional hurdle.

In 1910, as we have mentioned, Congress passed a law requiring that some kinds of federal question/civil rights cases could *not* be heard by an ordinary single-judge district court, but had to be heard by a three-judge district court. The cases that were directed by the law into three-judge courts included those in which the plaintiff (1) was alleging that a state statute violated the U.S. Constitution and (2) was requesting the district court to issue an injunction against further enforcement of the statute.

Between 1948 and 1976, the relevant congressional statute was codified as 28 U.S.C. #2281. It stipulated that "An . . . injunction restraining the enforcement . . . of any State statute . . . shall not be granted by any district court . . . upon the ground of the unconstitutionality of such statute unless the application therefor is heard and determined by a district court of three judges."

Neither Section 2281 nor any other provision of federal law *requires* a plaintiff in a federal question case to file his or her case in federal court. The effect of Section 2281 was to prescribe that *if* the plaintiff wished to file in federal court, and *if* the lawsuit included a request for injunctive relief, then the *only* federal court that could hear the case was a three-judge district court. The purpose of the law was to ensure that cases which could result in the issuance of an injunction against a state statute would be heard by a court with slightly more "status" than an ordinary U.S. District Court.

From the perspective of most plaintiffs, of course, the requirement embodied in Section 2281 was a godsend. It meant that their case would be heard by a court that was particularly likely to be receptive to the argument that a state law or other official practice was unconstitutional. It also meant that they could appeal from a loss in the lower courts directly to the U.S. Supreme Court, thus saving substantial amounts of time and money.

Beginning in the 1950s, constitutional challenges to the validity of state statutes became prevalent. Because most such challenges included a request for injunctive relief, there was a steady increase in requests by plaintiffs for the formation of three-judge courts. Three-judge courts became popular, in effect, because the requirements of federal law coincided perfectly with the strategic interests of plaintiffs.

The Repeal of Section 2281

In the 1970s the political mood in the country and in Congress became more conservative. Some members of Congress believed that three-judge courts had become too popular with plaintiffs intent upon challenging the constitutional validity of state statutes. In 1976 Congress enacted legislation restricting the jurisdiction of three-judge courts. The legislation repealed Section 2281 (along with a companion provision, 28 U.S.C. #2282, which required three-judge courts in lawsuits seeking to enjoin a congressional statute).

As a result of the 1976 legislation, three-judge courts are now required only in cases involving alleged malapportionment of state and federal legislative districts and in a few other specific cases. Cases that formerly would have been filed in three-judge district court—cases such as *Barnette, Brown, Schempp*, and *Roe*, which are discussed in Part II of this book—would be filed today in an ordinary (i.e., single-judge) district court. Since the decision of such a court cannot be appealed directly to the Supreme Court, but must proceed first to a court of appeal, the effect of the 1976 legislation has been to reduce the attractiveness of the federal courts as a forum for challenging the constitutional validity of state statutes.

Modern Constitutional Litigation:
Roe v. *Wade* in the Federal Courts

We discuss the Supreme Court's controversial abortion decision—*Roe* v. *Wade* (1973)—in Chapter 10. It may be useful to "preview" the case at this point, however, because it clearly illustrates the *jurisdictional* issues that arise in a modern civil liberties case. *Roe* was a case filed by an individual in federal court which challenged the constitutional validity of a state statute. In this sense, *Roe* is typical of much of the contemporary business of the federal courts.

In 1969 Norma McCorvey became pregnant and decided to seek an abortion. At the time, however, abortion was illegal in Texas except to save the life of the mother. McCorvey's life was not threatened by her pregnancy, and therefore she was not eligible for a legal abortion. She decided to file a legal challenge to the constitutional validity of the Texas statute. For purposes of the case, she adopted the pseudonym of "Roe."

Norma McCorvey filed her lawsuit in U.S. District Court in Dallas on May 3, 1970.[19] She needed to address five main issues in the jurisdictional portions of her complaint. First, her case was in essence a challenge to the constitutional validity of the Texas abortion statute. Thus, she needed to establish that she was entitled to sue state officials for violating what she believed was her constitutional right to obtain a legal abortion. Second, she needed to identify the constitutional basis of her complaint, that is, the constitutional right or rights that allegedly were violated by the Texas statute. Third, she needed to establish that her case fell within the jurisdiction of the federal courts. Fourth, she needed to specify what "relief" she was seeking from the federal courts. Finally, she needed to establish that her case should be heard by a three-judge district court.

Norma McCorvey's first task was to establish that she had a "right of action" against the defendant, Henry Wade. Wade was the district attorney of Dallas County and was responsible for enforcing the Texas abortion statute, and all other state statutes, in Dallas County. For purposes of establishing that she had a right of action against Wade, McCorvey cited 42 U.S.C. #1983. As we have seen, Section 1983 authorizes citizens to sue anyone who has deprived them of their constitutional or legal rights "under color of state law."

Norma McCorvey's next task was to identify which of her constitutional or legal rights were violated by the existence and enforcement of the Texas statute. In the *Roe* litigation, this was a rather delicate problem. The Constitution does not mention abortion, nor does it explicitly protect the right of privacy. As we will see in Chapter 10, the Supreme Court had recognized the existence of a right of privacy in previous cases, but the sources of the right were not well established.

Norma McCorvey and her lawyers were convinced, however, that the Constitution did protect a woman's right to choose to have an abortion. In their complaint, they cited the First, Fourth, Fifth, Eighth, Ninth, and Fourteenth amendments. The citation of so many constitutional provisions was indicative of the fact that, ultimately, the constitutional basis of McCorvey's challenge to the Texas abortion statute was unclear.

The next thing that Norma McCorvey needed to do was to invoke the jurisdiction of the federal courts. For this purpose, she cited both 28 U.S.C. #1331 and 28 U.S.C. #1343(3). Section 1331, as we have seen, authorizes the federal courts to exercise original jurisdiction "of all civil actions arising under the Constitution." Section 1343(3) authorizes the federal courts to exercise jurisdiction in cases seeking "[t]o redress the deprivation, under color of any State law . . . of any right . . . secured by the Constitution."

Fourth, Norma McCorvey needed to specify the types of relief she was seeking from the federal courts. Like most other plaintiffs in modern cases, she was seeking two types of relief. First, she wanted a "declaratory judgment" that the Texas statute was unconstitutional. For this purpose, she cited 28 U.S.C. #2201, which confers upon "any court of the United States" — that is, any federal court — the power to "declare the rights and other legal relations of any interested party seeking such a declaration." Second, she wanted an injunction against further enforcement of the Texas statute. For this purpose, she cited 28 U.S.C. #2202, which authorizes the federal courts to grant "[f]urther necessary or proper relief based on [the] declaratory judgment." The citation of Section 2202 served to alert the defendant and the federal court that Norma McCorvey intended to request an injunction against further enforcement of the Texas statute.

Finally, since McCorvey was requesting an injunction against the Texas statute, her case fell within the terms of 28 U.S.C. #2281, which requires the formation of the three-judge district court. McCorvey, like most other plaintiffs in civil liberties cases, was quite happy to file her case in three-judge court. In her complaint, she cited Section 2281, which stipulates that injunctive relief in cases alleging that a state statute is unconstitutional cannot be granted "unless the application therefor is heard and determined by a district court of three judges."

The litigation in *Roe* v. *Wade* contained all the elements commonly found in a modern constitutional challenge to state law in federal court. After 1976, the need to request a three-judge court was no longer part of the framework of such cases. In every other respect, however, the strategy pursued by Norma McCorvey and her attorneys was typical of modern cases.

Conclusion

In any given year, an unknown number of social, political, and economic disputes arise in the United States. Most of these disputes never reach the courts. Those that cannot be settled out of court, however, are transformed into legal disputes and are distributed, by a complex set of jurisdictional rules, to one or another of the various courts that comprise the American judicial system.

Most American courts fall into one of two categories — state courts or federal courts. Each state has its own system of courts. In addition, the federal government is served by a separate set of federal courts. Most legal disputes begin at the trial level in either the state or federal courts. Those cases that are appealed move upward to the appellate courts. Eventually, a few of these cases — but only a few — will reach the U.S. Supreme Court.

The federal judicial system consists of three levels of courts. The district courts are the trial courts of the federal system; the intermediate tier of federal courts consists of the courts of appeal; and at the pinnacle of the system is the U.S. Supreme Court. The Supreme Court is the final court of appeal for cases originating in both the state courts and the lower federal courts.

The federal courts were established during the founding period of American history. The politics of the founding period were exceptionally divisive, in part because they involved fundamental questions of how much power should be withdrawn from existing state governments and transferred to the new national government. The controversy surrounding the establishment of the federal courts was part of a larger political struggle over the shape and structure of the new nation.

Everyone recognized that the creation of a separate system of federal courts would greatly enlarge the power of the national government. Some citizens — known as Federalists — were enthusiastic about this result. Other citizens — known as Anti-Federalists — were appalled. In the end, the controversy over establishment of the federal courts was resolved by a series of compromises.

Those compromises were embodied primarily in Article III of the Constitution and the Judiciary Act of 1789. Article III created the Supreme Court, but it left to Congress the task of deciding whether to establish any "inferior" federal courts. In 1789, when Congress assembled for the first time, its first important task was to draft legislation to implement the provisions of Article III.

In the Judiciary Act of 1789, Congress made four important decisions, two of which favored the Federalists and two of which favored the Anti-Federalists. First, Congress established a system of federal courts, a victory for the Federalists. Second, Congress located the federal courts within states and specified that federal judges must be selected from the local population, a victory for the Anti-Federalists. Third, in a further victory for the Anti-Federalists, Congress withheld from the federal courts large chunks of the jurisdiction to which they were theoretically entitled by the terms of Article III. Finally, however, responding to the Federalists' concerns, Congress specified that appeals from state court decisions which could threaten national unity could be heard — in fact, must be heard — by the highest court of the federal system, the U.S. Supreme Court.

The Judiciary Act of 1789 represented the Congress's first exercise of its power to define the jurisdiction of the federal courts. On countless occasions since that time, Congress has enacted legislation designating which kinds of cases the federal courts may or may not hear. Each time Congress acts, it affects the calculations of litigants and alters the delicate balance between state and federal courts.

Today, the jurisdiction of the federal courts includes several important categories of cases. First, federal courts are empowered to decide diversity of citizenship cases. Second, all cases to which the United States is a party fall within the jurisdiction of the federal courts. Third, the federal courts may entertain petitions for a writ of habeas corpus filed by state and federal prisoners. Fourth, federal courts are the principal forum for litigation based on congressional statutes authorizing citizens to recover damages or obtain other forms of judicial relief for a variety of specified injuries and deprivations. Finally, federal courts have jurisdiction over cases involving the alleged deprivation by government officials of citizens' constitutional and legal rights.

The federal courts are now more than two hundred years old, and they are an established part of the judicial landscape. Even today, however, issues of the scope of their jurisdiction continue to excite controversy. As recently as 1976, for instance, Congress voted to restrict the jurisdiction of three-judge district courts. A principal purpose of the legislation was to render the federal courts less attractive to plaintiffs as a forum in which to challenge the constitutional validity of state statutes.

The courts that comprise the American judicial system are organized in a hierarchical fashion. In this chapter, we have focused on the overall organization of the American judicial system and on the jurisdiction of the lowest courts in the federal system — the U.S. District Courts. It is now time to turn our attention to the process by which cases are appealed from the lower courts to the U.S. Supreme Court.

Notes

1. Our focus will be on federal courts, but this is not meant to disparage the importance of state courts. State courts decide far more legal disputes than do federal courts. Moreover, many state court decisions have far-reaching effects. Finally, of course, state courts are the source of many cases that eventually reach the U.S. Supreme Court. For information on state courts in the United States, see Harry P. Stumpf and John H. Culver, *The Politics of State Courts* (1992); Henry R. Glick, *Courts, Politics, and Justice* (1988); G. Alan Tarr and Mary Cornelia Porter, *State Supreme Courts in State and Nation* (1988); Susan P. Fino, *The Role of State Supreme Courts in the New Judicial Federalism* (1987); and Henry J. Abraham, *The Judicial Process: An Introductory Analysis of Courts of the United States, England, and France* (1986).

2. Raoul Berger, *Federalism: The Founders' Design* (1987); and C. Herman Pritchett, *Constitutional Law of the Federal System* (1984).

3. The Constitution was officially adopted on June 21, 1788, when New Jersey became the ninth state (out of thirteen) to vote for ratification. Conventions in the important states of New York and Virginia voted for ratification shortly thereafter, on June 25 and July 26, respectively. North Carolina ratified on November 21, 1789, and Rhode Island made ratification unanimous by voting affirmatively on May 29, 1790.

4. The history and organization of the federal courts are examined in detail in Robert A. Carp and Ronald Stidham, *The Federal Courts* (1991); Howard Ball, *Courts and Politics: The Federal Judicial System* (1987); Sheldon Goldman and Thomas P. Jahnige, *The Federal Courts as a Political System* (1985); Stephen T. Early, Jr., *Constitutional Courts of the U.S.* (1977); and Richard J. Richardson and Kenneth N. Vines, *The Politics of Federal Courts* (1970).

5. District judges and their work are the subject of several interesting studies. See Robert A. Carp and C. K. Rowland, *Policymaking and Politics in the Federal District Courts* (1983); William Kitchin, *Federal District Judges* (1978); Joseph C. Goulden, *The Benchwarmers: The Private World of the Powerful Federal Judges* (1974); and Jack W. Peltason, *Fifty-Eight Lonely Men: Southern Federal Judges and School Desegregation* (1961).

6. The appointment and work of appellate judges (including court of appeals judges and Supreme Court justices) is the subject of John R. Schmidhauser's *Judges and Justices: The Federal Appellate Judiciary* (1979). Recent studies of the courts of appeal include Deborah J. Barrow and Thomas G. Walker, *A Court Divided: The Fifth Circuit Court of Appeals and the Politics of Judicial Reform* (1988); and J. Woodford Howard, *Courts of Appeals in the Federal Judicial System* (1981).

7. Creation of the federal courts is discussed in Farber and Sherry, *A History of the American Constitution*, Ch. 3; David Eisenberg, Christine R. Jordan, Maeva Marcus, and Emily F. Van Tassel, "The Birth of the Federal Court System," 17 *this Constitution* 18 (1987); Philip B. Kurland, "The Origins of the National Judiciary," in *this Constitution: Our Enduring Legacy* (1986), pp. 87–95.

8. The appointment and removal of federal judges, including Supreme Court justices, is explored more fully in Chapter 13. On the "local" background and orientation of district judges—which is no longer prescribed by law but continues to be the norm—see Richardson and Vines, *The Politics of Federal Courts*, Chs. 2 and 3; and Carp and Stidham, *The Federal Courts*, Chs. 4 and 5, especially pp. 147–55.

9. The federal system also contains several courts of specialized or limited jurisdiction. Among them are the U.S. Tax Court, which decides tax cases, and the U.S. Court of Military Appeals, which hears appeals from court martial proceedings. See Fisher, *Constitution Dialogues*, pp. 126–35; Ball, *Courts and Politics*, pp. 74–79.

10. This generalization about the scope of congressional power over the jurisdiction of the federal courts—like almost every generalization about the meaning of the Constitution—is subject to qualification. For a further discussion of the scope of congressional power over the jurisdiction of the federal courts, see Chapter 12.

11. Article III also specifies two less important categories of "Controversies:" (1) those "between Citizens of the same State claiming Lands under Grants of different States" and (2) those "between a State, or the Citizens thereof, and foreign States, Citizens or Subjects." As originally written, Article III also empowered the federal courts to decide controversies "between a State and Citizens of another State." However, in *Chisholm v. Georgia* (1793), the Supreme Court injudiciously held that this provision allowed a state to be sued (as defendant) by someone (as plaintiff) who was a citizen of another state. The Court's decision was deeply offensive to Anti-Federalists and was promptly reversed by passage and ratification (in 1798) of the Eleventh Amendment. This amendment—the first to be added to the Constitution after the Bill of Rights itself—stipulated that "The Judicial power of the United States shall not be construed to extend to any suit . . . commenced or prosecuted against one of the United States by Citizens of another State. . . ."

12. One study reports that the Supreme Court has exercised original jurisdiction in only about 150 cases since 1789. See Joel B. Grossman and Richard W. Wells (eds.), *Constitutional Law and Judicial Policy Making* (1988), p. 38.

13. The Removal Act of 1875 was so named because, in addition to stipulating that federal question cases could now begin in federal court, it stipulated that such cases, if begun in state court, could be "removed" by the defendant to federal court.

14. The Judiciary Act of 1789 resolved two additional issues left open by Article III. First, it established the position of chief justice. This position is not mentioned in Article III, although there is a reference to it in Article I, Section 3, which prescribes that when the president is being tried by the Senate for the commission of an impeachable offense, "the Chief Justice shall preside." Second, the Judiciary Act fixed the size of the Supreme Court—another issue on which Article III is silent—at six.

15. The Judiciary Act of 1789 is a uniquely important piece of congressional legislation. In the words of a leading scholar of the federal courts, it has "acquired a status almost as exalted as the Constitution itself." Charles Alan Wright, *Law of Federal Courts* (1983), p. 3.

16. Cf. *Stone* v. *Powell* (1976) (holding that state prisoners are ineligible for habeas corpus relief if they already had an opportunity for "full and fair litigation" in the state courts of their Fourth Amendment constitutional claim that illegally seized evidence was used against them); and *McCleskey* v. *Zant* (1991) (restricting availability of habeas corpus for state prisoners in capital cases).

17. Statistics on the work of the federal courts are presented in the *Annual Report of the Director of the Administrative Office of the United States Courts*. In 1986, 40,427 criminal cases and 254,828 civil cases were commenced in the federal courts. Of the civil cases, 11.5 percent, or 29,305 cases, were state prisoner petitions. See id. (1986 volume) at 13.

18. See, generally, Peter W. Low and John Calvin Jeffries, Jr. (eds.), *Civil Rights Actions: Section 1983 and Related Statutes* (1988); and Note, "Developments in the Law—Section 1983 and Federalism," 90 *Harv. L. Rev.* 1133 (1977).

19. *Roe* v. *Wade*, 314 F.Supp. 1217 (N.D.Tex 1970).

CHAPTER 3

The Appellate Process

T he U.S. Supreme Court is almost purely an appellate court. With few exceptions, every case it decides has previously been considered by at least one lower court. Our concern in this chapter is with what kinds of cases reach the Supreme Court and how they get there.

In Section I, we explore the congressional statutes and institutional practices that govern the process of selecting cases for appellate review. Section II examines the strategic considerations that influence justices and litigants in deciding what cases the Court should hear. Finally, Section III offers an overview of the Supreme Court's workload in recent years.

Appellate Review in the Supreme Court

The Supreme Court makes two decisions in connection with every case it is asked to hear: whether to hear the case, and, assuming it decides to hear it, how the case should be decided. This is an important point. Many Supreme Court decisions are dramatic in their content and have a substantial impact on national life. But the cases the Supreme Court elects to decide represent only a fraction of the cases it could decide. Thus, it is important to focus on the question of why certain issues are singled out for Supreme Court resolution, while others are decided elsewhere or are not decided at all.[1]

The Supreme Court's Annual Activity: An Overview

The Supreme Court's annual activity provides dramatic evidence that most of its decisions are actually "decisions not to decide." In any given year, approximately five thousand cases will be appealed to the Court. Of these, the Court will decide only about 250 (or 5 percent) and will decline to review the remaining cases—fully 95 percent of the total.

In fact, the Court's decision-making activities are even more limited than these figures indicate. Of the 250 cases which the Court decides each year, only about 120 to 150 will be given what is called *plenary consideration*. A plenary case is defined as one that (1) is decided after the submission of written briefs *and* the presentation of oral argument and (2) is accompanied, when it is handed down, by a written opinion of the Court. Plenary cases represent the core of the Supreme Court's affirmative decision-making activities. They also represent less than 5 percent of the cases it has been asked to decide.[2]

Congressional Control of the Appellate Process

Primary responsibility for structuring the appellate process rests with Congress. Congress specifies which cases fall within the Supreme Court's basic appellate jurisdiction and divides those cases into two separate categories. Some cases, known as *certiorari cases*, fall within the Court's discretionary appellate jurisdiction. When a case is classified as a certiorari case, the Supreme Court may decide for itself whether or not to hear the case. Other cases—known as *appeal cases*—fall within the mandatory appellate jurisdiction of the Supreme Court. When a case is classified by congressional legislation as an appeal case, the Supreme Court is obligated to hear and decide the case.

The distinction between discretionary (or certiorari) cases and mandatory (or appeal) cases is embodied in congressional statutes and goes back many years. We look first at how congressional statutes define the basic appellate jurisdiction of the Supreme Court and divide cases into certiorari and appeal cases. Following that, we turn to the actual practice of Supreme Court appellate review in recent years.

Congressional Statutes and the Basic Appellate Jurisdiction of the Supreme Court

Among the cases that fall within the Court's basic appellate jurisdiction are those decided by lower federal courts. Jurisdiction to review such cases is conferred by congressional statutes (28 U.S.C. #1253–1254). Any dissatisfied litigant who is a party to a case decided by a lower federal court can attempt to appeal to the Supreme Court.

The Supreme Court is also authorized by congressional statute (28 U.S.C. #1257) to exercise appellate jurisdiction in cases coming from state courts. Such cases must involve a federal question, that is, a question of federal statutory or constitutional law. Apart from this limitation, there is, theoretically, no other limitation on the types of state cases that can be appealed to the Supreme Court.

The Distinction between Certiorari Cases and Appeal Cases

The Supreme Court is thus authorized by Congress to exercise appellate jurisdiction over two broad types of cases — cases that come from lower federal courts and federal question cases that originate in state courts. These cases constitute the Court's basic *appellate jurisdiction*. Among the cases that the Court is authorized to decide, however, Congress has created a distinction between certiorari cases and appeal cases. In effect, Congress has carved out of the whole group of cases which constitute the basic appellate jurisdiction of the Supreme Court a small group of cases that are designated as appeal cases and that therefore fall within the Court's mandatory appellate jurisdiction. By default, the remaining cases within the Court's appellate jurisdiction become certiorari cases, that is, cases that the Court may review, or decline to review, at its discretion.

Prior to 1988, five main categories of cases were classified by congressional legislation as appeal cases. Among them were two types of cases that we have already encountered. As we noted in Chapter 2, the authors of the Judiciary Act of 1789 believed there were two types of state court decisions which, unless they were reviewed by the Supreme Court, could threaten national unity. In Section 25 of the Judiciary Act, therefore, Congress specifically identified those two categories of state cases — (1) state court decisions invalidating a federal law and (2) state court decisions upholding a state law that had been challenged as being repugnant to the U.S. Constitution or federal law — and made them subject to mandatory review by the Supreme Court. Between 1789 and 1988, any case falling into either of these two categories could be appealed to the Supreme Court, and the Court was required to hear and decide the case.

Prior to 1988, congressional statutes also obligated the Supreme Court to exercise appellate review in three additional categories of cases: (1) cases in which a U.S. Court of Appeals had struck down a state law, (2) civil cases in which a lower federal court had struck down an act of Congress, and (3) all equity decisions (i.e., those granting or denying an injunction) of three-judge district courts.

Prior to 1988, cases falling into the five categories classified by Congress as appeal cases constituted only 5 to 10 percent of the cases appealed to the Supreme Court. In numerical terms, therefore, appeal cases did not make up a large proportion of the Court's potential workload. Remember, however, that these were cases that the Supreme Court was *obligated* to hear and decide. From this perspective, appeal cases constituted an unavoidable and time-consuming segment of the Supreme Court's decision-making responsibilities.

The 1988 Congressional Legislation

In the 1970s Congress began to consider legislation to reduce the scope of the Supreme Court's mandatory jurisdiction. These proposals had strong support from the justices themselves. For various reasons, however, the legislation never actually passed, and the Court continued to be obligated by congressional statute to decide all five categories of appeal cases.

In 1988 Congress finally enacted legislation to reduce the Court's mandatory jurisdiction. The legislation accomplished this goal by converting four of the five existing categories of appeal cases into certiorari cases. The effect was to substantially increase the proportion of cases over which the Court may exercise discretionary jurisdiction. Since 1988, only one type of case — equity decisions of three-judge district courts — has continued to be classified as an appeal case. As we learned in Chapter 2, however, in 1976 Congress drastically reduced the jurisdiction of three-judge district courts. Since then the number of cases being appealed to the Supreme Court from three-judge district courts has dwindled to a trickle.

Table 3.1 summarizes the way in which congressional statutes classify cases that fall within the Court's appellate jurisdiction. The table also notes the changes in the law that took effect in 1988. The net result of the congressional actions in 1976 and 1988 was to eliminate practically all of the Court's mandatory jurisdiction. Henceforth the Court will be in a position to

---

TABLE 3.1

The Supreme Court's Appellate Jurisdiction

I. CASES THE SUPREME COURT *CAN* DECIDE (CERTIORARI CASES)
   A. Cases coming from lower federal courts (28 U.S.C. #1253–1254)
   B. Cases coming from state court courts, provided they involve a federal question (28 U.S.C. #1257)

II. CASES THE SUPREME COURT *MUST* DECIDE (APPEAL CASES)
   A. CASES COMING FROM LOWER FEDERAL COURTS
      1. Cases in which a lower federal court has held an act of Congress unconstitutional in a civil case to which the United States is a party (28 U.S.C. #1252) (*repealed in 1988*)
      2. Cases in which a three-judge district court has either granted or denied an injunction (28 U.S.C. #1253)
      3. Cases in which a court of appeals has invalidated a state statute as repugnant to the Constitution (28 U.S.C. #1254(2)) (*repealed in 1988*)
   B. CASES COMING FROM STATE COURTS
      1. Cases in which a state court (ordinarily a state supreme court) has invalidated a federal law (28 U.S.C. #1257(1)) (*repealed in 1988*)
      2. Cases in which a state court (ordinarily a state supreme court) has upheld a state law that was challenged as being repugnant to the U.S. Constitution or to federal law (28 U.S.C. #1257(2)) (*repealed in 1988*)

Note: Since 1988, the only federal cases classified as appeal cases have been those coming from three-judge U.S. District Courts. All other cases coming from lower federal courts, and all federal question cases coming from state courts, are now classified as certiorari cases.

exercise almost complete discretion in the choice of cases it will hear and decide.

The Judiciary Act of 1925 and the Writ of Certiorari

Over the years, the basic trend of congressional legislation has been to reduce pressure on the Supreme Court by enlarging the Court's ability to control the content of its *plenary docket*. The Court's plenary docket consists of those cases to which it devotes plenary consideration, that is, those cases that the Court decides (1) after oral argument and (2) with full opinions. In recent years, the Court's plenary docket has consisted of about 120 to 150 cases per year.

Prior to 1988 the principal piece of congressional legislation supporting the Supreme Court's effort to control the composition of its plenary docket was the Judiciary Act of 1925. The act substantially enlarged the scope of the Court's discretion to choose the cases to which it would give plenary consideration.[3] The act also created the particular device by which litigants attempt to effect an appeal to the Supreme Court in cases falling within the Court's discretionary jurisdiction. That device is known as the *petition for a writ of certiorari*, and it is for this reason that cases in which the Court exercises discretionary review are known today as certiorari cases.

Would-be appellants in certiorari cases are required to petition the Supreme Court for a writ of certiorari. The Court examines all such petitions and decides which ones it wishes to grant and which ones it wishes to deny. When the Supreme Court agrees to grant certiorari, the court below is required to send up to the Supreme Court, for the Court's attention, the record in a particular case.

The Rule of Four

Soon after the Judiciary Act of 1925 was passed, the Supreme Court adopted the institutional practice of voting on all petitions for certiorari and granting only those that were supported by at least four justices. This so-called *Rule of Four* persists to the present. No petition for a writ of certiorari will be granted unless it receives the support of at least four justices.[4]

The overall process of selecting cases for inclusion on the plenary docket involves several steps. The basic pool of cases from which the Court eventually constitutes its plenary docket includes all those requests for review which have been filed with the Supreme Court over a one-year period. This pool of cases is often described as the Court's *jurisdictional agenda* or, more simply, as *filings*. From this pool of cases, the chief justice prepares what is known as a *discuss list*. This list consists of cases which, in the chief justice's view, are potential candidates for inclusion on the Court's plenary docket. Each term, about 20 to 30 percent of certiorari cases (and all appeal cases) are placed on the discuss list. Petitions for certiorari which are not included on the discuss list are relegated to the *dead list*. These cases are automatically denied unless, as occasionally happens, a particular case is rescued from the dead list and placed before the Court by one or more of the associate justices.

Inclusion of a case on the discuss list means that the chief justice or one or more of the associate justices has made a preliminary judgment that the case is *certworthy*, that is, worth considering for possible inclusion on the plenary docket. The discuss list therefore constitutes the pool of cases from which the Court makes its certiorari decisions.[5]

Once the discuss list has been prepared, the Rule of Four goes into effect. If four or more of the justices wish to hear a case, the case will be removed from the discuss list and placed on the Court's plenary docket. Ordinarily, the case will be taken up in the following term of the Court, at which time the justices will hear oral argument, discuss the case among themselves, and render a decision.

The Rule of Four in Appeal Cases

Technically, the Rule of Four applies only to certiorari cases, that is, cases the Supreme Court is authorized to review or decline to review at its discretion. Cases classified as appeal cases are not supposed to be governed by the Rule of Four, because the Court, in theory, is obligated to hear and decide *any* case that satisfies the congressional definition of an appeal case.

Prior to 1988, however, a substantial number of cases on the Supreme Court's jurisdictional docket qualified as appeal cases. In the 1970s and early 1980s the Court's jurisdictional docket consisted of about four thousand cases per term, of which 5 to 10 percent were classified as appeal cases. That meant that the Court was theoretically obligated to give plenary consideration to between two hundred and four hundred cases per year in addition to those cases that the Court deemed worthy of review on certiorari.

The Court's response to the special burden posed by appeal cases was to treat such cases, as a matter of institutional practice, as if they were certiorari cases. If four or more justices wished to place a particular appeal case on the plenary docket, the Court would issue a brief order in which it would note *probable jurisdiction*. The issuance of an order noting probable jurisdiction, as opposed to an order granting certiorari, was a signal that the Court viewed the case as an appeal case rather than a certiorari case. The case would then be brought to the Supreme Court for plenary consideration.

Appeal cases that at least four justices did not regard as worthy of plenary consideration were decided summarily, that is, by a mechanism known as the *summary judgment*. The Court's practice in cases coming from state courts was to "dismiss the appeal for want of a substantial federal question" (reflecting the fact that the presence of a federal question was critical to qualifying the case for Supreme Court review in the first place). The Court's practice in cases coming from lower federal courts was to summarily affirm the decision of the court below. The effect of issuing a summary judgment in either a state

Law Clerks and the Certiorari Process

The opportunity to "clerk" for a Supreme Court justice is the coveted goal of practically every American law student. Each of the justices employs three or four clerks every year. Generally, clerks are recent graduates of prestigious law schools. Most have compiled distinguished academic records and have served for a year or more as clerks to a lower federal court judge. From there, they are chosen to work for a year or more as clerk to a Supreme Court justice.

In view of the large number of petitions filed with the Court each year — about five thousand — few if any of the justices can personally examine each petition for certiorari, or even each petition that survives the "first cut" and ends up on the discuss list. The job of reviewing petitions and preparing recommendations for the justices is among the primary responsibilities of the justices' clerks.

As the number of petitions for certiorari filed with the Supreme Court has increased, the role of clerks in reviewing those petitions has undergone changes. For many years, all petitions were reviewed by at least one clerk working for each of the justices. In the 1972 term, however, five justices — Warren Burger, Harry Blackmun, William Rehnquist, Lewis Powell, and Byron White — organized their clerks into a *cert pool*. The job of examining the annual crop of petitions for certiorari was distributed among the members of the cert pool, and the participating justices agreed to rely on recommendations prepared by any member of the pool.

The remaining four members of the Court — Potter Stewart, William Brennan, Thurgood Marshall, and William Douglas — declined to participate in the cert pool. They continued to accept recommendations only from their own clerks.

Prior to Justice Marshall's retirement from the Court in 1991, only he and Justice John Paul Stevens did not participate in the cert pool.

For a clerk's account of the work of the Supreme Court during the 1971 and 1972 terms, see J. Harvie Wilkinson III, *Serving Justice: A Supreme Court Clerk's View* (1974). In the early 1950s, the current chief justice, William Rehnquist, clerked for Associate Justice Robert Jackson. Rehnquist discusses his experiences as a clerk in William H. Rehnquist, *The Supreme Court: How It Was, How It Is* (1987).

or a federal case was to rebuff the attempt by a dissatisfied litigant to appeal to the Supreme Court and to affirm the decision of the court from which the case was being appealed.

The 1988 congressional legislation converting four categories of appeal cases into certiorari cases will substantially reduce the pressure on the Supreme Court to issue summary judgments. In the years immediately preceding 1988, the Court issued as many as two hundred summary judgments every term. Most of these judgments were appeal cases that the Court was theoretically obliged to hear but that fewer than four justices regarded as sufficiently important to warrant plenary consideration. Since the number of cases classified as appeal cases has now been drastically reduced, the Court is under much less pressure to issue a large number of decisions in the form of summary judgments.

The Criteria for Selection in Certiorari Cases

As we have said, most congressional legislation affecting the appellate process over the years has expanded the Supreme Court's ability to control the composition of its plenary docket. Today, the Court's plenary docket consists almost exclusively of certiorari cases. It thus becomes important to focus on the question of how the Supreme Court exercises its almost total discretion to select cases for plenary review.

The criteria on which the Supreme Court ostensibly bases its decisions to grant or deny certiorari are enunciated in Rule 10 of the Rules of the Supreme Court. This rule states that "review on writ of certiorari is not a matter of right, but of judicial discretion, and will be granted only where there are special and important reasons therefor." The rule goes on to suggest that among the reasons for granting certiorari are the existence of

1. Conflict between the decisions of two or more U.S. Courts of Appeal.
2. Conflict between the decision of a U.S. Court of Appeal and that of a state supreme court.
3. Conflict between the decision of a state or federal court and the "applicable decisions of this [i.e., the Supreme] Court."

Rule 10 enumerates the formal criteria governing the Supreme Court's decision to grant certiorari. Those criteria obviously emphasize the Court's role in resolving intercourt doctrinal conflict and integrating and rationalizing the content of federal constitutional law.

For some time, however, practicing lawyers, legal scholars, and political scientists have been aware that Rule 10 may offer an incomplete guide to the criteria that actually govern Supreme Court decisions to grant certiorari. Indeed, scholars have discovered that at least five factors, in addition to intercourt conflict, are useful predictors of whether or not the Court will accept and decide a case. These factors are often known as *cues* because they indicate whether the Supreme Court will actually exercise its discretionary power of appellate review. These cues are (1) whether the U.S. government is a party to the case and is the party asking for review; (2) whether a civil rights or civil liberties issue is involved in the case; (3) whether the case was decided by a divided (rather than a unanimous) lower court; (4) whether any *amicus curiae* (or "friend of the court") briefs have been filed in connection with the petition for certiorari; and (5) whether the lower court's decision is ideologically abhorrent to a majority of the Supreme Court. All of these factors (including the official factor of intercourt conflict) have proved to be useful guides to the Court's actual practice of appellate review in certiorari cases.[6]

Agenda Setting on the Supreme Court

Since the Supreme Court has almost complete control of its plenary docket, we can learn a great deal about the Court and its changing priorities by examining trends in the composition of that docket. In Sections II and III of this chapter, we will see that there are measurable changes over time in the types of cases the Supreme Court chooses to hear and in the types of litigants who are successful in getting the Supreme Court to hear their cases. Before we turn to these questions, however, we should note briefly what happens to the cases the Supreme Court decides *not* to decide. As noted earlier, cases in which the Court denies (rather than grants) certiorari constitute about 95 percent of its "decisions" every year, and there is sometimes confusion about their significance.

Since a denial of certiorari leaves a lower court decision undisturbed, the natural tendency is to view a denial of certiorari as an affirmation of the lower court's decision. The Supreme Court has frequently cautioned, however, that it is improper to attach any such significance to its denial of certiorari in a particular case. Unlike Supreme Court decisions in plenary cases, denials of certiorari do not represent nationwide legal precedents and are not considered to be decisions "on the merits." Their immediate effect—and, in the official view of the Supreme Court, their only effect—is to leave in place the decision of the court from which the case was appealed.[7]

From the vantage point of the appealing litigant, of course, a denial of certiorari is just as disappointing as an adverse decision on the merits. It means that the decision from which the litigant is appealing will be left in place. It is the rest of the world—that is, everyone *except* the parties to the particular case—who can best appreciate the difference between denials of certiorari and decisions on the merits. When the Supreme Court denies certiorari, the sole effect of its decision is to leave in place the decision of a particular lower court. In contrast, a plenary decision is a decision on the merits and constitutes a formal precedent of the Supreme Court which has nationwide effect and remains in force until overruled by the Supreme Court itself.

Conclusion

In its capacity as the nation's highest appellate court, the U.S. Supreme Court reviews cases emanating from a variety of lower courts, including both state and federal courts. The Supreme Court's decisions in appellate cases, as well as the handful of cases that fall within its original jurisdiction, become nationally binding legal precedents.

The Court's appellate jurisdiction is defined by congressional statutes. Today, statutes permit the Court to exercise discretionary control over almost all of its appellate docket. Unlike most lower courts in the American judicial system, the Supreme Court is obligated to hear very few cases. Instead, it is permitted, by law, to pick and choose the cases it will hear.

Over the years the Supreme Court has developed a variety of techniques for exercising its discretionary appellate jurisdiction. Among them are the "discuss list" — a short list of potentially "certworthy" cases — and the "Rule of Four" — by which four or more justices may indicate their desire to "grant certiorari" or "note probable jurisdiction" in a particular case.

Cases that the Court agrees to decide are placed on the Court's plenary docket for eventual decision on the merits. Each year about 120 to 150 cases receive plenary consideration, which means they are decided after oral argument and, when they are handed down, they are accompanied by a written opinion of the Court. The Court's remaining decisions take the form of summary judgments.

The discretionary character of the Supreme Court's exercise of the power of appellate review means that the Court is in a key position not only to make public policy, but also to control the timing and circumstances of its involvement in the policy-making process. This draws attention to some of the strategic considerations that may influence both judges and litigants in channeling cases to the Supreme Court.

Strategy, Ideology, and the Judicial Process

For public consumption, the Supreme Court maintains that its decisions to exercise appellate review are influenced primarily by the importance of the legal issues in a case and the need to enunciate uniform principles of national law. The Supreme Court, however, is a human institution, and it operates as part of a political system. It would be naive to think that cases are selected for plenary review purely because they raise important legal issues or purely because the Supreme Court as an institution is engaged in the altruistic process of illuminating the true meaning of the Constitution. The decision to give plenary consideration to particular cases is influenced by political, ideological, and strategic considerations. It is worthwhile examining what some of those considerations may be.[8]

The Plenary Docket and Judicial Strategy

Under the Rule of Four, as we have seen, an affirmative vote by four members of the Court is enough to grant certiorari (or, in practice, to hear a mandatory appeal case). In the end, however, it is a majority of five which has the power to decide a case in a particular direction on the merits. From these rudimentary mathematical facts, certain strategic considerations inexorably follow.[9] It is obvious, for instance, that for some justices (e.g., committed liberals) voting in favor of certiorari in certain situations (e.g., when the Court as a whole includes five committed conservatives) is not very astute. The net effect will be to bring to the Court a case which will almost certainly be decided on the merits in a way that directly conflicts with the preferences of our hypothetical "cert-granting" liberal justices.

Such a Machiavellian interpretation of the justices' behavior cannot, of course, be taken too far. First, major elements of uncertainty are implicit in any case that is brought to the Supreme Court. No case is completely devoid of factual surprises or unexpected legal issues. Thus, it is impossible to predict the outcome of a particular case with complete certainty. Second, rarely if ever does the membership of the Court consist exclusively of rigidly predictable liberals and conservatives. At least in recent years, the Court has always contained a middle group of moderate justices or *swing votes*. On certain issues, these justices could vote either way, thereby affecting the outcome of the case.[10] Finally, many, if not most, Court justices are notoriously independent. Their vote on the merits of an issue, no matter how strongly they may be identified with a particular point of view or ideological persuasion, can never be taken for granted.

Behind-the-scenes accounts of Supreme Court decision making abound with illustrations of the unpredictable character of the decision to grant or not to grant certiorari. The Supreme Court's decision in *Cohen* v. *California* (1971)—the so-called Fuck the Draft case—is an example. Paul Robert Cohen was convicted of disturbing the peace for wearing a jacket inscribed with the slogan "Fuck the Draft" in the corridor of a Los Angeles courthouse.[11] When Cohen appealed to the Supreme Court, Justice Harlan termed the case a "peewee" and was reluctant to grant review, while Justice Black was so outraged by what he perceived as a self-evident violation of First Amendment rights that he urged the Court to summarily reverse the conviction.[12] When the case was finally decided on its merits, however, Justice Harlan voted to overturn Cohen's conviction and wrote the opinion of the Court in the case. Justice Black, on the other hand, had become convinced that Cohen's conviction did not violate his constitutional rights. Black therefore voted with the minority, joining Justice Blackmun's dissenting opinion in the case.

Ideological Stability on the Supreme Court

Clearly, once a case has been accepted for plenary consideration, no one can predict its outcome with total certainty. Nonetheless, it is also clear that for extended periods of time the ideological composition of the Supreme Court may be relatively stable and also relatively lopsided. When these conditions prevail, a controlling majority on the Court can accept particular cases for review, secure in the knowledge that it will have the votes to decide those cases in a particular way.

In fact, the justices who enjoy the greatest strategic advantage will be those who constitute the hard core of a comfortable majority of either liberals or conservatives. Such a core of activists can vote to hear a particular case in the assurance that when the time comes to decide the case on the merits, there will be enough peripheral votes among sympathetic (but not crusading) justices to produce the desired outcome. In the end, there is no way around the fact that an ideologically unified majority on the Supreme Court is in a position to exercise the Court's nearly unrestricted discretionary power to bring particular cases to the Court for decision and to decide those cases in particular ways.

Interest Groups and Supreme Court Decision Making

The existence of a stable and/or lopsided ideological majority on the Supreme Court shifts the burden of strategic planning from the justices to actual litigants. The criminal defendant or political dissident who loses his or her case in the trial court during a period when conservatives dominate the Supreme Court must calculate the costs and benefits of appealing. The Court may contain four justices who are willing to hear the case. The real question, however, is whether there is any chance that the Supreme Court will reverse the lower court decision. A Court containing a maximum of four justices who are sympathetic to an appellant's claim is of no use when a minimum of five sympathetic justices is necessary to achieve victory.

In fact, calculating strategic advantage is somewhat more complicated than this analysis suggests. In particular, the perspective of an individual litigant may differ significantly from the perspective of an organization that specializes in helping individual litigants bring their cases to the Supreme Court.

An individual litigant may have everything to gain and nothing to lose by appealing to the Supreme Court, provided at least that others, as is often the case, bear the expense of appealing. Even in an era of conservative dominance of the Court, therefore, an individual litigant will not necessarily be disinclined to appeal even an unpromising civil liberties claim "all the way to the Supreme Court."

On the other hand, an organization whose primary goal is to elicit favorable policy judgments from the courts will have a very different perspective. The primary concern of such an organization — for example, the American Civil Liberties Union or the NAACP Legal Defense Fund — will be to avoid the establishment of an unfavorable precedent with nationwide force. The individual litigant may be oblivious to such considerations and concerned only with exercising his or her last personal option for achieving victory. In contrast, a civil liberties organization will adopt a wider and longer range perspective and may prefer to forego the opportunity to take a hopeless case to the Court.

For similar reasons, a civil liberties organization in an era of conservative dominance of the Supreme Court may actually prefer to *lose* rather than to *win* in trial court. In such circumstances, the organization can console itself that at least it retains the option of whether or not to appeal. It may take a hard look at reality and decide to bide its time until the Supreme Court is once again favorable to the views it espouses. In the meantime, the policy damage will be confined to the geographical area served by the lower court.

If the civil liberties organization is victorious in the lower courts, however, both the option and the incentive to appeal revert to "the other side" — the side which, in the example we are using, will often be the government. Once that option is exercised and the conservative majority on the Supreme Court detects a lower court policy pronouncement in need of rectification, there is little to prevent that majority from accepting the case for review and reversing the decision of the court from which it came.[13]

Conclusion

A complicated mixture of strategic and ideological considerations affects whether a particular case is appealed to the Supreme Court. Each of the players in the process — lawyers, litigants, interest groups, and justices — will have a distinctive perspective on the question of whether the Supreme Court should exercise its power of appellate review. Often there is disagreement within the Court about whether a particular case should be heard. It is also possible that individual litigants and the organizations that specialize in representing them will have conflicting perceptions of the wisdom of appealing to the Supreme Court.

Over time, the mixture of individual and organizational motivations that propel certain cases to the Supreme Court will produce patterns and trends in litigation. In the concluding section of this chapter, we look at historical trends in the types of cases that make their way to the Supreme Court.

The Supreme Court's Appellate Agenda in Historical Perspective

The Supreme Court's appellate agenda has undergone significant changes over time. Here we focus on historical trends in two sets of cases: (1) cases that litigants attempt to appeal to the Supreme Court and (2) cases that the Supreme Court agrees to review. Note that we will not consider how the Supreme Court actually decides the cases it has agreed to review. That question — the question of outcomes in Supreme Court cases — is taken up in Chapter 4.

The first set of cases we examine — cases that litigants attempt to appeal to the Supreme Court — is often described as the Court's jurisdictional agenda or, more simply, as filings. The second set of cases — the Supreme Court's plenary docket — consists of cases that the Court agrees to review. More particularly, it consists of cases to which the Court has agreed to give plenary consideration.

The Jurisdictional Agenda:
Cases the Court Could Decide

As we have noted, approximately five thousand cases are appealed to the Supreme Court each term. Actually, the number of cases on the Court's jurisdictional agenda in any given year is closer to six thousand. Of these, however, between five hundred and one thousand will be cases left from the previous term, and so in any given term, the Court will receive approximately five thousand fresh cases.

These cases can be subdivided in various ways. As we have seen, prior to recent changes in the law, approximately 90 to 95 percent were classified as certiorari cases, while the remainder, about 5 to 10 percent, were classified as appeal cases. In 1988, however, Congress eliminated several categories of appeal cases. In the future, only a minute proportion of cases on the Supreme Court's jurisdictional agenda will consist of mandatory appeal cases.

It is also common to divide cases appealed to the Supreme Court into two categories which, during most of the 1980s, were roughly equal in size. About half of the cases appealed to the Court are accompanied by printed transcripts of the trial record and by filing fees. These so-called *paid cases* are assigned to what is known as the *Appellate Docket*. In recent years, the Court has received about two thousand paid cases each term.

The remainder of the Court's jurisdictional agenda consists of cases filed *in forma pauperis*, that is, without transcripts or filing fees. Most of these cases are brought by inmates of state and federal prisons. Prior to 1988, the Court received about equal numbers of paid cases and pauper cases, that is, about two thousand each term. Beginning in 1988, however, there was a major increase in the number of cases filed *in forma pauperis*, and in the 1991–1992 term, the Court received more than thirty-seven hundred such cases. Cases filed *in forma pauperis* are assigned to what is known as the *Miscellaneous Docket*.[14]

The Growth of the Jurisdictional Agenda

The Supreme Court's jurisdictional agenda was at one time much smaller than it is today. In fact, as recently as the 1950s the jurisdictional agenda was only about one-third as large as it is today. Thus, the number of cases filed in the Court has increased substantially—indeed exponentially—in recent decades. In the meantime, the Court's annual output of plenary decisions has risen much more slowly and in recent years has actually declined.

Trends in the size of the Supreme Court's jurisdictional agenda and plenary docket are illustrated in Figure 3.1. In the early 1950s about 1,400 cases were filed each term in the Supreme Court. From this number, the Court selected approximately one hundred cases for plenary consideration. By the mid- to late 1960s, the number of filings had doubled—to about three thousand cases per term—while the number of plenary decisions rose by

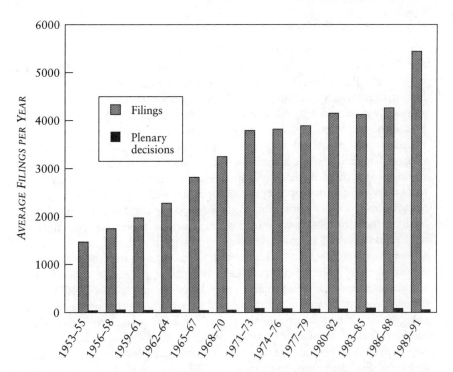

FIGURE 3.1 Trends in Filings and Plenary Decisions, 1953–1991 Terms

SOURCES: Arthur D. Hellman, "Case Selection in the Burger Court: A Preliminary Inquiry," 60 *Notre Dame L. Rev.* 947, 951 (1985); 54 *U.S. Law Week* 3038 (July 30, 1985); 57 *U.S. Law Week* 3074 (July 26, 1988); 60 *U.S. Law Week* 3056 (July 23, 1991); 61 *U.S. Law Week* 3098 (August 11, 1992).

about 15 percent. By the early 1980s an additional one thousand cases were being filed in the Supreme Court, bringing the total to more than four thousand cases per term, while plenary decisions rose only an additional 30 percent. As the 1980s drew to a close, the Court's jurisdictional docket continued to grow—reflecting the substantial upsurge in petitions filed *in forma pauperis*—while the output of plenary decisions reversed its previous trend and actually began to decline. In the 1990 and 1991 terms, respectively, the Court issued only 116 and 110 plenary decisions, a record low for recent years.

The overall trend is clear. At the beginning of the four-decade period on which we are focusing, the Court was issuing plenary decisions in about 5 to 7 percent of cases in which appellate review was requested. By the end of the 1980s, however, the ratio of plenary decisions to filings had fallen to between 2 and 3 percent.

Responses to the Growing Caseload

The sharp rise in filings in the 1950s and 1960s raised concerns about whether the Supreme Court could continue to function effectively as the nation's highest appellate court. In 1971, in response to these concerns, Chief Justice Burger appointed a committee to study the Court's workload. The committee was known as the Freund Committee, after its chairman, Professor Paul Freund of the Harvard Law School. It recommended the creation of a new national court of appeals, which would be positioned between the regional courts of appeals and the Supreme Court.[15] Shortly thereafter, a congressional commission chaired by Senator Roman Hruska issued a report that also called for creation of a national court of appeals, although one with different features and powers than that recommended by the Freund Committee.[16] Each of these proposals was given careful consideration. To date, however, neither has resulted in any definitive congressional action.[17]

In the meantime, as we have noted, Congress and the Court have taken various steps to cope with increases in the size of the Court's jurisdictional agenda. In 1976 Congress enacted legislation reducing the jurisdiction of three-judge district courts. Since appeals from such courts go directly to the Supreme Court and fall within the Court's mandatory jurisdiction, the 1976 legislation eased the pressure on the Court. In 1988 Congress took the further step of excluding several types of cases from the category of appeal cases. As a result of this legislation, the proportion of cases over which the Supreme Court could exercise discretionary (as opposed to mandatory) jurisdiction increased.

The justices were highly supportive of these congressional efforts to enlarge the scope of their discretion. In addition, the Court itself has taken various steps to cope with its growing caseload. Over the years, for instance, the number of clerks assigned to work with each of the justices has increased. A few years ago, each justice was served by one or two clerks; today the number is three or four per justice. In addition, in 1972 some members of the Court took an explicit step toward greater efficiency when they authorized their clerks to function as a cert pool, that is, to share responsibility for reviewing petitions for certiorari.

Most of the responses to the growing caseload of the Supreme Court have not actually helped reduce the Court's jurisdictional agenda. Rather, they have expanded the scope of the Court's discretion to be selective about which cases it will pluck from its jurisdictional agenda and actually decide. In the 1990s, compared to the earlier decades, the Supreme Court has more cases from which to choose *and* more freedom, as an institution, to make unhindered choices.

In the end, a relatively small number of cases — approximately 120 to 150 per year — will end up on the Supreme Court's plenary docket. It is now time to turn our attention to the plenary docket itself.

The Plenary Docket: Cases the Court Does Decide

Earlier in this chapter, we discussed the strategic considerations that may influence both justices and litigants in deciding whether the Supreme Court should accept a case for plenary consideration. Many of our conclusions were derived from assumptions about the political and ideological preferences of justices, litigants, and the groups that represent litigants in constitutional cases.

Obviously, the single most powerful influence on the composition of the plenary docket is the collective judgment of a majority of the justices about which cases the Court should review and decide. Changes in the composition of the plenary docket therefore represent changes in the priorities of the Court as an institution. The Court's changing priorities are reflected in trends in the *issue areas* addressed by the Court. They are also reflected in trends in the *identity of the litigants* who appeal to the Supreme Court. Each of these trends tells us something important about the changing role of the Supreme Court in American democracy.

Issue Areas and the Plenary Docket

Political scientist Richard Pacelle has documented the changes that occurred in the plenary docket of the Supreme Court between 1933 and 1988.[18] The results of his research are shown in Figure 3.2.

The figure shows that the Court's plenary docket has undergone substantial changes in the past fifty years. The most notable changes involved the increase in the number of cases dealing with civil rights and civil liberties and the corresponding decline in the number of cases touching on issues of economic and regulatory policy. The figure indicates that in the 1930s about three-fourths of the Court's plenary docket consisted of cases dealing with economic and regulatory policy. Today, however, such cases comprise less than one-third of the docket.

During the same period, as Figure 3.2 shows, an increasing proportion of the Court's plenary docket consisted of cases involving civil rights and civil liberties. Such cases—those in which the Court resolves issues of equal protection, due process of law, freedom of speech, freedom of religion, and privacy—were once a miniscule proportion of the plenary docket. Today they constitute about half of all cases to which the Court gives plenary consideration.

Within the general area of civil rights and civil liberties, there have also been detectable short-run changes in the focus of the Court. On several occasions since the 1940s, the Court has handed down decisions that opened new areas of public policy to judicial examination. Such decisions are almost invariably followed by several years in which the Court is "kept busy elabo-

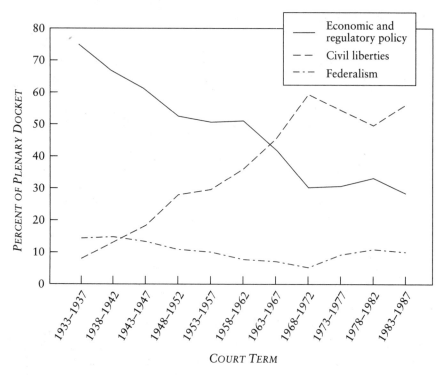

FIGURE 3.2 Trends in the Composition of the Supreme Court's Plenary Docket, 1933 to 1987 Terms

SOURCE: Richard L. Pacelle, Jr. *The Transformation of the Supreme Court's Agenda* (Boulder, Colo.: Westview Press, 1991), pp. 56–57.

rating and clarifying the scope of the newly recognized rights."[19] In the early 1960s, for instance, the Supreme Court entered the area of legislative reapportionment.[20] The initial decisions were followed by others in which the Court struggled to clarify the meaning of the judicial doctrine of "one person, one vote." Followup cases also populated the Court's plenary docket in the aftermath of its pathbreaking decisions on obscenity,[21] libel,[22] confessions,[23] sex discrimination,[24] the death penalty,[25] and abortion.[26]

Figure 3.2 also suggests that issues of federalism represent an important and relatively constant component of the Supreme Court's plenary docket. Supreme Court scholars emphasize that one of the Court's most important responsibilities over time has been to assist in "mark[ing] the boundaries between state and national power."[27] In its early history, as we have seen, the Court played a major role in resolving issues of federalism. Figure 3.2 indicates that the federal structure of the American polity continues to generate a significant number of plenary cases.

The clearest indication from the figure, however, is that civil rights and civil liberties represent a major preoccupation of the contemporary Court. Such cases now constitute about half of all cases it decides. This information, however, leaves unanswered two very basic questions: (1) *Whose* requests for appellate review is the Court granting? and (2) How is the Court deciding the cases it agrees to hear? We will take up the second question in the next chapter. Here let us focus on the first question — that of the identity of the litigants whose cases are being heard by the Supreme Court. It is particularly interesting to examine this question in the context of the transition from the Warren Court (1953–1969) to the Burger Court (1969–1986).

Litigant Status and the Plenary Docket

Before we look at empirical data on changes in the identity of litigants in plenary cases, let us engage in a bit of informed speculation. Using our imagination, we may be able to predict with considerable accuracy how the composition of the plenary docket has changed in the past four decades.

Let us imagine, for instance, an era in which the constitutional law of individual rights is relatively undeveloped and legislative bodies and lower courts are relatively insensitive to claims of abridgment of civil liberties. Suppose that at about this time, the political climate begins to change, and through the vagaries of the appointment process, the membership of the Supreme Court becomes more liberal and the protection of individual rights becomes a decision-making priority of a majority of the Court.

Under the circumstances, we would expect to find a measurable change in the identity of the litigants whose cases appear on the Supreme Court's plenary docket. We are assuming that in cases involving a challenge to governmental action — that is, in cases we would classify as civil liberties cases — the lower courts have tended to decide in favor of the government. We are also assuming that the Supreme Court has become receptive to constitutional challenges to governmental action and is prepared to reverse these lower court decisions. Before it can do so, however, it must agree to review them. Thus, we would expect to find that an increasing proportion of the Court's plenary docket consists of cases being reviewed at the request of individual and group litigants.

Suppose now, however, that things change again. Suppose that the constitutional law of individual rights has undergone an extended period of expansion, that lower courts have absorbed many of the doctrinal changes in the content of the law, and that federal courts are staffed by a new generation of judges who are more sympathetic than their predecessors to alleged governmental violations of individual rights. Suppose also, however, that in the meantime the political climate has become more conservative and that this political change is reflected in the membership of the Supreme Court. Let us suppose, in short, that the membership of the Supreme Court has become *less* receptive to allegations of governmental abridgment of individual rights just at the time that lower courts have become *more* receptive to such claims.

Under these circumstances, we would expect to find a reversal of the earlier trend. In particular, we would expect to find that the Supreme Court was reviewing fewer appeals brought by individuals challenging governmental action and more appeals brought by governments. In short, we would expect to find that an increasing proportion of the plenary docket of the Supreme Court consists of cases in which the government, rather than individual or group litigants, is the petitioning party.

The Supreme Court since 1953

Obviously, the foregoing hypothetical scenario bears a certain resemblance to reality. In the 1950s and 1960s a burgeoning array of groups and individuals came to believe that government was violating their constitutional rights, and the Supreme Court displayed an increasing willingness to agree that this was indeed the case. By the late 1970s, however, the Court had become noticeably less sympathetic to challenges to governmental action and more inclined to side with government in disputes between government and the individual.

The liberal trend in Supreme Court decision making commenced in the 1940s and 1950s and picked up considerable steam in the 1960s. By the mid-1960s the Supreme Court under the leadership of Chief Justice Earl Warren consisted of a solid core of liberal justices (including Warren himself and Associate Justices Hugo Black, William Douglas, William Brennan, and Arthur Goldberg). Moreover, the remaining justices on the Court — John Harlan, Potter Stewart, Byron White, and Tom Clark — were of moderate to conservative bent, and no member of the Court could fittingly be described as an archconservative. The replacement of Justice Goldberg by Justice Abe Fortas (in 1965) perpetuated the liberal complexion of the Court, and the replacement of Justice Clark by Justice Marshall (in 1967) served to strengthen it further.

The year 1969, however, represented an important transition year. With the appointment of Warren Burger to replace Earl Warren as chief justice, not only was there an instantaneous transition to the Burger Court, but also the beginnings of a gradual transition to the more conservative Court of the 1990s. All membership changes after 1969 involved the replacement of departing justices with successors who were comparatively conservative (Blackmun for Fortas in 1970, Powell for Black and Rehnquist for Harlan in 1971, Stevens for Douglas in 1975, O'Connor for Stewart in 1981, Rehnquist for Burger and Scalia for Rehnquist in 1986, Kennedy for Powell in 1988, Souter for Brennan in 1990, and Thomas for Marshall in 1991).

In the meantime, however, the doctrinal innovations of the Warren Court had been absorbed into the law and had diffused to the lower federal courts and to many state courts. Moreover, President Carter, who had no opportunity to make an appointment to the Supreme Court, did have an unusual number of opportunities to appoint lower federal court judges. He used those opportunities to greatly enhance the representation of women and minorities among the federal judiciary.[28]

The political climate has therefore had an ongoing impact on the composition of both the Supreme Court and the lower federal courts. The stage was set in the 1960s for a clash between the Supreme Court, which was relatively liberal, and legislative bodies and lower courts, which were relatively conservative. The stage was reset in the 1970s and 1980s, however, for a new clash between the Supreme Court, which was becoming increasingly conservative, and lower courts which, in the meantime, had begun to produce an array of relatively liberal decisions.

The Petitioning Party in Plenary Cases

The empirical evidence we possess tends to bear out the predictions we have made. Tables 3.2 and 3.3 present empirical data on changes in the composition of the plenary docket. Table 3.2 shows trends in the identity of the petitioning party in criminal procedure cases, that is, cases involving an alleged denial of the right to counsel, the right to a jury trial, the right against self-incrimination, or the right against unreasonable searches and seizures. This table clearly reveals that in criminal procedure cases reaching the plenary docket during the Warren Court (1953–1969), the petitioning party was almost always a criminal defendant (rather than the government). Fully 90 percent of the criminal procedure cases on the plenary docket during the Warren years fit this description.

When Chief Justice Burger replaced Chief Justice Warren, the picture changed dramatically. By the mid-1970s, as Table 3.2 shows, the petitioning party in a majority of criminal procedure cases on the Supreme Court's plenary docket was the government (rather than a criminal defendant). With the transition from the Warren Court to the Burger Court, therefore, an

TABLE 3.2

Litigant Status and the Plenary Docket in Criminal
Procedure Cases

	Percentage of Plenary Cases Being Reviewed at the Request of	
Court Term	State or Federal Government	Criminal Defendants
1953–1968[a]	10	90
1974–1976[a]	55	45
1980–1981[b]	58	42
1985–1986[b]	56	44
1988–1989[b]	54	46

[a]*SOURCE*: Arthur D. Hellman, "The Supreme Court, the National Law, and the Selection of cases for the Plenary Docket," 44 *U. Pitt. L. Rev.* 521, 548–9 (1983).
[b]*SOURCE*: Lawrence Baum, *The Supreme Court*, 4th ed. (Washington, D.C.: Congressional Quarterly, 1992), p. 106.

TABLE 3.3

Litigant Status and the Plenary Docket in Civil
Rights and Civil Liberties Cases

| Court Term | Percentage of Plenary Cases Being Reviewed at the Request of | |
	State or Federal Government	Groups or Individuals
1959–1964	14	86
1965–1970	39	61
1971–1976	48	52

SOURCES: Arthur D. Hellman, "The Business of the Supreme Court under the Judiciary Act of 1925: The Plenary Docket in the 1970's," 91 *Harv. L. Rev.* 1709, 1758 n. 182 (1978); and Arthur D. Hellman, "The Supreme Court and Civil Rights: The Plenary Docket in the 1970's," 58 *Ore. L. Rev.* 3 (1979).

increasing proportion of the scarce places on the plenary docket were being allocated to cases in which the government, not a criminal defendant, was requesting review of an adverse lower court decision.

Table 3.3 presents data on a more general category of cases — cases involving civil rights and civil liberties. Like Table 3.2, it suggests that, with the passage of time, an increasing proportion of the Court's plenary docket has come to consist of cases appealed by government (rather than individuals or groups). Only 14 percent of the civil rights and civil liberties cases on the plenary docket in the 1959–1964 period were cases appealed by state governments or the federal government. By 1971–1976 such cases comprised 48 percent of the plenary docket.[29]

Tables 3.2 and 3.3 indicate that the transition from the Warren Court to the Burger Court was marked by an increase in the Court's willingness to accept cases brought by government and a decrease in its willingness to accept cases brought by groups and individuals alleging that government had interfered with their constitutional rights. This in turn tends to confirm the more general suspicion that, as the Warren Court years receded and the decades of the 1970s and the 1980s unfolded, the Supreme Court was becoming increasingly conservative in outlook.

Conclusion

The Supreme Court must make two decisions in connection with every case it is asked to hear: whether to hear the case and how the case should be decided. These two decisions are not independent of one another. The distribution of opinion among the justices about how a particular case should be decided exerts a powerful influence on the Court's decision whether to hear the case in the first place.

Every year, the Supreme Court is presented with about five thousand opportunities to exercise its power of appellate review. These cases — or filings — comprise the Court's jurisdictional agenda. From among these cases, the Court selects about 120 to 150 cases for plenary consideration. The Supreme Court's exercise of appellate review is therefore confined to a severely restricted subset of the cases that appear on its jurisdictional agenda.

A complex set of statutory requirements and institutional norms govern the process by which cases are selected for inclusion on the plenary docket. Most of the cases on the Supreme Court's jurisdictional agenda (after 1988, nearly all) are classified as certiorari cases. The Supreme Court is authorized by congressional statute to decide for itself which of these cases it will hear.

The decision whether or not to grant certiorari is governed by the Rule of Four. An affirmative decision by four or more justices elevates a case from the jurisdictional agenda to the plenary docket.

In a small number of cases — known as appeal cases — litigants are theoretically entitled to invoke the mandatory appellate jurisdiction of the Supreme Court. In practice, however, such cases, like certiorari cases, are governed by the Rule of Four. A vote of four or more justices is a precondition of noting probable jurisdiction in an appeal case and slating it for plenary consideration.

Over the years, the Supreme Court's discretionary control of its decision-making agenda has gradually increased. Today we may safely assume that most cases that appear on the Supreme Court's plenary docket are there for a reason. If the Supreme Court's plenary docket is changing, it is due in large part to the fact that the Court as an institution wants it to change.

This leads naturally to a search for factors that influence the process of selecting cases for plenary consideration. In making their choices, justices are motivated by their perceptions of the facts of a case, by their political ideology, and by the rules of the game of politics.

A primary consideration for any justice who must select cases for the plenary docket is the correctness or incorrectness of the decision of the court from which the case is being appealed. In addition, each justice is well aware that he or she is only one member of a nine-person voting body and that selecting cases for review is only a prelude to reaching a decision on the merits.

Measurable changes have taken place in recent decades in the types of issues the Supreme Court agrees to decide and in the identity of the petitioning party in plenary cases. These trends reflect the broad transformations that have occurred in American society since the 1930s. They also reflect the impact of the appointment process on the composition of the Supreme Court and on the relationship between the Supreme Court and the lower courts.

Beginning in the 1930s an increasing proportion of the plenary docket of the Supreme Court consisted of cases involving issues of civil rights and civil liberties. By the 1960s about half of the plenary docket consisted of such cases. Since the 1960s, moreover, the representation of civil liberties cases on the plenary docket has remained relatively constant.

The composition of the plenary docket has not remained constant, how-ever, in every respect. In particular, since the 1960s measurable changes have occurred in the identity of the petitioning party in civil liberties cases. The Warren Court was receptive to the constitutional claims of criminal defend-ants, political dissidents, and racial minorities. As a result, its plenary docket was populated by large numbers of cases brought by such litigants. With the transition to the Burger Court, the identity of the petitioning party in plenary cases began to change. Beginning in 1969 the justices appointed to the Supreme Court were almost invariably less receptive than their predecessors to allegations of governmental interference with constitutional rights. As a result, an increasing proportion of the plenary docket has consisted of cases in which the government, rather than the opponents of government, is the petitioning party.

Once the Supreme Court has selected a case for inclusion on its plenary docket, the parties to the case will be notified and the case will be scheduled for oral argument, usually in the following term of the Court. Oral argument represents a further step in the lengthy process by which selected legal disputes rise through the American judicial system and eventually reach the highest court in the land. In the next chapter, we turn to the internal dynamics of the decision-making process and to patterns and trends in Supreme Court policy making.

Notes

1. There are several excellent empirical studies of the Supreme Court's exercise of appellate review. See, for example, H. W. Perry, Jr., *Deciding to Decide: Agenda Setting in the United States Supreme Court* (1991); Doris Marie Provine, *Case Selection in the United States Supreme Court* (1980); Arthur D. Hellman, "Case Selection in the Burger Court: A Preliminary Inquiry," 60 *Notre Dame L. Rev.* 947 (1985); Arthur D. Hellman, "The Supreme Court, the National Law, and the Selection of Cases for the Plenary Docket," 44 *U. Pitt. L. Rev.* 521 (1983); Arthur D. Hellman, "Error Correc-tion, Lawmaking, and the Supreme Court's Exercise of Discretionary Review," 44 *U. Pitt. L. Rev.* 795 (1983); and Arthur D. Hellman, "The Business of the Supreme Court under the Judiciary Act of 1925: The Plenary Docket in the 1970's," 91 *Harv. L. Rev.* 1709 (1978).

2. Annual statistics on the Court's decision-making activity are available in several places. Two of the most useful summaries appear in the *Harvard Law Review* and *U.S. Law Week.*

3. See, generally, Hellman, "The Business of the Supreme Court under the Judiciary Act of 1925." An important step was taken prior to 1925 in the Court of Appeals Act of 1891, which created the original counterparts of the modern courts of appeal and permitted them to have the final say—subject to discretionary review by the Supreme Court—in a broad category of cases. See Richard J. Richardson and Kenneth N. Vines, *The Politics of Federal Courts* (1970), pp. 26–33.

4. Associate Justice John Paul Stevens has discussed the history of the Rule of Four in an article entitled "The Life Span of a Judge-made Rule," 58 *New York Univ. L. Rev.* 1 (1983).

5. The history and uses of the discuss list are examined in Gregory A. Caldeira and John R. Wright, "The Discuss List: Agenda Building in the Supreme Court," 24 *Law and Soc. Rev.* 807 (1990). See also Perry, *Deciding to Decide*, Ch. 3.

6. There is a voluminous literature on *cue theory*. Its purpose is to predict what characteristics of individual cases will enhance the likelihood of their being chosen by the Supreme Court for plenary consideration. Recent contributions include Perry, *Deciding to Decide*, Chs. 5 and 8; Gregory A. Caldeira and John R. Wright, "Organized Interests and Agenda Setting in the U.S. Supreme Court," 82 *Am. Pol. Sci. Rev.* 1109 (1988); S. Sidney Ulmer, "The Supreme Court's Certiorari Decisions: 'Conflict' as a Predictive Variable," 78 *Am. Pol. Sci. Rev.* 901 (1984); S. Sidney Ulmer, "Conflict with Supreme Court Precedents and the Granting of Plenary Review," 45 *J. of Pol.* 474 (1983); Virginia C. Armstrong and Charles A. Johnson, "Certiorari Decisions by the Warren and Burger Courts: Is Cue Theory Time Bound?," 15 *Polity* 141 (1982); S. Sidney Ulmer, "Selecting Cases for Supreme Court Review: Litigant Status in the Warren and Burger Courts," in S. Sidney Ulmer (ed.), *Courts, Law, and Judicial Processes* (1981), pp. 284–98; and Provine, *Case Selection in the United States Supreme Court*.

7. See, for example, Justice Frankfurter's opinion in *Maryland* v. *Baltimore Radio Show*, 338 U.S. 912, 919 (1950): "[A]ll that a denial of a petition for a writ of certiorari means is that fewer than four members of the Court thought it should be granted. . . . [S]uch a denial carries with it no implication whatever regarding the Court's views on the merits of a case which it has declined to review."

8. The classic exposition of strategic considerations in judicial decision making is Walter F. Murphy, *Elements of Judicial Strategy* (1964).

9. We cannot explore these considerations in detail. For additional discussions, see Perry, *Deciding to Decide*, Chs. 6–9; John F. Krol and Saul Brenner, "Strategies in Certiorari Voting in the United States Supreme Court: A Reevaluation," 43 *Western Pol. Q.* 335 (1990); Saul Brenner and John F. Krol, "Strategies in Certiorari Voting on the United States Supreme Court," 51 *J. of Pol.* 828 (1989); Caldeira and Wright, "Organized Interests and Agenda Setting in the U.S. Supreme Court"; Provine, *Case Selection in the United States Supreme Court*; Saul Brenner, "The New Certiorari Game," 41 *J. of Pol.* 649 (1979); Peter Linzer, "The Meaning of Certiorari Denials," 79 *Columbia L. Rev.* 1227 (1979); and S. Sidney Ulmer, "Selecting Cases for Supreme Court Review: An Underdog Model," 72 *Am. Pol. Sci. Rev.* 902 (1978).

10. Justice Powell acquired a substantial reputation as a moderate "swing vote" on the Court. For a study disputing this perception, see Janet L. Blasecki, "Justice Lewis F. Powell: Swing Vote or Staunch Conservative?" 52 *J. of Pol.* 530 (1990).

11. The background of the case is recounted in Richard C. Cortner, *The Supreme Court and Civil Liberties Policy* (1975), Ch. 3.

12. Bob Woodward and Scott Armstrong, *The Brethren: Inside the Supreme Court* (1979), pp. 127–33.

13. The role of interest groups in Supreme Court litigation is examined in several recent studies. See, for example, Lee Epstein and C. K. Rowland, "Debunking the Myth of Interest Group Invincibility in the Courts," 85 *Am. Pol. Sci. Rev.* 205 (1991); Samuel Walker, *In Defense of American Liberties: A History of the ACLU* (1990); Susan E. Lawrence, *The Poor in Court: The Legal Services Program and Supreme Court Decision Making* (1990); Gregory A. Caldeira and John R. Wright, "Amici Curiae before the Supreme Court: Who Participates, When, and How Much?" 52 *J. of Pol.* 782 (1990); Lee Epstein and Charles D. Hadley, "On the Treatment of Political Parties

in the U.S. Supreme Court, 1900–1986," 52 *J. of Pol.* 413 (1990); Joseph F. Kobylka, "A Court-Created Context for Group Litigation: Libertarian Groups and Obscenity," 49 *J. of Pol.* 1061 (1987); Lee Epstein, *Conservatives in Court* (1985); Timothy J. O'Neill, *Bakke and the Politics of Equality* (1985); James L. Gibson and Richard D. Bingham, *Civil Liberties and Nazis: The Skokie Free Speech Controversy* (1985); and Karen O'Connor, *Women's Organizations' Use of the Courts* (1980).

14. Be careful not to confuse the various terms that are used to describe different portions of the Court's agenda. The term *Appellate Docket* is not used to describe the full set of cases appealed to the Court every year, but only that portion consisting of *paid cases*. Note also that the Appellate Docket, to which about half of the cases appealed to the Court are assigned, is not the equivalent of appeal cases. Appeal cases are those that fall within the Court's mandatory appellate jurisdiction. Today they constitute only a small proportion of the Court's jurisdictional agenda.

15. Federal Judicial Center, *Report of the Study Group on the Caseload of the Supreme Court* (Washington, D.C.: Administrative Office of the U.S. Courts, 1972).

16. Commission on Revision of the Federal Court Appellate System, *Structure and Internal Procedures: Recommendations for Change* (1975).

17. For additional discussions of the Supreme Court's workload and the various proposals to reduce it, see David M. O'Brien, *Storm Center: The Supreme Court in American Politics* (1990), pp. 181–92, 216–53; Arthur D. Hellman, "Caseload, Conflicts, and Decisional Capacity: Does the Supreme Court Need Help?" 67 *Judicature* 28 (1983); and Note, "Of High Designs: A Compendium of Proposals to Reduce the Workload of the Supreme Court," 97 *Harv. L. Rev.* 307 (1983).

18. Richard L. Pacelle, Jr., *The Transformation of the Supreme Court's Agenda: From the New Deal to the Reagan Administration* (1991).

19. Hellman, "The Business of the Supreme Court under the Judiciary Act of 1925," p. 1751.

20. *Baker* v. *Carr* (1962); *Reynolds* v. *Sims* (1964).

21. *Roth* v. *United States* (1957).

22. *New York Times Co.* v. *Sullivan* (1964).

23. *Miranda* v. *Arizona* (1966).

24. *Reed* v. *Reed* (1971).

25. *Furman* v. *Georgia* (1972).

26. *Roe* v. *Wade* (1973). For a detailed discussion of changes in the composition of the plenary docket since 1954, see Hellman, "Case Selection in the Burger Court," pp. 970–1010.

27. Hellman, "The Business of the Supreme Court under the Judiciary Act of 1925," p. 1716.

28. More than one-third of President Carter's appointees to the federal bench (116 out of 318) were women and minorities. See Thomas G. Walker and Deborah J. Barrow, "The Diversification of the Federal Bench: Policy and Process Ramifications," 47 *J. of Pol.* 596 (1985); Jon Gottschall, "Carter's Judicial Appointments: The Influence of Affirmative Action and Merit Selection on Voting on the U.S. Courts of Appeals," 67 *Judicature* 167 (1983); and Sheldon Goldman, "Carter's Judicial Appointments: A Lasting Legacy," 64 *Judicature* 344 (1981). President Carter's federal judicial appointments are compared with those of President Reagan in Sheldon Goldman, "Reaganizing the Judiciary: The First Term Appointments," 68 *Judicature* 313 (1985); and Sheldon Goldman, "Reagan's Judicial Legacy: Completing the Puzzle and Summing Up," 72 *Judicature* 318 (1989).

29. Tables 3.2 and 3.3 illuminate the changing priorities of the Supreme Court by focusing on changes in the composition of the plenary docket. For studies that employ alternative strategies for detecting changes in the case-selection priorities of the Supreme Court, see Caldeira and Wright, "The Discuss List"; Caldeira and Wright, "Organized Interests and Agenda Setting in the U.S. Supreme Court"; and Ulmer, "Selecting Cases for Supreme Court Review."

CHAPTER 4

Supreme Court
Decision Making

Only rarely does a case survive the gauntlet of the appellate process. Many litigants are discouraged by the time and money required to appeal a case all the way to the Supreme Court. In addition, as we have seen, the Supreme Court has discretionary control over most of its docket and declines to review about 95 percent of appeals and petitions for certiorari. Those cases which the Court does "decide to decide" become the chief vehicles for the policy pronouncements of the Supreme Court in American politics.

In this chapter, we begin by exploring the internal dynamics of the decision-making process of the Supreme Court in plenary cases. In Section II, we review the history of Supreme Court decision making and note some of the Court's most important decisions. In Section III, we look at empirical evidence of trends and patterns in Supreme Court decision making.

The Decisional Process in the Supreme Court

Every case accepted and decided by the Supreme Court has its own special characteristics. At the same time, the decisional process in the Supreme Court has remained relatively constant over the years. The job facing the Court is the same in every case accepted for plenary consideration—to hear from the contending parties, to reach a decision, and to justify that decision in a written opinion. These basic features of the judicial process shape the activities of the Court as it sets about deciding cases.[1]

Oral Argument

When the Supreme Court agrees to hear a case, it schedules oral argument for a particular day during its October to June term. Prior to oral argument, the justices will receive and peruse the written submissions—or *briefs*—of the opposing parties. In addition, the Court may receive *amicus curiae*, or friend of the court, briefs. In controversial cases, the flood of *amicus* briefs may be substantial. In the *Bakke* case (see Chapter 11) and in *Webster* v. *Reproductive Health Services* (a 1989 abortion case, discussed in Chapter 10), the Court received more than seventy-five such briefs.[2]

Once the Court has assembled for oral argument and the lawyers for each side begin presentation of the case, the justices will interrupt frequently with questions and comments. Indeed, quite commonly a lawyer is unable to present more than a small portion of his or her prepared remarks before facing a barrage of questions from the justices.

The Role of the Solicitor General in Supreme Court Decision Making

In cases to which the U.S. government is a party, or in which it is interested, responsibility for preparing and submitting a primary brief or an *amicus* brief rests with the solicitor general of the United States. This official also represents the federal government before the Supreme Court in oral argument.

The solicitor general is an official of the Justice Department and is thus ultimately responsible to the president. Traditionally, however, the solicitor general has maintained a degree of independence from the rest of the executive branch.

Over the years, the Supreme Court has come to expect that the solicitor general's office will exercise great restraint in appealing cases to the Court and will do so only when the government has a strong chance of winning. In addition, the Court has come to expect the solicitor general to submit highly professional briefs in those cases that it does decide to appeal or to join.

The special relationship between the solicitor general and the Supreme Court is reflected in the high proportion of the U.S. government's petitions for certiorari which are granted plenary review (between 75 and 90 percent; see H. W. Perry, Jr., *Deciding to Decide: Agenda Setting in the United States Supreme Court* [1991], pp. 128 – 33), and in the high proportion of cases in which the U.S. government is a winner on the merits (73 percent in the 1984 – 1989 terms; see Lawrence Baum, *The Supreme Court*, [1992] p. 140).

In sum, the solicitor general plays a uniquely important role in the appellate process. For additional discussion of this official's role, see Charles Fried, *Order and Law: Arguing the Reagan Revolution — A Firsthand Account* (1991); Jeffrey A. Segal, "Supreme Court Support for the Solicitor General: The Effects of Presidential Appointments," 43 *Western Pol. Q.* 137 (1990); and Lincoln Caplan, *The Tenth Justice: The Solicitor General and the Rule of Law* (1987).

Each side is normally allotted one half hour for argument. The typical case will therefore be heard in an hour's time. The half-hour limitation, moreover, is strictly enforced. There is a famous anecdote that serves as a reminder of this fact to anyone who plans to argue before the Supreme Court: It is said that Chief Justice Hughes once enforced the time limitation on the length of oral argument by cutting off an attorney in the middle of the word "if."

The Conference

Shortly after a particular case has been argued, the justices will assemble in *conference* to discuss the case and to reach at least a tentative decision on its outcome. Conference sessions of the Court are attended only by the justices themselves. Discussion is inaugurated by the chief justice, and succeeding contributions are made by the associate justices in order of seniority of service on the Court. On occasion, a separate, formal vote on the case will be taken following discussion. More commonly, at some appropriate point during the discussion itself, the justices will indicate the direction of their vote or perhaps their intention to "pass," that is, to reserve their vote for the time being.

The result of the conference will be a tentative decision on the merits of the case. By tradition, if the chief justice is a member of the majority, he has the option of selecting someone — including himself — to write the opinion of the Court. In the event the chief justice is in the minority, responsibility for assigning the opinion falls to the most senior justice in the majority.

Opinion Assignment

The power to assign opinions is an important one. Even though the Court's decision in a particular case may be settled by the vote in conference, responsibility for formulating the grounds for the decision and the reasoning of the Court will rest with the justice who is assigned the task of writing the opinion of the Court. The designated author may choose to write a "narrow" opinion, that is, one that is based strictly on the facts of the case and disclaims any intention to announce sweeping principles of law. Alternatively, the opinion writer may choose to prepare a "broad" opinion, that is, one that aims for wide impact by including language that could apply to a variety of factual situations other than those on which the case itself was based. The Court member who controls the opinion assignment also controls, to a considerable extent, the content of the opinion itself — and through it the scope and meaning of the Court's decision.[3]

The power to assign opinions is not only important; it is also delicate. An impolitic choice may result in the preparation of an opinion which, when circulated to the rest of the provisional majority, fails to attract the support of at least four additional justices. The result, of course, is that the original conference majority may evaporate and be replaced by a new—and perhaps very different—alignment of justices.

Numerous examples of shifts in the composition of the majority, and consequently the outcome of the case, emerge from inside accounts of the work of the Court. One such shift occurred in the 1986 case of *Bowers* v. *Hardwick*, in which the Supreme Court refused to invalidate a Georgia law against homosexual sodomy. At the end of the conference, there were five votes to overturn the law. Among them was Justice Powell. The senior justice in the majority, Justice Brennan, assigned Justice Blackmun, another member of the majority, the task of writing an opinion in the case. When Powell saw Blackmun's opinion, however, he felt unable to subscribe to its contents, and he informed Chief Justice Burger that he was changing his vote. As a result, the opinion that Justice White had drafted for a dissenting minority of four became the opinion of the Court for a majority of five.[4]

It is important to maintain a proper perspective on the foregoing phenomenon—a phenomenon that one scholar has called "the fluidity of judicial choice."[5] Empirical studies of the extent of such fluidity in two periods—1946–1956 and 1956–1967—suggest that justices change their minds only about 10 percent of the time and that most such changes served to increase the size of the original majority and only rarely caused it to disappear.[6] Thus, even though justices on occasion will change their minds, such change or fluidity is the exception and not the rule. Moreover, the prevailing pattern of change on the Supreme Court is in the direction of increased rather than decreased consensus.

Unanimity and Dissent: The Public Voice of the Court

The plenary decisions of the Supreme Court are presented to the public in several forms. Sometimes the Court will reach a unanimous decision. When this occurs, the Court will issue an opinion representing the views of the entire membership of the Court. More commonly, however, the Court will be divided. On those occasions, the Court will issue a *majority opinion*—an opinion representing the views of a majority of the Court. The majority opinion will be accompanied by one or more *concurring opinions* and *dissenting opinions*.

On occasion, the Court is divided almost down the middle. When that happens, the case may be decided by a proverbial 5–4 vote. A 5–4 decision represents a victory for one side or the other in the case. However, it is a victory achieved by the narrowest of margins.

Occasionally, the Court finds itself not only divided, but also fragmented. After the circulation of draft opinions, it may be that no single opinion can gain the assent of even a five-person majority. When that happens, the Court will issue a plurality opinion—an opinion representing the views of a minority of the Court—accompanied by various concurrences and dissents. The ex-

/77

a *plurality decision*, of course, is one in which each member
es his or her own separate opinion.[7]

the Supreme Court

ᵣₑₘₑ Court decision that commands the assent of every justice represents an emphatic statement of the law. When the Court is able to reach
complete agreement on the outcome of a case, and on the reasons for that
outcome, it will issue a unanimous opinion.

In several notable cases, the chief justice has gone to extraordinary
lengths to achieve unanimity. Chief Justice Earl Warren delayed a decision in
Brown v. *Board of Education* owing in part to his desire to produce a
unanimous decision on the issue of school segregation. As we will see in
Chapter 6, Warren's strategy paid off: The Court reached a unanimous
decision in the *Brown* case and also united behind a single opinion authored
by Warren himself.

In *Cooper* v. *Aaron* in 1958, the Court issued a unanimous decision with
an added twist: The opinion of the Court was personally signed by each of the
nine justices. The Court took this unusual step because it was concerned that
the facts of the case — defiance by public officials in Little Rock, Arkansas, of
a lower court desegregation order — constituted a particularly serious threat
to the authority of the federal courts.[8]

In the so-called Nixon Tapes Cases — *United States* v. *Nixon* (1974) —
Chief Justice Burger was also concerned about safeguarding the authority of
federal courts. The case arose out of the investigation by a special prosecutor
into the Watergate scandal — the alleged bugging of Democratic party head-
quarters by agents of President Nixon's reelection committee and the subsequent White House coverup of the episode.[9] The special prosecutor issued a
subpoena to President Nixon requesting various tapes of conversations that
had taken place in the White House, but the president resisted the subpoena
on the ground that it violated "executive privilege." When the case reached
the Supreme Court, Chief Justice Burger was concerned that if the decision
of the Court were not unanimous, President Nixon might be tempted to defy
the Court and refuse to relinquish the potentially incriminating evidence. The
Court eventually held, by a vote of 8 to 0, that Nixon must relinquish the
tapes.[10]

Unanimity and Division in
Historical Perspective

The foregoing cases are noteworthy, but they represent the exception, not the
rule. The contemporary Court is unanimous only about 25 to 30 percent of
the time; the remainder of its decisions are reached by a divided vote.

This represents a major change from the nineteenth and early twentieth
centuries. Prior to the 1940s, the Court was unanimous about 80 to 90
percent of the time. The low rate of dissent and concurrence did not mean

there was no disagreement among the justices. Instead it meant that the justices chose to subordinate their differences to the institutional norm that the Court should present a united front to the public whenever possible. Thus, disagreements among the justices tended to remain private and were rarely revealed to the public in the form of published dissents or concurrences.[11]

The institutional norm of unanimity was abruptly shattered during the tenure of Chief Justice Stone (1941 – 1946).[12] Unlike many of his predecessors, Stone did not discourage his fellow justices from writing dissents and concurrences, and he himself dissented frequently. The pattern established by Stone has persisted, and today the Court's decisions are nonunanimous about two-thirds to three-fourths of the time.[13]

When the Court Divides: Majority Opinions, Concurrences, and Dissents

When the Court reaches a decision supported by a majority of between five and nine justices, the views of the majority are embodied in a single "opinion of the Court." On occasion, the majority opinion will be issued *per curiam*, that is, from the Court as a body. More commonly, the majority opinion will be authored by a particular justice — the justice who was assigned the task of writing the opinion after the vote in conference. When five or more justices agree to join a particular opinion, the published decision will open with the phrase "Mr. Justice Smith delivered the opinion of the Court."

A majority decision that is not unanimous will usually be accompanied by at least one dissenting opinion. Such an opinion represents an expression by a justice (or group of justices) of disagreement with the result reached by the Court, that is, with the outcome of the case. A dissenting opinion will almost always argue that the case should have been decided in the opposite direction from the way it was.

Majority opinions are also accompanied, quite frequently, by one or more concurring opinions. Some concurring opinions represent the expression of additional remarks by a justice (or group of justices) who are otherwise in agreement with the content of the majority opinion. As long as at least a five-person majority coalesces around one result and one opinion, the presence of concurring opinions will not disturb the clarity of the victory achieved by one side or the other. Moreover, the published decision will open with the distinctive phrase "Mr. Justice Smith delivered the opinion of the Court."

The Fragmented Court: Plurality Opinions in Supreme Court Cases

On occasion, however, one or more of the justices may issue a concurring opinion whose purpose goes beyond the expression of additional views or comments. The distinctive feature of such a concurring opinion is that, while it expresses agreement with other members of the Court about the *result* of the case, it usually takes exception to the *reasons* on which that result is based. When the Court is divided in this way, the case will be resolved by the device of a *plurality opinion*. Issuance of a plurality opinion usually signifies that, while a majority of the Court has agreed on the result of the case, there is no agreement *within* the majority on the reasons for that result.[14]

Plurality Opinions in Constitutional Cases

The Supreme Court's decisions on capital punishment in the 1970s offer an example of the significance of reasons as well as results in Supreme Court decision making.

By a fragmented majority of 5–4, the Court in *Furman* v. *Georgia* (1972), struck down the death penalty as it was then being administered by the states. The judgment of the Court was announced in a *per curiam* opinion, but each of the five justices in the majority, as well as each of the four justices in the minority, wrote a separate opinion.

Observers quickly realized that among the majority justices — that is, among the five justices who voted to overturn the death penalty — there were several very different theories of why the death penalty was unconstitutional. Justice Douglas emphasized evidence of racial discrimination in administration of the death penalty. Justices Brennan and Marshall emphasized their opposition to capital punishment under any circumstances. Justice Stewart focused on the randomness and capriciousness of the process by which defendants were actually chosen for execution. And Justice White expressed his skepticism that the death penalty could serve as an effective deterrent to murder when in practice it was so rarely imposed.

Obviously, Justice Stewart's opposition to capital punishment could be overcome by reducing the level of capriciousness in imposition of the death penalty. Justice White's opposition, moreover, could be overcome by evidence that states intended to use the death penalty on a more frequent and consistent basis.

When the Court reexamined the issue of capital punishment in *Gregg* v. *Georgia* (1976), it did so in the context of revised state statutes that provided more guidance to juries in imposing the death sentence. The Court concluded, by a 7–2 margin, that execution was a permissible punishment for murder.

Four members of the original *Furman* "majority" remained on the Court. (Justice Douglas had retired.) Of the four, however, only Brennan and Marshall continued to oppose the use of capital punishment. The doubts about capital punishment expressed by Justices Stewart and White in their *Furman* opinions had been resolved by the new state statutes.

In a typical situation, a total of five justices may conclude that Litigant X should win, but they may divide 3–2 over the reasons for this result. When this happens, the opinion of one segment of the majority—for example, the group of three justices—will be designated as the plurality opinion. The published decision of the Court will open with the phrase "Mr. Justice Smith announced the judgment of the Court [i.e., the *result* in the case] and delivered an opinion in which Justices Jones and Brown joined." The remaining two justices in the majority will add their opinion, in the form of a concurrence, while the four justices who endorse neither the result nor the reasoning of the majority will contribute their views in the form of a dissent. The result is a 5–4 decision which, in essence, is a 3–2–4 decision. Observers of the Court will note the existence of deep divisions within the majority and will predict, with justification, that in a future case involving similar issues the majority will not necessarily remain intact.[15]

Division on the Court: Recent Trends

We have already mentioned that the proportion of unanimous Supreme Court decisions declined from 80 to 90 percent in the nineteenth and early twentieth centuries to 25 to 30 percent since 1941. A further indicator of the trend toward greater public division on the Court is the contemporary prevalence of 5–4 decisions and plurality opinions. During the nineteenth century, an average of only one case per term was decided by a 5–4 majority, but the average rose to sixteen during most of the Warren Court (1956–1969) and to eighteen during the first three years of the Burger Court (1969–1972).[16] In the nine most recent terms of the Court (1982–1990), the Court averaged more than thirty 5–4 decisions per term.[17]

Plurality opinions are also much more prevalent than they used to be. There were only 10 such opinions in the entire nineteenth century, but that number rose to 51 for the years between 1901 and 1969, and to 116 in the Burger Court (1969–1986).[18] Clearly, the contemporary Supreme Court is much more willing to reveal its internal differences to the public than was the Court in earlier years.

With the consolidation of a conservative majority on the Supreme Court, these recent trends are likely to be reversed. The Burger Court was a transitional Court, spanning the period between the end of the 1960s and the waning years of the Reagan Administration. As liberal members of the Court were gradually replaced by more conservative justices, the basic political orientation of the Court underwent a fitful but profound transformation. With the departure of Justices Brennan and Marshall—the two most liberal members of the Court—the transformation is complete. No one is predicting a return to the days when the Court was unanimous 80 to 90 percent of the time. Almost certainly, however, there will be a decline—perhaps a rather sharp decline—in the proportion of cases decided by 5–4 majorities and by plurality opinions.

Decisional Norms in
Comparative Perspective

The American approach to judicial decision making represents a compromise between two alternatives found in other countries. In some judicial systems, for instance, those of England and India, the norm is for each member of a judicial tribunal to present his or her views seriatim, that is, one after the other. The challenging task of deciphering which party actually won the case — and for what reasons — is left to observers.

In other judicial systems, for instance, those of Italy and France, there is a presumption against dissent and strong pressure on judges to reach consensus. Regardless of the depth of dissension among the judges themselves, the public eventually sees a unanimous decision.

In the United States, it was Chief Justice John Marshall who persuaded his fellow judges of the merits of departing from British practice and presenting, whenever possible, a single opinion of the Court. Not surprisingly, Marshall himself was a prominent beneficiary of the more structured system that he had managed to introduce. During his tenure as chief justice (1801–1835), Marshall personally authored more than half of the constitutional rulings of the Court and was obliged to dissent from a constitutional ruling only once.[19]

Conclusion

The decisional process in plenary cases consists of several steps that do not vary much from case to case. The Supreme Court receives written briefs and schedules oral argument. Following oral argument, the Court meets in conference to discuss the case. After the conference discussion, the chief justice (or, if the chief justice is in the minority, the senior justice in the majority) assigns the opinion. The draft opinion of the majority, as well as concurring and dissenting opinions, will circulate among the justices over a period of weeks or months. Eventually, usually during the spring, the Court will announce decisions in the cases it has heard during the term.

Supreme Court decisions take various forms. Some (about 25 to 30 percent in recent years) are unanimous. Of the nonunanimous decisions, most are majority decisions. The majority coalition will include from five to eight justices, some of whom, in addition to joining in the majority opinion, may issue concurring opinions. Between one and four justices, either singly or in groups, will dissent. Occasionally — and in fact fairly frequently during the Burger Court — the justices in the majority will disagree among themselves about the reasons for reaching a particular result. When that happens, a case will be decided by the device of a plurality opinion.

Majority opinions of the Supreme Court (as well as unanimous decisions of the Court) are almost always the product of an intense process of negotiation and compromise. Once that process is over, however, the public is offered a single decision of the Supreme Court and a single set of reasons for that decision. The advantage of achieving agreement on a single opinion of the Court is that the world at large — and more importantly lower court judges and practicing lawyers — will learn not only *how* the case was decided but also *why* it was decided the way it was.

The issuance of a plurality opinion, on the other hand, means that the law remains unclear and unsettled. The Supreme Court is divided not only about the outcome of a case, but also about the reasons for reaching a particular result. The constitutional issue posed by the case will not be resolved in any definitive fashion until one or more justices has a change of mind or until the composition of the Court itself is altered by the appointment process.

Most of the cases the Supreme Court accepts for plenary review are treated in roughly the same fashion. The cases themselves, however, vary widely. Each case incorporates a distinctive set of facts, generates a distinctive set of interactions among the justices, and culminates in a judicial decision that has a distinctive impact on American society. We now turn our attention, therefore, to the content of Supreme Court decisions and to patterns and trends in Supreme Court decision making.

Supreme Court Decision Making in Historical Perspective

The Supreme Court changes relatively slowly. As a result, an entire generation can absorb a uniform perception of what the Court is really like. Some Americans grew up during a time when the Court was renowned for its economic conservatism. Others came of age when the Court had a strong reputation for liberal activism. Still others — including, presumably, most of the readers of this book — have grown up during a time when the liberal and activist members of the Court were being methodically replaced by justices who promised to be more conservative and restrained in their approach to constitutional problems.

Each generation, therefore, will have a distinctive image of both the political orientation and decision-making philosophy of the Supreme Court. It becomes particularly important to remember that the Court, like any political institution, does change. It used to be very different than it is today, and in ten or twenty years, if not tomorrow or the next day, it will have changed again, perhaps in major ways. Nothing is more critical to understanding the Supreme Court as a political institution than gaining a working familiarity with its overall history.

A great deal of thoughtful historical scholarship on the Supreme Court is available. In a book such as this, obviously we cannot provide a complete history of the Court. However, we can allude to some of the leading historical accounts of the Supreme Court and to the conclusions they reach about the distinctive characteristics of different eras of Supreme Court decision making.[20]

The Early Years: The Supreme Court under John Marshall

In the first decades of the Republic, the Supreme Court was preoccupied with a distinctive set of interrelated issues. First, the Court was called upon to play a role in resolving the balance of power between the states and the federal government. Second, the Court was drawn into several controversies involving the power of government to interfere with property rights and other vested interests. Finally, the Court was concerned with defining its own role in the emerging political order.[21]

John Marshall, who served as chief justice between 1801 and 1835, was by far the dominant figure on the Court and was primarily responsible for shaping its response to the twin issues of nation-state relations and property rights. Never far from Marshall's mind, moreover, was the third issue — the role of the Supreme Court in the American system of government. Among Marshall's many talents was an uncanny ability to enhance the prestige of the Supreme Court as a byproduct of his decisions on other critical issues of the day.

Marbury v. *Madison* (1803) is the preeminent example of Marshall's extraordinary combination of political and legal skills. As we saw in Chapter 1, the facts in *Marbury* presented Marshall with a seemingly hopeless political dilemma. Instead of shrinking from the challenge, he audaciously capitalized on his predicament and used it to establish the Supreme Court's prerogative to review the constitutional validity of congressional legislation.

Marshall provided equally forceful answers to the other pressing issues of the day. In *McCulloch* v. *Maryland* (1819), he offered an expansive interpretation of congressional power under the Necessary and Proper Clause of the Constitution. In *Gibbons* v. *Ogden* (1824), Marshall threw the weight of the Court behind the policy of national economic integration. In *Dartmouth College* v. *Woodward* (1819), he inaugurated a tradition of judicial protection of property rights which would last well into the next century.

Marshall's impact on the development of the Supreme Court as an institution cannot be overstated. "It was Marshall," one scholar has written, "who by his courage, his convictions, and his intellectual vigor raised the Supreme Court from a third-rate status to a position of constitutional equality with President and Congress."[22]

The Race Issue: Dred Scott and Its Consequences

The Supreme Court's first major misstep occurred in *Dred Scott* v. *Sandford* in 1857. The Court had convinced itself that it could resolve the impasse over slavery, and in a sense, it was right. The issue of slavery was resolved by the Civil War, and most historians regard the *Dred Scott* decision as one of the factors that precipitated the war.

In an opinion by Chief Justice Roger Taney, the Court rejected a claim by

Dred Scott, a slave, that he had become a free man by virtue of his journeys into areas where slavery was illegal under state law or under congressional legislation known as the Missouri Compromise. The Court declared the Missouri Compromise unconstitutional and also held that persons of African ancestry, whether or not they were slaves, were not citizens of the United States.[23]

Dred Scott was the first case since *Marbury* in which the Supreme Court had overturned an act of Congress. It was also a low point in the history of the Court. The prestige of the Court recovered relatively quickly. In the apt description of one scholar, however, the *Dred Scott* decision itself was "a political error of the highest magnitude."[24]

In the wake of the Civil War, much of the energy of the Reconstruction Congress was devoted to clarifying and improving the legal and political status of the newly freed slaves. In particular, one of the Supreme Court's holdings in *Dred Scott*—that blacks were not citizens—was overturned by passage and ratification, in 1868, of the Fourteenth Amendment to the Constitution. The first sentence of the Amendment stipulated that "All persons born or naturalized in the United States, and subject to the jurisdiction thereof, are citizens of the United States and of the State wherein they reside."[25]

The Supreme Court and Economic Expansion

By the 1870s the Court had recovered its prestige and was once again a prominent participant in the political process. The years following the Civil War were characterized by extraordinary economic expansion and by new governmental initiatives to regulate economic growth. The Court became heavily involved in the struggle to define the limits of governmental power to regulate the economy.

The rapid economic expansion spawned two conflicting schools of thought. Some believed fervently in laissez-faire capitalism, that is, the theory that economic activity should be completely free of governmental control. Others believed, just as fervently, that it was imperative for government to play an increased role in regulating business activity. The Court sided with the advocates of laissez faire and manifested its sympathies by overturning numerous state and federal regulatory laws between the 1890s and 1937. Historians emphasize that the Court was not uniformly hostile to government regulation. Without doubt, however, that was the prevailing tenor of its decisions.

The years during which the Court was dominated by justices who espoused doctrines of laissez-faire capitalism are known as the era of *substantive due process*. The phrase derives from the fact that the Court frequently used the Due Process Clause of the Fourteenth Amendment as a basis for its decisions overturning state regulatory legislation. The Due Process Clause prevented the states from "depriv[ing] any person of life, liberty, or property, without due process of law." The Court interpreted this language to mean that state legislation that protected workers or regulated businesses was unconstitutional, because it deprived people of their liberty or property without due process of law.

The doctrine of substantive due process was not very logical, because the Due Process Clause, as written, does not protect life, liberty, or property *as such*. It merely guarantees that persons cannot be deprived of these things "without due process of law." For a period of about forty years, however, a majority of the Supreme Court supported the idea that the Due Process Clause protected persons (and corporations) from interference by state governments with their substantive right to liberty and property.[26] The doctrine of substantive due process provided a pretext for striking down legislation which, in the view of a majority of the Court, would inhibit rapid economic expansion, and it enabled the Court to play a key role in the process of defining the limits of governmental regulation of economic affairs.[27]

Confrontation: The Supreme Court and the New Deal

The conflict between the Supreme Court and advocates of governmental control of the economy came to a head in the 1930s. Franklin D. Roosevelt was elected president in 1932, in the midst of the Great Depression, and as soon as he took office, he launched a wide range of economic reforms that together were known as the New Deal. Many of Roosevelt's programs substantially increased the role of government, especially the federal government, in the regulation of economic affairs.

Given the Supreme Court's conservative economic outlook, it was inevitable that the Court would have a negative reaction to the New Deal. Between 1933 and 1937, the Court used its power of judicial review to overturn several key pieces of New Deal legislation.[28]

President Roosevelt had no opportunity to appoint anyone to the Supreme Court during his first term in office. By February 1937, he had become so frustrated by the Court's opposition to his program of economic recovery that he proposed enlarging the Court to fifteen members. The official explanation that Roosevelt gave for his proposal was that the Court was overworked and that a new justice should be added to the Court for every sitting justice who was over seventy years old. Almost everyone understood, however, that the real purpose of the so-called *Court-packing* plan was to open the way for appointment of six new justices who would be sympathetic to the aims of the New Deal.[29]

Roosevelt's plan to enlarge the Court was eventually defeated by the Senate.[30] In the meantime, however, the impasse between the Court and the Roosevelt Administration was moving toward resolution. In June 1937, Justice Van Devanter, a steadfast opponent of the New Deal, announced his retirement from the Court. Moreover, earlier in the spring Justice Roberts had voted to uphold a state minimum wage law, altering his previous stance on the issue. Roberts's decision was promptly dubbed "the switch in time that saved nine," because it helped to defuse the president's campaign to enlarge the Court.[31]

By the summer of 1937 the constitutional crisis of the 1930s was effectively over. By acquiescing to the legislative initiatives of the New Deal, the Court tacitly conceded that it would no longer play an active role in assessing the constitutional validity of economic legislation and that henceforth Congress and the president would have the final say in this area of public policy.

Footnote Four and the New Emphasis on Civil Liberties

Once the Court had abdicated its traditional role as a major participant in the policy-making process on economic issues — a role it had played since the 1890s — it was temporarily bereft of a clear set of constitutional responsibilities. The Court's loss of direction was short-lived. Within months, the Court began to carve out a new niche for itself as a principal policy-making voice on civil liberties issues.

Prior to the 1930s, as we saw in Chapter 3, civil liberties cases were almost completely absent from the Supreme Court's plenary docket. Moreover, of the civil liberties cases that the Court did decide, few were decided in favor of individuals or minority groups claiming that government had violated their constitutional rights.[32] Beginning in the 1930s, however, the Court began to decide substantial numbers of civil liberties cases. Within a short time, as we have seen, civil liberties cases came to comprise about 50 percent of the Court's plenary docket and have maintained this level of representation ever since.[33]

The Court's transformation from protector of property rights to guardian of civil liberties was marked, in somewhat unlikely fashion, by a *footnote* to one of its decisions! In 1938, in a case called *United States* v. *Carolene Products Co.*, the Court voted to uphold a challenged piece of congressional economic legislation.[34] The Court's decision was in keeping with its newfound deference to Congress on economic issues. In his opinion for the Court, however, Justice Stone appended a footnote — *Footnote Four* — in which he suggested that in cases involving alleged violations of the civil rights and civil liberties of individuals and minority groups — in contrast to cases involving property rights and economic legislation — the Court, in the future, would be especially vigilant. Footnote Four is now widely regarded as the Supreme Court's deliberate statement of its intention to withdraw from active participation in the policy-making process on economic issues and to redirect its energies to the protection of civil liberties and individual rights.[35]

We will take a closer look at the contents of Footnote Four in upcoming portions of this book, especially in the Introduction to Part II and in Chapter 14. Footnote Four appears so often in our discussions because it represents a seminal statement of the Supreme Court's modern conception of its role in the political process. Moreover, the Footnote accurately predicted the new directions that Supreme Court decision making was about to take. Almost immediately, the Court began to decide additional cases involving issues of freedom of speech, press, assembly, and religion, due process for criminal defendants, equal protection of the laws, and privacy.

The Supreme Court under Earl Warren

The accession of Earl Warren to the chief justiceship in 1953 solidified the new orientation of the Court. Within months, the Supreme Court handed down its decision in *Brown* v. *Board of Education*, in which it ruled unanimously that racial segregation of public schools was unconstitutional. Many judicial scholars regard *Brown* as the most important civil liberties decision of this century.

The judicial activism of the Warren Court intensified in the 1960s. Between 1962 and 1967, Presidents Kennedy and Johnson made several key appointments to the Court, including Justices Goldberg, Fortas, and Marshall. The Court's decisions reflected the liberal sentiments of these and other justices. The period of liberal dominance of the Supreme Court did not last long—by 1971 Justices Fortas and Black, as well as Chief Justice Warren, were gone from the Court. However, the 1960s produced some of the Court's most celebrated civil liberties decisions. Among them were *Mapp* v. *Ohio* (1961) (applying the exclusionary rule to the states), *Baker* v. *Carr* (1962) (extending federal court jurisdiction to reapportionment cases), *Engel* v. *Vitale* (1962) and *Abington Township* v. *Schempp* (1963) (the school prayer cases; these cases are examined in detail in Chapter 8), *Gideon* v. *Wainwright* (1963) and numerous other decisions protecting criminal defendants and applying provisions of the Bill of Rights to the states (these cases are examined in detail in Chapter 9), *New York Times* v. *Sullivan* (1964) (extending First Amendment protection to newspapers accused of publishing libelous statements about public officials), and *Griswold* v. *Connecticut* (1965) (discovering a right of privacy in the Constitution).[36]

The Burger Court

The transition to the Burger Court was marked by President Nixon's appointment of Chief Justice Burger in 1969, followed by three further appointments (Blackmun, Rehnquist, and Powell) in 1970 and 1971. It was widely expected that the new Court would overrule at least some Warren Court decisions. However, while the Burger Court was clearly disinclined to expand the protections established by the Warren Court, neither did it engage in any wholesale repudiation of existing law. In addition, the Burger Court was responsible for the Supreme Court's first-ever decisions protecting women (and men) from alleged sex discrimination. Moreover, when the Court issued its controversial decision in *Roe* v. *Wade*, holding that women had a constitutionally protected right to obtain an abortion, three Nixon appointees— Blackmun, Burger, and Powell—were part of the majority.[37]

It was primarily in cases involving criminal procedure that the Burger Court began to revise the doctrines of the Warren Court. Even here, however, a majority of the Court was unwilling to overturn past decisions. The overall caution of the Burger Court, combined with its willingness to open up new areas of constitutional protection of individual rights, led many observers to retract or modify their original predictions about the impact of the new appointments.[38]

The Rehnquist Court

With the ascension of William Rehnquist to the chief justiceship in 1986, the Burger Court has come to be regarded, in restrospect, as a transitional court. The Burger Court included two justices — Brennan and Marshall — who rank among the most liberal in the history of the Supreme Court. In addition, several Burger Court justices, including Blackmun, Powell, Stevens, and White, displayed liberal voting tendencies on selected issues. As a result, the

The Supreme Court in 1992. Only one member of the current Court — Byron White, a Kennedy appointee — was appointed by a Democratic president. The remaining justices were appointed by four successive Republican presidents — Richard Nixon, Gerald Ford, Ronald Reagan, and George Bush. *Standing (left to right):* David Souter, Antonin Scalia, Anthony M. Kennedy, and Clarence Thomas. *Seated (left to right):* John Paul Stevens, Byron R. White, William H. Rehnquist, Harry A. Blackmun, and Sandra Day O'Connor.

SOURCE: Collection of the Supreme Court of the United States

Supreme Court under Chief Justice Burger never gelled into a consistently conservative decision-making institution.

In 1986, however, Burger was replaced as chief justice by William Rehnquist and Rehnquist's place was taken by Antonin Scalia. In fairly rapid succession, additional justices with conservative views on constitutional issues were added to the Court (Anthony Kennedy in 1988, David Souter in 1990, and Clarence Thomas in 1991). Souter and Thomas replaced Brennan and Marshall, the Court's veteran liberal justices. These membership changes have completed the Court's transformation from a bastion of liberal judicial activism into an institution with a profoundly different set of perspectives on contemporary constitutional questions.[39]

Conclusion

This brief survey of the history of the Supreme Court suggests how dangerous it is to try to stereotype the Court. In the first era of its history, the Court was preoccupied with issues of federalism and property rights (and incidentally with the status of the Supreme Court in the American system of government). In the last years of the nineteenth century and during the first decades of this century, the Court viewed itself as a key defender of conservative economic values. During all this time — that is, from the very beginning of American history to the 1930s — civil liberties cases were almost entirely absent from its agenda. Moreover, when such cases did reach the Court, the Court rarely ruled in favor of underprivileged minorities or powerless individuals.

In recent decades, however, the Court has focused heavily on cases arising under the Bill of Rights and the Fourteenth Amendment. Beginning in the 1940s, moreover, the Court became increasingly likely to decide those cases in favor of groups and individuals who were challenging governmental action. The liberalism of the Supreme Court became particularly pronounced during the 1960s, when, under Chief Justice Earl Warren, the Court gained a substantial reputation as a champion of individual rights.

With the transition to the Burger Court in 1969, however, the orientation of the Court again began to change. Between 1969 and 1981, Republican presidents had six opportunities to appoint new justices (Burger, Blackmun, Rehnquist, Powell, Stevens, and O'Connor). In 1986 Justice Rehnquist became chief justice, and Antonin Scalia took Rehnquist's place as associate justice. Between 1988 and 1991, Presidents Reagan and Bush made three additional appointments to the Court (Kennedy, Souter, and Thomas). By the end of 1991, the Court included only one justice — Justice White — who had been appointed by a Democratic president.

In the 1960s it was often argued — sometimes with glee, sometimes with dismay — that the Supreme Court as an institution is by its very nature a staunch defender of individual rights. Events in recent decades, however, suggest that the outburst of support for individual rights may have been one more passing phase in the history of the Supreme Court. To confirm whether the Court has in fact changed direction in recent years, and if we turn to empirical evidence of historical trends in Supreme C making.

Supreme Court Decision Making: Patterns and Trends

In the previous section, we highlighted several important Supreme Court decisions and reviewed historical scholarship on its decision making during different periods. By examining its work from the perspective of history, we were able to dispel the notion that the Supreme Court is essentially liberal, essentially conservative, essentially activist, or essentially anything else. Over time, the Supreme Court has displayed a wide variety of ideological and decision-making tendencies.

In this section, we turn to additional evidence that can help us to understand the nature of Supreme Court. This evidence, like that which we reviewed in the previous section, is historical. However, it consists primarily of quantitative measures of Supreme Court decision making. In conjunction with traditional historical scholarship, these quantitative measures can greatly enhance our ability to make sense of the Court's policy-making role in the political system.

We look at two distinct bodies of information. First, we examine evidence of the incidence of Supreme Court decisions overturning state and federal laws. We will see how often, and in what kinds of cases, the Court has chosen to exercise its power of judicial review of legislation. Second, we look at the direction of Supreme Court decisions in constitutional cases. We will see which kinds of litigants have been "winning" and "losing" in the Supreme Court over time.

Judicial Review in Historical Perspective

A common criticism of the Supreme Court—one that has been raised in almost every period of American history—is that the Supreme Court has overstepped the boundaries of its proper role in the political system and is engaging in judicial activism. It is important, therefore, to place the judicial activism of the Supreme Court in historical perspective.

Judicial activism can be defined in a variety of ways.[40] In the case of the Supreme Court, one common definition of judicial activism is that it consists of those instances in which the Court has overturned the decision of a legislative body. Under this definition, judicial activism is measured by looking at the frequency with which the Court has exercised its power of judicial review to invalidate state and federal laws.

The Congressional Research Service (CRS), an office of the Library of Congress, has compiled a complete list of the Supreme Court's decisions overturning state and federal laws.[41] The CRS list has served as the basis of several recent attempts to assess the Court's judicial activism over time.[42]

The CRS list of decisions overturning state laws begins with *United States v. Peters* (1809) and *Fletcher v. Peck* (1810).[43] The list of decisions overturning federal laws begins, of course, with *Marbury v. Madison* (1803), in which Chief Justice Marshall, inspired in part by the political predicament in which he found himself, concluded that a portion of the Judiciary Act of 1789 was unconstitutional. These decisions were the first of many in which the Supreme Court exercised its power of judicial review. According to the Congressional Research Service, between 1803 and 1988 the Court handed down 130 decisions overturning federal laws and 1,058 decisions overturning state laws. The record of these decisions provides a portrait of the history of judicial activism on the part of the Supreme Court.

Historical Fluctuations in Judicial Activism

Figure 4.1 charts the trend of Supreme Court activism on a decade-by-decade basis. It indicates that, the frequency with which the Court has exercised its power of judicial review has fluctuated substantially. It also indicates that

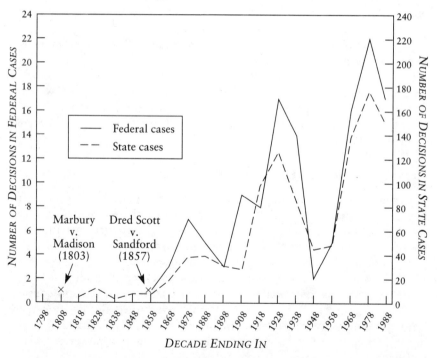

FIGURE 4.1 Frequency of Supreme Court Decisions Overturning State and Federal Laws

SOURCE: Congressional Research Service, *Constitution of the United States of America: Analysis and Interpretation* (Washington, D.C.: U.S. Government Printing Office, 1987); *1988 Supplement.*

Court decisions overturning state and federal laws have tended to fluctuate in tandem. Finally, it shows that decisions overturning state laws have in general been about ten times as numerous as decisions overturning federal laws.

Figure 4.1 indicates that, prior to 1858, the Court had overturned a federal law on only two occasions — in *Marbury* v. *Madison* (1803) and *Dred Scott* v. *Sandford* (1857). Moreover, Court decisions overturning state laws hovered in the range of about five to ten per year. After the Civil War, however, the frequency of Supreme Court decisions overturning legislation began to increase. It reached a peak in the decade ending in 1928, during which the Court decided 125 cases overturning state laws and 17 cases overturning federal laws.

The effects of the constitutional crisis of the 1930s are clearly depicted in Figure 4.1. Supreme Court decisions overturning legislation fell during the

Judicial Review and Electoral Realignment

The 1930s were years of major political upheaval in the United States, one of a handful of such periods in American history. The conservative Republican majority that had dominated American politics for several decades was replaced by the coalition of liberal forces that elected Franklin Roosevelt in 1932.

There is a lively debate among scholars about the role of the Supreme Court during these periods of so-called "critical realignment." The premise of the debate is that the Supreme Court is appointed, not elected. In the wake of one or more critical elections, therefore, the Court will consist of justices who were appointed by previous presidents and who reflect the old rather than the new majority in American politics. Some scholars argue that in these periods of critical realignment, the Court is particularly likely to be out of step with the rest of the political system. As a result, there will be a temporary but measurable increase in Supreme Court decisions overturning legislation.

Contributions to the debate over the role of the Court during periods of critical realignment include John B. Gates, *The Supreme Court and Partisan Realignment* (1992); William Lasser, "The Supreme Court in Periods of Critical Realignment," 47 *J. of Pol.* 1174 (1985); David Adamany, "The Supreme Court's Role in Critical Elections," in Bruce A. Campbell and Richard J. Trilling (eds.), *Realignment in American Politics* (1980), pp. 229–59; Richard Funston, "The Supreme Court and Critical Elections," 69 *Am. Pol. Sci. Rev.* 795 (1975); David Adamany, "Legitimacy, Realigning Elections, and the Supreme Court," 1973 *Wis. L. Rev.* 790 (1973); and Robert A. Dahl, "Decision-making in a Democracy: The Supreme Court as a National Policy-maker," 6 *J. of Pub. L.* 279 (1957).

decade ending in 1938 and dropped precipitously during the following decade. The Court's principal use of its power of judicial review up to 1937 had been to overturn legislation regulating the economy. The outcome of the crisis of 1937 was to oust the Court from this area of policy making. As a result, the Court was deprived — at least temporarily — of any significant role in the policy-making process.

Figure 4.1 also indicates that the Court recovered relatively quickly from the debacle of 1937. The downward trend of decisions overturning legislation was reversed, and by the 1960s the Court was as active as it had been in the 1930s. Between 1969 and 1978, moreover, the Court invoked its power of judicial review to overturn 22 federal laws and 176 state laws, thereby pushing its reputation for activism to new heights.

The Subject Matter of Supreme Court Decisions Overturning Legislation

What Figure 4.1 does not reveal, of course, is the subject matter of the cases in which the Court has exercised its power of judicial review in different periods. Table 4.1 focuses on this question. The history of the Court is divided into four periods, and the Court's decisions overturning state laws are divided into several categories according to their purpose or effect.

The table graphically underlines what historians have concluded about trends in Supreme Court decision making. During the first three periods of Supreme Court history — that is, up to 1938 — decisions protecting civil liberties constituted only a tiny proportion of the instances of judicial review of state laws. After 1938, however, such cases expanded rapidly and soon constituted almost two-thirds of the Court's decisions overturning state laws.

Table 4.1 also illustrates several subsidiary trends in Supreme Court decision making. For instance, we see that Court decisions protecting business from state regulation and taxation peaked in the second period (1869–1888). Moreover, such decisions continued to be numerous — and were joined by decisions protecting business from social welfare legislation — in the third period, the era of substantive due process (1889–1938).

Finally, the proportion of decisions whose purpose is to protect federal institutions or enforce the supremacy of federal law (many of which are based on the Supremacy Clause) has remained relatively constant (with the exception of the 1869–1888 period) at 20 to 25 percent of all decisions. This suggests the ongoing importance of the Court's role in supervising federal-state relations and protecting the supremacy of federal law.

A Note of Caution

The foregoing statistics suggest that Supreme Court activism has fluctuated substantially over time. They also suggest that its activism has been directed at different types of issues in different historical periods. In an earlier era, the Supreme Court frequently used its power of judicial review to overturn

TABLE 4.1

Purpose or Effect of Supreme Court Decisions Declaring State Laws Unconstitutional

Purpose or Effect of Decision	Percent of Decisions				
	1809–1868	1869–1888	1889–1938	1939–1988	1809–1988
Protect property rights and other vested interests[a]	45	30	9	1	8
Protect business from state regulation and taxation[b]	15	50	31	7	19
Protect business from state social welfare legislation[c]	0	4	27	2	11
Protect federal institutions and enforce the supremacy of federal law[d]	25	6	21	24	22
Protect civil liberties[e]	0	2	6	62	35
Miscellaneous	15	8	6	4	5
Total	100	100	100	100	100
	(n = 53)	(n = 77)	(n = 374)	(n = 554)	(n = 1058)

[a]Cases overturning state laws affecting property rights, contract or charter guarantees, tax exemptions, and the claims of creditors and mortgagors.

[b]Cases overturning state laws imposing formal or monetary restraints on business (e.g., tariffs, taxes, and licensing requirements).

[c]Cases overturning state laws intended to promote various welfare goals (e.g., public health and safety, more peaceful labor relations, and greater business responsibility toward workers and consumers).

[d]Cases overturning state laws interfering with banks, Indian lands, the U.S. mail, military operations, and the federal courts, and cases enforcing the supremacy of federal law in areas such as transportation rates, the liability of interstate carriers, standards of purity in food and drugs, bankruptcy, natural resource exploitation, and labor relations.

[e]Cases overturning state laws discriminating against racial and other minorities, laws abridging due process rights of criminal defendants and others, laws abridging First Amendment rights, and laws abridging the right of privacy.

SOURCES: Congressional Research Service, *Constitution of the United States of America: Analysis and Interpretation* (Washington, D.C.: U.S. Government Printing Office, 1987); 1988 *Supplement.*

legislation regulating economic activity. In the recent period, it has exercised its power of judicial review most frequently in cases involving civil rights and civil liberties.

The foregoing statistics are revealing. Unfortunately, they also have a variety of weaknesses. Recall, first, that the statistics themselves consist of the absolute number of cases in which the Court has overturned a state or federal law on constitutional grounds. Consequently, they ignore the "other side of the coin," that is, the cases in which the Court is asked to overturn a state or federal law but declines to do so.

A second weakness of statistics showing how often the Supreme Court has overturned a state or federal law is that they are confined to judicial review of the validity of legislation. By definition, they ignore an additional category of important cases, namely, those in which the Supreme Court ruled for or against an individual litigant, even on constitutional grounds, without being obliged to consider the constitutional validity of a written law.[44]

Finally, a substantial proportion of Supreme Court decisions — particularly in federal cases — are examples of *statutory construction* rather than judicial review. Such decisions can significantly alter the meaning of a federal law, but they do not actually invalidate the law on constitutional grounds. As a result, they will not be included in any list of Supreme Court decisions overturning legislation, even though, in practical effect, they may be equivalent to such decisions.[45]

While statistics on the incidence of judicial review are valuable, then, they are not without their limitations. In particular, they fail to focus directly on the very question in which we may be most interested, namely, who is winning and who is losing in the Supreme Court. For insights into trends in the outcome or direction of Supreme Court decision making, we turn to an additional body of data.

The Direction of Supreme Court Decision Making

In the last few years, judicial scholars have accelerated their collection of quantitative data on Supreme Court decision making. Individual scholars have collected their own bodies of data. In addition, a collaborative project involving several scholars has generated what is known as the Supreme Court Data Base. Among other things, the Data Base includes quantitative information on the direction (or outcome) of civil liberties cases decided by the Supreme Court under Chief Justices Warren, Burger, and Rehnquist.

Studies of the direction of Supreme Court decision making in civil liberties cases usually begin by identifying certain types of litigants who are likely to be involved in bringing constitutional challenges to governmental policy. Litigants in such cases may include racial and ethnic minorities, women, criminal defendants, political dissidents, and others. The governmental policy being challenged may be embodied in a written statute. Alternatively, it may take the form of the decision or action of someone in a position of governmental authority, that is, a school principal, a public employer, a police officer, or an administrative official. Judgments about trends in Supreme Court decision making are based on information about how often anti-government litigants are victorious in their attempts to challenge governmental power.

Table 4.2 reproduces findings on the direction of Supreme Court decision making in a sample of 1,283 civil liberties cases decided between 1903 and 1969.[46] Each of the cases pitted a "governmental litigant" against an "underdog," that is, "any litigant characterized as Black, Black organization, labor union, union member, alien, criminal defendant, subversive, or alleged subversive person or organization."[47]

The table suggests three important conclusions. First, in both federal and state cases, the success rate of governmental litigants fell between 1903 and 1968. In the early part of the century, government was winning most of the time in federal cases and almost all of the time in state cases. During the Warren Court, however, government victories fell below 50 percent in both federal and state cases.

Second, the declining success of government in civil liberties cases is most dramatic in state cases. The Supreme Court ruled in favor of government in state cases more than 90 percent of the time in the early years — that is, before 1930 — but state governments prevailed less than one-fourth of the time in civil liberties cases decided by the Warren Court.

Finally, the declining success of government — or, if you will, the Supreme Court's increasing tendency to rule in favor of underdog litigants — seems to fall into three stages. There is a drop in governmental victories between the Taft Court and Hughes Court (particularly in state cases). This is

TABLE 4.2

Support for Government Litigants over Underdogs in
Civil Liberties Cases, 1903–1968 Terms

Court	Percentage of Victories for Government	
	Federal Cases	State Cases
Fuller (1888–1910)	69.2	96.9
White (1910–1921)	70.8	90.5
Taft (1921–1930)	65.8	93.6
Hughes (1930–1941)	57.3	56.3
Stone (1941–1946)	47.8	42.1
Vinson (1946–1953)	55.8	52.2
Warren (1953–1968)	41.8	24.2

SOURCE: S. Sidney Ulmer, "Governmental Litigants, Underdogs, and Civil Liberties in the Supreme Court: 1903–1968 Terms," 47 *J. of Pol.* 899, 907 (1985).

followed by a period of relative stability between 1930 and 1953. Then there is a further substantial drop in governmental victories coinciding with the transition from the Vinson Court to the Warren Court.[48]

The information in Table 4.2 is based on Supreme Court decisions up to the end of the Warren Court. It was widely expected, of course, that the transition to the Burger Court would bring a reversal of these historical trends in Supreme Court decision making. The empirical evidence suggests that the success rate of individual litigants in civil liberties cases in fact fell appreciably in the Burger Court.

Figure 4.2 presents data from a recent study based on the Supreme Court Data Base.[49] The figures in the table represent the proportion of liberal decisions of the Supreme Court during the 1953 through 1985 terms of the Court. A liberal decision in a civil liberties case is defined as one that results in victory for (1) a person accused or convicted of a crime, (2) a civil liberties or civil rights claimant, (3) an indigent litigant, (4) an Indian litigant, (5) someone alleging that government has violated his or her right to due process of law, or (6) someone alleging that government has violated his or her right of privacy.

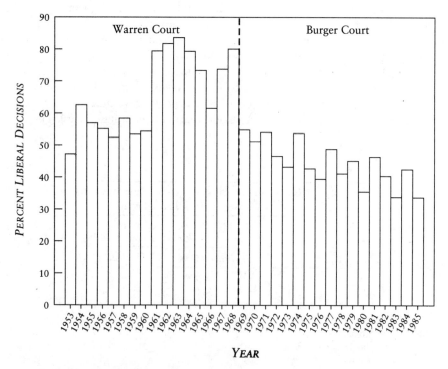

FIGURE 4.2 Ideological Trends in Civil Liberties Cases

SOURCE: Jeffrey A. Segal and Harold J. Spaeth, "Decisional Trends on the Warren and Burger Courts: Results from the Supreme Court Data Base Project," 73 *Judicature* 103, 104 (1989).

Figure 4.2 indicates that liberal decisions usually constituted a majority of the decisions of the early Warren Court — that is, the Court in the 1953– 1960 terms — but exceeded the 60 percent mark on only one occasion during that period (the 1954 term). During the next few years, however, liberal decisions constituted more than 70 percent of the Court's decisions in every year except one (the 1966 term). In 1969, the year that Chief Justice Burger replaced Chief Justice Warren, liberal decisions in civil liberties cases fell abruptly, and have remained at a new and much lower level ever since. Indeed, in some years (1980, 1983, and 1985) they have constituted only about one-third of the Court's decisions in civil liberties cases.[50]

Civil rights and civil liberties continue to be among the Supreme Court's central concerns. At the same time, it is clear that the Court is becoming measurably less sympathetic to the types of litigants who once viewed the Court as a trustworthy friend. As we saw in Chapter 3, the petitioning party in a growing proportion of civil liberties cases is the government rather than the opponents of government. Moreover, as the data in Figure 4.2 indicate, in an increasing number of those cases, the Court eventually rules in favor of government and rejects the claims of individuals and groups alleging that their constitutional rights had been violated.[51]

Conclusion

The Supreme Court changes slowly, but, given time, it can change profoundly. During the nineteenth century, the Court was preoccupied with issues of property rights and the relationship between government and business. The outcome of many of the Court's most celebrated cases reflected the fact that a majority of the Court held a highly restrictive view of the government's proper role in regulating economic affairs.

Civil liberties were at best a marginal concern of the Supreme Court until the 1930s. Very few civil liberties cases appeared on the Court's plenary docket. In those cases that did raise civil liberties issues, the Court seldom ruled in favor of individuals and underprivileged minorities.

Following the constitutional crisis of the 1930s, the Court moved aggressively into the area of civil rights and civil liberties. An increasing proportion of the plenary docket consisted of cases arising under provisions of the Bill of Rights and the Thirteenth, Fourteenth, and Fifteenth Amendments. The Court was receptive to the constitutional claims of a variety of underprivileged groups, including criminal defendants, racial minorities, and political dissidents. By the end of the 1960s, the Court had substantially expanded the scope of constitutional protection of individual rights.

The years since 1969 have been characterized by a fitful but inexorable decline in the Supreme Court's willingness to support the constitutional claims of underprivileged minorities. An increasing proportion of the Court's plenary docket consists of cases that are being reviewed at the government's request. Moreover, an increasing proportion of the Court's decisions are favorable to government. At the very least, the rapid expansion of constitutional rights that began in the 1940s has been brought to a halt.

The decision-making trends of the last twenty years establish that Supreme Court support for the constitutional claims of underprivileged minorities is not inevitable. The Court is capable of protecting individual rights from governmental abuse, but only if it wants to. When the Supreme Court is populated with justices who are unsympathetic to allegations that government has violated someone's constitutional rights, the Court will rule in favor of government and against the individual. It is as simple as that.

Even though the Court is far more conservative than it once was, however, it has thus far shown a marked reluctance to engage in outright reversal — let alone wholesale reversal — of its important precedents. It is clear that most, if not all, of the constitutional innovations of the last sixty years are here to stay. The Court is not about to dismantle the edifice of First Amendment law that dates from the 1930s, to overrule *Brown* v. *Board of Education*, to immunize the police from judicial scrutiny, or to hold that the right of privacy has no constitutional foundation whatsoever.

This is not to say, of course, that selected Supreme Court precedents are not in jeopardy. Many Supreme Court decisions handed down in the period between the mid-1950s and the mid-1970s substantially enhanced the constitutional rights of individuals and minority groups. Clearly, the Supreme Court in the 1990s will be offered plentiful opportunities — some of which it may choose to accept — to redefine the relationship between government and the individual. The bulk of constitutional doctrine enunciated by the Court since the 1930s, however, is secure. It is now an integral part of the meaning of the Constitution.

Notes

1. Three recent studies explore the internal workings of the Supreme Court. Each is based on extensive interviews with justices and clerks. See Perry, *Deciding to Decide* (focusing on the 1976–1980 terms); Bernard Schwartz, *The Ascent of Pragmatism: The Burger Court in Action* (1990); and Bob Woodward and Scott Armstrong, *The Brethren: Inside the Supreme Court* (1979) (focusing on the 1969–1975 terms).

2. For a study of *amicus* participation in cases decided during the 1982 term, see Gregory A. Caldeira and John R. Wright, "Amici Curiae Before the Supreme Court: Who Participates, When, and How Much?" 52 *J. of Pol.* 782 (1990).

3. Several studies examine the strategic considerations affecting opinion assignment on the Supreme Court. See Saul Brenner and Harold J. Spaeth, "Majority Opinion Assignments and the Maintenance of the Original Coalition on the Warren Court," 32 *Am. J. Pol. Sci.* 72 (1988); Harold J. Spaeth, "Distributive Justice: Majority Opinion Assignments in the Burger Court," 67 *Judicature* 299 (1984); Saul Brenner, "Strategic Choice and Opinion Assignment on the U.S. Supreme Court: A Reexamination," 35 *Western Pol. Q.* 204 (1982); Elliott E. Slotnick, "Who Speaks for the Court? Majority Opinion Assignment from Taft to Burger," 23 *Am. J. Pol. Sci.* 60 (1979); Saul

Brenner, "Minimum Winning Coalitions on the U.S. Supreme Court," 7 *Am. Pol. Q.* 384 (1979); Elliott E. Slotnick, "The Chief Justice and Self-Assignment of Majority Opinions: A Research Note," 31 *Western Pol. Q.* 219 (1978); David W. Rohde, "Policy Goals and Opinion Coalitions in the Supreme Court," 16 *Midwest J. Pol. Sci* 208 (1972); and David W. Rohde, "Policy Goals, Strategic Choice and Majority Opinion Assignments in the U.S. Supreme Court," 16 *Midwest J. Pol. Sci.* 652 (1972).

4. See David M. O'Brien, *Storm Center: The Supreme Court in American Politics* (1990), pp. 255–57. For additional background on the *Hardwick* case, see Peter Irons, *The Courage of Their Convictions: Sixteen Americans Who Fought Their Way to the Supreme Court* (1988), Ch. 16.

5. J. Woodford Howard, "On the Fluidity of Judicial Choice," 62 *Am. Pol. Sci. Rev.* 43 (1968).

6. Saul Brenner, "Fluidity on the United States Supreme Court: A Reexamination," 24 *Am. J. Pol. Sci.* 526 (1980); and Saul Brenner, "Fluidity on the Supreme Court: 1956–1967," 26 *Am. J. Pol. Sci.* 388 (1982).

7. On rare occasions, the Court is reduced in size due to an unfilled vacancy, the temporary illness of a justice, or a justice's decision not to participate in a particular case. If the Court is reduced to eight members, and if the vote is a 4–4 tie, the effect is to leave in place the decision of the lower court. The Court will not announce how the individual justices voted, and the tie vote will not constitute a precedent of the Supreme Court. The Supreme Court may (and often does) vote to rehear the case when membership is at full strength. Since a quorum of the Court is six, it is also technically possible for a case to be decided by a 3–3 tie, but such an outcome is extremely unlikely.

8. See O'Brien, *Storm Center*, p. 258.

9. The Watergate scandal is the subject of many books, among them Carl Bernstein and Bob Woodward, *All the President's Men* (1974); Bob Woodward and Carl Bernstein, *The Final Days* (1976); John Dean, *Blind Ambition* (1977); James Doyle, *Not Above the Law: The Battles of Watergate Prosecutors Cox and Jaworski* (1977); Leon Jaworski, *The Right and the Power: The Prosecution of Watergate* (1977); and Richard Ben-Veniste and George Frampton, Jr., *Stonewall: The Real Story of the Watergate Prosecution* (1977).

10. Justice Rehnquist disqualified himself, without giving any reason, but presumably because before being appointed to the Supreme Court he had worked professionally in the Justice Department with many of the key figures in the Watergate scandal. For a discussion of the Court's deliberations in the Nixon tapes case, see Woodward and Armstrong, *The Brethren*, pp. 285–347; and O'Brien, *Storm Center*, pp. 259–66.

11. See O'Brien, *Storm Center*, pp. 319–20.

12. Thomas G. Walker, Lee Epstein, and William J. Dixon, "On the Mysterious Demise of Consensual Norms in the United States Supreme Court," 50 *J. of Pol.* 361 (1988); and S. Sidney Ulmer, "Exploring the Dissent Patterns of the Chief Justices: John Marshall to Warren Burger," in Sheldon Goldman and Charles M. Lamb (eds.), *Judicial Conflict and Consensus: Behavioral Studies of Appellate Courts* (1986), pp. 50–67.

13. The proportion of unanimous versus nonunanimous decisions of the Supreme Court is reported annually in the November issue of the *Harvard Law Review*.

14. For a discussion of concurring opinions on the Rehnquist Court, see Laura

Krugman Ray, "The Justices Write Separately: Uses of the Concurrence by the Rehnquist Court," 23 *U.C. Davis L. Rev.* 777 (1990).

15. See Note, "Plurality Decisions and Judicial Decisionmaking," 94 *Harv. L. Rev.* 1127 (1981).

16. O'Brien, *Storm Center*, p. 312.

17. The November issue of the *Harvard Law Review* reports the number of 5–4 decisions in the preceding term of the Court as well as the composition of the five-person majority. This information can help to identify ideological trends in Supreme Court decision making. In the 1988 term, for instance, thirty-three cases were decided by a 5–4 majority. In nineteen of these cases, the majority consisted of Rehnquist, White, O'Connor, Scalia, and Kennedy, that is, the five most conservative members of the Court.

18. O'Brien, *Storm Center*, p. 313.

19. Lawrence Tribe, *God Save This Honorable Court: How the Choice of Supreme Court Justices Shapes Our History* (1985), p. 37.

20. Recently published histories of the Court include David P. Currie, *The Constitution in the Supreme Court: The First Hundred Years, 1789–1888* (1985); David P. Currie, *The Constitution in the Supreme Court: The Second Century, 1888–1986* (1990); Elder Witt (ed.), *Congressional Quarterly's Guide to the U.S. Supreme Court* (1990), Part I; William Lasser, *The Limits of Judicial Power: The Supreme Court in American Politics* (1988); and William M. Wiecek, *Liberty under Law: The Supreme Court in American Life* (1988).

21. There are several excellent accounts of the Supreme Court in the nineteenth century, including Robert G. McCloskey, *The American Supreme Court* (1960); Charles Evans Hughes, *The Supreme Court of the United States* (1936); and Charles Warren, *The Supreme Court in United States History* (1947).

22. C. Herman Pritchett, *Constitutional Law of the Federal System* (1984), p. 43. For studies of John Marshall and the Marshall Court, see Albert J. Beveridge, *The Life of John Marshall* (1916); Robert K. Faulkner, *The Jurisprudence of John Marshall* (1968); George L. Haskins and Herbert A. Johnson, *History of the Supreme Court of the United States: Foundations of Power: John Marshall, 1801–1815* (1981); G. Edward White, *History of the Supreme Court of the United States: The Marshall Court and Cultural Change, 1815–1835* (1988); and Leonard Baker, *John Marshall: A Life in Law* (1974).

23. The *Dred Scott* case is explored in Lasser, *The Limits of Judicial Power*, Ch. 2. See also Don E. Fehrenbacher, *The Dred Scott Case: Its Significance in American Law and Politics* (1978).

24. Lasser, *The Limits of Judicial Power*, p. 20.

25. The Reconstruction period is discussed in Lasser, *The Limits of Judicial Power*, Ch. 3. Other histories of the Taney Court and the Reconstruction period include Carl B. Swisher, *History of the Supreme Court of the United States: The Taney Period, 1836–1864* (1974); and Charles Fairman, *History of the Supreme Court of the United States: Reconstruction and Reunion, 1864–1888*, Part One (1971) and Part Two (1987).

26. For helpful explanations of the illogical doctrine of substantive due process, see McCloskey, *The American Supreme Court*, Chs. 5 and 6; and C. Herman Pritchett, *Constitutional Civil Liberties* (1984), Ch. 11.

27. Oliver Wendell Holmes, Jr., served on the Supreme Court between 1902 and 1932 and is widely regarded as one of the great justices. His reputation is based in part

on his outspoken opposition to the Court's use of the Due Process Clause to protect substantive economic rights. For a recent biography, see Liva Baker, *The Justice from Beacon Hill: The Life and Times of Oliver Wendell Holmes* (1991).

28. Robert H. Jackson served as solicitor general, and later as attorney general, in the Roosevelt Administration. For his classic account of the confrontation between the New Deal and the Supreme Court, written just prior to his own appointment to the Supreme Court, see *The Struggle for Judicial Supremacy* (1941). This critical period of American history is also the subject of Chapter 4 of Lasser, *The Limits of Judicial Power*.

29. For discussions of the Court-packing episode, see Michael Nelson, "The President and the Court: Reinterpreting the Court-packing Episode of 1937," 103 *Pol. Sci. Q.* 267 (1988); Gregory A. Caldeira, "Public Opinion and the U.S. Supreme Court: FDR's Court-Packing Plan," 81 *Am. Pol. Sci. Rev.* 1139 (1987); and William E. Leuchtenburg, "The Origins of Franklin D. Roosevelt's 'Court-Packing' Plan," 1966 *Sup. Ct. Rev.* 347 (1966).

30. The Senate voted to recommit the bill in July 1937.

31. The quote is attributed to Abe Fortas, at the time a New Deal lawyer and later (from 1965 to 1969) a member of the Supreme Court. See Tribe, *God Save This Honorable Court*, p. 66.

32. See Robert A. Dahl, "Decision-Making in a Democracy: The Supreme Court as a National Policy-Maker," 6 *J. of Pub. L.* 279 (1957); and Henry Steele Commager, *Majority Rule and Minority Rights* (1943). For a critical but less negative appraisal of the civil liberties decision making of the pre-1937 Court, see John Braeman, *Before the Civil Rights Revolution: The Old Court and Individual Rights* (1988).

33. For an exploration of the Court's behavior during the transitional years between 1937 and 1953, see C. Herman Pritchett, *The Roosevelt Court: A Study in Judicial Politics and Values, 1937–1947* (1948); and C. Herman Pritchett, *Civil Liberties and the Vinson Court* (1954).

34. 304 U.S. 144 (1938).

35. Discussions of the significance of Footnote Four can be found in J. A. Balkin, "The Footnote," 83 *Nw. U. L. Rev.* 275 (1989); Geoffrey P. Miller, "The True Story of Carolene Products," 1987 *Sup. Ct. Rev.* 397 (1987); and Bruce A. Ackerman, "Beyond Carolene Products," 98 *Harv. L. Rev.* 713 (1985).

36. *Griswold* is discussed in Chapter 10. These cases represent a minute sample of the important civil liberties decisions of the Warren Court. For detailed discussion of the civil liberties decisions of the modern Court, including the Warren Court, see Melvin Urofsky, *Continuity and Change: The Supreme Court and Individual Liberties 1953–1986* (1991); Laurence H. Tribe, *American Constitutional Law* (1988); Henry J. Abraham, *Freedom and the Court: Civil Rights and Liberties in the United States* (1988); and Pritchett, *Constitutional Civil Liberties*.

37. For a collection of essays on each of the justices of the Burger Court, see Charles M. Lamb and Stephen C. Halpern (eds.), *The Burger Court: Political and Judicial Profiles* (1991).

38. See Vincent Blasi (ed.), *The Burger Court: The Counter-Revolution That Wasn't* (1983); Mark Silverstein and Benjamin Ginsberg, "The Supreme Court and the New Politics of Judicial Power," 102 *Pol. Sci. Q.* 371 (1987); and Lamb and Halpern, *The Burger Court*, Chs. 1 and 15.

39. Chief Justice Rehnquist's approach to constitutional issues is examined in Sue Davis, *Justice Rehnquist and the Constitution* (1989).

40. For a useful discussion of the various meanings of the term *judicial activism,* see Bradley C. Canon, "Defining the Dimensions of Judicial Activism," 66 *Judicature* 236 (1983).

41. Congressional Research Service, *The Constitution of the United States of America: Analysis and Interpretation* (1987).

42. See, for example, Lawrence Baum, *The Supreme Court* (1992), pp. 185–92; and Gregory A. Caldeira and Donald J. McCrone, "Of Time and Judicial Activism: A Study of the U.S. Supreme Court, 1800–1973," in Stephen C. Halpern and Charles M. Lamb (eds.), *Supreme Court Activism and Restraint* (1982), pp. 103–27.

43. Many analyses identify *Fletcher* v. *Peck* (1810) as the first instance of judicial invalidation of a state statute.

44. The Supreme Court's decision in *Miranda* v. *Arizona* (1966) is a good example of this kind of case. *Miranda* held that police officers are required by the Constitution to read defendants their rights before they are questioned. The decision is among the most controversial and far-reaching ever handed down by the Supreme Court. However, it is not an example of judicial review of legislation. The Supreme Court in *Miranda* did not overturn a law that required police officers not to read defendants their rights. Rather, the Court declared unconstitutional the widespread police practice of not reading defendants their rights. Since the practice was not embodied in written law, the Court was not obliged, in reaching its decision, to overturn any law on constitutional grounds.

45. A good example of the Supreme Court's use of statutory construction is *Yates* v. *United States,* a case we examine in detail in Chapter 7.

46. S. Sidney Ulmer, "Governmental Litigants, Underdogs, and Civil Liberties in the Supreme Court: 1903–1968 Terms," 47 *J. of Pol.* 899 (1985).

47. Id. at 903.

48. For a quantitative study comparing (1) the success rate of government in constitutional cases in two widely separated periods (1816–1827 and 1950–1969) and (2) the judicial activism of the U.S. and Canadian Supreme Courts in the 1950s and 1960s, see Carl Baar, "Judicial Behavior and Comparative Rights Policy," in Richard P. Claude (ed.), *Comparative Human Rights* (1976), pp. 353–81.

49. Jeffrey A. Segal and Harold J. Spaeth, "Decisional Trends on the Warren and Burger Courts: Results from the Supreme Court Data Base Project," 73 *Judicature* 103 (1989).

50. For detailed studies of decision making in the Warren Court, see Russell W. Galloway, Jr., "The Early Years of the Warren Court: Emergence of Judicial Liberalism (1953–1957)," 18 *Santa Clara L. Rev.* 609 (1978); Russell W. Galloway, Jr., "The Second Period of the Warren Court: The Liberal Trend Abates (1957–1961)," 19 *Santa Clara L. Rev.* 947 (1979); and Russell W. Galloway, Jr., "The Third Period of the Warren Court: Liberal Dominance (1962–1969)," 20 *Santa Clara L. Rev.* 773 (1980).

For additional analysis of policy making on civil liberties issues in the Burger Court, see Harold J. Spaeth, "Burger Court Review of State Court Civil Liberties Decisions," 68 *Judicature* 285 (1985); Gayle Binion, "The Disadvantaged before the Burger Court," 4 *Law and Policy Q.* 37 (1982); and Robert C. Welsh, "Whose Federalism? The Burger Court's Treatment of State Civil Liberties Judgments," 10 *Hastings Cons. L. Q.* 819 (1983).

Voting patterns on the Warren and Burger courts are compared in Edward V. Heck, "Changing Voting Patterns in the Warren and Burger Courts," in Goldman and

Lamb, *Judicial Conflict and Consensus*, pp. 68–86; and Lamb and Halpern, *The Burger Court*, Chs. 1 and 15.

51. The proportion of cases in which the Supreme Court rules for or against the government is affected by a number of factors, including the types of cases that are being decided by the lower courts, the way in which those cases are being decided, and the way in which the Supreme Court chooses to exercise its power of discretionary review. If lower courts are acceding to an increasingly radical array of civil liberties claims, and if the Supreme Court is unwilling to affirm these lower court rulings, the Supreme Court may *appear* to be moving in a conservative direction, even though it is in fact maintaining a consistent ideological position. For attempts to cope with this impediment to the accurate interpretation of trends in Supreme Court decision making, see Lawrence Baum, "Comparing the Policy Positions of Supreme Court Justices from Different Periods," 42 *Western Pol. Q.* 509 (1989); Lawrence Baum, "Measuring Policy Change in the U.S. Supreme Court," 82 *Am. Pol. Sci. Rev.* 905 (1988); and Jeffrey A. Segal, "Measuring Change on the Supreme Court: Examining Alternative Models," 29 *Am. J. Pol. Sci.* 461 (1985).

PART II

Constitutional Litigation in American Politics

CHAPTER 5
Jehovah's Witnesses and the American Flag:
*West Virginia State Board of
Education* v. *Barnette* (1943)

CHAPTER 6
Racial Segregation of Public Schools:
Brown v. *Board of Education* (1954)

CHAPTER 7
The Communist Party and Cold War Politics:
Yates v. *United States* (1957)

CHAPTER 8
The Supreme Court Confronts
Prayer in Public Schools:
*School District of Abington
Township* v. *Schempp* (1963)

CHAPTER 9
The Incorporation Debate and
the Right to Counsel:
Gideon v. *Wainwright* (1963)

CHAPTER 10
The Abortion Issue in American Politics:
Roe v. *Wade* (1973)

CHAPTER 11
The Agonizing Issue of Affirmative Action:
*Regents of the University of
California* v. *Bakke* (1978)

IN THE CHAPTERS THAT comprise this portion of the book, we explore seven leading episodes of Supreme Court decision making. The cases were decided over a thirty-five year period. The first case, the so-called flag salute case, was decided in 1943. The most recent case, the Supreme Court's first major encounter with the issue of affirmative action, was decided in 1978.

The seven cases on which we focus do not constitute a representative sample of Supreme Court decisions. No seven cases could successfully replicate the full range of issues with which the Supreme Court deals. The cases were chosen, instead, because they are extraordinarily interesting, because they illustrate not only the legal but also the political dimensions of Supreme Court decision making, and because they are widely regarded as being among the most significant Supreme Court decisions of recent decades. Each case deals with an important contemporary social issue and occupies an important place in the development of American constitutional law.

These seven cases would all be classified, in a general sense, as civil liberties cases. They deal with issues of freedom of speech, race relations, religious freedom, privacy, due process for criminal defendants, and related questions. They have arisen under the Bill of Rights and other provisions of the Constitution that identify and protect the fundamental rights of individuals and groups in our society.

As we saw in Chapters 3 and 4, issues of civil rights and civil liberties occupy a prominent place in the decision-making activities of the contemporary Supreme Court. About half of the Court's decisions — and almost all of its widely publicized decisions — touch on one or another aspect of constitutional rights. In this sense, these seven cases lie at the core of the decision-making responsibilities of the modern Court.

The first case we examine — *West Virginia State Board of Education* v. *Barnette* (1943) — represents a relatively early example of Supreme Court decision making in the civil liberties area. The Court had established some

108

important civil liberties precedents in the 1920s and 1930s and had even decided a handful of important civil liberties cases in the nineteenth century, but it was not until the 1940s and 1950s that civil rights and civil liberties became one of the Court's major concerns. The *Barnette* decision is widely viewed as a prime early example of the modern Court's approach to civil liberties issues.

It is important to note, however, that the *Barnette* case was not decided in an historical vacuum. As we discussed in Chapter 4, the Court in the 1930s had been involved in an extended confrontation with the Roosevelt Administration. A principal outcome of the constitutional crisis of the 1930s was that the Supreme Court abandoned any pretensions of playing a major role in the policy-making process on economic issues. An additional outcome was that the Court resolved to redirect its attention to issues of civil rights and civil liberties.

The case in which the Court announced its intention to become more vigilant in protecting individual rights was *United States* v. *Carolene Products Co.*, decided in 1938. As we mentioned in Chapter 4, the case itself involved the power of Congress to regulate aspects of interstate commerce, and the opinion of the Court, written by Justice Stone, *upheld* the congressional statute at issue in the case. In a footnote to his opinion, however, Stone indicated that in areas *other* than economic regulation, the Court intended to play a particularly vigilant role in the future.[1]

Stone identified three categories of cases in which the Court might be especially willing to exercise its power of judicial review. The first category included cases in which legislation was being challenged on the ground that it violated "a specific prohibition of the Constitution, such as those of the first ten Amendments." Stone's purpose in the first paragraph of Footnote Four was to renounce the Court's history of using the Due Process Clause of the Fourteenth Amendment to strike down economic legislation. He sought to restrict the Court, in the future, to relying not only on specific provisions of the Constitution, but also on specific provisions, such as those in the Bill of Rights, which protect *noneconomic* individual rights.

The second category of legislation that the Court might subject "to more exacting judicial scrutiny," Stone said, was "legislation which restricts those political processes which can ordinarily be expected to bring about repeal of undesirable legislation." The language of the second paragraph of Footnote Four is somewhat convoluted, but Stone's point is clear. The Court, he was saying, will exercise its power of judicial review to overturn legislation that is aimed at undermining the integrity of the democratic process. Pursuant to the rationale identified in paragraph two, the Court could be expected to intervene in cases involving legislation which imposed restrictions on citizens' freedom of speech or freedom of the press or on the right of citizens to vote their preferences in free elections.

The third paragraph of Footnote Four identifies a final category of statutes to which the Court will apply special scrutiny, namely, statutes "directed at particular religious, or national, or racial minorities." The clear purpose of this language was to signal the Court's intention to cease using its power of judicial review to protect the economic interests of powerful corporations and to direct its energies instead to protecting the rights of relatively powerless groups such as racial, ethnic, and religious minorities.

The principal purpose of Stone's "Footnote Four" was to draw a distinction between the *restraint* with which the Court intended to approach issues of economic regulation and the *activism* with which it intended to approach issues of civil rights and civil liberties. To a striking extent, the Supreme Court since 1938 has fulfilled the intentions embodied in Footnote Four.

In *West Virginia State Board of Education* v. *Barnette* (1943), the case to which we turn in Chapter 5, the Court kept its promise to apply "more exacting judicial scrutiny" to legislation aimed at restricting the constitutional rights of religious minorities. The Court in *Barnette* overturned a West Virginia statute under which children who were members of the Jehovah's Witnesses had been expelled from school for refusing to salute the flag.

Chapter 6 deals with the case that most observers regard as the Supreme Court's most important decision in this century. In the early 1950s public schools in the southern and border states were racially segregated by law. In *Brown* v. *Board of Education* (1954), the Supreme Court declared that such segregation violated the constitutional guarantee of equal protection of the laws.

Chapter 7 takes up an issue that preoccupied the Supreme Court — and much of the country — during the 1950s. During the first half of the twentieth century, Congress and state legislatures passed a variety of laws aimed at the Communist party and other radical organizations. In *Yates* v. *United States* (1957), the Supreme Court examined congressional legislation aimed at those who advocate the overthrow of government and overturned the criminal convictions of several leaders of the Communist party.

In the early 1960s the Supreme Court encountered for the first time an issue that continues to stimulate litigation. In *School District of Abington Township* v. *Schempp* (1963), the Court held that prayer in public schools violated the constitutional requirement of the separation of church and state. In Chapter 8, we will look at the Court's decision in the *Schempp* case and at the Court's subsequent encounters with the issue of school prayer.

Chapter 9 explores the question of how the Constitution protects the rights of criminal defendants. The specific focus of the chapter is the Court's decision in *Gideon* v. *Wainwright* (1963). The Court in *Gideon* held that the constitutional guarantee of "Assistance of Counsel" means that states must provide indigent defendants with free legal counsel in serious criminal cases.

Chapter 10 takes up one of the most controversial issues in contemporary American life. In *Roe* v. *Wade* (1973), the Supreme Court held that a pregnant woman has a constitutionally protected right to obtain an abortion during the first two-thirds of her pregnancy. *Roe* v. *Wade* has been the center of intense political and legal controversy ever since it was decided, and many believe the decision will be overruled by the Supreme Court sometime in the near future.

Finally, in Chapter 11, we examine an issue that excites almost as much controversy as abortion. The constitutional validity of affirmative action in university admissions was at issue in the Supreme Court's 1978 decision in *Regents of the University of California* v. *Bakke*. Like abortion, the issue of affirmative action has returned to the Supreme Court on a regular basis and does not appear likely to disappear anytime soon.

Note

1. *United States* v. *Carolene Products Co.*, 304 U.S. 144, 152 n. 4 (1938).

CHAPTER 5

Jehovah's Witnesses and the American Flag: *West Virginia State Board of Education* v. *Barnette* (1943)

The Jehovah's Witnesses originated as a religious sect in 1870 and had grown, by the late 1930s, to include between twenty-five thousand and seventy thousand active members. Members of the sect believed, among other things, "that their divinely sanctioned work was properly subject to no restraints of time, place or propriety whatever."[1] As a result, they often ran afoul of local law. In 1936 alone, Jehovah's Witnesses were arrested on 1,149 occasions for offenses such as parading without a permit, distributing literature without a license, and disturbing the peace.[2]

Among the beliefs of Jehovah's Witnesses was one that made them particularly unpopular in some communities: Jehovah's Witnesses are instructed by Chapter 20 of the Book of Exodus to have "no other gods before me" and not to "bow down" to "a graven image." As a result, Jehovah's Witnesses are steadfastly opposed to participating in any ceremony that involves saluting the flag.

The flag of the United States became the official symbol of the nation by an act of Congress in 1794, but the flag salute ceremonies that eventually became a major point of tension between Jehovah's Witnesses and local communities did not originate until the late nineteenth century. The first flag salute statute was passed by the state legislature of New York in 1898. It imposed on the state superintendent of public instruction "the duty . . . to prepare . . . a program providing for a salute to the flag at the opening of each school day."[3] In due course, flag salute ceremonies became an institutionalized feature of public school life in many states.[4]

On December 7, 1941, the Japanese attacked Pearl Harbor. In response, the United States declared war on Japan and formally entered World War II on the side of the Allies. Not surprisingly, the country was swept with a wave of patriotic fervor. In West Virginia, one manifestation of the new patriotism was a decision by the State Board of Education to institute flag salute ceremonies in the state's public schools. In January 1942 the Board passed a resolution "order[ing] that the commonly accepted salute to the Flag of the United States . . . now becomes a regular part of the program of activities in the public schools." The resolution went on to say that teachers and pupils were "required to participate" and that refusal would be regarded as "an act of insubordination."[5]

Walter Barnette's family was one of those affected by the new policy. The Barnette family were Jehovah's Witnesses, and two of the Barnette daughters were enrolled in a public school near Charleston. The daughters refused to participate in the flag salute ceremony. By the end of January 1942 they had been expelled from school.

Flag Salute Requirements in the Supreme Court

Barnette immediately contemplated legal action. The prospects for success, however, did not seem very good. Two years earlier, in *Minersville School District* v. *Gobitis* (1940), the U.S. Supreme Court had ruled *in favor* of the power of school officials to compel children to participate in flag salute ceremonies. Thus, there was a recent precedent suggesting that the Supreme Court did not view compulsory flag salute ceremonies as a violation of the Constitution.

The *Gobitis* case had arisen when two Jehovah's Witness children refused to salute the flag and were expelled from a Pennsylvania public school. Two lower federal courts ruled in favor of the children — holding that compulsory flag salute ceremony was a violation of their constitutional rights — but the Supreme Court reversed. The vote in the Supreme Court was 8 to 1, with Justice Stone the sole dissenter.[6] Justice Frankfurter wrote the opinion of the Court. He held that the flag salute requirement did not violate the Fourteenth Amendment's guarantee against being deprived of liberty without due process of law.[7]

The situation facing Walter Barnette and his children did not, therefore, seem very promising. As recently as 1940 — and by an overwhelming margin — the Supreme Court had affirmed the constitutional validity of flag salute requirements. Under ordinary circumstances, it would not have been a propitious time to challenge such requirements in the lower courts.

Some Justices Have Second Thoughts

The circumstances, however, were not altogether ordinary. In particular, there was evidence that the Supreme Court's position on issues of religious freedom was undergoing rapid change. On June 8, 1942, only a few months after the Barnette children had been expelled from school, the Court decided a case — *Jones* v. *Opelika* — involving the constitutional validity of "occupational license taxes" as applied to persons engaged in the door-to-door selling of religious literature. Although the Court upheld the license taxes, the margin by which it did so was only 5 to 4.[8]

Even more important than the narrowness of the vote to uphold the law, however, was the reason *why* it was so narrow. Three of the justices who comprised the *Gobitis* majority had switched their position on the issue of religious liberty and were now part of the dissenting bloc of the Court in *Opelika*. Moreover, in a most unusual move, these three justices—Hugo Black, William O. Douglas, and Frank Murphy—not only dissented from the Court's decision in *Opelika*, but also wrote a separate dissent. In this dissent they stated that, although they had joined in the majority opinion in *Gobitis*, they now believed that the case had been "wrongly decided."[9]

In addition to this public retraction by three members of the *Gobitis* majority, two other significant events had occurred since the *Gobitis* decision in 1940. First, Justice Stone, the sole dissenter in *Gobitis*, had been elevated to the position of chief justice by President Roosevelt in 1941. Second, President Roosevelt (also in 1941) had appointed Justice Robert H. Jackson to the Court, and Jackson was thought to be an opponent of flag salute statute requirements. This combination of events made it clear that the Supreme Court might be willing to reconsider its decision in *Gobitis*. By the summer of 1942, the Court consisted of four members—Stone, Black, Douglas, and Murphy—who were on record as opposing the *Gobitis* decision—and a fifth member—Jackson—who was probably opposed to the decision.

Armed with this information, attorneys for the Jehovah's Witnesses resolved to file a lawsuit on behalf of Walter Barnette and his children. For the second time in two years, the issue of the constitutional validity of compulsory flag salute ceremonies was on its way to the U.S. Supreme Court.

The *Barnette* Case Is Filed in Three-Judge District Court

The attorneys for Walter Barnette had definite ideas about where they wanted to file their lawsuit. They strongly preferred to file the suit in federal (as opposed to state) court. In addition, they wanted to file the case, if possible, in a three-judge district court. Their preference for a three-judge district court was not difficult to understand. They were convinced that the U.S. Supreme Court was prepared to overrule *Gobitis*. Their principal goal, therefore, was to reach the Supreme Court as expeditiously as possible. Given this goal, a three-judge court was ideal, because the losing party in a case decided by such a Court is entitled to appeal directly to the U.S. Supreme Court.

When they examined the relevant federal statutes, Barnette and his lawyers discovered that their case indeed fell within the jurisdiction of the federal courts, and in particular the jurisdiction of a three-judge district court. Barnette and his lawyers intended to ask the judge (1) to rule that the West Virginia flag salute statute was unconstitutional and (2) to issue an injunction against further enforcement of the statute. As we saw in Chapter 2, congressional statutes conferred jurisdiction to decide such lawsuits (up to 1976) on three-judge district courts.

The Lower Court Decides

Barnette and his lawyers filed their case in three-judge district court in August 1942. Two months later, on October 6, the Court handed down its decision. The Court decided, unanimously, that the West Virginia flag salute requirement was unconstitutional.[10] Judge Parker wrote the opinion of the Court. He held that children who have "conscientious scruples . . . against saluting the flag" are, if they are expelled from school for refusing to salute the flag, "unquestionably denied that religious freedom which the Constitution guarantees."[11]

Judge Parker acknowledged in his opinion that the Supreme Court in *Minersville School District* v. *Gobitis* had upheld a flag salute requirement. He also acknowledged that "ordinarily" the lower federal courts should "follow an unreversed decision of the Supreme Court."[12] He noted, however, that some members of the present Court had "given public expression to the view that [*Gobitis*] is unsound."[13] Under the circumstances, Judge Parker felt that he and the two other judges for whom he spoke were correct in holding that flag salute requirements did indeed violate the Constitution.

The School Board Appeals

School authorities in West Virginia complied with the decision of the three-judge court and readmitted the Barnette children to school. On October 23, 1942, however, the State Board of Education voted to appeal the case to the U.S. Supreme Court. School officials were convinced that the Supreme Court would not be willing to overrule *Gobitis* only three years after it was handed down.

Federal statutes dictated how the appeal would proceed. Because the *Barnette* decision had been reached by a three-judge district court, the School Board was entitled, under federal statutes, to appeal directly to the Supreme Court. In addition, as we saw in Chapter 3, the case fell within one of the five categories of cases classified by Congress as appeal cases. As a result, the losing party had a right to invoke the mandatory appellate jurisdiction of the Supreme Court.

Barnette Reaches the Supreme Court

On January 4, 1943, the Supreme Court noted "probable jurisdiction" in the *Barnette* case. The choice to note probable jurisdiction, as opposed to the more common practice of granting certiorari, was dictated by the fact that *Barnette* was an example of a mandatory appeal case.

On March 11, 1943, the Supreme Court heard oral argument in the *Barnette* case. Three months later, on June 14, 1943, the Court handed down its decision. The Board of Education had hoped the Supreme Court would reverse the decision of the three-judge court and reaffirm its 1940 *Gobitis* holding in favor of flag salute requirements. Instead, by a vote of 6 to 3, the

The Supreme Court in 1943. The *Barnette* Court included one justice (Owen Roberts) appointed by President Herbert Hoover. The remaining members of the *Barnette* Court had all been appointed by President Franklin Roosevelt. *Standing (left to right):* Robert H. Jackson, William O. Douglas, Frank Murphy, and Wiley B. Rutledge. *Seated (left to right):* Stanley F. Reed, Owen J. Roberts, Harlan Fiske Stone, Hugo L. Black, and Felix Frankfurter.

SOURCE: Collection of the Supreme Court of the United States

Supreme Court affirmed the decision of the three-judge Court and overruled its own previous decision in *Gobitis*.[14]

Justice Jackson's *Barnette* Opinion

The Supreme Court's decision in *Barnette* was destined to become one of the leading precedents of the Court in the area of constitutional protection of individual rights. At the time the case was decided, as we have seen, the Court was in a period of transition. It had recently been known as an institution dedicated to protecting property rights and big business. In 1938, however, in Footnote Four to the majority opinion in the *Carolene Products* case, the Court had indicated its intention to assume greater responsibility for protecting civil rights and civil liberties. The *Barnette* decision represented a crucial further step in the metamorphosis of the Court.

Justice Jackson's opinion for the Court in *Barnette* was in part a point-by-point response to Justice Frankfurter's opinion for the Court in *Gobitis*. Jackson noted that Justice Frankfurter had assumed that schoolchildren could be required to salute the flag and that the only question for the Court was whether the Jehovah's Witnesses should be granted an exemption.[15] Jackson insisted, however, that the real issue was not whether Jehovah's Witnesses (or any other religious group) should be exempt from saluting the flag, but whether government had the power to compel *anyone* to salute the flag. "The question which underlies the flag salute controversy," Jackson said, "is whether such a ceremony so touching matters of opinion and political attitude may be imposed upon the individual by official authority . . . under our Constitution."[16]

In the course of his opinion, Justice Jackson alluded to several passages of Justice Frankfurter's opinion in *Gobitis*. One of Frankfurter's arguments had been that judicial review is "a fundamental part of our constitutional scheme" but is also "a limitation on popular government." Frankfurter argued that it was preferable to "fight out the wise use of legislative authority in the forum of public opinion and before legislative assemblies rather than to transfer such a contest to the judicial arena."[17]

Justice Jackson responded to Frankfurter's call for judicial restraint by crafting what is perhaps the single most famous defense of the role of the courts in a constitutional democracy. "The very purpose of a Bill of Rights," Jackson wrote, "was to withdraw certain subjects from the vicissitudes of political controversy, to place them beyond the reach of majorities and officials and to establish them as legal principles to be applied by the courts. One's right to life, liberty, and property, to free speech, a free press, freedom of worship and assembly, and other fundamental rights may not be submitted to vote; they depend on the outcome of no elections.[18]"

Justice Jackson's description of "the very purpose of a Bill of Rights" is regarded as a classic statement of the modern role of the courts in the democratic process. Jackson's thinking—and even his choice of words— were obviously influenced, however, by the opinion that Judge Parker had written for the three-judge court in the *Barnette* case. "The tyranny of majorities over the rights of individuals or helpless minorities," Judge Parker said,

> has always been recognized as one of the great dangers of popular government. The [founding] fathers sought to guard against this danger by writing into the Constitution a bill of rights guaranteeing to every individual certain fundamental liberties, of which he might not be deprived by any exercise whatever of governmental power. This bill of rights is not a mere guide for the exercise of legislative discretion. It is a part of the fundamental law of the land, and is to be enforced as such by the courts.[19]

The *Barnette* case reached the Supreme Court at a time when some of its members were prepared to redefine the role of the courts in protecting individual rights and to reevaluate the choice of rights that should benefit from judicial protection. The Supreme Court majority for whom Jackson spoke was clearly offended by the idea that government would attempt to punish an individual for adhering to a particular set of personal or religious values and would attempt to compel citizens to show their patriotic allegiance to the American flag. Jackson concluded his opinion by declaring that

If there is any fixed star in our constitutional constellation, it is that no official, high or petty, can prescribe what shall be orthodox in politics, nationalism, religion, or other matters of opinion or force citizens to confess by word or act their faith therein. . . . We think the action of the local authorities in compelling the flag salute and pledge transcends constitutional limitations on their power and invades the sphere of intellect and spirit which it is the purpose of the First Amendment to our Constitution to reserve from all official control.[20]

The Significance of *Barnette*

It was clear from Justice Jackson's opinion in *Barnette* that the Supreme Court was actively groping for a new conception of its role in the political process. Since the 1890s the Court had been an active defender of the rich and powerful. In the constitutional crisis of the 1930s, however, the Court had been forced to accept that it could no longer challenge decisions of the president and Congress on issues of economic and regulatory policy. The Court urgently needed to redefine its role in the policy-making process. The *Barnette* decision represented a significant step in the Court's transition from an institution dedicated to defending property rights and resisting social change to an institution dedicated to safeguarding the civil rights and civil liberties of underprivileged groups.[21]

In fact, the Court was rapidly becoming a magnet for groups and individuals seeking to vindicate their constitutional rights. Among the groups that began to look to the Supreme Court for help were America's racial minorities, and in particular, its black citizens. We turn next to litigation that presented the Supreme Court with one of the most sensitive and momentous issues of the twentieth century — the issue of racial segregation of public schools.

Notes

1. David R. Manwaring, *Render unto Caesar: The Flag Salute Controversy* (1962), p. 26. This book examines the history, beliefs, and principal constitutional battles of the Jehovah's Witnesses.

2. Id. at 28.

3. Id. at 3.

4. Id. at 3–16. Flag salute ceremonies were usually accompanied by recitation of the "Pledge of Allegiance." In 1942, because a salute was reminiscent of the "stiff-arm" gesture used by the Nazis in Germany, Congress provided that respect for the flag should be shown by placing the right hand over the heart. Id. at 3.

5. Id. at 209. The resolution had been passed pursuant to a West Virginia statute, enacted in 1923, which required every school to give instruction in history and civics "for the purpose of teaching, fostering and perpetuating the ideals, principles and spirit of Americanism." Id. at 208–9.

6. The Supreme Court's deliberations in the *Gobitis* case are discussed in Alice Fleetwood Bartee, *Cases Lost, Causes Won* (1984), Ch. 2. The *Gobitis* case is also discussed in Peter Irons, *The Courage of Their Convictions: Sixteen Americans Who Fought Their Way to the Supreme Court* (1988), Ch. 1.

7. In the wake of the *Gobitis* decision, and in part because of it, Jehovah's Witnesses were the object of widespread acts of persecution, including arrests, violence, and the passage and enforcement of new flag salute requirements (of which the West Virginia resolution was one). Manwaring, *Render unto Caesar*, pp. 163–95.

8. *Jones* v. *Opelika*, 316 U.S. 584 (1942).

9. Id. at 623–34 (Black, Douglas, and Murphy, JJ., dissenting).

10. *Barnette* v. *West Virginia State Board of Education*, 47 F.Supp. 251 (S.D.W.Va. 1942).

11. Id. at 253.

12. Id. at 252.

13. Id. at 254.

14. *West Virginia State Board of Education* v. *Barnette*, 319 U.S. 624 (1943).

15. Id. at 634–35.

16. Id. at 635–36.

17. *Minersville School District* v. *Gobitis*, 310 U.S. 586, 600 (1940).

18. 319 U.S. at 638 (1943).

19. *Barnette* v. *West Virginia State Board of Education*, 47 F.Supp. at 254.

20. 319 U.S. at 642.

21. For additional discussions of this key period of Supreme Court history — and the justices who shaped it — see Howard Ball and Phillip J. Cooper, *Of Power and Right: Hugo Black, William O. Douglas, and America's Constitutional Revolution* (1992); Stephen L. Wasby (ed.), *"He Shall Not Pass This Way Again": The Legacy of Justice William O. Douglas* (1991); Melvin I. Urofsky, *Felix Frankfurter: Judicial Restraint and Individual Liberties* (1991); James F. Simon, *The Antagonists: Hugo Black, Felix Frankfurter and Civil Liberties in Modern America* (1989); Mark Silverstein, *Constitutional Faiths: Felix Frankfurter, Hugo Black, and the Process of Decision* (1984); H. N. Hirsch, *The Enigma of Felix Frankfurter* (1981); James F. Simon, *Independent Journey: The Life of William O. Douglas* (1980); Sidney Fine, *Frank Murphy: The New Deal Years* (1979); Charles A. Leonard, *A Search for a Judicial Philosophy: Mr. Justice Roberts and the Constitutional Revolution of 1937* (1971); J. Woodford Howard, *Mr. Justice Murphy: A Political Biography* (1968); and Alpheus T. Mason, *Harlan Fiske Stone: Pillar of the Law* (1956).

CHAPTER 6

Racial Segregation of Public Schools: *Brown* v. *Board of Education* (1954)

T he first African slaves were brought to the Eastern Seaboard of the United States in the early seventeenth century. By 1787, when the Constitution was being drafted, the institution of slavery — the "peculiar institution," as it was sometimes called — was well established. Slavery served as the foundation of the southern economy and affected every aspect of politics and social relations in both the North and the South.[1]

The Constitution itself contained three references to slavery. In Article I, Section 9, Congress was prevented from prohibiting, prior to 1808, "[t]he Migration or Importation of such Persons as any of the States now existing shall think proper to admit." In Article I, Section 2 — in a further oblique reference to slavery — the Constitution made population the basis of each state's representation in the House of Representatives and prescribed that population would be determined "by adding the whole Number of free Persons . . . and . . . three fifths of all other Persons." Finally, in Article IV, Section 2, the framers dealt with the problem of fugitive slaves. They provided that "No Person held to Service or Labour in one State . . . escaping into another, shall . . . be discharged from such Service or Labour, but shall be delivered up on Claim of the Party to whom such Service or Labour may be due."

The Civil War brought an end to slavery, but racism and racial inequality persisted. In the last decades of the nineteenth century, southern states began to enact an elaborate system of laws designed to relegate blacks to second-class status. These Jim Crow Laws, as they were called, deprived blacks of the right to vote, excluded blacks from the mainstream of economic and professional life, and enforced a comprehensive system of racial segregation of public facilities.[2]

In the nineteenth century the Supreme Court made several ignominious contributions of its own to the woeful status of blacks in American society.[3] In 1857, in *Dred Scott* v. *Sandford*, the Court held that blacks were not citizens and were not entitled to sue in the courts. In 1883, in a group of cases known as the Civil Rights Cases, the Court examined the Civil Rights Act of 1875, in which Congress had outlawed racial discrimination in public accommodations such as inns, conveyances, and theaters, and declared the law unconstitutional. Finally, in *Plessy* v. *Ferguson* in 1896, the Court examined a Louisiana law that required railway passenger cars to have "equal but separate accommodations for the white, and colored races."[4] The Court held that the Constitution did not prevent states from enacting laws to enforce racial segregation of public facilities, provided the facilities themselves were "equal."[5]

The *Plessy* decision formalized the doctrine of "separate but equal" and signaled the legislatures of the several states that the Supreme Court was willing to tolerate racial segregation of public facilities. The southern states, in particular, made the most of the Supreme Court's pronouncement. By the early part of the twentieth century, practically every aspect of southern life — from the hospitals in which people were born to the graveyards in which they were buried — was segregated.

Racial Segregation of Public Schools

No form of segregation was more widespread or more significant, however, than segregation of the schools. At the time the litigation in *Brown* v. *Board of Education* began, in the early 1950s, seventeen states and the District of Columbia had statutes or constitutional provisions (or both) which either required or permitted racial segregation of public schools. Such de jure segregation (i.e., segregation enforced by law) was a critical component of the complex web of laws and customs that relegated blacks to second-class citizenship.[6]

The Supreme Court's decision in *Brown* v. *Board of Education* was actually a consolidated group of cases originating in four states — South Carolina, Virginia, Delaware, and Kansas. The text of the South Carolina state constitution gives some idea of the depth and breadth of the practice of segregation. The document prescribed that "Separate schools shall be provided for children of the white and colored races, and no child of either race shall ever be permitted to attend a school provided for children of the other race."[7]

The NAACP and the Legal Attack on School Segregation

The attack on segregation was coordinated by the National Association for the Advancement of Colored People (NAACP). The cases that eventually reached the Supreme Court under the title of *Brown* v. *Board of Education* were not initiated by the NAACP as part of a calculated master plan. Each case had arisen in a particular locality for particular reasons. But the NAACP, as a national organization, assumed overall responsibility for conduct of the litigation.

The NAACP was founded in 1909 and began its involvement with issues of race and education in the 1920s. Initially, the NAACP despaired of ending segregation itself and focused instead on equalizing white and black schools. The NAACP brought suits to end discrimination in the salaries paid to white and black teachers and to force states, at the graduate school and professional level, either to desegregate public institutions or else to provide black students with equal, if separate, facilities.[8]

In the early 1950s, the NAACP began to focus on elementary and secondary schools. In addition, it replaced the strategy of attempting to force states to provide equal but segregated facilities with a direct attack on racial segregation. The NAACP believed that school segregation was a critical component of the overall system of racial segregation and racial inequality. It therefore resolved to launch an attack on school segregation in the courts.

The *Brown* Litigation Takes Shape

The NAACP's attack on segregation consisted of cases that had originated in South Carolina, Virginia, Delaware, and Kansas. For purposes of preparing an appeal to the Supreme Court, these cases were consolidated into a single package of cases.

By the time the school desegregation cases reached the Supreme Court, a

Thurgood Marshall and the School Cases

Thurgood Marshall was a principal architect of the NAACP's legal attack on school segregation. Marshall was born in Baltimore in 1908 and received his law degree from Howard University in 1933.

In 1936 Marshall joined the staff of the NAACP. At the time of the *Brown* decision, he was chief counsel for the NAACP Legal Defense and Education Fund.

Marshall subsequently served as solicitor general of the United States (from 1965 to 1967). In 1967 he was appointed to the Supreme Court by President Johnson.

Marshall became an integral part of the liberal voting bloc on the Supreme Court. He served on the Court until his resignation in 1991.

Marshall's role in crafting legal and political strategies to end segregation is described in Richard Kluger, *Simple Justice* (1976) and Mark V. Tushnet, *The NAACP's Legal Strategy Against Segregated Education, 1925–1950* (1987).

fifth case, *Bolling* v. *Sharpe*, was added. In 1864 Congress had established separate schools for black children in Washington, D.C., the nation's capital. School segregation was not formally required by law, but District of Columbia schools were operated on a segregated basis. Furthermore, the courts had rebuffed all constitutional and legal challenges to segregation. The most recent pre-*Brown* defeat had come in *Carr* v. *Corning* in 1950.[9]

The particular dispute that lent its name to the school desegregation cases began in Topeka, Kansas. Statutes in effect in Kansas authorized, but did not require, school segregation. Pursuant to this authorization, the town of Topeka chose to operate its school system on a segregated basis. The plaintiff in the Kansas litigation was Oliver Brown, who was suing in behalf of his minor daughter, Linda Brown, a black pupil attending a segregated school in Topeka. Hence, the case became known as *Brown* v. *Board of Education of Topeka*.

School Segregation in the Lower Courts

The litigation that culminated in the Supreme Court's 1954 decision in *Brown* v. *Board of Education* thus consisted of five separate cases. Three were filed in three-judge district court;[10] the fourth began in state court in Delaware;[11] and the fifth, *Bolling* v. *Sharpe*, was filed in U.S. District Court for the District of Columbia.[12]

Each of the cases was resolved somewhat differently by the lower courts. Most of the lower courts, however, came to the same basic conclusion: segregation did not, in itself, violate the Constitution. This affirmation of the constitutional validity of segregation was consistent with the Supreme Court's 1896 decision in *Plessy* v. *Ferguson*, which had held that racial segregation was permissible as long as facilities for whites and blacks were equal. Most of the lower courts held that school facilities for whites and blacks were equal or were being equalized. Moreover, none of the lower courts, on its own initiative, was willing to overrule *Plessy*.

It was a three-judge district court in Kansas that decided the *Brown* case itself. The court held that the "separate but equal" requirement of *Plessy* was satisfied, because physical facilities in the white and black schools in Topeka, Kansas, were "comparable."[13] Since *Plessy* had never been overruled by the Supreme Court, it was "still . . . authority," the district court held, "for the maintenance of a segregated school system."[14] Accordingly, it was for the Supreme Court, rather than the district court, to evaluate the contention of the plaintiffs that "segregation in and of itself without more violates their rights guaranteed by the Fourteenth Amendment."[15]

The NAACP was disappointed but not surprised with the outcome in *Brown* (and in the other lower courts). It proceeded expeditiously to appeal to the U.S. Supreme Court. On June 9, 1952, the Court noted probable jurisdiction in *Brown* and in *Briggs* v. *Elliott* (from South Carolina). In October and November, it agreed to hear the remaining cases (from Virginia, Delaware, and the District of Columbia).

Oral Argument in the School Cases

Oral argument in the five cases comprising the *Brown* litigation occurred over a three-day period, December 9–11, 1952.[16] Shortly after oral argument, the justices met in conference to discuss the case. Reportedly, there were deep divisions over whether to overrule *Plessy* and declare segregation unconstitutional. Moreover, the divisions persisted into the spring.

Finally, with the term ending in June 1953—and with no consensus in sight—Justice Frankfurter drafted a memo to the Court suggesting that the cases be scheduled for reargument in the fall.[17] On June 8, 1953, the Court announced that the five cases would be "restored to the docket . . . for reargument on Monday, October 12, next."[18]

Earl Warren Becomes Chief Justice

Resolution of the issue of school segregation was thus postponed for another few months. In fact, there was one further delay. On September 8, 1953, Chief Justice Vinson died suddenly, and the search for a successor began. President Eisenhower chose Earl Warren, who at the time was governor of California, and Warren was sworn in on October 5. Because Congress was in recess, however, confirmation hearings in the Senate could not be scheduled until the first of the year. As a result, Warren assumed office on an interim basis.

Despite his tentative status, Warren began work in earnest in October. Soon he was making substantial progress in restoring a degree of harmony and civility to a Court that for several years had been deeply divided along lines of personality as well as ideology. Thus, the Court was already responding, as an institution, to the remarkable leadership talents of its new chief justice.[19]

Reargument in *Brown* occurred on December 8–9, 1953. In response to questions formulated by the Court, counsel for the parties focused on the historical issue of the intentions of those who participated in drafting and ratifying the Fourteenth Amendment in the 1860s. Not surprisingly, the historical evidence proved to be incomplete and ambiguous. In any case, it could not possibly offer an easy solution to the question of what to do about school segregation in the 1950s. The Court would be obliged to resolve this momentous social issue without the benefit of any clear guidance from either the text or the history of the Constitution.[20]

The Conference Meets

Following oral argument, the Court met in conference. Warren reportedly stated that he believed the Court had "finally arrived" at the moment when the issue of school segregation must be resolved and that he, personally, could no longer support the doctrine of "separate but equal."[21] The NAACP had been of the view since the early 1930s that segregation *necessarily* entailed inequality. Now the Supreme Court—or at least its forceful new chief justice—had come to the same conclusion.

It was also apparent at the conference, however, that to take an immedi-

The Supreme Court in 1954. In addition to five Roosevelt appointees, the *Brown* Court included three justices (Harold Burton, Tom C. Clark, and Sherman Minton) appointed by President Harry Truman. The Court's newest member, Chief Justice Earl Warren, had been appointed to the Court by President Dwight Eisenhower only a few months before the *Brown* decision itself. *Standing (left to right):* Tom C. Clark, Robert H. Jackson, Harold H. Burton, and Sherman Minton. *Seated (left to right):* Felix Frankfurter, Hugo L. Black, Earl Warren, Stanley F. Reed, and William O. Douglas.

SOURCE: Collection of the Supreme Court of the United States

ate vote on the question of ending school segregation would invite dissension. Some members of the Court were skeptical about overruling *Plessy*. In addition, since Warren himself had not yet been confirmed by the Senate, he was not anxious to force the issue. He wanted above all for the Court to be unified when it took the momentous step of declaring that segregation was unconstitutional. Thus, he was prepared to postpone a vote and to utilize the time to develop a consensus among the justices.

The Senate confirmed Earl Warren, by a unanimous vote, on March 1, 1954. At about the same time, the Court took a formal vote on the school segregation cases. Justice Stanley F. Reed was still unwilling to end segregation, and the division within the Court was therefore 8 to 1. Chief Justice Warren remained confident, however, that Reed could be won over. Warren assigned himself the delicate task of writing the majority opinion and went to work. In the end, Reed did join the Court's decision and Warren's opinion. The Supreme Court's unanimous decision ending racial segregation of public schools was announced to the world on May 17, 1954.

The Opinion in *Brown*

Justice Warren's opinion for the Court was brief and somewhat understated. He noted that the various lower courts in the *Brown* litigation had found that "Negro and white schools . . . have been equalized, or are being equalized, with respect to buildings, curricula, qualifications and salaries of teachers, and other 'tangible' factors." The decision of the Supreme Court, therefore, could not "turn on merely a comparison of these tangible factors . . . [but] must look instead to the effect of segregation itself on public education."[22]

Warren's ensuing observations on "the effect of segregation" are among the most memorable passages in any Supreme Court decision. "To separate [some children] from others of similar age and qualifications solely because of their race," Warren wrote, "generates a feeling of inferiority as to their status in the community that may affect their hearts and minds in a way unlikely ever to be undone."[23] Warren concluded that "in the field of public education the doctrine of 'separate but equal' has no place. Separate educational facilities are inherently unequal. Therefore, we hold that the plaintiffs and others similarly situated . . . are, by reason of the segregation complained of, deprived of the equal protection of the laws guaranteed by the Fourteenth Amendment."[24]

The Aftermath of *Brown*

Immediately after the Court's decision, Thurgood Marshall was, not surprisingly, both ecstatic and optimistic. He was quoted in the *New York Times* "as predicting that school segregation in America would be entirely stamped out in no more than five years."[25] A statement of the governor of Virginia made five weeks after the *Brown* decision, however, gave some indication of how misplaced Marshall's optimism might be. "I shall use every legal means at my command," the governor said, "to continue segregated schools in Virginia."[26]

In fact, there was almost no actual integration of public schools for a full decade after the *Brown* decision. In 1955, in a case often known as *Brown II*, the Supreme Court delegated principal responsibility for implementing the *Brown* decision to U.S. District Courts in the affected states and held that desegregation should proceed "with all deliberate speed."[27] In most southern states, however, judicial efforts to implement the *Brown* decision met with stiff resistance.[28] By 1963–1964 "only 1.17 percent of black schoolchildren in the eleven states of the Confederacy were attending public school with white classmates."[29]

At about this time, however, several factors combined to hasten the process of change, including additional Supreme Court decisions, a more aggressive enforcement posture on the part of the Kennedy and Johnson administrations, and the emergence of Congress as a force in the policy-making process on civil rights issues. By 1972–1973, "46.3 percent of the black children in eleven Southern states were attending schools in which the majority of children were white."[30]

Social Science and Constitutional Law

One element of Chief Justice Warren's opinion in *Brown* v. *Board of Education* has spawned a special controversy. Warren wrote that school segregation "generates a feeling of inferiority" among minority students, and, quoting from the District Court's opinion in *Brown*, Warren added that legally enforced segregation "has a tendency to [retard] the educational and mental development of Negro children." (347 U.S. at 494).

To support his conclusion that school segregation has a damaging effect on minority children, Warren cited several books and articles by social scientists. These citations were included in a footnote — Footnote Eleven — to Warren's opinion.

Some legal scholars immediately questioned whether it was wise to base a constitutional decision on social scientific evidence that might prove to be inaccurate or incomplete. The evidence provided critical support for the Court's holding that school segregation is unconstitutional. What if future research should discover, however, that minority children experience a greater sense of inferiority in integrated than in segregated schools, or that school integration has a detrimental rather than beneficial effect on the educational development of minority students? Would such discoveries, if they occurred, mean that *Brown* was wrongly decided?

The *Brown* Court's use of social scientific evidence is the subject of continuing debate. For discussions, see Edmond Cahn, "Jurisprudence," 30 *N.Y.U.L. Rev.* 150 (1955); Kenneth B. Clark, "The Social Scientists, the Brown Decision, and the Contemporary Confusion," in Leon Friedman (ed.), *Argument: The Oral Argument before the Supreme Court in Brown v. Board of Education, 1952–1955* (1969); Frank I. Goodman, "De Facto Segregation: A Constitutional and Empirical Analysis," 60 *Calif. L. Rev.* 275 (1972); Symposium, "The Courts, Social Science, and School Desegregation," 39 *Law & Contemp. Prob.* (Winter/Spring 1975); and Symposium, "School Desegregation: Lessons of the First Twenty-Five Years," 42 *Law & Contemp. Prob.* (Summer/Autumn 1978).

Footnote Eleven is one of two exceptionally famous Supreme Court footnotes. The other, of course, is Footnote Four to Justice Stone's opinion in *Carolene Products* (1938). Students of Supreme Court history may be interested to learn that the two footnotes have one thing in common. Both were initially written by clerks and eventually adopted by the justice who was the named author of the Court's opinion! See Bernard Schwartz, *The Unpublished Opinions of the Warren Court* (1985), pp. 458–59 (Footnote Eleven); Mason, *Harlan Fiske Stone: Pillar of the Law* (1956), pp. 513–15 (Footnote Four). For commentary by the clerk who authored the initial version of Footnote Four, see Louis Lusky, "Footnote Redux: A Carolene Products Reminiscence," 82 *Colum. L. Rev.* 1093 (1982).

Ironically, however, it was in this same period that so-called de facto segregation of schools in the North began to worsen. The term *de facto segregation* refers to the phenomenon of schools that are racially homogeneous—that is, either all-white or all-black—because the neighborhoods they serve are themselves racially homogeneous. By 1972–1973, only 28.3 percent of black children were attending majority-white schools in the North, compared to 46.3 percent in the South.[31] By the early 1970s, therefore, school desegregation was more extensive in the southern than in the northern states.

From a constitutional point of view, the problem of de facto school segregation is commonly regarded as being more complicated than the problem of de jure segregation. Experts disagree about whether courts possess the power under the Constitution to order an end to school segregation when the segregation is not enforced by written statutes, as such, but instead reflects the racial homogeneity of most American neighborhoods. In several cases in the 1970s—including *Keyes* v. *School District* (1973), *Milliken* v. *Bradley* (1974), *Columbus Board of Education* v. *Penick* (1979), and *Dayton Board of Education* v. *Brinkman* (1979)—the Supreme Court confronted but never clearly resolved the difficult question of the constitutional status of de facto school segregation. In the 1990s most American cities exhibit a substantial degree of residential segregation. A direct reflection of this segregation is the continuing existence of schools with racially homogeneous student populations.

Conclusion

Brown v. *Board of Education* was one of many episodes in America's long struggle with its racial problems. It is widely regarded as the most important Supreme Court decision of the twentieth century and as a milestone in the process of ending racial segregation and racial inequality. In retrospect, however, it is painfully clear that *Brown* was at best a small step in a continuing process. In a classic study published in the 1940s, Swedish sociologist Gunnar Myrdal referred to the problem of race in American society as the "American dilemma."[32] America's mixed success in attacking its racial problems in the wake of the *Brown* decision reinforces the conclusion that race is among the most difficult and stubborn of modern social problems.[33]

In the 1940s and 1950s America was troubled by other controversies, some of which had little or nothing to do with race. One of the most volatile of these controversies—the question of the legal status of the Communist party and other radical groups—was to culminate in the Supreme Court's important First Amendment decision in *Yates* v. *United States*. We turn next to the important question of the scope of political freedom under the First Amendment.

Notes

1. Kenneth M. Stampp, *The Peculiar Institution: Slavery in the Ante-Bellum South* (1956).

2. C. Vann Woodward, *The Strange Career of Jim Crow* (1974).

3. See, generally, Derrick A. Bell, *And We Are Not Saved: The Elusive Quest for Racial Justice* (1987); and Derrick A. Bell, *Race, Racism and American Law* (1980).

4. 163 U.S. 537, 540 (1896).

5. Charles A. Lofgren, *The Plessy Case: A Legal-Historical Interpretation* (1987); and Paul Oberst, "The Strange Career of Plessy v. Ferguson," 15 *Ariz. L. Rev.* 389 (1973).

6. For a brief history of American race relations, and an exhaustive examination of school segregation and the *Brown* litigation, see Richard Kluger, *Simple Justice* (1976). See also Dennis J. Hutchinson, "Unanimity and Desegregation: Decisionmaking in the Supreme Court, 1948–1958," 68 *Geo. L. J.* 1 (1979).

7. *Briggs* v. *Elliott* (I), 98 F.Supp. 529, 530 n. 1 (E.D.S.C. 1951).

8. The evolution of the NAACP's attack on segregation is traced in Mark V. Tushnet, *The NAACP's Legal Strategy against Segregated Education, 1925–1950* (1987).

9. See Kluger, *Simple Justice*, pp. 508–23.

10. *Brown* v. *Board of Education* (1951) (Kansas); *Briggs* v. *Elliott* (II) (South Carolina); *Davis* v. *Board of Education of Prince Edward County* (1952) (Virginia).

11. *Belton* v. *Gebhart* (1952).

12. The case was dismissed, without opinion, by the Court. See Kluger, *Simple Justice*, pp. 508–23, 538–40. The Supreme Court's eventual decision was *Bolling* v. *Sharpe* (1954).

13. *Brown* v. *Board of Education*, 98 F.Supp. 797, 798 (D.Kan. 1951).

14. Id. at 800.

15. Id. at 798

16. Oral argument in the *Brown* litigation is discussed in Kluger, *Simple Justice*, pp. 543–81.

17. See id. at 582–616.

18. 345 U.S. 972 (1953).

19. For biographies of Chief Justice Earl Warren, see Bernard Schwartz, *Super Chief: Earl Warren and His Supreme Court — A Judicial Biography* (1983); and G. Edward White, *Earl Warren: A Public Life* (1982).

20. The intent of the framers of the Fourteenth Amendment is explored in detail in Raoul Berger, *Government by Judiciary: The Transformation of the Fourteenth Amendment* (1977).

21. Kluger, *Simple Justice*, pp. 678–79.

22. *Brown* v. *Board of Education*, 347 U.S. 483, 492 (1954).

23. Id. at 494.

24. Id. at 495.

25. Kluger, *Simple Justice*, p. 714.

26. Quoted in id. at 714.

27. *Brown* v. *Board of Education* (II), 349 U.S. 294, 301 (1955).

28. See Jack Peltason, *Fifty-Eight Lonely Men: Southern Federal Judges and School Desegregation* (1961).

29. Kluger, *Simple Justice*, p. 758.

30. Id. at 768. For a thorough discussion of the impact of judicial decisions on the problem of school segregation, see Gerald N. Rosenberg, *The Hollow Hope: Can Courts Bring about Social Change?* (1991), Ch. 2.

31. Kluger, *Simple Justice*, p. 768.

32. Gunnar Myrdal, *An American Dilemma: The Negro Problem and Modern Democracy* (1944).

33. Recent examinations of race and inequality in American society include Andrew Hacker, *Two Nations: Black and White, Separate, Hostile, Unequal* (1992); Chistopher Jencks, *Rethinking Social Policy: Race, Poverty, and the Underclass* (1992); William Julius Wilson, *The Truly Disadvantaged: The Inner City, the Underclass, and Public Policy* (1987); Jennifer Hochschild, *The New American Dilemma: Liberal Democracy and School Desegregation* (1984).

CHAPTER 7

The Communist Party and
Cold War Politics:
Yates v. United States (1957)

From the beginning of its history, the United States has experienced periodic outbursts of patriotism. While these outbursts have often served the beneficial purpose of uniting the country in times of crisis, they have also had a darker side. Increased patriotism is usually accompanied by increased suspicion of anyone who is different and by the passage and enforcement of repressive legislation aimed at unpopular groups, unassimilated minorities, and dissenting citizens.

The Alien and Sedition Acts of 1798 were among the earliest attempts to enforce political loyalty and cultural purity through legislation. The acts were a pair of statutes enacted by the Federalist-controlled Congress. The Alien Act was aimed at immigrant groups, particularly the French and the Irish, whereas the Sedition Act was directed at persons who held anti-Federalist views, that is, the Jeffersonian Republicans. Sedition charges were brought against various Republican newspapers and Republican officeholders and resulted in at least twenty-five arrests and ten convictions.[1]

Jefferson's electoral victory in 1800 was fueled in part by resentment toward the Alien and Sedition Acts. Once in office, Jefferson allowed the acts to expire and pardoned those who remained in prison. In some local areas, however, Republicans could not resist the temptation to seek revenge and brought common law prosecutions for "seditious libel" against Federalists. Indeed, Jefferson himself was tempted to invoke the law to silence his critics in the press. Fortunately for his reputation, he never actually did so.[2]

The essence of the crime of *sedition* (or *seditious libel*, as it is also called) is the allegation that someone has published or uttered words that will bring the government or governmental leaders into "disrepute" or will "cast contempt" on public figures or political institutions. The Sedition Act of 1798, for instance, purported to punish "any false, scandalous and malicious . . . writings against . . . the Congress . . . or the President . . . with intent . . . to bring them . . . into contempt or disrepute;

or to excite against them . . . the hatred of the good people of the United States."[3]

Enforcement of the Alien and Sedition Acts was only the first example of a recurring phenomenon in American history. Whenever citizens have felt threatened by social forces over which they had no control, or by political ideologies that they could not understand or abide, they have endorsed the passage of legislation aimed at preventing change and stifling new political ideas.

The Suppression of Dissent in Recent History

The modern era of conflict between government and political dissenters dates from the end of the nineteenth century. The country was experiencing an unprecedented series of cultural shocks, including an upsurge in immigration from Europe, the emergence of a bewildering assortment of anticapitalist ideologies, and the rise of militant political agitation among workers and the poor. The reaction of state and local governments was predictable: many jurisdictions enacted statutes designed to inhibit change, suppress dissent, and control public order.

An early example of this type of statute was passed by the New York State Legislature in 1902. President McKinley had been assassinated in 1901 by a self-proclaimed anarchist. In response, New York enacted a law aimed at punishing the offense of criminal anarchy. The statute made it a crime to advocate "the doctrine that organized government should be overthrown by force or violence, or by assassination . . . or by any unlawful means."[4]

As the first two decades of the twentieth century unfolded, new developments shook the confidence of the American people. In 1914 World War I engulfed Europe, and Americans were soon engaged in a debate over whether to enter the war. One component of that debate was the allegation that persons of German extraction in the United States might constitute a threat to national security. Then, in 1917, the Bolsheviks seized power in Russia. This momentous occurrence generated new fears among many Americans that left-wing political movements would soon gain a foothold in the United States.

Legislative bodies responded by enacting new laws. In 1917 Idaho passed the first criminal syndicalism law, and within a short time, other states followed suit.[5] Between 1917 and 1921 approximately two-thirds of the states passed laws against criminal anarchy, criminal syndicalism, or sedition. Many states took the additional step of forbidding the public display of any red flag or other symbol of radical change.[6]

At the federal level, American entry into World War I in 1917 led to enactment of legislation aimed at curbing disagreement with the war and disaffection within the military. The Espionage Act of 1917 made it a crime (1) "to make . . . false reports . . . with intent to interfere with the operation or success of the military or naval forces," (2) to "cause or attempt to cause insubordination [or] disloyalty . . . in the military or naval forces," or (3) to "obstruct the recruiting or enlistment service of the United States."[7]

The Red Scare of 1919–1920

The plethora of legislative enactments at all levels of government contributed to events that historians call the "Red Scare" of 1919–1920. Hundreds of citizens were prosecuted for violating state and federal laws prohibiting criminal anarchy, criminal syndicalism, and related crimes. One historian estimates that about 1,400 persons were arrested and about 300 convicted under state laws in 1919 and 1920.[8] Under the federal Espionage Act of 1917, an estimated 1,956 persons were arrested, of whom 877 were convicted.[9]

The most notorious episode of the period of the Red Scare was a group of events known as the Palmer Raids. On January 2, 1920, A. Mitchell Palmer, the U.S. attorney general, ordered federal agents to conduct raids on union halls and other sites to look for deportable aliens who were members of the Communist party or the Communist Labor party. As many as five to ten thousand people may have been arrested in the raids. In the end, only a handful of aliens were actually deported, but the Palmer Raids, combined with the other governmental actions of the Red Scare, were effective in breaking the back of radical movements in the United States for many years to come.[10]

The Depression, the Cold War, and Anticommunist Legislation

Governmental repression of dissent subsided in the 1920s but revived in the 1930s. Most states still had laws against criminal anarchy, criminal syndicalism, and sedition, and in some states these laws had been supplemented by legislation aimed at enforcing loyalty among teachers and governmental employees. The political and economic tensions of the Great Depression produced a new wave of demands for the punishment of radical dissenters.[11]

At the federal level, renewed concern with disloyalty and dissent crystallized in congressional efforts to pass legislation aimed at the Communist party and other radical groups. The U.S. Code contained no statute equivalent to state laws against criminal anarchy or criminal syndicalism. A campaign to remedy this situation began in 1935 and culminated, in 1940, in passage of the Alien Registration Act, more commonly known as the Smith Act, after its sponsor, Congressman Howard W. Smith of Virginia. Title I of the Smith Act closely resembled the New York criminal anarchy statute. Under Title I, it was a crime "to advocate . . . the duty, necessity, desirability, or propriety of overthrowing . . . any government in the United States by force or violence." In addition, it was a crime "to organize . . . any society . . . of persons who teach, advocate, or encourage the overthrow . . . of . . . government" or "to conspire to commit any of the acts prohibited [by the law]."[12]

For a period of several years, the wartime alliance between the United States and the Soviet Union prevented any application of the Smith Act to the American Communist party. The onset of the Cold War, however, changed all that. On July 20, 1948, the government indicted twelve leaders of the Communist party for violation of the Smith Act. Eventually, eleven of the defendants were convicted. The tumultuous trial lasted nine months, cost about $1 million, and generated twenty thousand pages of testimony.[13]

The *Dennis* Case and Its Aftermath

The Smith Act convictions became known as the *Dennis* case — after Eugene Dennis, who was general secretary of the Communist party and one of eleven defendants in the case. In 1951 the case reached the U.S. Supreme Court on appeal. The Court declined to examine the sufficiency of the evidence and confined itself to deciding whether the Smith Act violated the Constitution. The Court concluded that the Smith Act was constitutional, and it upheld the convictions of all eleven defendants.[14]

The Supreme Court's decision in the *Dennis* case emboldened the government to bring further prosecutions under the Smith Act. In July 1951, one such prosecution commenced in Los Angeles. It focused on fourteen individuals, including Oleta Yates, organizational secretary of the Communist party in California.

Yates in the Lower Courts

The trial of Oleta Yates and her co-defendants took place in U.S. District Court in Los Angeles and lasted six months, almost as long as the nine-month ordeal in *Dennis*. The presiding judge was William Mathes. When the trial was over, the jury returned a verdict of guilty, and Judge Mathes sentenced all fourteen defendants to the maximum penalty under the law — five years in prison and a $10,000 fine.[15]

The *Yates* case followed the normal appeal route for a federal criminal case. It went from the district court to the U.S. Court of Appeals for the Ninth Circuit, whose jurisdiction includes cases appealed from district courts in California and neighboring western states. The appeal in *Yates* was heard by a three-judge panel consisting of Judges Stephens, Fee, and Chambers.[16]

Judge Fee authored the opinion of the court of appeals, and he rejected every claim raised by the defendants. He began by noting that "[t]he impressive feature of this case is that practically every [contention] urged in this appeal has been ruled upon by the Supreme Court of the United States in *Dennis* v. *United States*."[17] He went on to hold that the Smith Act was constitutional as applied to the *Yates* defendants, that the evidence was sufficient to support the verdict of the jury, that the instructions to the jury by Judge Mathes were correct, and that the trial was "impeccable from the standpoint of fairness."[18]

With the decision of the court of appeals in place, the defendants prepared to appeal to the Supreme Court. They relied on 28 U.S.C. #1254, which indicates that "Cases in the courts of appeals may be reviewed by the Supreme Court . . . [b]y writ of certiorari granted upon the petition of any party to any civil or criminal case."

On October 17, 1955, the Supreme Court granted certiorari in the *Yates* case. The Supreme Court had previously denied certiorari in two Smith Act cases. Thus, its decision to grant certiorari came as something of a surprise. The Court's decision on the merits came as an even greater surprise.

The Supreme Court Narrows the Smith Act

The Supreme Court handed down its decision in *Yates* on June 17, 1957.[19] To the surprise of the government — and almost everyone else — the Court used the case as the vehicle for an important decision circumscribing the meaning of the Smith Act and broadening the scope of constitutional protection of freedom of speech for radical dissenters.

Justice Harlan's opinion for the Court was an example of statutory construction rather than judicial review. He examined the language of the Smith Act and gave it a restrictive construction. The Court's reinterpretation of the Smith Act resolved the incompatibility that the Court believed would otherwise exist between the language of the act and the requirements of the First Amendment. Thus, the Court avoided the choice of whether to uphold or overturn the act itself on constitutional grounds. The net effect of Justice Harlan's construction of the law, however, was comparable to a decision that the law was unconstitutional. Harlan's interpretation of the law was sufficiently restrictive to render the law itself ineffectual as a weapon against the Communist party.[20]

Justice Harlan's opinion for the Court focused on the discrepancy between Judge Mathes's charge to the jury in the *Yates* trial and the "true" meaning of the Smith Act. In Harlan's view, Judge Mathes had permitted the jury to return a verdict of guilty, even though the advocacy with which the defendants were charged had not necessarily urged anyone to take concrete action to overthrow the government. "We are thus faced with the question," Harlan said, "whether the Smith Act prohibits advocacy and teaching of forcible overthrow as an abstract principle, divorced from any effort to instigate action to that end. . . . We hold that it does not."[21]

The Court held that the Smith Act, if properly construed, was not aimed at advocacy of abstract doctrine — *even* the doctrine that government should be overthrown by force and violence — but only at advocacy of concrete action to bring about that result. In passing the Smith Act, Harlan said, "Congress was aware of the distinction between the advocacy . . . of abstract doctrine and the advocacy . . . of action, and . . . it did not intend to disregard it. The statute was aimed at the advocacy . . . of concrete action for the forcible overthrow of the Government, and not of principles divorced from action."[22]

The Supreme Court in 1957. The *Yates* Court included justices appointed by Presidents Franklin Roosevelt, Harry Truman, and Dwight Eisenhower. The *Yates* decision itself, however, was reached by only seven justices. The two newest members of the Court — William Brennan and Charles Whittaker — had not yet joined the Court at the time of oral argument in the *Yates* case and therefore did not participate in the decision itself. *Standing (left to right):* William J. Brennan, Jr., Tom C. Clark, John M. Harlan, and Charles E. Whittaker. *Seated (left to right):* William O. Douglas, Hugo L. Black, Earl Warren, Felix Frankfurter, and Harold H. Burton.

SOURCE: Collection of the Supreme Court of the United States

Justice Harlan concluded that in light of the distinction that Congress had meant to incorporate into the Smith Act, "we are unable to regard the District Court's charge . . . as adequate."[23] Judge Mathes's charge to the jury had been too broad to faithfully reflect the intent of Congress, Harlan argued, and therefore the constitutional rights of the defendants had been violated.

Justice Harlan's decision that the charge to the jury in the *Yates* case was improper would have sufficed to overturn the convictions of the defendants and to order a new trial. Justice Harlan proceeded to take the somewhat unusual step, however, of examining the actual evidence in the case. He concluded that the evidence against nine of the defendants was strong enough to justify their retrial, but the evidence against five of the defendants was "so clearly insufficient that their acquittal should be ordered."[24] In the end, the case against the nine remaining defendants was also dismissed, because the

Statutory Construction and Constitutional Politics

The technique of statutory construction is a way for the Supreme Court to avoid a direct confrontation with Congress over the constitutional validity of legislation. Justice Harlan's opinion in the *Yates* case is a good example of the Court's use of this technique.

Justice Harlan held that the Smith Act did not punish advocacy of overthrow of the government as an abstract doctrine, *only* advocacy of action. Harlan gave the Smith Act a restrictive construction in order to avoid the constitutional issue of whether the Smith Act itself violated the First Amendment.

Since the *Yates* decision was an act of statutory construction, rather than judicial review, Congress could have reenacted the Smith Act, this time making it clear that the Act was intended to punish *all* types of advocacy, including abstract advocacy. Had Congress done so, the Court would have been presented squarely with the *constitutional* issue of whether the act, as reenacted by Congress, violated the First Amendment.

In the end, Congress chose not to exercise its prerogative to reenact the Smith Act. The Court's decision in *Yates* remained good law and effectively ended one prong of the government's campaign to destroy the Communist party by legal prosecutions.

government concluded that it could not "satisfy the evidentiary requirements laid down by the Supreme Court."[25]

The Aftermath of *Yates*

The Supreme Court's decision in *Yates* v. *United States* brought a halt to government prosecutions under the Smith Act and marked the beginning of the end of the anticommunist hysteria of the 1950s. Several pieces of legislation were introduced in Congress to restrict the jurisdiction of the Court or to reverse the *Yates* decision. Most of this legislation, however, was ultimately defeated.

Some have argued that one reason for the defeat of this so-called *Court-curbing legislation* is that, following *Yates*, the Supreme Court executed a tactical retreat. The Court sensed that it was reaching the limits of its ability to hand down controversial decisions without provoking retaliatory legislation from Congress. Therefore, the argument goes, it deliberately "pulled in its horns." In particular, it temporarily adopted a more moderate stance in a series of decisions in the late 1950s in order to avoid further antagonizing Congress.[26]

The *Yates* decision itself, however, was a milestone in the Supreme Court's assumption of responsibility for protecting First Amendment rights. In addition, it was not long before the Court waded back into the thick of political controversy. At about the time the Supreme Court was considering the *Yates* case, a new constitutional problem was brewing in the lower courts. The problem was whether it was permissible under the Constitution to require students in public schools to recite the Lord's Prayer or to engage in other types of religious observances. When the constitutional litigation generated by this problem reached the Supreme Court, the Court responded by issuing one of its most controversial decisions of all time.

Notes

1. The leading history of the Alien and Sedition Acts is James Morton Smith, *Freedom's Fetters: The Alien and Sedition Laws and American Civil Liberties* (1956).

2. Leonard W. Levy, *Legacy of Suppression: Freedom of Speech and Press in Early American History* (1960), pp. 297–307; see also Leonard W. Levy, *Jefferson and Civil Liberties: The Darker Side* (1963).

3. The text of the Alien and Sedition Acts is reprinted in Thomas I. Emerson, David Haber, and Norman Dorsen (eds.), *Political and Civil Rights in the United States*, Vol. I (1967), pp. 35–39. This volume is an invaluable source of citations to books and articles on legal and political aspects of freedom of speech, press, assembly, and association.

4. The Supreme Court upheld the constitutional validity of the New York statute in *Gitlow* v. *New York* (1925).

5. Criminal syndicalism statutes were similar to criminal anarchy statutes, except that they focused on the problem of militant labor unions and left-wing political parties. The California criminal syndicalism statute, for instance, punished anyone who advocated "crime, sabotage, [or] unlawful acts of force or violence . . . as a means of accomplishing a change in industrial ownership or control." The statute was upheld by the Supreme Court in *Whitney* v. *California* (1927).

6. Eldridge F. Dowell, *A History of Criminal Syndicalism Legislation in the United States* (1969).

7. The leading Supreme Court decision arising under the Espionage Act of 1917 is *Schenck* v. *United States* (1919). This was the case in which Justice Holmes enunciated the famous "clear and present danger test." See also *Abrams* v. *United States* (1919), a prosecution arising under 1918 amendments to the Espionage Act. The classic exposition of legal and political issues arising from prosecutions under the Espionage Act is Zechariah Chafee, Jr., *Free Speech in the United States* (1941).

8. Robert K. Murray, *Red Scare: A Study in National Hysteria, 1919–1920* (1955), pp. 233–35.

9. Chafee, *Free Speech*, pp. 51–52 n. 30.

10. See, generally, Robert Justin Goldstein, *Political Repression in Modern America* (1978).

11. Carol E. Jenson, *The Network of Control: State Supreme Courts and State Security Statutes, 1920–1970* (1982).

12. The history of the Smith Act, from its inception to its application to the

Communist party in the postwar period, is recounted in Michal R. Belknap, *Cold War Political Justice: The Smith Act, the Communist Party, and American Civil Liberties* (1977).

13. Belknap, *Cold War Political Justice*, Chs. 3 and 4.

14. *Dennis* v. *United States* (1951).

15. The conduct of the *Yates* trial is discussed in Belknap, *Cold War Political Justice*, Ch. 6.

16. *Yates* v. *United States*, 225 F.2d 146 (9th Cir. 1955).

17. Id. at 149.

18. Id. at 164.

19. *Yates* v. *United States*, 354 U.S. 298 (1957).

20. Justice Harlan was generally viewed as a moderate or even conservative member of the Warren Court. On several occasions, however, Harlan surprised both Court observers and his colleagues by crafting highly protective opinions. *Yates* was one example, and *Cohen* v. *California* (1971), discussed elsewhere in this book, was another. For a recent biography of Justice Harlan, see Tinsley E. Yarbrough, *John Marshall Harlan: Great Dissenter of the Warren Court* (1992).

21. Id. at 318.

22. Id. at 319–20.

23. Id. at 324.

24. Id. at 328–29.

25. *New York Times*, December 3, 1957.

26. See Walter F. Murphy, *Congress and the Court* (1962); and C. Herman Pritchett, *Congress versus the Supreme Court* (1961).

CHAPTER 8

The Supreme Court Confronts Prayer in Public Schools: *School District of Abington Township* v. *Schempp* (1963)

In traditional European politics, an established religion or established church was one that enjoyed the support of government and had a monopoly on the religious life of the nation. Citizens were required to profess belief in the doctrines of the established church, to attend its services, and to pay taxes to support its continued operation.

Political systems with an established church are often described as societies in which there is no separation of church and state. An almost unavoidable consequence of the absence of separation of church and state, of course, is that persons who do not belong to the established church are ostracized or even persecuted for their nonconformist beliefs.

Many of the early immigrants to the United States were fleeing such religious persecution. Often, however, their response to newfound religious freedom was to create a religious establishment of their own. "On the eve of the American Revolution," one scholar has written, "most of the colonies maintained establishments of religion. Those colonies, although resentful of British violations of American rights, discriminated against Roman Catholics, Jews, and even dissenting Protestants. . . . "[1]

The Establishment Clause

The Establishment Clause of the First Amendment to the Constitution, added to the Constitution in 1791, stipulated that "Congress shall make no law respecting an establishment of religion." At a minimum, the purpose of the Establishment Clause was to end, in the United States, the practice of established churches and the abuses that inevitably followed.

In fact, the picture in the new states was mixed. The Establishment Clause, on its face, only prohibited Congress from making laws "respecting an establishment of religion." Some states, however, persisted for some time in discriminating against particular religious groups. Discrimination often took the form of preventing anyone who was not a Protestant or at least a Christian from voting or holding public office. "The early constitutions of several states," for instance, "disenfranchised or excluded from office Catholics, Jews, and nonbelievers. In Massachusetts and Maryland, the office of governor was closed to all except Christians. In four more states, the governor had to be Protestant."[2]

The Supreme Court and the Establishment Clause

The first major Supreme Court decision under the Establishment Clause was handed down in 1947. In *Everson* v. *Board of Education of Ewing Township*, the Court examined a New Jersey law that authorized local school boards to make arrangements with parents for the transportation of children to school. The school board of Ewing Township decided to reimburse parents of Catholic-school children for the cost of bus transportation. The reimbursement program was challenged in court as an unconstitutional establishment of religion.

When the case reached the Supreme Court, the Court decided that the New Jersey law and the Ewing Township reimbursement program did not violate the Constitution.[3] In his opinion for the Court, however, Justice Black also announced that the Court was generally sympathetic to the position of Thomas Jefferson, who had argued that the purpose of the Establishment Clause was to erect "a wall of separation between Church and State."[4]

By the end of the 1950s a variety of cases arising under the Establishment Clause began to enter the courts. Among the issues that were beginning to surface in litigation was the question of whether prayer in public schools was a violation of the Constitution.[5]

Prayer and the American Public School

Surveys of school districts in the early 1960s revealed that various forms of devotional activity were common in public schools in the United States. One such activity was Bible reading. Approximately 40 to 50 percent of American schools included Bible reading in their daily routine.[6]

Not surprisingly, there were sharp regional variations in the incidence of Bible reading. Some 60 to 80 percent of schools in the East and South reported the practice, while only 10 to 20 percent of schools in the West and Midwest did so. Moreover, state laws governing the subject of Bible reading varied dramatically. In 1960 "eleven states (mostly in the West) had laws *prohibiting* Bible reading; eleven others (mainly in the South) had laws *requiring* Bible reading; and twenty-six others *permitted, but did not require*, the practice."[7]

Origins of the *Schempp* Case

Pennsylvania was one of the states in which Bible reading was required. State law prescribed that "[a]t least ten verses from the Holy Bible shall be read . . . at the opening of each public school on each school day." The law did not specify what sanction, if any, would be imposed on a student who refused to participate. It did prescribe, however, that if any teacher should "fail or omit" to read the Holy Bible, he or she would be "discharged."[8]

In 1956 a constitutional challenge to the Pennsylvania law was begun by Ellory Schempp, a sixteen-year-old junior in high school in Abington Township, Pennsylvania. The practice in Schempp's school included Bible reading followed by recitation of the Lord's Prayer. As a junior, Schempp declined to participate in these activities. Each day he spent the Bible-reading period in the school guidance office. In his senior year, under mounting pressure, he remained in class during the Bible reading and Lord's Prayer, but he continued to voice his objections to the policy. Eventually, he brought suit against the school district in federal court.

At about the time that Ellory Schempp was preparing to challenge the constitutional validity of Bible reading in his Pennsylvania school, another prayer case was taking shape in the state of New York. The litigants in the New York and Pennsylvania cases did not know one another and were not aware they had embarked on parallel courses of action. Eventually, however, both cases reached the U.S. Supreme Court. The Supreme Court's decision in the New York case—*Engel* v. *Vitale*—was handed down in 1962. The *Schempp* litigation—*School District of Abington Township* v. *Schempp*—was resolved by the Supreme Court in 1963. Together, these decisions became known as the "school prayer cases."

Engel v. *Vitale*: The First School Prayer Case

The New York litigation arose in response to what was known as the Regents' Prayer. In 1958, in accordance with a recommendation of the state Board of Regents, the school board of Nassau County instructed its staff to begin each day by leading students in the recitation of a prayer composed by the regents themselves. The prayer was deliberately brief, broad, and vague. Students were called upon to say "Almighty God, we acknowledge our dependence upon thee, and we beg thy blessings upon us, our parents, our teachers and our country." Presumably, the regents hoped that no one would object to such a bland prayer. They were wrong. Several families combined together to challenge the prayer in court.

The *Engel* litigation began in the state courts of New York. The plaintiffs commenced their lawsuit in the Supreme Court of Nassau County—the trial court of the state court system in New York—but their claim that the Regents' Prayer violated the Establishment Clause was rejected.[9] The decision of the Supreme Court was affirmed by two appellate courts—the Appellate

Division of the Supreme Court[10] and the Court of Appeals of New York (the highest court in the New York system)[11]—and the plaintiffs appealed to the U.S. Supreme Court.

The Supreme Court reversed.[12] In an opinion by Justice Black, an 8-to-1 majority of the Court held that "by using its public school system to encourage recitation of the Regents' prayer, the State of New York has adopted a practice wholly inconsistent with the Establishment Clause."[13] One reason the plaintiffs had objected to the Regents' Prayer was that it was "composed by governmental officials." The Supreme Court agreed that this was a critical point, saying that the Establishment Clause "must at least mean that in this country it is no part of the business of government to compose official prayers for any group of the American people to recite as part of a religious program carried on by government."[14]

The Court also rejected the state's claim that the Regents' Prayer did not violate the Establishment Clause because students were not required to recite the prayer but could, if they wished, "remain silent or be excused from the room." The fact that the prayer was voluntary, the Court said, did not serve "to free it from the limitations of the Establishment Clause."[15]

The *Engel* case presented a somewhat specialized example of school prayer—a prayer actually composed by governmental officials. Perhaps for this reason the Court moved expeditiously to take a further case involving the more common situation of school districts that required or encouraged students to recite verses from the Bible or to recite a traditional prayer such as the Lord's Prayer. The case the Court agreed to decide was the one begun by Ellory Schempp.

The *Schempp* Case in the Lower Courts

Ellory Schempp filed his lawsuit in a three-judge U.S. District Court in 1959. His basic contention was that the Pennsylvania statute—which prescribed that each school day should begin with the reading of "[a]t least ten verses from the Holy Bible"—was an unconstitutional violation of the First Amendment requirement that "Congress shall make no law respecting an establishment of religion."

The decision of the three-judge court, issued in September 1959, was unanimous and emphatic.[16] The Court decided, as a preliminary matter, that the practice required by the Pennsylvania statute was not, as the state contended, simply an additional educational experience. Instead, the Court viewed it as an activity that was "devotional in nature, intended to inculcate religious principles and religious beliefs."[17] The Court conceded that under the statute no sanction was "directly imposed" on a recalcitrant student, but the Court expressed its belief that "[t]he argument made by [the school district] that there was no compulsion ignores reality and the forces of social suasion."[18] The Court concluded that "a state supported practice of daily reading from [the Bible] in the public schools is, we believe, within the proscription of the First Amendment."[19]

In November 1959 Pennsylvania amended its statute to provide that any child could be excused from Bible reading "upon the written request of his parent or guardian." In 1962 the district court decided that the amended statute, like the original statute, was an unconstitutional violation of the Establishment Clause of the First Amendment.[20]

Following its second defeat in three-judge court, Abington Township prepared its appeal to the U.S. Supreme Court. The *Schempp* decision had been handed down by a three-judge district court and had been accompanied by an injunction against further enforcement of the school prayer statute. Under federal law, therefore, the case was classified as an appeal case falling within the mandatory appellate jurisdiction of the Supreme Court. On October 8, 1962, the Supreme Court, following its usual practice in appeal cases, noted probable jurisdiction.

The *Schempp* Case in the Supreme Court

On June 17, 1963, one year after *Engel* v. *Vitale*, the Supreme Court handed down its decision in *School District of Abington Township* v. *Schempp*.[21] The Court's decision in *Schempp* was authored by Justice Clark and built upon the foundation established in previous cases.[22]

Justice Clark conceded that the First Amendment does not proscribe study of the Bible or of religion "when presented objectively as part of a secular program of education." "But," he said, "the exercises here do not fall into those categories. They are religious exercises, required by the States in violation of the command of the First Amendment that the Government maintain strict neutrality, neither aiding nor opposing religion."[23] "[T]he practices at issue and the laws requiring them," Justice Clark concluded, "are unconstitutional under the Establishment Clause."[24]

With its decisions in *Engel* and *Schempp*, the Supreme Court had spoken on the subject of prayer in schools. However, the Court's decisions did not put the matter to rest. In fact, the issue of prayer in schools has continued to preoccupy both Congress and the courts.

The Legislative Response to *Engel* and *Schempp*

Congress reacted to the Court's decisions in *Engel* and *Schempp* by considering amendments to the Constitution which would legalize school prayer. Constitutional amendments authorizing school prayer obtained a simple majority in both houses of Congress in 1966 and 1971. However, since the Constitution requires a two-thirds vote in both houses before an amendment can be sent on to the states for ratification, the proposals died in Congress.[25]

Efforts to reverse the school prayer decisions by amending the Constitution were renewed in 1982. President Reagan proposed an amendment providing that "[n]othing in this Constitution shall be construed to prohibit individual or group prayer in public schools or other public institutions. No person shall be required by the United States or any state to participate in prayer." The amendment was approved by the Senate in 1984 by a vote of 56 to 44, and thus it fell eleven votes short of the required two-thirds majority.[26]

From a mathematical point of view, an easier method of reversing a Supreme Court decision is to deprive the Court—or the Supreme Court *and* the lower federal courts—of jurisdiction over particular kinds of cases. Beginning in 1979, Senator Jesse Helms of North Carolina introduced legislation in the Senate which would have deprived both the Supreme Court and the lower federal courts of jurisdiction to decide cases involving voluntary prayer. The legislation required only a majority vote for enactment. It was passed by the Senate, but not by the House, and subsequent attempts to pass Court-curbing legislation also failed.[27]

The Supreme Court and the Future of School Prayer

The issue of school prayer returned to the Court itself in the case of *Wallace* v. *Jaffree* (1985).[28] The Court heard a challenge to an Alabama law which authorized in all public schools a one-minute "period of silence . . . for meditation or voluntary prayer."[29] Relying on legislative history that indicated that the sponsor of the bill intended it "to return voluntary prayer" to the public schools, the Supreme Court held that the law was unconstitutional under the Establishment Clause. In his opinion for the Court, Justice Stevens concluded that the Alabama State Legislature enacted the law "for the sole purpose of expressing the State's endorsement of prayer activities. . . . Such an endorsement is not consistent with the established principle that the Government must pursue a course of complete neutrality toward religion."[30]

Despite the Court's ruling in *Jaffree*, it is clear that the Court, like the country, remains divided on the issue of school prayer. The *Jaffree* case itself included a lengthy opinion by Justice O'Connor. She concurred in the judgment of the Court—that is, the result in the case—but she noted that moment of silence laws are in effect in twenty-five states and she expressed her view that some of those laws, unlike the Alabama statute, might be valid.[31] In his dissenting opinion, Justice Rehnquist—then an associate justice but soon to be chief justice—was openly critical of the Court's approach to Establishment Clause issues. He reviewed the history of the Establishment Clause and questioned the wisdom of continuing to base constitutional doctrine on Thomas Jefferson's reference to the need for "a wall of separation between church and state."[32]

Although the current Court is deeply divided on issues arising under the Establishment Clause, it has so far resisted pressure to overrule the *Schempp* decision itself. In its most recent encounter with the issue of prayer in schools, the Court was asked to examine the constitutional validity of the practice of the Providence, Rhode Island, school system of inviting members of the clergy to offer prayers at graduation ceremonies. Writing for a 5–4 majority of the

Court, Justice Kennedy held that the challenged practice violated the Establishment Clause.[33] "The lessons of the First Amendment are as urgent in the modern world," Kennedy wrote, "as in the 18th century when it was written. One timeless lesson is that if citizens are subjected to state-sponsored religious exercises, the State disavows its own duty to guard and respect that sphere of inviolable conscience and belief which is the mark of a free people."[34]

Despite Justice Kennedy's reaffirmation of the Court's traditional position on school prayer, clearly the Court as an institution is moving towards a more moderate position on a variety of Establishment Clause issues and is ready to uphold practices that at one time it would almost certainly have condemned as unconstitutional. It is widely anticipated that one manifestation of the changing composition of the Supreme Court in the 1990s will be significant alterations in the Court's reaction to alleged violations by government of the constitutional requirement of separation of church and state.

The Supreme Court of the early 1960s, however, was a very different institution from the Supreme Court of the early 1990s. In the early 1960s the Supreme Court under the leadership of Earl Warren was anxious to expand the scope of individual rights in a variety of ways. One issue that the Court had an opportunity to resolve was the status of indigent defendants in criminal cases. By definition, such defendants could not afford to retain a lawyer. Under the Constitution, however, criminal defendants are entitled to "Assistance of Counsel." In the 1930s and 1940s the Supreme Court had decided several cases involving the right to counsel for indigent defendants. In 1963 it would decide another.

Notes

1. Leonard W. Levy, *The Establishment Clause: Religion and the First Amendment* (1986), p. 1. See also Lynda Beck Fenwick, *Should the Children Pray? A Historical, Judicial, and Political Examination of Public School Prayer* (1989).
2. C. Herman Pritchett, *Constitutional Civil Liberties* (1984), p. 131.
3. *Everson v. Board of Education of Ewing Township*, 330 U.S. 1 (1947).
4. Id. at 16.
5. For an examination of a cross-section of Establishment Clause cases in state and federal courts in the period 1951 to 1971, see Frank J. Sorauf, *The Wall of Separation: The Constitutional Politics of Church and State* (1976).
6. Kenneth M. Dolbeare and Phillip E. Hammond, *The School Prayer Decisions: From Court Policy to Local Practice* (1971), pp. 29–30.
7. Id. at 29 (emphasis added).
8. Quoted in *Schempp v. School District of Abington Township*, 177 F.Supp. 398, 399 n. 3 (E.D.Pa. 1959).
9. *Engel v. Vitale*, 191 N.Y.S.2d 453 (1959).
10. *Engel v. Vitale*, 206 N.Y.S.2d 183 (1960).
11. *Engel v. Vitale*, 10 N.Y.2d 174, 176 N.E.2d 579 (1961).
12. *Engel v. Vitale*, 370 U.S. 421 (1962).

13. Id. at 424.

14. Id. at 425.

15. Id. at 430.

16. *Schempp* v. *School District of Abington Township*, 177 F.Supp. 398 (E.D.Pa. 1959).

17. Id. at 406.

18. Id.

19. Id.

20. *Schempp* v. *School District of Abington Township*, 201 F.Supp. 815 (E.D.Pa. 1962).

21. 374 U.S. 203 (1963).

22. The Court's decision in *Schempp* also resolved a companion case — *Murray* v. *Curlett* — from Baltimore. Madalyn Murray O'Hair, the celebrated atheist, and her schoolage son, William Murray, launched a state court challenge to a policy of the Board of School Commissioners of Baltimore, dating from 1905, which prescribed that "[e]ach school . . . shall be opened by the reading . . . of a chapter in the Holy Bible and/or the use of the Lord's Prayer." The Supreme Court consolidated the appeals in *Schempp* and *Murray* and decided them with a single opinion. The facts of the *Murray* case are reviewed in the *Schempp* opinion, 374 U.S. 203, 211–12 (1963).

23. 374 U.S. at 225.

24. Id. at 205.

25. See Fenwick, *Should the Children Pray?*, Chs. 19 and 20. See also Edward Keynes, *The Court vs. Congress: Prayer, Busing, and Abortion* (1989), Ch. 7.

26. For further discussion of use of the amendment process to reverse Supreme Court decisions, see Chapter 12.

27. For further discussion of Congress's use of legislation to curb the Supreme Court, see Chapter 12.

28. 472 U.S. 38 (1985).

29. The background of the *Jaffree* case is discussed in Peter Irons, *The Courage of Their Convictions: Sixteen Americans Who Fought Their Way to the Supreme Court* (1988), pp. 337–67.

30. 472 U.S. at 60.

31. Id. at 70–79 (O'Connor, J., concurring).

32. Id. at 91–114 (Rehnquist, J., dissenting).

33. *Lee* v. *Weisman*, 112 S.Ct. 2649 (1992).

34. Id. at 2658. For a case study of the Supreme Court's decision in *Lynch* v. *Donnelly* (1984), holding that a city-sponsored Nativity scene did *not* violate the Establishment Clause, see Wayne R. Swanson, *The Christ Child Goes to Court* (1990).

The Incorporation Debate and the Right to Counsel: *Gideon* v. *Wainwright* (1963)

When the Fourteenth Amendment was added to the Constitution in 1868, it included, among other provisions, a Due Process Clause. The constitutional prohibition embodied in the Clause was that "No state shall . . . deprive any person of life, liberty, or property, without due process of law." The Due Process Clause of the Fourteenth Amendment was patterned directly on the Due Process Clause of the Fifth Amendment, which had been added to the Constitution in 1791. The Due Process Clause of the Fifth Amendment stipulated that "No person shall . . . be deprived of life, liberty, or property, without due process of law."

Obviously, the two clauses have a great deal in common. The only difference, in fact, is that the original clause was written from the perspective of the individual, whereas the more recent one is directed explicitly at the states. A straightforward reading of the original clause is that *no government* may deprive any person of life, liberty, or property, without due process of law. The most direct reading of the more recent clause is that *state governments*, in particular, may not deprive any person of life, liberty, or property, without due process of law.

At first glance, this state of affairs seems curious. If government in general was required to observe due process of law by the terms of the original Due Process Clause, why should a second Due Process Clause—one specifically directed at the states—be necessary?

The Bill of Rights and the Incorporation Debate

The explanation lies in the history of the Bill of Rights. The principal motivation behind the addition of the Bill of Rights to the Constitution was to establish a set of restrictions on the power of the federal government. In the founding period, many citizens believed that the new federal government represented a serious threat to their liberties. They were less afraid that state governments threatened their liberties. Moreover, state governments, in most cases, were already restricted by provisions of state constitutions. Thus, the primary purpose of adding the Bill of Rights to the Constitution was to protect citizens from the federal government, and not to identify rights that citizens could assert against government in general.

This understanding of the purpose of the Bill of Rights was confirmed by the Supreme Court in *Barron* v. *Baltimore* in 1833. The Court held that the Just Compensation Clause of the Fifth Amendment — which prohibits government from taking private property for public use, "without just compensation" — was not a restriction on the states but only a restriction on the federal government.

In the years after the *Barron* decision, judges accepted the view that none of the provisions of the Bill of Rights operated as a restriction on the power of the states. Citizens who believed that they had been deprived of their rights could look to their state constitution for protection. But if these citizens lived in a state whose constitution did not (for instance) protect freedom of speech, and if they believed that one of the laws of their state deprived them of their "freedom of speech," they could not claim that their federal constitutional rights had been violated, because they did not possess a *federal* constitutional right to freedom of speech.[1]

The Fourteenth Amendment and the Incorporation Debate

In 1868, however, the Fourteenth Amendment was added to the Constitution. It contained a Due Process Clause that explicitly restricted the states. Its effect, therefore, was to impose on the states at least one of the restrictions embodied in the original Bill of Rights. Henceforth, both the states and the federal government would be prohibited by the Constitution from depriving any person of "life, liberty, or property, without due process of law."

Almost immediately an important question arose: What was the relationship between the Due Process Clause of the Fourteenth Amendment and the various specific provisions of the Bill of Rights? The Due Process Clause, by itself, was extremely vague. It merely enjoined state governments to observe "due process of law." Did the Due Process Clause embody the specific protections of the Bill of Rights — in which case they would become operative against the states as well as the federal government — or did the Due Process Clause simply enunciate a general, autonomous criterion for judging the constitutional validity of state procedures in criminal cases?

The question was extremely important because the Bill of Rights, as a whole, contains a wide variety of specific protections for criminal defendants. Provisions of the Bill of Rights protect a criminal defendant from "unreasonable searches and seizures" (Fourth Amendment), from being "compelled in any criminal case to be a witness against himself" (Fifth Amendment), from having to defend himself in a criminal trial without the "Assistance of Counsel" (Sixth Amendment), and from being subjected to "cruel and unusual punishments" (Eighth Amendment). If the Fourteenth Amendment "embodied" these specific protections, they were now available not only to criminal defendants in federal cases, but also to criminal defendants in state cases.

For several decades following ratification of the Fourteenth Amendment, the Supreme Court took the position that nothing had changed. The specific protections of the Bill of Rights, the Court said, were not available to criminal defendants in state cases, but only to criminal defendants in federal cases. In state cases, therefore, the only *federal* constitutional question that a defendant could raise—no matter how specific his or her complaint might be, and no matter how clearly it might be covered by one of the existing provisions of the Bill of Rights—was whether he or she had been deprived of the general entitlement under the Fourteenth Amendment to "due process of law."

The Supreme Court and Defendants' Rights in State Cases

Even though the Supreme Court declined to apply the Bill of Rights to the states, it did gradually expand the rights of criminal defendants in state cases. By the 1920s and 1930s the Court had begun to focus with some frequency, in specific cases, on the general question of whether criminal defendants in state cases had been deprived of their Fourteenth Amendment entitlement to due process of law.

In two particularly notorious cases in the 1930s, the Court had occasion to review the process of criminal justice in the southern states. Both cases involved black defendants and white victims. In 1932, in *Powell* v. *Alabama* —known as the Scottsboro case, because it arose in Scottsboro, Alabama— the Supreme Court reviewed the convictions of seven black youths accused of raping two white girls.[2] No specific lawyer was ever appointed to assist the defendants. Nevertheless, they were convicted and sentenced to death within a few days of their arrest. On appeal, the Supreme Court held that in view of the circumstances—which included the fact that the defendants were young, poor, and illiterate—"the failure of the trial court to make an effective appointment of counsel was . . . a denial of due process within the meaning of the Fourteenth Amendment."[3]

A few years later, in *Brown* v. *Mississippi* (1936), the Supreme Court reviewed the convictions of three black defendants accused of murdering a white man in Mississippi.[4] The convictions rested solely on the confessions of the defendants, but those confessions had been obtained only after one of the defendants had been tied to a tree and whipped and the other two defendants had been taken to the jail where, in the words of the Supreme Court, "their backs were cut to pieces with a leather strap with buckles on it."[5] The Court concluded that "[i]t would be difficult to conceive of methods more revolting to the sense of justice than those taken to procure the confessions of these petitioners, and the use of the confessions thus obtained as the basis for conviction and sentence was a clear denial of due process."[6]

The *Powell* and *Brown* cases represented some of the first attempts by the Supreme Court to define the content of the federal requirement of due process of law in state criminal cases. In the 1940s the Supreme Court began to hear more and more such cases. Moreover, the way in which at least some members of the Court chose to approach these cases began to change.

The Incorporation Debate in the Supreme Court

The change came about because some members of the Court were frustrated with the inherent vagueness of the concept of due process of law. In addition, they were anxious to expand the role of the Supreme Court (and other federal courts) in defining the rights of criminal defendants in state cases. These motivations led them to argue that the Due Process Clause of the Fourteenth Amendment *did* embody the specific protections of the Bill of Rights. The direct consequence of this interpretation of the meaning of the Due Process Clause would be to convert the specific protections of the Bill of Rights into protections available to state as well as federal defendants.

As formulated by Justice Black, the new approach suggested that the true purpose of the Due Process Clause of the Fourteenth Amendment had been to "incorporate" the full range of specific protections to which criminal defendants were entitled under the Bill of Rights. If Black's theory of *total incorporation* were accepted, it would mean that criminal defendants in state cases would enjoy the same protections, under the federal Constitution, as did criminal defendants in federal cases.[7]

In the end, Justice Black did not succeed in convincing a majority of the Supreme Court that the Due Process Clause of the Fourteenth Amendment should incorporate the entire Bill of Rights. However, his insistence that the Bill of Rights should bind the states as well as the federal government eventually prompted the Court to embark on a process of so-called *selective incorporation*. This process meant that the Court was willing to examine the possibility, in a particular case, that a particular provision of the Bill of Rights should be transformed from a restriction on the federal government into a restriction on government in general. One by one, specific provisions of the Bill of Rights came before the Court, and one by one, they were incorporated. The process gathered momentum in the early 1960s, and by 1969 all the important provisions of the Bill of Rights had been incorporated. Criminal defendants in state cases now enjoy essentially the same rights, under the federal Constitution, as do criminal defendants in federal cases.[8]

Clarence Earl Gideon and the Right to Counsel

The Supreme Court's 1963 decision in *Gideon* v. *Wainwright* was an example of a decision based on the concept of selective incorporation. The case began as an ordinary criminal case, indistinguishable from thousands of other cases arising at the local level. For reasons having more to do with its own priorities than with the case itself, however, the Court chose to use the *Gideon* case to hold that the Sixth Amendment guarantee of "Assistance of Counsel" applies to the states as well as the federal government.

Clarence Earl Gideon was a fifty-one-year-old white man who had been convicted on four occasions between 1928 and 1951 of burglary and other nonviolent property crimes. On June 3, 1961, it was alleged, he had broken into the Bay Harbor Poolroom in Panama City, Florida, and had stolen money from the cigarette machine and the juke box. He was arrested and charged under Florida law with the felony offense of "breaking and entering with intent to commit petit larceny." On August 4, 1961, he went to trial before Judge Robert McCrary and a jury of six men in the Circuit Court of Bay County, Florida.[9]

As the trial was about to begin, Gideon indicated to Judge McCrary that he was not ready, and he gave as his reason the fact that he had no lawyer. He requested that the court appoint counsel for him. Judge McCrary replied, however, that under Florida law, "the only time the court can appoint counsel to represent a Defendant is when that person is charged with a capital offense." Since Gideon was charged with a felony, but not a capital offense, Judge McCrary denied his request for counsel.[10]

Following Judge McCrary's ruling, Gideon elected to serve as his own lawyer, and the trial proceeded. When the trial was over, the jury returned a verdict of guilty. Three weeks later, after examining the report of Gideon's prior record, Judge McCrary sentenced Gideon to five years in prison, the maximum penalty under the law.[11]

Clarence Gideon Prepares His Appeal

Gideon was sent to the State Prison at Raiford, Florida, to begin serving his sentence. He still believed, however, that he had been unfairly treated. In particular, he believed that he had been improperly denied his right to assistance of counsel. He was determined to take the question to a higher court. From his prison cell at Raiford, he began a campaign that would eventually take him — or at least the case of which he was a part — all the way to the Supreme Court.

In most states, at this point a person in Gideon's position would have appealed his conviction to the next highest state appellate court. In Florida, however, a prisoner could raise the issue of a constitutional defect in his trial by petitioning the state supreme court for a writ of habeas corpus. A petition for a writ of habeas corpus, as we have seen, is a request to a court to order the police or prison authorities — or whoever may be holding an individual — to "produce the body." In Gideon's case, the purpose of seeking a writ of habeas corpus was to reverse his allegedly unconstitutional conviction and thereby free himself from prison.

In his petition to the Supreme Court of Florida, Gideon reiterated his belief that under the U.S. Constitution he was entitled to be represented by state-appointed counsel. On October 30, 1961, the Supreme Court of Florida denied his request. It did so summarily, that is, without a written opinion. The order of the Court said only that "upon consideration [of the petition], it is ordered that said petition be and the same is hereby denied."[12]

As soon as his petition for a writ of habeas corpus was denied, Gideon began work on his petition for a writ of certiorari to the U.S. Supreme Court. Under ordinary circumstances, there would have been little chance that Gideon's petition would be granted. Gideon's petition was handwritten, not very articulate, and one of hundreds of petitions from convicted offenders, all of whom, like Gideon, were convinced that they were innocent, or at least that their constitutional rights had been violated. As it happened, however, Gideon was riding the tide of history. His handwritten petition propelled the case of *Gideon* v. *Wainwright* into the annals of American constitutional law.

Gideon Petitions the Supreme Court

Gideon prepared his petition to the Supreme Court from his prison cell at Raiford, Florida. The petition consisted of two parts: (1) a request to proceed *in forma pauperis*, that is, under separate rules governing petitions filed by indigent persons; and (2) the actual petition for a writ of certiorari. Both documents were handwritten in pencil. They arrived at the Supreme Court on January 8, 1962.

In his petition for a writ of certiorari, Gideon mentioned that he had asked for a lawyer at his trial but had been turned down by the judge. Gideon was convinced that the right to counsel was already a requirement under the U.S. Constitution and that Florida, by denying him counsel, was clearly violating his constitutional rights. He therefore asked the Supreme Court to reverse his conviction and order his release from prison.

Betts v. *Brady* and the "Special Circumstances" Rule

Gideon's belief that the Supreme Court had already ruled that indigent defendants were automatically entitled to state-appointed counsel was erroneous. In fact, in *Betts* v. *Brady*, decided in 1942, the Court had held that criminal defendants in state cases were *not* entitled to court-appointed legal counsel under the Sixth Amendment. Subsequent cases had evolved the principle that appointment of counsel was required by the Due Process Clause of the Fourteenth Amendment, but only in cases involving "special circumstances." Such circumstances could include, for instance, the fact that the defendant was illiterate or that the case against the defendant involved complex legal issues. In the absence of special circumstances, however, states were at liberty to refuse to appoint counsel for indigent defendants.

Gideon was therefore wrong that the Supreme Court had already ruled in his favor. What Gideon did not realize, however, was that the Supreme Court was poised to reconsider *Betts* v. *Brady* and the special circumstances rule.

The Supreme Court Takes Up Gideon's Petition

Gideon's submission to the Supreme Court was added to the Miscellaneous Docket, the docket to which petitions filed *in forma pauperis* are automatically assigned.[13] On June 1, 1962, the submission was among several items scheduled for discussion at the Court's regular Friday conference. The content of the discussion is not known. What is known is that at least four members of the Court—the minimum number necessary to grant a writ of certiorari—voted to hear Gideon's case. On Monday, June 4, the Court announced that "[t]he motion for leave to proceed *in forma pauperis* and the petition for writ of certiorari are granted."[14]

The Court also signaled to the world that it was contemplating the possibility of overruling *Betts* v. *Brady*. The final sentence of the brief order granting certiorari in Gideon's case stated that "In addition to other questions presented by this case, counsel are requested to discuss the following in their briefs and oral argument: "Should this Court's holding in Betts v. Brady be reconsidered?"[15]

The Court's final action in response to Gideon's submission was to arrange for someone to represent Gideon in his appeal to the Court. On June 22, 1962, the justices discussed this question, again at their Friday conference, and decided to ask Abe Fortas, then a prominent Washington lawyer, to represent Gideon. Fortas agreed, and the stage was set for the case of *Gideon* v. *Wainwright* to be argued before the U.S. Supreme Court.

The *Gideon* Decision and the Right to Counsel

By the time the case of Clarence Earl Gideon reached the Supreme Court in 1962, it had taken on two very important dimensions, neither of which had been present when Gideon was originally tried and convicted of breaking and entering in 1961. First, Gideon was now being represented by one of the most powerful lawyers in Washington and a future justice of the U.S. Supreme Court. In view of Gideon's basic claim—that under the Sixth Amendment indigent defendants in criminal cases were entitled to free legal counsel—this was, to say the least, a promising development. Second, the Supreme Court had sent a signal to the legal community that the *Betts* decision was in trouble. Evidently, the Court was actively looking for an opportunity to overrule the *Betts* decision and terminate the special circumstances rule.

Oral argument in *Gideon* v. *Wainwright* was held on January 15, 1963. In his presentation of Gideon's case, Abe Fortas argued that "you cannot have a fair trial without counsel." He noted also that in 1963 thirty-seven states already provided counsel for indigent defendants in all felony cases, while only five states restricted provision of counsel to capital cases or to cases that, for some other reason, involved special circumstances. Finally, he argued that *Betts* v. *Brady* should be overruled.[16]

The state of Florida was represented in the Supreme Court by a young and relatively inexperienced lawyer named Bruce Jacob. Jacob was clearly fighting both the tide of history and the inclinations of most, if not all, members of the Supreme Court. Nevertheless, he gamely contended that Florida and other states should retain discretion to decide whether to require appointment of counsel for indigent defendants. "By imposing an inflexible rule," he argued, "we feel this Court would be intruding into an area historically reserved to the states."[17]

The Supreme Court did not agree. On March 18, 1963, the Court announced its unanimous decision that Clarence Earl Gideon had been deprived of his constitutional rights when he was tried and convicted without the benefit of state-appointed counsel.[18]

The opinion of the Court was authored by Justice Black. Black, of course, was a proponent of the doctrine of total incorporation. He was also

The Supreme Court in 1963. The Court that decided *School District of Abington Township* v. *Schempp* and *Gideon* v. *Wainwright* included justices appointed by four presidents — Franklin Roosevelt, Harry Truman, Dwight Eisenhower, and John Kennedy. The two newest members of the Court were Kennedy appointees Byron White and Arthur Goldberg. *Standing (left to right):* Byron R. White, William J. Brennan, Jr., Potter Stewart, and Arthur Goldberg. *Seated (left to right):* Tom C. Clark, Hugo L. Black, Earl Warren, William O. Douglas, and John M. Harlan.

SOURCE: Collection of the Supreme Court of the United States

one of three justices who had dissented, twenty-one years earlier, from the Court's contrary decision in *Betts* v. *Brady.*

Black's Opinion in the *Gideon* Case

Justice Black began his opinion with a recitation of the facts in Gideon's case, but he quickly turned to the question of *Betts* v. *Brady.* The premise of the *Betts* decision, Black said, was that only those rights that are "fundamental" and "essential to a fair trial" are made applicable to the states by the Due Process Clause of the Fourteenth Amendment. The *Betts* majority had conceded that under the Sixth Amendment an indigent defendant in a federal case was automatically entitled to appointed counsel. But the *Betts* majority also believed that the right to appointed counsel, though important, was not "fundamental," and therefore was not among those rights which should be extended to the states under the Fourteenth Amendment."[19]

Once Black had framed the issue in this way, the path to his new conclusion was clear. "We accept Betts v. Brady's assumption," he said, ". . . that a provision of the Bill of Rights which is 'fundamental and essential to a fair trial' is made obligatory upon the States by the Fourteenth Amendment. We think the Court in *Betts* was wrong, however, in concluding that the Sixth Amendment's guarantee of counsel is not one of these fundamental rights."[20] Black then developed the argument that the right to counsel *is* fundamental—that "in our adversary system [an indigent defendant] cannot be assured a fair trial unless counsel is provided for him."[21] He concluded that the contrary holding of *Betts* v. *Brady* "should now be overruled."[22]

The Warren Court and Defendants' Rights

Gideon v. *Wainwright* was one of many Warren Court decisions protecting the rights of criminal defendants.[23] As we saw in Chapter 3, criminal defendants were the petitioning party in about 90 percent of plenary cases involving issues of criminal procedure in the period between 1953 and 1969. Moreover, in most of those cases, the Court eventually ruled in favor of defendants. Among the most celebrated and controversial decisions of the 1960s were *Mapp* v. *Ohio* (1961), which applied the exclusionary rule to the states, and *Miranda* v. *Arizona* (1966), which required the police to read criminal defendants their rights.[24]

A key issue in many of the Warren Court's criminal procedure decisions, including *Mapp* v. *Ohio* and *Gideon* v. *Wainwright*, was whether or not to "incorporate" a particular provision of the Bill of Rights. By 1969 the Court had held that all the important procedural guarantees of the Bill of Rights did apply to the states and in the process had substantially expanded the constitutional rights of criminal defendants.

As part of the immediate aftermath of the *Gideon* decision, two significant events occurred. First, Florida released almost one thousand prisoners—persons who had been tried originally without counsel—and the state made preparations to retry several hundred additional prisoners—this time with lawyers.[25] Second, one of those who was retried was Clarence Earl Gideon. In his second trial, the jury found him "not guilty."[26]

The long-term impact of the *Gideon* decision was also significant. The Court in *Gideon* had not defined the precise boundaries of the right to counsel for indigent defendants. In 1972, however, the Court held in *Argersinger* v. *Hamlin* that such defendants are entitled to appointed counsel whenever the actual outcome of their trial is imprisonment—regardless of whether the offense itself is defined as a felony or a misdemeanor. The net result is that in all jurisdictions and for virtually all offenses, public defenders are now available to indigent defendants.

In 1969, of course, the era of the Warren Court came to an end. Warren himself resigned and was replaced by Chief Justice Burger, and shortly thereafter Fortas, Black, and Harlan also left the Court. The more conservative orientation of the Court was evident almost immediately in decisions involving defendants' rights. On other issues, however, the Burger Court produced some surprises. One of those surprises was its decision on the issue of abortion.

Notes

1. The original understanding of the Bill of Rights is particularly evident in the text of the First Amendment, which stipulates that "*Congress* shall make no law. . . ."

2. See Dan T. Carter, *Scottsboro: A Tragedy of the American South* (1979).

3. *Powell* v. *Alabama*, 287 U.S. 45, 71 (1932).

4. See Richard C. Cortner, *A "Scottsboro" Case in Mississippi: The Supreme Court and Brown v. Mississippi* (1986).

5. *Brown* v. *Mississippi*, 297 U.S. 278, 282 (1936).

6. Id. at 286.

7. Perhaps the fullest exposition of Justice Black's position appears in his dissenting opinion in *Adamson* v. *California* (1947).

8. For discussions of the Supreme Court's incorporation decisions, see Raoul Berger, *The Fourteenth Amendment and the Bill of Rights* (1989); and Richard C. Cortner, *The Supreme Court and the Second Bill of Rights: The Fourteenth Amendment and the Nationalization of Civil Liberties* (1981).

9. The classic exposition of Gideon's fight to present his case to the Supreme Court is Anthony Lewis, *Gideon's Trumpet* (1964).

10. Id. at 10.

11. Id. at 57–62.

12. Id. at 33.

13. As we discussed in Chapter 3, "paid cases" are placed on the Supreme Court's Appellate Docket, while petitions filed *in forma pauperis* are placed on the Miscellaneous Docket.

14. *Gideon* v. *Cochran*, 370 U.S. 908 (1962).

15. Id.

16. Lewis, *Gideon's Trumpet*, pp. 169–75.

17. Id. at 176–78.

18. *Gideon v. Wainwright*, 372 U.S. 335 (1963).

19. Id. at 339–40.

20. Id. at 342.

21. Id. at 344.

22. Id. at 345.

23. Justice Black was among the majority in most of these decisions, as well as other decisions on which the Warren Court's reputation for judicial activism is based. Toward the end of his career, however, Black developed reservations about some of the directions in which the Warren Court was taking the law, particularly in cases involving public demonstrations and freedom of assembly. For a biography of Justice Black, see Gerald T. Dunne, *Hugo Black and the Judicial Revolution* (1977). For Justice Black's own account of his service on the Supreme Court, see *A Constitutional Faith* (1968).

24. See Fred P. Graham, *The Due Process Revolution: The Warren Court's Impact on Criminal Law* (1970).

25. Lewis, *Gideon's Trumpet*, p. 205.

26. Id. at 237.

CHAPTER 10

The Abortion Issue in American Politics: *Roe* v. *Wade* (1973)

The Supreme Court decided *Roe* v. *Wade* in 1973. The Court's decision placed the abortion issue squarely at the forefront of American political controversy, and it has remained there ever since.[1]

Abortion is particularly controversial in part because it offers so little room for compromise. Either a woman is granted the right to choose to terminate her pregnancy—in which case she is authorized to make a choice that some regard as tantamount to murder—or she is prohibited by law from making that choice—in which case, in the view of others, she has been deprived of the right to control her own body and has been forced either to bear an unwanted child or to seek an illegal and perhaps unsafe abortion. On most political issues, it is possible for "objective" observers, and, eventually, for those who find themselves on opposing sides of the issue, to perceive an acceptable compromise. On the issue of abortion, it is not clear what such a compromise would be.

Historical Developments in Abortion Policy

In reaching its decision in *Roe* v. *Wade*, the Supreme Court was prompted to reexamine the entire history of abortion. It discovered considerable variation in the way different societies approach the subject of abortion. It also discovered that, even in the United States, the law governing abortion had not always been as strict as it was in 1973. The Court learned that in English common law, abortion was not necessarily a crime. The common law was the accumulated body of legal precedents enunciated by judges in specific cases. These precedents focused on the point in pregnancy that was known as quickening—the time, usually in the sixteenth to eighteenth week, when the fetus begins to exhibit some movement. According to common law, abortion was not a crime unless it was performed *after* quickening.[2]

In the United States, the states retained these common law principles in the first decades after Independence. In 1821, however, Connecticut enacted the first statutory proscription of abortion, making abortion a crime before quickening as well as after. In addition, the law did not contain any exceptions; that is, it did not permit abortion even in cases when a continuation of pregnancy might endanger the mother's life. The Connecticut law thus represented an unqualified prohibition of abortion.

In the next few years, additional states outlawed abortion. Most states followed the example of New York, which enacted a statute in 1830. The New York law outlawed abortion but did contain a single therapeutic exception. Abortion was legal in New York, as well as in the states that followed New York's example, if it was necessary to save the life of the mother.

By 1880, abortion was a crime in every state, and the statutory policies established by 1880 prevailed until the end of the 1950s. Abortion was regarded in most states as a serious criminal offense. Moreover, it was punishable regardless of the stage in pregnancy during which it was performed. Finally, the only abortions that were classified as therapeutic, and were therefore legal, were those that were necessary to save the life of the mother.

Pressures for Liberalization

Political pressure to liberalize the laws against abortion began to build in the early 1960s. The women's movement was gathering strength, and among its priorities was an end to restrictive abortion laws. In addition, one particular incident in 1962 brought nationwide attention to the problem. Sherri Finkbine was a television personality in Phoenix, Arizona, and was married and the mother of four children. When she became pregnant with her fifth child, she learned that a drug she had obtained in Europe to help her sleep — Thalidomide — was suspected of causing serious birth defects, and in particular, the birth of children without arms or legs. Mrs. Finkbine was unable to secure a legal abortion in Arizona, because Arizona law, like that of most states, permitted abortion only to save the life of the mother. Mrs. Finkbine eventually traveled to Sweden and obtained an abortion there.

The Finkbine case and other events prompted several states to reconsider their anti-abortion statutes. By the early 1970s, four states (Alaska, Hawaii, Washington, and New York) had repealed their laws against abortion. Moreover, fourteen states had enacted abortion statutes patterned after the model penal code of the American Law Institute (ALI), an organization that drafts law reform proposals for possible adoption by the states. The ALI statute on abortion expanded the range of circumstances under which abortion would be legal. Whereas most state laws permitted abortion only to save the life of the mother, the ALI statute defined a "justifiable abortion" as one that was performed because "[1] continuation of the pregnancy would gravely impair the physical or mental health of the mother or . . . [2] the child would be born with grave physical or mental defect, or . . . [3] the pregnancy resulted from rape, incest, or other felonious intercourse."[3]

Public Opinion on the Abortion Issue

There were also indications that the American public in the late 1960s was growing more receptive to the idea that abortion should be legal in some circumstances. Americans were asked in public opinion polls whether they approved of legal abortion for the reasons embodied in the ALI model statute—that is, if the mother's health was in danger, if the pregnancy resulted from rape or incest, or if there was a chance of serious birth defects. In the seven-year period between 1965 and 1972, public support for legalized abortion in such circumstances rose from the range of 50–75 percent to the range of 80–90 percent.

The justifications embodied in the ALI model statute are not the only reasons, however, why a woman might consider having an abortion. In fact, in the overwhelming proportion of cases, the motivation for seeking an abortion is likely to relate to a woman's economic or family circumstances. A woman might seek an abortion, for instance, because her family cannot afford another child, because she is unmarried, or because (even if she is married) she does not want any more children.

To most Americans, these so-called discretionary reasons for seeking an abortion did not seem nearly as compelling as those embodied in the ALI statute. Nevertheless, public support for abortion for discretionary reasons, like public support for abortion for other reasons, was growing. In 1965 support for abortion for a variety of discretionary reasons was quite low— in the range of 16 to 22 percent. By 1972, however, 49 percent of Americans supported legalized abortion if a family has "very low income and cannot afford any more children" (compared to 22 percent in 1965). Public approval of legalized abortion if a woman "is married and does not want to have any more children" had risen (between 1965 and 1972) from 16 to 40 percent.[4]

Despite these trends in public opinion, and the response of some state legislatures, it was difficult or impossible in many jurisdictions to obtain a legal abortion. As a result, many women turned to illegal abortions. Estimating the number of illegal abortions in the United States prior to 1973 is almost impossible, but some observers place the figure as high as 1 million each year.[5]

Norma McCorvey and the Texas Anti-Abortion Statute

It was in this context that a twenty-one-year-old Dallas woman named Norma McCorvey became pregnant. The year was 1969. Norma McCorvey was unmarried, had no permanent home, and was working as a waitress. Not wanting to have a child, she decided to seek an abortion. When she examined the Texas statute governing abortion, however, she realized that she was not entitled to obtain a legal abortion. The Texas law, which dated from 1856, was similar to the laws in effect in most other states. It permitted abortion only "by medical advice for the purpose of saving the life of the mother."[6]

Under the circumstances, the choices available to Norma McCorvey were clear. She could travel to another state where abortion was legal; she could obtain an illegal abortion in Texas; or she could challenge the constitutional validity of the Texas law in court. Norma McCorvey chose the third option. On March 3, 1970, she filed suit in the U.S. District Court for the Northern District of Texas. For purposes of the suit, she adopted the pseudonym "Jane Roe." She named as her defendant Henry Wade, the district attorney of Dallas County. Henceforth, the case became known as *Roe* v. *Wade*.

The Right of Privacy in American Constitutional Law

Norma McCorvey's chances of convincing the district court to strike down the Texas statute were problematic. They hinged in large part on the Supreme Court's willingness to expand the constitutional concept of the right of privacy. This concept had emerged in constitutional litigation only a few years earlier, and it was exceedingly controversial. In 1965, in *Griswold* v. *Connecticut*, the U.S. Supreme Court examined a Connecticut law that made it a crime to use contraceptives or to counsel others to do so.[7] The principal argument made to the Court was that the law violated the constitutional right of privacy. Unfortunately, the right of privacy is not explicitly mentioned in the Constitution. Thus, however unwise or unenforceable the Connecticut law might be, it was not clear that the Supreme Court was justified in coming to the conclusion that it was unconstitutional.

When it came time to decide the case, however, a majority of the Court swept aside these doubts. In an opinion by Justice Douglas, the Court conceded that the right of privacy is not explicitly mentioned in the Constitution. However, Douglas held, the right of privacy is protected by the "penumbras . . . formed by emanations" from specific guarantees of the Bill of Rights.[8] In any case, Douglas held, privacy—at least as it applies to the institution of marriage—is a right that is "older than the Bill of Rights."[9]

The Douglas opinion drew heavy criticism from dissenting Justices Black and Stewart. Black argued that "I get nowhere in this case by talk about a constitutional 'right of privacy' as an emanation from one or more constitutional provisions. I like my privacy as well as the next one, but I am nevertheless compelled to admit that government has a right to invade it unless prohibited by some specific constitutional provision."[10] Justice Stewart's dissent was even more scathing. He wrote that he found the Connecticut law "uncommonly silly," but, he said, "we are not asked in this case to say whether we think this law is unwise, or even asinine. We are asked to hold that it violates the United States Constitution. And that I cannot do."[11]

It was clear, therefore, that the Supreme Court in the late 1960s was deeply divided on the question of whether the Constitution protects the right of privacy and, if so, precisely what the right of privacy would include. It was in the midst of these conflicting and not altogether promising signals that

Norma McCorvey decided to challenge the constitutional validity of the Texas abortion statute.

Roe v. *Wade* in the Lower Courts

As we discussed in Chapter 2, *Roe* v. *Wade* was a classic example of a modern civil liberties case. McCorvey was challenging the constitutional validity of the Texas abortion statute. In addition, she was seeking an injunction against further enforcement of the statute. For these reasons, she was entitled to invoke the jurisdiction of a three-judge U.S. District Court. On May 3, 1970, Norma McCorvey filed her lawsuit in three-judge district court in Dallas.

On June 17, 1970, the three-judge court handed down its decision.[12] It concluded that the Texas statute did violate Norma McCorvey's constitutional right to obtain an abortion. What was perhaps even more surprising than the decision itself, however, was the constitutional foundation on which the decision was based.

The three-judge court chose to base its decision on the Ninth Amendment to the Constitution. In a *per curiam* opinion, the Court held, unanimously, that "the Texas Abortion Laws must be declared unconstitutional because they deprive single women and married couples of their right, secured by the Ninth Amendment, to choose whether to have children."[13]

The Ninth Amendment in Constitutional Law

The Ninth Amendment was part of the original group of ten amendments that are known as the Bill of Rights. It stipulates that "[t]he enumeration in the Constitution, of certain rights shall not be construed to deny or disparage others retained by the people." On its face, it seems to suggest that Americans possess an inexhaustible supply of "unenumerated" constitutional rights.

When the language of the Ninth Amendment is combined with the existence of the power of judicial review, however, a somewhat disturbing prospect arises. If judges have the power to decide what the Constitution means, and if the Constitution protects unenumerated rights, then judges, in effect, possess the power to rewrite the Constitution, that is, to identify new constitutional rights as the occasion arises. Theoretically, of course, the only way to rewrite the Constitution is to undertake the formal process of constitutional amendment. The Ninth Amendment seems to provide a way to circumvent the amendment process and amend the Constitution by judicial fiat.[14]

Perhaps in part because of its apparently boundless connotations, the Ninth Amendment had rarely been invoked by the Supreme Court or other courts. Indeed, it had achieved rather sudden notoriety only a few years earlier, in *Griswold* v. *Connecticut*, when it served as the centerpiece of Justice Goldberg's concurring opinion in the case.[15] Goldberg argued that the Ninth Amendment did indicate that the framers of the Constitution believed that American citizens possessed "fundamental personal rights" other than those enumerated in the Constitution. Moreover, he expressed confidence that judges could be trusted with the power to determine what those rights might be.[16]

When the three-judge district court decided to base its holding in *Roe* on the Ninth Amendment, therefore, it was exploring relatively new constitutional territory. As we have already seen, however, the Constitution does not contain an explicit right of privacy. Thus, a court that wishes to rule in favor of a claim based on the notion of a constitutional right of privacy must be prepared to entertain one of a handful of controversial and innovative theories of the meaning of the Constitution.

The Relief in *Roe*

Having decided that the Texas abortion statute was unconstitutional, the district court next needed to decide whether to issue an injunction restraining its further enforcement. The plaintiff, Norma McCorvey, wanted an injunction, because it would then be clear that she could proceed to seek a legal abortion in Texas. Moreover, the district court had the basic power to grant such relief. It was also clear, however, that the district court's decision was going to be appealed to the U.S. Supreme Court. Under the circumstances — that is, before the Supreme Court had ruled on the issue — the district court was reluctant to order an actual cessation of enforcement of the Texas statute. Thus, it declined to accompany its declaratory judgment with an injunction.[17]

In view of the "mixed" holding of the district court — overturning the abortion statute, but refusing to enjoin its enforcement — neither party to the litigation was fully satisfied. The consequence was that both sides in the case of *Roe* v. *Wade* prepared to take appeals to the U.S. Supreme Court.

Roe v. *Wade* Reaches the Supreme Court

On May 3, 1971, the Supreme Court noted probable jurisdiction in *Roe* v. *Wade*, and preparations began for oral argument in the fall. As it turned out, however, there was a major delay in the Court's consideration of the case. Oral argument did take place that fall — on December 13, 1971 — but the Court at the time consisted of only seven justices. On September 17, Justice Black, who was gravely ill, had resigned from the Court, and only a few days later, on September 25, he died. Two days before Black's death, Justice Harlan, who was also very ill, submitted his resignation. Therefore, as the Court began its October term, it was short two justices.

On October 21, President Nixon nominated Lewis Powell to succeed Justice Black and William Rehnquist to succeed Justice Harlan. The confirmation process in the Senate occurred over the next few weeks. Powell was confirmed, by a vote of 89 to 1, on December 6, and Rehnquist was confirmed, by a vote of 68 to 26, on December 10. Swearing in, however, was not scheduled until after the Christmas holidays. Thus, the December 13 oral argument in *Roe* v. *Wade* took place without the new appointees.

Following oral argument, the Court met in conference to discuss *Roe* and other cases. The discussion, it seems, was inconclusive. In fact, the justices emerged from the conference with conflicting interpretations of how the vote on *Roe* v. *Wade* had come out. Some believed it was 5 to 2 to overturn the Texas law, while others concluded that the division was 4 to 3 to uphold the law.[18]

Despite this uncertainty — or perhaps because of it — Chief Justice Burger asserted his prerogative to assign the opinion in *Roe*, and he chose Justice Blackmun for the job. Burger's assertion of the power to assign the opinion was challenged, however, by those on the Court who believed that a majority of the Court was in favor of overturning the law and that Burger was not a member of that majority. If that were indeed the case, the prerogative to assign the opinion belonged to Justice Douglas, the senior justice in the majority. Chief Justice Burger defended his decision by arguing that the division of the justices after the conference was unclear. As a result, he said, the ultimate resolution of the case would have to depend on the content of Justice Blackmun's opinion and whether a majority of justices in fact agreed to join it.[19]

Chief Justice Burger's decision to assign the opinion to Justice Blackmun prevailed, and Blackmun set to work on the task. The resulting draft of Blackmun's opinion was not circulated until May, however, and when it reached the other justices, some members of the majority for whom Blackmun was by then presumably speaking — that is, the justices who favored striking down the Texas law — were not very enthusiastic about its contents. In addition, of course, some uneasiness remained within the Court that a decision in *Roe* that spring would be based on the votes of seven rather than nine justices. On June 3, 1972, therefore, Blackmun notified the other members of the Court that he wished to withdraw the opinion. The Court thereupon decided to schedule *Roe* v. *Wade* for reargument in the fall.

The Court Decides the Abortion Question

When *Roe* v. *Wade* was reargued in the Supreme Court on October 10, 1972, the Court was at full strength and final resolution of the abortion issue was at hand. Following oral argument, the Court met in conference on October 12, 1972. The tentative vote among the justices appeared to be 6 to 3 to strike down the Texas statute. The minority consisted of White, Burger, and the newly appointed Rehnquist. The majority consisted of Blackmun, Douglas, Brennan, Marshall, Stewart, and the other new member of the Court, Powell.[20]

Blackmun's opinion in the case had been in preparation for almost a year.

The latest version was circulated among the justices in late October. Each of the justices in the presumed majority made suggestions for changes, most of which Blackmun incorporated into his draft opinion. White and Rehnquist prepared dissents, which were also circulated among the justices. Only Chief Justice Burger remained a question mark. Most of the other justices assumed he would vote to uphold the Texas law, but he had never stated his position with finality. At the Court's conference on January 12, however, Burger announced he was joining the majority. His decision to join the majority brought to a total of seven the number of justices voting to strike down the Texas law.[21]

The Opinion in *Roe*

The Court's decision in *Roe* v. *Wade* was announced on January 22, 1973. The Court held that a woman had a constitutional right to obtain a legal abortion during the first two-thirds of her pregnancy and that state laws which interfered with the exercise of that right were unconstitutional. At the

The Supreme Court in 1973. *Roe* v. *Wade* was decided by a Court consisting of justices appointed over a span of three decades. William Douglas, appointed by Franklin Roosevelt, had been on the Court since 1939, while the two newest members of the Court — Lewis Powell and William Rehnquist — had been there for just over a year. *Standing (left to right):* Lewis F. Powell, Jr., Thurgood Marshall, Harry A. Blackmun, and William H. Rehnquist. *Seated (left to right):* Potter Stewart, William O. Douglas, Warren E. Burger, William J. Brennan, Jr., and Byron R. White.

SOURCE: Collection of the Supreme Court of the United States

time of the Court's decision, four states (Alaska, Hawaii, Washington, and New York) had repealed their laws against abortion. In the remaining states, however, abortion was illegal except in specified circumstances. The effect of the Court's decision, therefore, was to overturn abortion statutes in forty-six states.

Justice Blackmun's opinion in *Roe* v. *Wade* was—and remains to this day—a controversial document. Blackmun knew that few issues disturbed the American people as profoundly as the abortion issue. Thus, he began his opinion by saying that "[w]e forthwith acknowledge our awareness of the sensitive and emotional nature of the abortion controversy, of the vigorous opposing views . . . and of the deep and seemingly absolute convictions that the subject inspires."[22]

When he turned to the question of the constitutional basis for the Court's decision, Blackmun conceded that "[t]he Constitution does not explicitly mention any right of privacy." He concluded, however, that "the Court has recognized that a right of personal privacy . . . does exist under the Constitution." He asserted that previous cases "make it clear that the right has some extension to activities relating to marriage, procreation, contraception, family relationships, and child rearing and education."[23]

Once he had reaffirmed the existence of a constitutional right of privacy, Blackmun proceeded to enunciate the Court's specific holding on the issue of abortion. "This right of privacy," he said, "[is] founded in the Fourteenth Amendment's concept of personal liberty . . . [and] is broad enough to encompass a woman's decision whether or not to terminate her pregnancy."[24]

In this single sentence, Blackmun confronted and resolved not one, but two, important issues. First, he decided that the right of privacy was "founded" in the Due Process Clause of the Fourteenth Amendment. The three-judge district court had concluded that the right of privacy was protected by the Ninth Amendment, and in 1965, in *Griswold* v. *Connecticut*, the Supreme Court had held that the right of privacy was protected by the "penumbras" of specific provisions of the Bill of Rights. Blackmun's opinion in *Roe* chose to locate the right of privacy in the Due Process Clause of the Fourteenth Amendment.

Second, Blackmun extended the right of privacy to "encompass" a woman's decision to terminate her pregnancy. In *Griswold*, the effect of judicial invocation of the right of privacy was to confer constitutional protection on the decision whether or not to use contraceptives. Extension of the right of privacy to protect a woman's decision to terminate an ongoing pregnancy represented a significant and controversial step.[25]

Blackmun thus articulated the majority's basic conclusion that women have a constitutional right to obtain abortions. He noted immediately, however, that "this right is not unqualified and must be considered against important state interests in regulation."[26] He identified two such interests— "preserving the . . . health of the pregnant woman" and "protecting the potentiality of human life"—and he held that each of these interests "grows in substantiality as the woman approaches term."[27] He concluded that subsequent to the end of the first trimester, the state may not prohibit abortion, but it may "regulate the abortion procedure in ways that are reasonably related to maternal health." In the third trimester—that is, when the fetus becomes viable and is capable of life outside the womb—the state "in promoting its interest in the potentiality of human life may . . . proscribe . . . abortion."[28]

The Unending Controversy over Abortion

The Supreme Court's decision in *Roe* v. *Wade* marked the beginning, not the end, of the modern controversy over abortion. The decision stimulated considerable grassroots political activity. Many Americans became active participants in the "pro-life" or "pro-choice" movements. Politicians at all levels of government were forced to confront the abortion issue, and legislation aimed at limiting or reversing *Roe* v. *Wade* was passed by Congress and various state legislatures. Prospective nominees to the Supreme Court were questioned about their views on abortion, and each new appointment to the Court raised the possibility that *Roe* v. *Wade* might be overturned.

Polls show that the American public continues to be deeply and evenly divided on the abortion issue. About 50 to 60 percent of Americans express support for the Supreme Court's decision in *Roe* v. *Wade*, while about 35 percent believe the decision was wrong.[29] At the same time, only about 30 to 50 percent of Americans support abortion for the various "discretionary" reasons that are most likely to lie behind a woman's decision to seek an abortion—for example, that she is unmarried or that she and her husband cannot afford, or do not want, another child.[30]

Congressional Reaction to *Roe* v. *Wade*

Congress has made several efforts to counter the Supreme Court's decision in *Roe* v. *Wade*. Most of them are similar to efforts made to reverse the Court's decisions on school prayer. Like the school prayer decisions, *Roe* v. *Wade* has thus far not been directly reversed by Congress.

One congressional strategy has been to withdraw abortion cases from the original jurisdiction of the lower federal courts, or from the appellate jurisdiction of the Supreme Court, or both. A second strategy has been to seek the passage of legislation declaring that human life begins at conception. In 1981 Representative Henry Hyde and Senator Jesse Helms introduced legislation that combined the two strategies in a single bill. Section 1 of their "Human Life Statute" stipulated that "The Congress finds that the life of each human being begins at conception." Section 2 stipulated that "no inferior federal court . . . shall have jurisdiction to issue any . . . injunction . . . or declaratory judgment in any case involving . . . any state law or municipal ordinance that . . . prohibits, limits, or regulates . . . the performance of abortions." As yet, Congress has passed neither a human life statute nor any legislation depriving the federal courts of their jurisdiction over abortion cases.[31]

The most direct way in which Congress can overturn a decision of the Supreme Court is to pass and send a constitutional amendment to the states. Beginning in 1973, Congress has attempted to pass an amendment either (1) returning control of abortion to the states or (2) defining the fetus as a "person" entitled to "the right to life." Only one amendment has reached the floor of either house of Congress for a vote. In 1983 Senator Orrin Hatch (R-Utah) sponsored an amendment that stated, simply, that "A right to abortion is not guaranteed by the Constitution."[32] When it came to a vote in the Senate, the tally was 49 for and 50 against. It thus fell 18 votes short of the 67 needed to pass by a two-thirds majority.[33]

Abortion Funding in Legislatures and Courts

A common legislative strategy to reduce the impact of *Roe* v. *Wade*, if not reverse the decision itself, is to prohibit the use of public funds to pay for abortions. In Congress, legislation has been introduced every year since 1976 to prohibit the use of federal funds to reimburse states for Medicaid abortions, that is, abortions for poor women who are eligible, under the Medicaid program, for government-funded medical care. In 1980, by a 5–4 vote, the Supreme Court held that this legislation—known as the Hyde Amendment after its principal sponsor, Representative Henry Hyde—was not unconstitutional.[34]

Some individual states have also passed legislation to restrict the availability of public funds for abortions. In 1977 the Supreme Court voted 6–3 to uphold a Connecticut law that permits Medicaid funds to be used for childbirth but not for abortion.[35] As of 1992, some thirty-one states withheld Medicaid funding from all abortions except those in which the mother's life was in danger.[36]

Other Legislative Attacks on *Roe* v. *Wade*

Other types of legislation aimed at restricting or reversing *Roe* v. *Wade* have not, until recently, fared so well in the Supreme Court. In 1976, in *Planned Parenthood of Central Missouri* v. *Danforth*, the Court voted 6–3 to overturn a Missouri statute requiring a married woman to obtain her husband's consent to an abortion and an unmarried woman under eighteen to obtain her parents' consent.[37] In 1983, in *Akron* v. *Akron Center for Reproductive Health*, the Court, also by a vote of 6–3, overturned several provisions of an Akron ordinance regulating abortion and explicitly reaffirmed its decision in *Roe*. In 1986, in *Thornburgh* v. *American College of Obstetricians and Gynecologists*, by a vote of 5–4, the Court overturned a Pennsylvania law which, like the Akron ordinance, contained a variety of restrictions on abortion.

In recent years, however, the Court's approach to legislative restrictions on abortion has begun to change. A major turning point came in 1989, with the Court's decision in *Webster* v. *Reproductive Health Services*.[38] By a 5-4 margin, the Court upheld a provision of a Missouri law that requires physicians to perform various tests to determine whether a fetus is viable if the physician "has reason to believe [the fetus is] twenty or more weeks gestational age." In a plurality opinion, in which he spoke for himself and Justices White and Kennedy, Chief Justice Rehnquist declined to overrule *Roe* v. *Wade* on the ground that "[t]he facts of the present case . . . differ from those at issue in *Roe*."[39] In his concurring opinion, however, Justice Scalia argued that the time *had* come to reconsider *Roe* v. *Wade*.[40]

The combination of opinions in *Webster* supporting the Missouri law provoked Justice Blackmun to write an emotional dissent. "For today, at least," he said, "the law of abortion stands undisturbed. For today, the women of this Nation still retain the liberty to control their destinies. But the signs are evident and very ominous, and a chill wind blows."[41]

The *Webster* decision was followed in 1990 and 1991 by two additional decisions indicative of the Court's changing position on abortion. In *Hodgson* v. *Minnesota* (1990), a 5-4 majority upheld a law requiring that both parents of an unemancipated minor must be notified before an abortion can be performed, but providing—under a so-called "judicial by-pass" provision— that judicial authorization for the abortion may in some cases be substituted for parental notification. In another 5-4 decision, *Rust* v. *Sullivan* (1991), the Court upheld federal regulations that forbid government-funded family planning clinics from counseling women that abortion is one option available to them to end an unwanted pregnancy.

Political observers predicted that the immediate effect of the Court's decision in *Webster* would be to encourage states to pass new laws banning or restricting abortion. In fact, in the aftermath of *Webster*, about six hundred bills relating to abortion were introduced in state legislatures. Some states voted to ban abortion outright, while others enacted restrictions on abortion. The most common restrictions require that a minor either notify or obtain the consent of her parents before having an abortion, that a married woman either notify or obtain the consent of her husband before having an abortion, and that a woman seeking an abortion must be informed of her options and must wait twenty-four hours (or a comparable period of time) before having an abortion.

Pennsylvania was among the states that enacted new restrictions on abortion in the late 1980s. The Pennsylvania law required (1) that women under eighteen obtain parental consent—or a court order substituting for parental consent—before having an abortion, (2) that all abortions must be based on "informed consent," that is, must be preceded by mandatory counseling followed by a twenty-four-hour waiting period before the abortion is performed, and (3) that married women must notify their husbands before seeking an abortion.

In October, 1991, in *Casey* v. *Planned Parenthood of Southeastern Pennsylvania*, the U.S. Court of Appeals for the Third Circuit upheld the parental consent and informed consent provisions of the law, but it struck down the spousal notification provision,[42] and on January 21, 1992, the Supreme Court granted certiorari in the case.[43] On June 29, 1992, the Supreme Court issued a decision that closely tracked the decision of the court of appeals. A 7–2 majority of the Court voted to uphold the parental consent and informed consent provisions of the law, while a 5–4 majority voted to overturn the spousal notification provision.[44]

The Court's decision in *Casey* satisfied almost no one. For abortion rights activists, *Casey* was a disappointing decision because it imposed further onerous restrictions on abortion and, more importantly, because it signaled the imminent demise of *Roe* v. *Wade* itself. For anti-abortion activists, however, the Court's decision in *Casey* was equally disappointing, because it stopped short of the essential goal of overruling *Roe* v. *Wade* and returning the abortion issue to the states. If abortion were an ordinary political issue, the *Casey* decision might have been viewed as an acceptable compromise between two opposing positions. Given the nature of the abortion issue, however, it was in fact viewed as one more inconclusive battle in an ongoing war.

Most observers are convinced, however, that *Roe* v. *Wade* is closer to being overruled than ever before. The precarious status of *Roe* was sharply illuminated by the distribution of the justices on the *Casey* Court. Four members of the Court—Rehnquist, White, Scalia, and Thomas—said they were ready to overrule *Roe*. Moreover, while a bare majority of five members of the Court declined to overrule *Roe*, that majority included only two justices—Blackmun and Stevens—who voiced support for the substance of *Roe*. The remaining justices in the majority, O'Connor, Kennedy, and Souter, based their refusal to overrule *Roe* v. *Wade* on the principle of *stare decisis* (which translates as "let the decision stand" and which embodies the bias in our legal system in favor of preserving established judicial precedents) and on their concern, as expressed in their plurality opinion, that "to overrule under fire in the absence of the most compelling reason to reexamine a watershed decision would subvert the Court's legitimacy beyond any serious question."[45] It is therefore clear that the existence of a basic constitutional right to abortion will not survive the replacement of any one of the five justices in the majority by an appointee who is willing to overrule *Roe* v. *Wade* itself.

The abortion issue is probably the most controversial issue to reach the Supreme Court in recent years. Not far behind, however, is the issue of affirmative action. Few questions perplex and agitate the American people more deeply than the question of whether racial minorities and other disadvantaged groups should qualify for preferential treatment in educational institutions and the job market.

Notes

1. See, for example, Roger Rosenblatt, *Life Itself: Abortion in the American Mind* (1992); Marian Faux, *Roe v. Wade: The Untold Story of the Landmark Supreme*

Court Decision That Made Abortion Legal (1988); Eva R. Rubin, *Abortion, Politics, and the Courts* (1987); Hyman Rodman, Betty Sarvis, and Joy Walker Bonar, *The Abortion Question* (1987); and Kristin Luker, *Abortion and the Politics of Motherhood* (1984).

2. *Roe v. Wade*, 410 U.S. 113, 132–36 (1973).

3. Quoted in id. at 205–6.

4. See Judith Blake, "The Abortion Decisions: Judicial Review and Public Opinion," in Edward Manier, William Liu, and David Solomon (eds.), *Abortion: New Directions for Policy Studies* (1977), pp. 51–82. See also Rodman et al., *The Abortion Question*, pp. 136–37.

5. Rubin, *Abortion, Politics, and the Courts*, p. 17; Rodman et al., *The Abortion Question*, p. 23.

6. *Roe v. Wade*, 410 U.S. at 117–18.

7. *Griswold v. Connecticut*, 381 U.S. 479 (1965).

8. Id. at 484.

9. Id. at 486.

10. Id. at 510 (Black, J., dissenting).

11. Id. at 527 (Stewart, J., dissenting).

12. *Roe v. Wade*, 314 F.Supp. 1217 (N.D.Tex 1970).

13. Id. at 1221.

14. Among the outspoken critics of the Ninth Amendment—or rather, the Supreme Court's willingness to use the Ninth Amendment to rewrite the Constitution—is Robert Bork, President Reagan's unsuccessful nominee to the Supreme Court. See Robert H. Bork, *The Tempting of America: The Political Seduction of the Law* (1990).

15. 381 U.S. 479, 486–99 (1965) (Goldberg, J., concurring).

16. 381 U.S. at 492. For a recent collection of articles on the Ninth Amendment, see Randy E. Barnett (ed.), *The Rights Retained by the People: The History and Meaning of the Ninth Amendment* (1989).

17. 314 F.Supp. at 1224.

18. See Bob Woodward and Scott Armstrong, *The Brethren: Inside the Supreme Court* (1976), pp. 169–70.

19. See id. at 171–72. See also David M. O'Brien, *Storm Center: The Supreme Court in American Politics*, p. 284.

20. Woodward and Armstrong, *The Brethren*, pp. 229–31.

21. Id. at 231–40.

22. 410 U.S. at 114.

23. Id. at 152–53.

24. Id. at 153.

25. Blackmun was aware of the magnitude of that step. In a subsequent passage of his opinion, he noted that "[t]he pregnant woman cannot be isolated in her privacy. She carries an embryo and, later, a fetus. . . . The situation therefore is inherently different from marital privacy . . . with which . . . *Griswold* . . . [was] concerned." Id. at 159.

26. Id. at 154.

27. Id. at 162–63.

28. Id. at 164–65.

29. *Gallup Report* (No. 289), October 1989, p. 17; "Whose Life Is It?" *Time Magazine*, May 1, 1989, pp. 20–24.

30. See National Opinion Research Center, *General Social Surveys, 1972–1991: Cumulative Codebook* (1991); Richard G. Niemi, John Mueller, and Tom W. Smith,

Trends in Public Opinion: A Compendium of Survey Data (1989), pp. 201–13; Benjamin I. Page and Robert Y. Shapiro, *The Rational Public: Fifty Years of Trends in Americans' Policy Preferences* (1992), pp. 63–64, 105–10; "Pro-Choice: 'A Sleeping Giant' Awakes," *Newsweek Magazine*, April 24, 1989, pp. 39–40; and Charles H. Franklin and Liane C. Kosaki, "Republican Schoolmaster: The U.S. Supreme Court, Public Opinion, and Abortion," 83 *Am. Pol. Sci. Rev.* 751 (1989). For additional discussion of trends in public opinion on abortion, see Chapter 15.

31. See Rodman et al., *The Abortion Question*, pp. 126–34; and Rubin, *Abortion, Politics, and the Courts*, pp. 151–83.

32. The Hatch amendment would return control of abortion to the states. It is thus an example of the states' rights rather than the right to life approach to reversing *Roe v. Wade.*

33. See Edward Keynes, *The Court vs. Congress: Prayer, Busing, and Abortion* (1989), pp. 280–85.

34. *Harris v. McRae* (1980).

35. *Maher v. Roe* (1977).

36. "Abortion: The Future is Already Here," *Time Magazine*, May 4, 1992, pp. 27–32.

37. See also *Bellotti v. Baird* (1979) (overturning a Massachusetts law requiring an unmarried minor to obtain parental consent or judicial consent to abortion).

38. 109 S.Ct. 3040 (1989).

39. Id. at 3058.

40. Id. at 3064–67.

41. Id. at 3079.

42. 947 F.2d 682 (3rd Cir., 1991).

43. *Planned Parenthood of Southeastern Pennsylvania v. Casey*, 112 S.Ct. 931 (1992).

44. *Planned Parenthood of Southeastern Pennsylvania v. Casey*, 112 S.Ct. 2791 (1992).

45. Id. at 2815.

CHAPTER 11

The Agonizing Issue of
Affirmative Action: *Regents of*
the University of California v.
Bakke (1978)

Race is almost certainly the most intractable issue in American politics. It bedeviled the Constitutional Convention.[1] It provoked the American Civil War, and, a century later, the Civil Rights Movement of the 1950s and 1960s.[2] It is capable of bringing out the best and the worst in the American people and their governmental institutions, including the Supreme Court.[3]

The issue of race returned to the Supreme Court yet again in *Regents of the University of California* v. *Bakke* in 1978. The *Bakke* case, however, raised the issue in a totally new guise. In previous cases, the Supreme Court had been concerned with allegations of discrimination against racial and ethnic minorities. In *Bakke*, the Court was concerned with the constitutional validity of preferential treatment of racial minorities. Not surprisingly, *Bakke* became one of the most prominent and controversial cases of the 1970s.[4]

One indication of the exceptional ability of affirmative action to divide Americans is the fact that participants in the debate cannot even agree on terminology. The term *affirmative action* dates from the early 1960s, when Presidents Kennedy and Johnson issued executive orders calling for special efforts by federal contractors to employ minorities on federal projects.[5] Today, supporters of efforts to achieve racial equality through special programs for racial minorities prefer the term *affirmative action*, while opponents of special programs are more likely to characterize them as examples of preferential treatment, reverse discrimination, or racial quotas. Over the years, various compromise descriptions have been offered, including benign discrimination, compensatory discrimination, and compensatory justice. Each is designed in one fashion or another to frame the issues and set the tone for one of the most important debates in American history.

The Case for Affirmative Action

The basic theory of affirmative action is relatively easy to articulate. It is that various groups — including blacks, women, ethnic minorities, and Native

175

Americans — have long been the victims of discrimination in American society. Moreover, this discrimination was in some cases, notably in the case of blacks, practically all-pervasive. Even after the end of slavery, legal rules and social practices prevented blacks from owning property, holding certain jobs, attending integrated schools, enjoying equal access to public accommodations, and participating in the political process. In short, from the moment they set foot on American soil, blacks were victims of what supporters of affirmative action call "societal discrimination," that is, discrimination in a multitude of formal and informal manifestations that affected practically every aspect of the lives of individual blacks.[6]

Supporters of affirmative action concede that, beginning in the 1940s, the edifice of formal discrimination began to crumble and that by the end of the 1960s, most (though not all) of the formal barriers to equal participation had been removed. The problem, of course, is that by this time blacks had, for generations, been relegated to second-class status. In the process, they had effectively been deprived of the ability to compete on an equal basis with dominant groups in the society. In widely quoted remarks delivered at commencement ceremonies at Howard University in 1965, President Johnson identified the problem. "You do not take a person," he said, "who, for years, has been hobbled by chains and liberate him, bring him up to the starting line of a race and then say, 'You are free to compete with all the others,' and still justly believe that you have been completely fair."[7]

The results of decades of discrimination against blacks are evident in statistics showing that blacks are underrepresented in higher education and the professions and overrepresented among the ranks of the poor. In 1970 blacks comprised nearly 12 percent of the population, but only 2.2 percent of doctors, 2.8 percent of medical students, and 1 percent of lawyers.[8] In 1969 black families were almost four times as likely as white families to have incomes below the poverty line.[9] By almost every measure, blacks as a group were — and are — clearly less fortunate than most other Americans.[10]

The theory of affirmative action is premised on these grim statistics and the shameful history that produced them. The theory asserts that ending discrimination against blacks is not enough to ensure that blacks will take their rightful place in the mainstream of American society. Even if there is never again an instance of discrimination against blacks — itself an optimistic assumption — the legacy of past discrimination will guarantee that blacks remain second-class citizens for the indefinite future. It follows that we as a society must resort to drastic means to overcome racial inequality. The only strategy that can be expected to obliterate the effects of past discrimination is one that allows businesses and institutions to accord preferential treatment to blacks on a temporary basis.

Perhaps the most succinct statement of the philosophy of affirmative action is found in Justice Blackmun's opinion in the *Bakke* case. It encapsulates the grave reservations that almost everyone shares about using race to effectuate social goals, as well as the conviction that the use of so-called "race-conscious remedies" is a necessity if American society ever hopes to overcome the effects of past discrimination. "I yield to no one," Justice Blackmun said, "in my earnest hope that the time will come when an 'affirmative action' program is unnecessary."[11] But, he continued, "[i]n order to get beyond racism, we must first take account of race. There is no other way."[12]

Affirmative Action and the Constitution

Although many regard the arguments for affirmative action as thoroughly compelling, others find the very concept of affirmative action to be repugnant. Before venturing further into the debate over affirmative action, however, it may be useful to clarify why affirmative action is such an important *constitutional* issue, as well as such an important public policy issue.

Years ago, in his dissent to the Supreme Court's decision in *Plessy* v. *Ferguson,* Justice Harlan expressed the view that "Our Constitution is color blind."[13] This simple sentence captured the essence of one understanding of the Equal Protection Clause — the view that the Equal Protection Clause represents an absolute bar to the use of race to achieve policy objectives, regardless of whether those objectives are to *further degrade* an already oppressed racial group or to *uplift* that group through the preferential treatment of its members.

Applied to the modern era, the theory that the Constitution is color blind would mean that the United States must be firmly committed to ending positive discrimination against racial minorities. Once that goal had been accomplished, however, society would be prevented from turning around and using racial criteria for the purpose of rectifying the effects of past discrimination. Under the theory of a color-blind Constitution, once discrimination has been eliminated, each individual should henceforth be judged on his or her individual merit according to neutral, that is, nonracial, criteria.

From the perspective of those who support affirmative action, of course, the prospective application of neutral criteria is precisely the sort of policy that would, in practice, perpetuate the effects of past discrimination. Thus, the basic question that ultimately needed to be decided in the *Bakke* case was whether the Constitution is or is not completely color blind: Does the Constitution permit government some discretion to use race to rectify the effects of past discrimination, or does it absolutely preclude government from adopting race-conscious means to uplift underprivileged racial groups?

The question of whether the Constitution is or should be absolutely color blind therefore lies at the heart of the constitutional debate over affirmative action. For obvious reasons, opponents of affirmative action ordinarily take the position that the Constitution *is* color blind. However, the argument that the Constitution is color blind is only one of the objections to affirmative action.

The Case against Affirmative Action

The basic argument against affirmative action is that it constitutes, in effect, reverse discrimination. That is, that its differential treatment of blacks and whites works to the detriment of individual whites whose qualifications are at least as strong, and perhaps stronger, than those of their black competitors. Under affirmative action programs, relatively well-qualified whites are displaced by relatively less qualified blacks for opportunities such as vocational training, professional education, employment, and promotion.

The argument against affirmative action also focuses on those who are intended to be its beneficiaries. What renders an individual eligible for benefits under an affirmative action program, the argument goes, is his or her race per se. The use of race as the criterion of eligibility, however, leads to two anomalies. First, particular blacks may be poorly qualified to take advantage of particular educational or employment opportunities for the same reasons as particular whites: that is, not because they are the victims of past discrimination, but because they are not very bright, not very motivated, or not very talented. Under many affirmative action schemes, however, they will be eligible for special consideration because they are black and for that reason alone.

One way around this situation, of course, is to confer benefits within the category of those who are eligible — that is, blacks — based on traditional criteria for determining who is best qualified. This, however, leads to a second anomaly, which is especially obvious in the case of affirmative action programs aimed at increasing the number of minorities in graduate and professional schools. From the perspective of those who administer such programs, the most promising candidates for preferential treatment will be individuals who are poised to capitalize on new opportunities. In many, if not most, cases, however, blacks who fit this description will come from middle-class backgrounds and will have experienced little or no personal deprivation or discrimination. In the meantime, the most deserving candidates for preferential treatment will be those who have actually suffered past discrimination. Almost by definition, however, such candidates will find it particularly difficult to survive, after years of deprivation, in a highly competitive educational environment. The anomaly of affirmative action arises because the most deserving candidates for special treatment will be those who are least capable of competing successfully, while those who are best equipped to compete successfully will be individuals who were not in fact the victims of past racial discrimination.[14]

Opponents of affirmative action also point to additional difficulties with the use of race-conscious remedies to achieve racial equality. They argue that many affirmative action programs use quotas in hopes that one day blacks or other minorities will be represented in particular sectors of public or private life in proportion to their numbers in the overall population. Efforts to achieve such proportionality will ultimately fail, however, because, opponents of affirmative action argue, they ignore the obvious fact that groups differ in both their aspirations and their abilities.

Opponents of affirmative action also argue that affirmative action programs may include not only those who are less qualified, but also those who are absolutely unqualified. Opponents of affirmative action argue further that members of particular minority groups, whether or not they have been the beneficiaries of affirmative action, must forever live with the stigma that they have achieved success not on their own merits but because of special treatment. Finally, opponents of affirmative action argue that serious difficulties arise in trying to determine which minorities deserve preferential treatment, in trying to determine how generous society should be in setting aside places for specified minorities, and in trying to determine when it will be appropriate to end affirmative action programs and revert to the use of neutral criteria for determining eligibility for opportunities and rewards.[15]

The Ongoing Argument over Affirmative Action

The proponents of affirmative action often respond to these arguments with assertions that are designed to sidestep, at least in part, the moral and practical dilemmas inherent in treating some groups more favorably than others for the purpose of rectifying past discrimination. They argue that the true purposes of affirmative action are essentially "forward-looking." If affirmative action programs are implemented with care and sensitivity, they argue, the result will be to enrich and diversify higher education and the professions, to break down negative stereotypes about traditionally underprivileged groups, to provide the next generation of blacks (and women and others) with positive role models, and to strengthen the economic and professional infrastructure of minority communities. Each of these arguments is designed to emphasize the advantages to American society of the active pursuit of affirmative action regardless of one's opinion about the precise role of past discrimination in producing current conditions.

The proponents of affirmative action also display confidence in the old adage that "the best defense is a good offense." They refuse to concede one of the central premises of the argument against affirmative action, namely, that racial minorities who benefit from affirmative action programs are, by definition, less qualified than their white counterparts. They argue that in many situations the question of who is best qualified is itself riddled with ambiguity. In any case, they assert, those who oppose affirmative action are operating, either implicitly or explicitly, on an arbitrarily narrow definition of what constitutes a qualification. Allocating places in college or graduate school based wholly or mostly on test scores, for instance, overlooks a host of other useful predictors of academic success, while hiring people for job opportunities based purely on formal credentials will similarly exclude many promising employees.

A particularly forceful version of this argument incorporates the proposition that in the United States, with its long history of racism and discrimination, simply being black represents an important qualification for many educational and job opportunities. Therefore, any business or institution that purports to be interested in identifying those who will make the most useful contribution to American society should give race at least as much weight as test scores or academic grades.[16]

Clearly, the debate over the merits of affirmative action will not be resolved in the near future. Some believe that preferential treatment of racial minorities is the only method by which the goal of racial equality can be achieved. Others, most of whom fully endorse the goal of racial equality, are nevertheless skeptical of the wisdom of using race-conscious methods to achieve that goal. The conflicting views on affirmative action came to a head in Allan Bakke's challenge to the admissions practices of the Davis Medical School.

Allan Bakke and the Davis Medical School

The University of California Medical School at Davis opened in 1968. In 1969, responding in part to the fact that no blacks or Chicanos had been among the entering class of fifty students, the school decided to institute a "special admissions program." The school's catalog described the program as one that was meant for applicants who were "economically or educationally disadvantaged."[17]

By 1971 the Medical School had enlarged its entering class to one hundred seats, sixteen of which were reserved for students selected under the special admissions program. At the time, the special admissions program was ostensibly open to any student who qualified as "disadvantaged." Between 1971 and 1974, however, no whites were actually admitted under the program, even though about 272 white applicants qualified, in the eyes of the school, as disadvantaged. During the same period, twenty-one black and thirty Chicano students were admitted under the special program. Beginning in 1974, applicants were explicitly asked (on the school's application form) to place themselves in one or another of several categories, including Black/Afro-American, American Indian, White/Caucasian, and Mexican/American or Chicano.

The discrepancy in qualifications of students admitted under the special admissions and the regular admissions program was substantial. In 1973 the average GPA (grade-point average) of regular admittees was 3.49 (on a 4-point scale), while that of special admittees was 2.88. Regular admittees, on average, were in the seventy-seventh percentile based on their scores on four sections of the Medical College Admissions Test (MCAT). Special admittees, on average, were in the thirty-fourth percentile.

For the one hundred seats in its 1973 entering class, Davis Medical School received 2,464 applications. One of those applications was from Allan Bakke.

In his application, Bakke did not indicate that he was disadvantaged. Neither was he a member of any of the minority groups eligible, in practice, for consideration under the special admissions program. Thus, his application placed him in contention for one of the eighty-four seats available to applicants under the regular admissions program.

A Determined Plaintiff Challenges Affirmative Action

Allan Bakke's father was a mailman and his mother was a teacher. He graduated from the University of Minnesota with an engineering degree in the early 1960s and then served four years in the Marine Corps, including seven months as commanding officer of an antiaircraft unit in Vietnam. He subsequently earned a master's degree from Stanford University and began work in 1967 as an engineer at the Ames Research Center (a research facility of the National Aeronautics and Space Administration) in the Bay Area of Northern California.

At some point during this period, Allan Bakke decided he wanted to become a doctor. While holding a full-time job at the Ames Center, he completed the prerequisites for medical school (courses in biology and chemistry). In addition, he served as a volunteer in a local hospital emergency room. In the fall of 1972, at the age of thirty-two, he applied to eleven medical schools, including the University of California at Davis.

Allan Bakke and the Admissions Process

Bakke's credentials made him a strong candidate for admission to the Davis Medical School, even compared to other nonminority applicants and certainly compared to the students eligible for admission under the special admissions program. His GPA was 3.46, which was very close to the average GPA of regular admittees. The average of his scores on the MCAT placed him in the eighty-ninth percentile, well above the average of regular admittees.

Despite these impressive credentials, Bakke was denied admission to Davis — and to all the other schools to which he applied. There were apparently two main reasons for his lack of success. The first was his age, which was above that of the typical applicant and which some schools explicitly cited as their reason for rejecting him. The second, which particularly applied to Davis, was that Bakke had completed his application rather late (in January 1973). By the time he was interviewed by Davis (in March), many acceptance letters had already been mailed, and only thirty-seven seats remained in the 1973 entering class.

Bakke reapplied to Davis in the fall of 1973. In the meantime, he had become increasingly concerned about the possibility that the school was operating a separate special admissions program for which he, as a nonminority, was not eligible. In July 1973 he wrote to Dr. George Lowrey, chairman of the admissions committee, expressing his belief that

Applicants chosen to be our doctors should be those presenting the best qualifications. . . . [B]ut I am convinced that a significant fraction of every current medical class is judged by a separate criterion. I am referring to quotas, open or covert, for racial minorities. . . . I realize that the rationale for these quotas is that they attempt to atone for past racial discrimination. But instituting a new racial bias, in favor of minorities, is not a just solution.[18]

In late September 1973 Bakke learned that he would not be admitted under the early admissions plan. In January 1974 he contacted a San Francisco attorney, Reynold H. Colvin, who agreed to represent him. In early April 1974 Bakke received a form letter informing him of his final rejection. He thereupon resolved to bring a lawsuit against the Davis Medical School.

The Supreme Court's Initial Encounter with Affirmative Action

In January 1974 when Bakke met Colvin for the first time, Colvin informed him that the Supreme Court was about to decide a case involving a white law student who had been rejected by the University of Washington Law School. The plaintiff in the case, Marco DeFunis, Jr., believed he had been unfairly displaced by minority applicants whose qualifications were not as strong as his own. Colvin suggested that Bakke postpone his lawsuit against the Davis Medical School until the *DeFunis* decision was handed down.

When the Supreme Court decision in *DeFunis* was issued, however, it proved to be a nondecision. In 1971, at the commencement of his lawsuit against the University of Washington, DeFunis had obtained a court order admitting him to law school pending the outcome of the case. By the time the Supreme Court was ready to decide the case, in April 1974, DeFunis was in his final quarter of school. The Supreme Court seized upon this fact to decide, by a 5-to-4 majority, that the case was "moot" and did not need to be decided "on the merits."[19]

Since the *DeFunis* decision provided little guidance to the Court's views on the subject of affirmative action — let alone a definitive resolution of the issue — it was clearly appropriate for Bakke to proceed with his suit. On June 20, 1974, Bakke and his attorney filed their complaint in California state court. The exceedingly difficult issue of the constitutional validity of affirmative action in professional school admissions was on its way back to the Supreme Court.

Affirmative Action and the Equal Protection Clause

The constitutional basis of Bakke's challenge to the Davis special admissions program was the Equal Protection Clause of the Fourteenth Amendment. The clause stipulates that "No state shall . . . deny to any person within its jurisdiction the equal protection of the laws." The gist of Bakke's lawsuit was the allegation that when the Davis Medical School classified applicants into minority and nonminority categories, and precluded him from competing for any of the seats allocated to minority applicants, it had denied him his constitutional right to "the equal protection of the laws."

In the spring of 1978, four years after the *Bakke* case was originally filed, the Supreme Court handed down its decision. The case had provoked an exceptional amount of discussion and negotiation within the Court. The intensity and complexity of the Court's internal debate was reflected in the Court's decision, which, when it was announced, consisted of a complicated set of interlocking judgments. The Court's decision was a vivid reminder that the issue of affirmative action is second to none in complexity and emotional content.

The *Bakke* Case in the Lower Courts

The posture of the case as it came up from the lower courts was as follows: The California Superior Court for Yolo County — the trial court — had concluded that the special admissions program of the Davis Medical School did violate the Fourteenth Amendment. However, the trial court declined to issue an injunction ordering Bakke's immediate admission to medical school.[20]

Until the trial court held that the special admissions program of the Davis Medical School was unconstitutional, the *Bakke* case had received little attention from anyone but the immediate participants. Once the trial court issued its decision, however, the case was transformed into a *cause célèbre*. A clear indication of the new importance of the case was the fact that the California Supreme Court ordered the case brought directly to itself, bypassing the California Court of Appeals, to which it ordinarily would have gone.

The decision of the California Supreme Court was issued on September 16, 1976, and was a complete victory for Allan Bakke.[21] The Court held (1) that the Davis special admissions program was unconstitutional, (2) that Davis was enjoined from taking race into consideration in the admissions process, and (3) that Allan Bakke was entitled to admission to the Medical School.

In early November 1976 the regents of the University of California voted to appeal to the U.S. Supreme Court. On November 15, the U.S. Supreme Court granted the university's request that the order directing that Bakke be admitted to the Medical School be "stayed" pending disposition of the appeal to the U.S. Supreme Court. On February 22, 1977, the Supreme Court granted certiorari in the *Bakke* case.

It was now almost five years since Allan Bakke had initially applied to medical school. Because the U.S. Supreme Court had stayed the decision of the California Supreme Court ordering that he be admitted to Davis, he still had not succeeded in actually getting into medical school. At least he could console himself, however, that his case — and with it the important issue of the constitutional validity of affirmative action in graduate school admissions — was on its way to the U.S. Supreme Court.

The Burden of Proof in Constitutional Cases

The *Bakke* litigation illustrates the critical importance of the burden of proof in legal cases. The outcome in each of the courts that considered *Bakke* depended in part on how the court chose to allocate the burden of proof on one of the issues in the case.

The trial court held that the Davis special admissions program was unconstitutional but declined to order that Bakke be admitted to the Medical School. The trial judge believed that Bakke should bear the burden of proving that he would have been admitted in the absence of the now-invalidated special admissions program. Since Bakke could not do so, he was not entitled to injunctive relief.

In the California Supreme Court, Bakke's lawyer, Reynold Colvin, argued that once the university's special admissions program had been declared unconstitutional, the burden of proof should have shifted to the university to prove that Bakke would not have been admitted even if the special admissions program had not existed. The California Supreme Court accepted this theory and imposed on the university the burden of proving that the special admissions program had not resulted in Bakke's failure to gain admission.

As we have seen, Bakke's credentials were extremely competitive. It was therefore virtually impossible for the university to "prove" that Bakke would not have been admitted if he had been able to compete for all one hundred seats in the entering class, instead of the eighty-four seats that remained after minority students had been accommodated under the special admissions program. The university conceded that it could not meet its burden of proof. The California Supreme Court thereupon ruled that Bakke was entitled to an order admitting him to the Medical School.

In his opinion for the U.S. Supreme Court, Justice Powell affirmed the decision of the California Supreme Court. Powell noted that the university "had conceded that it could not carry its burden of proving that, but for the existence of its unlawful special admissions program, [Bakke] still would not have been admitted" (438 U.S. at 320). In view of this concession, Powell concluded that Bakke was entitled to an injunction admitting him to the Medical School.

The Supreme Court Gets the *Bakke* Case

The Supreme Court heard oral argument in *Regents of the University of California* v. *Bakke* on October 12, 1977. The petitioner in the case, the University of California, was represented by Archibald Cox, a member of the faculty of the Harvard Law School and former special prosecutor in the Watergate case. Bakke was represented by Reynold Colvin, the lawyer to whom Bakke had entrusted his case in January 1974, when he first resolved to sue the university. Also participating in the oral argument, at the invitation of the Supreme Court, was Wade McCree, solicitor general of the United States. His role was to present the U.S. government's position on the issues before the Court.[22]

The Court held its first conference on the *Bakke* case on October 14, 1977, two days after oral argument. The weeks that followed witnessed a blizzard of memoranda within the Court, as the individual justices formulated and communicated their opinions on the case. In a memorandum dated November 10, Justice Rehnquist argued, with reference to the apparently rigid reservation of sixteen places for minority students, that the Davis special admissions program seems "as difficult to sustain constitutionally as one conceivably could be." He also argued that while "the notion that past societal discrimination justifies these affirmative action programs . . . is not an unappealing rationale," it was, in his view, "ultimately . . . unacceptable."[23]

Not surprisingly, Justice Brennan took a very different view. In a memorandum dated November 23, he disputed the principle that the Constitution is absolutely "color blind," that is, that it cannot tolerate preferential treatment of either blacks or whites. He went on to conclude that "the decision to set aside 16 places out of 100 for *qualified minority* students . . . is [not] an unreasonable one, especially in California where far more than 16% of the population is minority."[24]

The Court had scheduled a conference for December 9 to continue its discussion of the *Bakke* case. As the conference approached, the situation seemed bleak for the justices who supported affirmative action and the Davis program. Justice Powell had circulated a lengthy memo on November 22 in which he concluded that "the Davis special admission program involves the use of an explicit racial classification never before countenanced by this Court." "The fatal flaw in petitioner's preferential program," he said, "is its disregard of individual rights as guaranteed by the Fourteenth Amendment."

Justice Powell's apparent determination to overturn the Davis program meant that the pro-Davis justices could prevail only if they were joined by both Justices Stewart and Blackmun. At the December 9 conference, however, Justice Stewart announced his opposition to the Davis program. Thus, even though Justice Blackmun's position was unknown — he was away from the Court awaiting surgery at the Mayo Clinic in Minnesota — there were apparently five votes to invalidate the Davis program (Rehnquist, Burger, Stevens, Stewart, and Powell). Justice Blackmun eventually joined the pro-Davis justices (Brennan, White, and Marshall). In the meantime, however, the fact that both Powell and Stewart had expressed their opposition to the Davis program meant that the pro-Davis group was left with a maximum of four justices.

The only ray of hope for the pro-Davis justices was the fact that in one passage of his November 22 memorandum, Justice Powell had extolled the virtues of the approach to affirmative action adopted by Harvard College. According to Powell, the Harvard program — in contrast to the Davis program, which set aside a specified number of places for racial minorities — treats race or ethnic background as "a 'plus' in a particular applicant's file, but it does not insulate the individual from fair comparison with all other candidates for the available seats." At the conference, Justice Brennan pointed out that if Justice Powell could support the Harvard program — in which race *could* be taken into account in the admissions process — it meant that Powell did not fully endorse the ruling of the California Supreme Court, which had held, in Brennan's view, that race could *never* be taken into account.

Brennan's argument at the conference elicited a concession from Powell: "I agree," Powell said, "that the judgment [of the California Supreme Court] must be reversed insofar as it enjoins Davis from taking race into account." Powell's concession paved the way for a mixed decision in the *Bakke* case. In the end, the Court invalidated the Davis special admissions program but declined to hold that the Constitution precludes university administrators from taking race into account in the admissions process. The author of the opinion that expressed these sentiments was Justice Powell. The justice who apparently deserves credit for forging this delicate compromise was Justice Brennan.[25]

The Court Announces a Complicated Decision

The Court announced its decision in the *Bakke* case on June 28, 1978. When the decision was issued, observers learned that the Court had divided 4 to 1 to 4 on the outcome of the case. One group of four justices voted to affirm the decision of the California Supreme Court, that is, to hold that the special admissions program was invalid and that Allan Bakke should be admitted to the Davis Medical School. An opinion for this group of justices was prepared by Justice Stevens, who spoke for himself, Chief Justice Burger, and Justices Rehnquist and Stewart.

A second group of four justices voted to reverse the decision of the California Supreme Court. In their opinion, the special admissions program at Davis was constitutional, Allan Bakke was not entitled to an order admitting him to medical school, and Davis and similar institutions should not be precluded, in the future, from taking race into account in making admissions decisions. An opinion for this group of justices was prepared by Justice Brennan, who spoke for himself and Justices White, Blackmun, and Marshall.[26]

Standing in the middle, and bridging the gap between the two groups of justices, was Justice Powell. He wrote an opinion in which he expressed agreement, but only in part, with the "Brennan group" of justices, and also expressed agreement, but only in part, with the "Stevens group" of justices. He thus represented the proverbial "swing vote" in this particularly complicated Supreme Court decision.

Justice Powell agreed with the Stevens group of justices that the special admissions program was invalid and that Allan Bakke was entitled to an order admitting him to the Davis Medical School. The Supreme Court's *Bakke* decision was therefore a personal victory for Allan Bakke and a pronouncement that affirmative action programs such as the one in place at the Davis Medical School were invalid. Justice Powell agreed with the Brennan group of justices, however, that the Constitution does not prohibit institutions from "taking race into account" in the admissions process. The Supreme Court's *Bakke* decision therefore preserved a place for affirmative action in American public policy.

The Powell Opinion in the *Bakke* Case

Justice Powell began his opinion in the *Bakke* case in the conventional way — by reciting the facts. When he moved to the substance of the case, he listed four purposes that Davis said it was trying to accomplish with its special admissions program. Eventually, he focused on two of these purposes.

Davis had told the Court that one of its purposes in operating a special admissions program was to remedy the effects of "past societal discrimination" against blacks and other minorities. Justice Powell was not unsympathetic to this goal. Earlier in his opinion he had noted that "[n]o one denies the regrettable fact that there has been societal discrimination in this country against various racial and ethnic groups."[27] Ultimately, however, he concluded that the concept of "past societal discrimination" was too amorphous to serve as the basis for discrimination against individual nonminority applicants. "[T]he purpose of helping certain groups whom the faculty of the Davis Medical School perceived as victims of 'societal discrimination'," he wrote, "does not justify a classification that imposes disadvantages upon persons like [Bakke], who bear no responsibility for whatever harm the beneficiaries of the special admissions program are thought to have suffered."[28]

The other goal of the special admissions program to which Powell gave particular attention was "the attainment of a diverse student body."[29] Powell argued that "[t]his clearly is a constitutionally permissible goal for an institution of higher education." As Powell approached the case, however, a further question remained before he could conclude that the Davis special admissions program did not deny equal protection. Powell needed to determine whether the *means* that Davis had chosen to accomplish its goal of diversity were truly "necessary," that is, whether there really was no alternative, other than reserving a specific number of places for minority applicants, by which Davis could achieve its stated goal.

Powell concluded that alternatives did exist. Alluding to the Harvard program, he argued that it was possible to take race into account in order to achieve educational diversity without, as Davis had done, setting aside a specific number of places for minority applicants.[30] Powell's ultimate conclusion, therefore, was that, although Allan Bakke had been denied his constitutional right to equal protection of the laws and was entitled to admission to

The *Bakke* Decision
as a Plurality Opinion

As our summary of the *Bakke* decision suggests, the issue of affirmative action produced a highly fragmented Court. In fact, our summary, complicated as it must seem to anyone encountering the case for the first time, is a substantial oversimplification of the Court's actual decision.

In the first place, Justice Powell concluded that the special admissions program was unconstitutional under the Fourteenth Amendment, while the Stevens group concluded that the program was illegal under a congressional statute, Title VI of the Civil Rights Act of 1964. Thus, although Justice Powell and the Stevens group agreed that the Davis program should be invalidated, they had different reasons for reaching this conclusion.

In addition, while Justice Powell agreed with the Brennan group that institutions should be allowed to take race into account, he based his conclusion on different reasons than those articulated by Justice Brennan. In particular, Powell rejected the proposition that past societal discrimination against a racial minority was sufficient to justify remedial measures that included all members of the disadvantaged group.

Thus, the various positions enunciated in the Powell opinion did not constitute a set of majority opinions of the Supreme Court. Rather, they constituted a set of "judgments" of the Court, that is, results supported by Justice Powell's plurality opinion, in which, technically, he spoke only for himself.

Anyone wishing to fully understand this important case should read the fascinating and carefully crafted opinions of the justices in their entirety. Before embarking on this useful adventure, however, be forewarned that the combined length of the various opinions in the case is 156 pages!

the Davis Medical School, the Equal Protection Clause did not preclude Davis or any other educational institution from furthering the substantial interest in educational diversity "by a properly devised admissions program involving the competitive consideration of race and ethnic origin."[31]

Overcoming Inequality:
The New American Dilemma

The path that Justice Powell charts in his *Bakke* opinion through the minefield of affirmative action has become a mainstay among politicians and others who are pressed to explain what they think should be done about the persistent problem of racial inequality in American society. Powell declines to base his support for affirmative action on the need to rectify the effects of "past societal discrimination." Instead, he emphasizes the present and future benefits to all of society of an active policy of inclusion. He goes on to suggest that a principal benefit of affirmative action is the attainment of diversity on college and university campuses. As a means of achieving diversity, he draws a distinction between using "quotas"—which, he says, the Constitution prohibits—and "taking race into account"—which, he says, the Constitution does condone. Not everyone is convinced that the various distinctions propounded by Justice Powell are real. They have nevertheless become standard ingredients of the debate over the wisdom of affirmative action.

In the *Bakke* case, the Supreme Court issued a fractured judgment that the public identified with Justice Powell's conciliatory opinion. Both features of the *Bakke* case—the fractured judgment and the conciliatory opinion— were symbolic, each in its own way, of America's struggle to come to terms with the difficult problem of overcoming racial inequality.

The Aftermath of *Bakke*

Since deciding *Bakke* in 1978, the Supreme Court has not revisited the issue of racial preferences in college and university admissions. However, the Court has decided several other cases involving affirmative action. Most of these cases, like *Bakke*, have produced a splintered Court and clearly advertised the fact that neither the Court nor the country is very close to reaching a consensus on how to deal with the problem of racial inequality.

A majority of the Court has continued to express skepticism about the sufficiency of using past societal discrimination as a justification for affirmative action. In the important recent case of *Richmond v. J. A. Croson Co.,*[32] the Court struck down a municipal "set-aside" program that required prime contractors to award a fixed percentage of their subcontracts to minority-owned businesses. Speaking for the Court, Justice O'Connor said that before they may resort to "race-conscious remedies" for past discrimination, cities and states must identify the alleged discrimination—whether it be their own or that of private parties operating within their jurisdiction—"with some specificity."[33]

Justice O'Connor's opinion in *Croson* clearly indicated that a majority of the Court had lost patience with affirmative action programs that were unsupported by documentary evidence of past discrimination against minorities. Moreover, of the three dissenters in *Croson*, two—Justices Brennan and Marshall—have since left the Court. Therefore, the Court today is less likely than ever to support race-conscious remedies as a way of rectifying generalized past discrimination against minorities.

The future of *Bakke* itself, however, raises separate issues. The Court in *Bakke* cautioned colleges and universities against basing admissions decisions on rigid quotas. Not surprisingly, colleges and universities have taken this admonition to heart. Moreover, complying with the Court's decision has not been difficult, since the Court also explicitly authorized educational institutions to "take race into account."

In retrospect, therefore, the principal effect of Powell's opinion in *Bakke* has been to camouflage the use of race as a criterion in the admissions process and to immunize institutions from lawsuits by nonminority applicants. Ironically, this perception of the effect of the Powell opinion may be one of the few things on which supporters and opponents of affirmative action agree.

The departure of Brennan and Marshall, however, means that *Bakke* itself may be in trouble. Some members of the Court—notably Scalia and Kennedy—are vehemently opposed to the use of race as a criterion for making policy decisions. The fragile "majority" for which Powell spoke in *Bakke* may have collapsed, therefore, and been replaced by a majority unwilling to condone the use of race, even covertly and even as only one factor among many, in the educational admissions process.[34]

As for Allan Bakke himself, the Supreme Court's decision in the case that bears his name ended his long quest to enter medical school. He began his studies at Davis in September 1978, a few months after the Court's decision. He graduated four years later and is now practicing medicine.[35]

Notes

1. William M. Wiecek, "The Witch at the Christening: Slavery and the Constitution's Origins," in Leonard W. Levy and Dennis J. Mahoney (eds.), *The Framing and Ratification of the Constitution* (1987), pp. 167–84.

2. Robert Weisbrot, *Freedom Bound: A History of America's Civil Rights Movement* (1990); Hugh Davis Graham, *The Civil Rights Era: Origins and Development of National Policy, 1960–1972* (1990); Taylor Branch, *Parting the Waters: America in the King Years* (1988); and David J. Garrow, *Bearing the Cross: Martin Luther King, Jr., and the Southern Christian Leadership Conference* (1986).

3. For a provocative and readable analysis of the Supreme Court's recent encounters with race, see J. Harvie Wilkinson III, *From Brown to Bakke: The Supreme Court and School Integration: 1954–1978* (1979).

4. Discussions of *Bakke* and its implications include Allan P. Sindler, *Bakke, DeFunis, and Minority Admissions: The Quest for Equal Opportunity* (1978); Joel Dreyfuss and Charles Lawrence III, *The Bakke Case: The Politics of Inequality* (1979); Terry Eastland and William J. Bennett, *Counting by Race* (1979); Timothy J. O'Neill, *Bakke and the Politics of Equality* (1985); and Bernard Schwartz, *Behind Bakke: Affirmative Action and the Supreme Court* (1988).

5. Executive Order 10925, 26 *Federal Register* 1977 (March 6, 1961); Executive Order 11246, 30 *Federal Register* 12319 (September 24, 1965).

6. Our discussion will focus on discrimination against blacks. It is well to remember, however, that societal discrimination has allegedly restricted other groups —including women, ethnic minorities, racial minorities other than blacks, and Native Americans—and that many affirmative action programs either target or include these other groups. For a general introduction to the topic of affirmative action, see Ger-

trude Ezorsky, *Racism and Justice: The Case for Affirmative Action* (1992); and Russell Nieli (ed.), *Racial Preference and Racial Justice: The New Affirmative Action Controversy* (1991). For an exploration of the personal and constitutional dimensions of affirmative action, see Stephen L. Carter, *Reflections of an Affirmative Action Baby* (1991). For a discussion of affirmative action which draws on philosophical and constitutional sources, see Michael Rosenfeld, *Affirmative Action and Justice* (1991). For discussions of employment discrimination and affirmative action, see Melvin I. Urofsky, *A Conflict of Rights: The Supreme Court and Affirmative Action* (1991); Herman Belz, *Equality Transformed: A Quarter-Century of Affirmative Action* (1991); and Kathanne W. Greene, *Affirmative Action and Principles of Justice* (1989).

7. Lyndon B. Johnson, *The Vantage Point: Perspectives on the Presidency, 1963–1969* (1971), p. 166.

8. Wilkinson, *From Brown to Bakke*, p. 267.

9. O'Neill, *Bakke and the Politics of Equality*, p. 56.

10. Recent studies of race and inequality in American society are cited in Chapter 6, note 33.

11. *Regents of University of California* v. *Bakke*, 438 U.S. 265, 403 (1978).

12. Id. at 407.

13. 163 U.S. 537, 559 (1896).

14. There is, of course, a rejoinder to this argument. It was articulated by Justice Marshall in his opinion in the *Bakke* case: "It is unnecessary in 20th-century America to have individual Negroes demonstrate that they have been victims of racial discrimination; the racism of our society has been so pervasive that none, regardless of wealth or position, has managed to escape its impact. The experience of Negroes in America has been different in kind, not just in degree, from that of other ethnic groups." 438 U.S. at 400.

15. The arguments against affirmative action are forcefully presented in Thomas Sowell, *Civil Rights: Rhetoric or Reality?* (1984); and Thomas Sowell, *Preferential Policies: An International Perspective* (1990).

16. For a discussion of the *Bakke* case that emphasizes this point, see Dreyfuss and Lawrence, *The Bakke Case*.

17. The facts of the *Bakke* case are recounted in several places, including the Supreme Court's decision in the case.

18. The text of Bakke's letter is reprinted in Dreyfuss and Lawrence, *The Bakke Case*, p. 14.

19. *DeFunis* v. *Odegaard*, 416 U.S. 312 (1974).

20. The text of the trial court's judgment is reprinted in the Supreme Court's *Bakke* decision, 438 U.S. 265, 409 n. 2 (1978).

21. *Bakke* v. *Regents of University of California*, 553 P.2d 1152 (Cal. Sup. Ct. 1976).

22. Oral argument in the *Bakke* case is recounted in Schwartz, *Behind Bakke*, pp. 47–54.

23. The various memoranda circulated by the justices in the *Bakke* case are reprinted in Schwartz, *Behind Bakke*, Appendices A–E.

24. Emphasis in the original.

25. The events that transpired at the December 9 conference are recounted in Schwartz, *Behind Bakke*, pp. 93–98.

26. Justices White, Blackmun, and Marshall also each wrote a separate opinion.

27. 438 U.S. at 296 n. 36.

28. Id. at 310.

29. Id. at 311.

30. Id. at 316–19.

31. Id. at 320.

32. 109 S.Ct. 706 (1989).

33. Id. at 727.

34. For a sample of the views of Justices Scalia and Kennedy, see their concurring opinions in *Richmond* v. *J. A. Croson Co.* (1989), and Kennedy's dissenting opinion, in which Scalia joins, in *Metro Broadcasting, Inc.* v. *FCC* (1990).

35. Schwartz, *Behind Bakke*, p. 163.

PART III

The Supreme Court in American Democracy

T he cases examined in Part II show that in recent years the Supreme Court has assumed responsibility for resolving a broad array of highly complex and volatile questions of public policy. From its flag salute decision in 1943 to its flag burning decisions in 1989 and 1990, from its school desegregation decision in 1954 to its affirmative action decisions in the 1970s and 1980s, from its school prayer and abortion decisions in the 1960s and 1970s to its school prayer and abortion decisions in 1992, the Supreme Court has become deeply embroiled in some of the most contentious and intractable issues in American politics.

The Supreme Court's involvement in deciding these and other issues has been accompanied by substantial controversy. We can point to at least two reasons why. First, of course, the issues themselves have not been easy ones. They have gone to the core of what it means to be an American and what it means to live in American society. Second, they have generated sharp divisions among the American people and have provoked not only impassioned debate but also widespread political action.

Given the types of issues that the Supreme Court has agreed to decide in recent years, controversy is inevitable. When the Supreme Court agrees to resolve a difficult issue of public policy, however, the controversy that results has an additional dimension. In a political democracy, most such issues are resolved by decision makers who are accountable, through the electoral process, to the people. The Supreme Court, however, consists of nine justices who are not elected and who enjoy what amounts to life tenure in their positions. When the Court decides that citizens have a constitutionally protected right to advocate the overthrow of government or to obtain an abortion, or that government is prohibited by the Constitution from sponsoring prayer in schools or punishing those who burn the flag, it is permissible to ask whether the Supreme Court is or should be authorized to decide such questions. In doing so, the Court would seem to be violating the fundamental principle that policy decisions in a political democracy should be made by public officials who are ultimately accountable to the people.

Part III looks directly at the question of whether the unelected Supreme Court is or should be authorized to craft enforceable decisions on policy issues. Only after this question is confronted and resolved can we rest assured that we have achieved an informed position on the role of the Supreme Court in American democracy.

Each of the next four chapters explores a different option for reconciling the Supreme Court's power of judicial review with fundamental principles of American democracy. In Chapter 12, we look at various external restraints on the Supreme Court. Supreme Court justices are not altogether immune from the political pressures that influence the behavior of other decision makers in American democracy. In Chapter 12, we examine various mechanisms for applying external pressure on the Supreme Court and ask whether these mechanisms constitute an adequate check on the policy-making pretensions of the Supreme Court.

In Chapter 13, we focus on the appointment process. One way to change the political orientation of the Supreme Court is to reconstitute the Court with justices whose views are different from those of the justices they have replaced. In a sense, therefore, the appointment process is a form of "internal restraint" on Supreme Court decision making. It is also a mechanism whereby the views of a current majority of the American people can find expression in Supreme Court decisions. Chapter 13 explores whether the appointment process is an effective mechanism for subjecting the Supreme Court to majoritarian political control.

Chapter 14 deals with normative justifications of judicial review. The premise of the chapter is that the tension between judicial review and majoritarian principles is not necessarily an unhealthy or unwelcome feature of American democracy. We reopen the question of what it means to describe a country as a democracy, and we argue that the United States is an example of a "constitutional democracy," rather than a "majoritarian democracy." We then discuss various theories that claim to provide an affirmative defense of judicial review.

Chapter 15 examines whether and how often the Supreme Court actually contradicts the will of the majority. We discuss trends in nationwide public opinion on various issues that have come before the Supreme Court for decision. We then ask whether it is factually accurate to describe particular Supreme Court decisions as examples of countermajoritarian judicial policy making. We conclude that the Supreme Court may not contradict the preferences of a majority of the American people quite as often as either its supporters or its detractors sometimes allege.

Chapter 16 offers concluding remarks on the role of the Supreme Court in American democracy.

CHAPTER 12

External Restraints on the
Supreme Court

T he Supreme Court wields great power. At the same time, its members are not regularly or directly accountable to the people. In a democracy, such an institution is unusual. Few institutions in American democracy possess as much political power, while simultaneously enjoying as much political independence, as the United States Supreme Court.

It would be wholly incorrect to conclude, however, that the Court operates in a political vacuum. On the contrary, it is but one component of the complicated system of checks and balances devised by the framers of the American Constitution. The Court and its members enjoy extraordinary political independence. Because Supreme Court justices are not elected, they are free from one of the key restraints on political leaders in a democratic system. Even so, the Supreme Court and its members are not wholly unaccountable to the people and institutions with which they share the political arena.

Our focus in this chapter is on external restraints on the Supreme Court —those political pressures that originate outside the Court itself and may influence the decision-making behavior of the Court or of individual justices. The discussion is divided into two parts. In Section I, we examine a variety of informal restraints on the Supreme Court. By *informal restraints* we mean those methods of exerting pressure on the Court which are not explicitly or formally authorized by the Constitution. In Section II, we turn to a set of restraints that are more formal in nature.

Informal Restraints on the Supreme Court

There are a surprising number of informal ways in which those outside the Supreme Court can apprise the Court of their negative views and feelings. They range from public attacks on the Court by powerful political figures to grassroots resistance to Court decisions by people who cannot abide the policy choices promulgated by a majority of the justices. Each form of political pressure represents, in its own way, a challenge to the Court's decision-making authority.

Public Reactions from Political Leaders

The United States, we are often reminded, is a "free country." One manifestation of that freedom is the fact that prominent politicians and other influential citizens are at liberty to criticize the justices of the Supreme Court, the Court as an institution, and the Court's decisions. The Supreme Court probably receives less criticism than some other institutions, but it does not escape entirely.

For obvious reasons, the president's views on the Supreme Court may carry special weight. In 1937, as we have seen, President Roosevelt proposed to enlarge the Court to fifteen members. He recommended adding one justice to the Court for every sitting justice over the age of seventy. Defending his plan in a "fireside chat" to the nation, Roosevelt said that "[w]e have . . . reached the point as a Nation where we must take action to save the Constitution from the Court and the Court from itself." Sharpening his political rhetoric, Roosevelt went on to say that his plan to appoint additional justices to the Court would bring into the judicial system "new and younger blood" and would "save our National Constitution from hardening of the judicial arteries."[1]

More recently, President Nixon used the occasion of his nomination of Justices Powell and Rehnquist to express his opinion of the Court's approach to issues of criminal justice. He argued that "some Court decisions have gone too far in the past in weakening the peace forces as against the criminal forces in our society."[2] Nixon's remarks were an extension of a theme he stressed throughout his 1968 presidential campaign — that the Supreme Court under Earl Warren had been too lenient on criminals.[3]

In the 1980s President Reagan criticized the Supreme Court on several occasions. However, the remarks made by Reagan's attorney general, Edwin Meese, drew the most attention. In his 1985 speech calling for a "jurisprudence of original intention," Meese warned that "a drift back toward the radical egalitarianism and expansive civil libertarianism of the Warren court would . . . be a threat to the notion of limited but energetic government."[4] In other speeches during this period, Meese argued that the Supreme Court's interpretation of the Constitution was not entitled to the same deference as the Constitution itself.[5]

Presidents are not the only political figures, of course, who express their opinion of the Supreme Court or its decisions. Some recent Court decisions have received extensive media coverage and been lavishly praised or roundly condemned by affected segments of the society. The Court's decision in *Roe v. Wade*, for instance, was followed by a flood of statements from religious leaders (decrying the Court's decision) and from leaders of the women's movement (extolling it).[6] All of the Court's controversial decisions — on abortion, school prayer, desegregation, busing, criminal procedure, the death penalty, and affirmative action—have elicited strong public reactions from interest groups and their leaders.[7]

The Supreme Court and the American People

The frequency with which elected officials and other political leaders criticize the Supreme Court indicates that Supreme Court decisions often provoke strong reactions from the public itself. Public reactions can take various forms. First, opinion polls may reveal how the public in general feels about the Court and its decisions. Second, public reaction may be sufficiently intense to produce actual demonstrations for or against the Court's decisions. Third, public reaction can become more ominous and manifest itself in the form of intimidation of members of the judiciary. Finally, the public can react to Supreme Court decisions by resisting or ignoring the Court's pronouncements.

Public Opinion and the Supreme Court

The relationship between public opinion and the Supreme Court is in fact rather poorly understood. It is not always clear how the public feels about the Court or why it feels the way it does. Nor is the impact of public opinion on Supreme Court decision making very clearcut.

The content of public attitudes toward the Supreme Court presents the first mystery. Several studies over the years have shown that the public extends to the Supreme Court a measure of what is known as diffuse support, that is, support for the Court as an institution and for the basic legitimacy of its decision-making role in the political system. At the same time, there is reason to be skeptical about the breadth and depth of such support. Polls consistently show that large numbers of citizens are uninformed about the Supreme Court, its members, and its work.[8] Moreover, even among citizens who do have an opinion about the Court, approval of the Court as an institution is often contingent upon approval of its decisions in specific cases. Many of the Court's supporters, in other words, are at best "fair weather friends."[9]

Even when we have a clear picture of the content of public opinion about the Supreme Court, we cannot always know what significance to attribute to the patterns that emerge. Certainly the justices are aware of the content of public opinion and sometimes take it into account—at least when it suits their purposes—in deciding cases. A good example is *Gregg* v. *Georgia*, the Court's 1976 decision upholding revised state statutes authorizing capital punishment for some offenses. In one of the opinions in the case, Justice Stewart concluded that the death penalty for murder did not constitute "cruel and unusual punishment." As support for his conclusion, he cited various indications of "society's endorsement of the death penalty for murder," including public opinion polls and state referenda.[10]

Individual justices, then, are aware of the content of public opinion on specific issues, but it is not usually clear whether public opinion has actually influenced a justice's thinking or is instead part of the process of rationalizing a preexisting view. Not surprisingly, those justices whose views are supported by public opinion are the ones who actually cite the results of polls. Justices whose views are out of step with public opinion are likely either to maintain a studied silence on the subject or to argue that it is improper for the Court to allow public opinion to influence its decisions.[11]

It is also unclear how often public opinion exerts an influence on the Court as a whole, as opposed to individual justices. Studies of the relationship between the Court's decisions and public opinion have found that the Court agrees with public opinion about 62 to 63 percent of the time.[12] Other studies, however, have found similar levels of agreement on policy issues between the American public, on the one hand, and Congress and the president, on the other. Somewhat surprisingly, then, it appears that the Supreme Court is neither more nor less influenced by public opinion than other institutions, including those that are explicitly designed to be responsive to the public.[13]

The fact that Congress and the president are no more responsive to public opinion than the Supreme Court raises interesting questions of democratic theory. It also raises the possibility that levels of agreement between the American people and their decision-making institutions, including the Supreme Court, may be a matter of sheer coincidence rather than cause and effect. Researchers have encountered persistent difficulties in determining whether public opinion actually influences decision makers, or whether agreement between public opinion and decision makers is a function of other mechanisms, including chance. These and other problems have impeded our ability to come to firm conclusions about the impact of public opinion on Supreme Court decision making.[14]

We will return to the question of public opinion and Supreme Court decision making in Chapter 15. For now we must admit that we do not have particularly advanced knowledge of whether public opinion exerts an influence on the Supreme Court, and if so, when and how it may do so.[15]

Other Public Reactions to Supreme Court Decisions

Ordinarily, our only insight into how the public views the Supreme Court and its decisions derives from opinion polls and public statements by political leaders. On occasion, however, public reaction to Supreme Court decisions moves beyond the expression of opinions. *Roe* v. *Wade* is, of course, one of the Court's most controversial recent decisions. It has aroused public feelings so intensely that demonstrations by both pro-life and pro-choice groups occur every year, on the anniversary of the Court's decision, on the grounds of the Supreme Court.

On occasion, public reaction to Supreme Court decisions has taken the form of attempted intimidation of members of the judiciary. Such attempts are rare, but they do occur. Following its decision in *Brown* v. *Board of Education* in 1954, for example, the Supreme Court delegated responsibility for implementing the ruling to U.S. District Judges in the southern states. Not surprisingly, these judges were subjected to intense pressure and occasional intimidation from their local communities.[16]

Supreme Court justices are well insulated from direct public pressure. If they want to know what the public thinks about their decisions, however, all they have to do is read their mail or venture outside the confines of the Court. In the wake of *Roe* v. *Wade*, Justice Blackmun, author of the Court's decision, received numerous death threats by phone and mail and was greeted by anti-abortion pickets during a speaking engagement in Iowa.[17]

Grassroots Resistance to Supreme Court Decisions

A final informal, but sometimes very effective, political mechanism for exerting pressure on the Supreme Court is for the public simply to resist or ignore the Court's decision. A rapidly growing literature documents the impact of Supreme Court decisions on the lower courts and local communities.[18] Especially well documented is the impact of the Court's decisions in the areas of reapportionment,[19] school desegregation,[20] criminal procedure,[21] abortion,[22] and school prayer.[23] While some studies have found expeditious and thorough compliance with the Court's decisions, most studies — perhaps because they tend to deal with exceptionally controversial areas of Supreme Court decision making — have found substantial resistance and delay.

Conclusion

A variety of informal mechanisms may exert pressure on the Supreme Court. They include public criticism of the Court by the president and other political leaders and grassroots resistance to the Court's decisions by local communities. Not all of these mechanisms for pressuring the Court are equally legitimate. At one time or another, however, all have been used.

We do not know whether any or all of these mechanisms have had any actual impact on the decision-making behavior of the Supreme Court. The framers designed the Court to be an institution capable of withstanding political pressure. Moreover, most of its members are exceptionally strong-willed and independent. The Court and its members are therefore, well suited to resist the pressures directed at them from the remainder of the political system.

Informal restraints, however, represent only a portion of the pressures to which the Court is subjected. Before we reach a final judgment about the relationship of the Court to its political environment, it is important to examine the many formal restraints on the Court.

Formal Restraints on the Supreme Court

Numerous formal mechanisms for restraining the Supreme Court are available to various political actors, and in particular, Congress and the president. Each of them is basically legitimate; that is, each of them is either explicitly authorized by the Constitution or at least not precluded by it. All these mechanisms are part of the elaborate system of checks and balances devised by the framers of the Constitution in order, as James Madison said in his "Federalist No. 51," to "oblige [the government] to control itself."[24]

Even though all the various formal mechanisms for restraining the Supreme Court are basically legitimate, they differ considerably in terms of their probable effectiveness in actually restraining the Court. It is therefore useful to distinguish between minor restraints, and major restraints. Let us begin by examining various methods of restraining the Supreme Court whose effectiveness is open to question. Following that, we turn to other, more important formal mechanisms of external political control of the Supreme Court.

Minor Mechanisms of Political Control

Congress and the president have at their disposal several minor mechanisms for exerting political pressure on the Supreme Court. Some of these mechanisms are explicitly authorized by the Constitution, and others are available because the Constitution is silent on key issues relating to the Supreme Court. Whenever such a constitutional vacuum exists — that is, whenever the Constitution does not prohibit a particular action from being taken — Congress and the president may see an opportunity to flex their political muscles.

Members and Majorities

The Constitution says nothing about the size of the Supreme Court. Congress or the president is therefore free to propose changes in the size of the Court. The Judiciary Act of 1789 specified that the Court would consist of six members. Over the next few decades, however, the size of the Court was enlarged or reduced — from a minimum of five to a maximum of ten — on several occasions. In 1869 Congress decided that the Supreme Court should consist of nine members. The Court's membership has remained at that level ever since.[25]

The most celebrated attempt to manipulate the size of the Court was President Roosevelt's 1937 Court-packing proposal. In response to the Court's stubborn refusal to give constitutional approval to the legislative initiatives of the New Deal, President Roosevelt proposed to enlarge the Court to fifteen members. In July 1937 the Senate rejected his plan. In the meantime, the Court had begun to show signs of a more favorable attitude toward New Deal legislation. Thus, Roosevelt's "threat" to enlarge the Court, even though it was never carried out, may have had some impact on the justices' behavior.

The Constitution is also silent on the question of the size of the majority among the justices which is necessary to reach a valid decision. One method by which the president or Congress can express disapproval of Supreme Court decision making, therefore, is to alter — or to threaten to alter — the number of justices needed to constitute a majority. On several occasions legislation has been introduced in Congress to prohibit the Court from achieving certain types of outcomes (e.g., invalidation of a state or federal law) unless it does so by an extraordinary majority of justices (e.g., six or seven out of nine). To date, however, none of this legislation has ever been enacted.[26]

Congressional Control of the Court's Budget

Congress also controls the operating budget of the federal courts, and it has something to say about federal judicial salaries. The Constitution stipulates (in Article III, Section 1) that the salaries of federal judges "shall not be diminished during their Continuance in Office." Congress, however, may refuse to grant raises and may do so, if it wishes, to express its displeasure with particular judicial rulings. In 1964, in response to the Supreme Court's reapportionment decisions, Congress purposely increased the salaries of lower federal court judges more than those of Supreme Court justices. In general, however, Congress has not chosen to use its power over the Court's budget and the justices' salaries as a punitive weapon.[27]

Impeachment

Congress possesses one additional formal but minor method of political control — impeachment. Under Article II, Section 4 of the Constitution, Supreme Court justices, like "[t]he President, Vice President and all civil Officers of the United States," are subject to removal from office "on Impeachment for, and Conviction of, Treason, Bribery, or other high Crimes and Misdemeanors." The full process involves impeachment by a majority vote of the House of Representatives (Article I, Section 2, Para. 5), followed by conviction in the Senate by a two-thirds vote of the members who are present (Article I, Section 3, Para. 6).

It may seem curious to classify impeachment as a "minor" method of political control of the Supreme Court. Obviously, impeachment of a Supreme Court justice would not be a minor matter for either the justice or the Court. Precisely because it is such a drastic step, however, impeachment is not regarded as a particularly useful method of political control.

Only once in history has the threat to impeach a Supreme Court justice ever matured into congressional action. Samuel Chase, an ardent Federalist, was impeached by Jeffersonian Republicans in the House of Representatives in 1804. When the case moved to the Senate in early 1805, however, it proved impossible for Republicans to muster the necessary two-thirds majority for conviction and removal from office. Republican leaders had contended that impeachment "must be considered a means of keeping the courts in reasonable harmony with the will of the nation, as expressed through Congress and the executive."[28] Chase's acquittal permanently discredited the use of impeachment to intimidate justices whose political views arouse congressional hostility.

This is not to say, of course, that tentative attempts to impeach Supreme Court justices do not occur. Numerous efforts were made to impeach Chief Justice Warren, although none of them ever resulted in a vote in Congress. The most recent impeachment campaign was orchestrated by the Nixon Administration (in the wake of Senate rejection in 1969 and 1970 of Supreme Court nominees Clement Haynsworth and Harrold Carswell) and was aimed at Justice Douglas. The effort included a call for Douglas's impeachment on the floor of the House in April 1970 by then House Minority Leader Gerald Ford. It reached the stage of hearings by a Subcommittee of the House Judiciary Committee, but the Subcommittee found no grounds for impeachment, and the matter was allowed to die.[29]

Impeachment is clearly a potent weapon of political control of the Supreme Court. However, its extreme character renders it unsuitable for use in cases where a justice or group of justices is perceived as being out of step — even seriously out of step — with the will of the majority. Impeachment represents a strong statement by the people of their disagreement with the policy-making behavior of a public official. The framers of the Constitution, however, did not intend it to be a routine method of popular control of the Supreme Court, nor has it been treated this way by subsequent generations.[30]

Major Mechanisms of Political Control

The Constitution specifies several formal mechanisms of political control of the Supreme Court that may be classified as having major importance. They represent potent alternatives whereby the American people and their elected representatives can exert pressure on the Supreme Court in response to what they perceive to be objectionable judicial decisions.

Not surprisingly, most of the formal methods of political control find their source in the constitutional powers and political resources of the president and Congress. These two "political branches" of American government inherit the lion's share of responsibility for restraining the Court.

The president and Congress are in a special position to restrain the Supreme Court because they are explicitly authorized by the Constitution to exercise certain Court-curbing powers. In addition, and perhaps more importantly, the Supreme Court must never forget that enforcement of its decisions almost always requires some degree of cooperation from the president or Congress, or both. As Alexander Hamilton wrote some two hundred years ago in "Federalist No. 78," the judiciary "has no influence over either the sword or the purse." Those powers — the executive power to field armies and organize police forces and the legislative power to collect taxes and spend money — are in the hands of the president and the Congress. As a result, it is no exaggeration to conclude, as Hamilton did, that the judiciary "must ultimately depend upon the aid of the executive arm even for the efficacy of its judgments."[31]

Presidential Cooperation and Supreme Court Decision Making

The Constitution empowers the president to "take Care that the Laws be faithfully executed" (Article II, Section 3). The president's basic power to enforce the law, however, necessarily enables the president to enforce the law less "faithfully" — that is, less consistently or less vigorously — than some would like. On occasion, presidents have undermined the effectiveness of a Supreme Court decision — or for that matter of a congressional law — by adopting a tepid approach to enforcement.

President Jackson's famous reaction to an 1832 decision of the Marshall Court nicely illustrates that presidential cooperation may be crucial to implementing Supreme Court decisions. "John Marshall has made his decision," Jackson is supposed to have said. "Now let him enforce it." In the end, Marshall did not need Jackson. At other times, the Court's dependence on the president has been more evident.[32]

Before and during the Civil War, for instance, President Lincoln was frequently at odds with Chief Justice Taney over the nature of presidential obligations to enforce the law. Both in his debates with Stephen Douglas during the Senatorial campaign in 1858 and in his first inaugural address, Lincoln questioned the rightness and the binding force of the Supreme Court's decision in *Dred Scott* v. *Sandford*.[33] Early in the Civil War itself, Taney and Lincoln clashed over the power of the president to suspend the writ of habeas corpus in emergency situations.[34]

A more recent example of the delicate relationship between the president and the Supreme Court is provided by President Eisenhower's reaction to *Brown* v. *Board of Education*. The president was not enthusiastic about the decision and gave it only qualified support in his public statements. Eisenhower's failure to unequivocally endorse the *Brown* ruling contributed to already grave difficulties of enforcement. Eventually, in 1957, Eisenhower was forced to dispatch troops to Little Rock, Arkansas, to assist the federal courts in enforcing orders to desegregate the city's schools. The president's earlier ambivalent reaction to *Brown* had helped to create a situation where federal military intervention was necessary.[35]

Presidential noncooperation is not always fatal to effectuating Supreme Court rulings, but it may have a significant negative impact. The president is in a unique position to enhance or undermine public confidence in the Supreme Court. When the president even hints that he is opposed to what the Supreme Court has done, the task of implementing the Court's decision becomes substantially more difficult.

Congressional Cooperation and
Supreme Court Decision Making

The Supreme Court is dependent not only on the president, but also on Congress. In fact, Congress may employ a variety of strategies to express its displeasure with the Court. One particular form of congressional leverage, however, resembles that which the president possesses: Congress can undermine the Supreme Court simply by failing to cooperate with the Court in implementing its decisions.

A favorite congressional strategy for undermining particular Supreme Court decisions is to prohibit the use of federal funds to pay for constitutionally protected activities. In 1973, for instance, the Court in *Roe* v. *Wade* upheld the right of women to choose to have abortions. Since 1976, however, Congress has imposed restrictions on the use of federal funds to reimburse women for the cost of abortions under the Medicaid program. In 1980 the Supreme Court by a 5–4 margin upheld these restrictions—known as the Hyde Amendment—in *Harris* v. *McRae.*[36]

Congressional reaction to court-ordered busing in school desegregation cases offers an additional example of the importance of legislative control of the purse. The Supreme Court ordered an end to school segregation in *Brown* v. *Board of Education* in 1954 and endorsed the use of busing to achieve integration in *Swann* v. *Charlotte-Mecklenburg Board of Education* in 1971. Beginning in the mid-1970s, however, legislation was repeatedly introduced in Congress, in the form of riders to appropriations bills, which prohibited the expenditure of federal funds in support of busing orders.[37]

Of course, congressional and presidential reactions to Supreme Court decisions affecting minority rights have not always been unhelpful. On occasion, the coordinate branches have provided crucial support for Court decisions. Congress agreed to use its funding power to support rather than oppose the Court when, in the Civil Rights Act of 1964, it provided for the withholding of federal funds from school districts that were not in compliance with the Court's desegregation decision in *Brown* v. *Board of Education*. The Court's decision had produced very little actual desegregation between 1954 and 1964. Following the congressional action, however, the pace of desegregation picked up considerably.[38]

In addition to inducing greater grassroots compliance with *Brown*, congressional passage of the Civil Rights Act also had a positive impact on decisional outcomes in lower federal courts. One study shows that, in their approach to desegregation cases, such courts became significantly more liberal in 1965–1969 than they had been in 1960–1964.[39]

As these examples indicate, Congress and the president are not uniformly unsupportive of the Supreme Court. Indeed, the Court enjoys the support of the political branches the overwhelming proportion of the time. On occasion, however, successful implementation of a Supreme Court decision may be contingent on the cooperation of Congress or the president, or both. When such cooperation is withheld, the Supreme Court's ability to gain compliance with its decisions may be greatly diminished.[40]

Congressional Reversal of
Supreme Court Decisions

Declining to cooperate with the Supreme Court is only one way in which the political branches can exert pressure on the Court. The political branches, especially Congress, have additional options for expressing their displeasure with the Court. We must remember that the Supreme Court is only one component of a complicated political system. On issues with a highly charged political content, the political branches may consider playing "hardball" with the Supreme Court by resorting to various direct mechanisms for reversing the Court.

In this section, we look at ways in which Congress can use its ordinary legislative powers to reverse or circumvent a Supreme Court decision. We look first at the options available to Congress to reverse a Supreme Court decision that is based not on the Constitution, but on the Court's power to construe statutory language. After that, we examine the options available to Congress to reverse one of the Supreme Court's constitutional decisions.

CONGRESSIONAL REVERSAL OF STATUTORY DECISIONS A substantial proportion of the Supreme Court's decisions every year involves interpretation of a statute — usually a congressional statute — rather than interpretation of the Constitution itself. Such decisions are examples of the Court's exercise of its power of statutory construction, rather than its power of judicial review. In such cases the Court gives meaning to statutory language which, for one reason or another, is ambiguous or unclear. Because the Court has not based its decision on the Constitution, but has simply made a choice about what Congress must have meant when it drafted particular statutory language, Congress is free to disagree with the Court's interpretation and to redraft the statute in question. In doing so, Congress can make its policy position unmistakably clear and can foreclose the courts from adopting any alternative interpretations of the meaning of the statute.

Congress may exercise its option to redraft a statute regardless of the political or ideological basis of its disagreement with the Court. Congress may feel the Court has been too conservative or too liberal in its interpretation of statutory language, or it may disagree with the Court for reasons that have nothing to do with ideology. As long as the Court has reached its decision by construing statutory language, rather than interpreting the Constitution, Congress is free to react to the Court's decision by ordinary legislative means.

Yates v. *United States* is a good example of a "liberal" decision that Congress could have reversed by enacting new legislation. As we saw in Chapter 7, the Supreme Court decided the *Yates* case by narrowly construing the language of the Smith Act. The Court's purpose in doing so was to "avoid" the constitutional issue of whether the Smith Act, as written, violated the First Amendment. The Court's narrow construction of the Smith Act, however, made it far more difficult for the government to successfully prosecute members of the Communist party, because the Court held that such defendants could be convicted only if they had advocated concrete action to overthrow the government. After the *Yates* decision, Congress had the option of re-passing the Smith Act to make it clear that it applied to all forms of advocacy, and not merely advocacy of action, as the Court had said in its decision. Had Congress done so, the Court would have been faced with the question of whether the Smith Act, as newly rewritten by Congress, violated the Constitution. In fact, Congress failed to act, and the Court's construction of the Smith Act, as enunciated in *Yates*, prevailed.

Yates is an example of a case in which the Court narrowly construed an act of Congress for the purpose of giving added protection to constitutional rights. In the last decade, however, as the Supreme Court has become more conservative, the Court has more frequently given a restrictive construction to congressional legislation which is designed to confer rights, not abridge them. Congress is then presented with the question of whether it wants to re-pass the legislation to make it clear that the law has a broader scope than the politically conservative Supreme Court has said it does.

The most common situation that has arisen is that Congress has taken exception to the Supreme Court's restrictive interpretation of civil rights legislation.[41] The Civil Rights Act of 1990, for instance, was in part a response to the Court's decision in *Wards Cove Packing Co.* v. *Antonio* (1989), which made it more difficult for minority plaintiffs to establish employment discrimination claims under Title VII of the Civil Rights Act of 1964. (President Bush vetoed the legislation in 1990 but signed modified legislation in the form of the Civil Rights Act of 1991.)

A similar sequence of events occurred in 1984–1988. In *Grove City College* v. *Bell* (1984), the Supreme Court held that Title IX of the Education Act Amendments (1972), which prohibits sex discrimination in federally assisted educational programs, did not mean that federal assistance could be withheld from an entire institution because of sex discrimination in a particular program of the institution. Four years later, Congress passed legislation specifying that sex discrimination in a single program *would* disqualify an entire institution from receiving federal funds. President Reagan, who agreed with the Court and disagreed with Congress, vetoed the legislation, but Congress overrode his veto.[42]

Theoretically, it should not be difficult for Congress to reenact legislation given an "unacceptable" construction by the Court. Since the Court has avoided basing its decision on the Constitution itself, Congress can reverse the Court's position without amending the Constitution, which, of course, requires a two-thirds vote in both houses of Congress. As the above examples indicate, however, if the president is in sympathy with a majority of the Court, Congress may have to contend with a presidential veto. When that is the case, Congress will need to be sufficiently united to muster a two-thirds majority in both houses, just as it must do in order to pass a constitutional amendment.

Even without the complication of a presidential veto, however, it appears that Congress exercises its power to overcome the Supreme Court's statutory interpretations relatively rarely. One study found that between 1950 and

1972, Congress in antitrust and labor cases attempted to reverse only 27 out of 222 Supreme Court decisions and succeeded in reversing the Court on only nine occasions.[43] Once the Court has given congressional legislation new meaning—whether that meaning is more liberal or more conservative than what Congress may have intended—it appears to be difficult for Congress to bestir itself to reverse the Court.

STATUTORY REVERSAL OF CONSTITUTIONAL DECISIONS If a Supreme Court decision is based on the Constitution rather than the Court's interpretation of statutory language, theoretically the Court can be reversed in only one way: by passing and ratifying a constitutional amendment. In the real world of constitutional politics, however, nothing is quite that simple. In fact, Congress and state legislatures have a number of purely *legislative* options for at least circumventing, if not reversing, the Court's constitutional decisions.

First, nothing in the Constitution prevents Congress or the states from going further than the Court in protecting rights. A state court may give more protection to criminal defendants under its own state constitution, for instance, than the Supreme Court believes is warranted under the U.S. Constitution. Moreover, Congress may pass legislation protecting individual rights, even though the Court has concluded that the Constitution itself does not do so. In *Zurcher* v. *Stanford Daily* (1978), for instance, the Court held that the Fourth Amendment did not prevent the police from searching a newspaper office provided they were armed with a search warrant. In 1980 Congress passed legislation that required police in most cases to proceed on the basis of a subpoena, rather than a search warrant, thereby affording the newspaper an opportunity to challenge the validity of the search before rather than after it has occurred.[44]

A second example of statutory reversal occurs when the Court, or more probably some portion of the Court, invites state legislatures or Congress to adopt new legislation that overcomes the particular constitutional problems identified by the Court. A good example is *Furman* v. *Georgia* (1972) in which the Court overturned state death penalty statutes. As we saw in Chapter 4, the distribution of opinions in the case showed that less than a majority of the Court was opposed to the death penalty *per se*. Moreover, Justice Stewart in his plurality opinion suggested that, if states could reduce the capriciousness with which the death penalty was actually imposed, he and other members of the Court might be disposed to reconsider their decision. Four years later, in *Gregg* v. *Georgia* (1976), the Court upheld death penalty statutes that provided for additional scrutiny by juries of the decision to impose the death penalty on particular defendants.

A third example of a statutory response to a constitutional decision—but one that did not succeed—was congressional passage of a national flag desecration statute. In *Texas* v. *Johnson* (1989), by a vote of 5 to 4, the Supreme Court overturned a Texas statute that prohibited desecrating the flag. In response to the Court's decision, Congress drafted and passed a national flag desecration statute which it believed would meet the Court's constitutional objections. Congress was wrong, however, and in *United States v. Eichman* (1990), by the same 5–4 margin, the Court overturned the statute. The Court's decision left Congress with only two alternatives—prohibiting the Supreme Court from exercising appellate jurisdiction in cases involving flag desecration or passing a constitutional amendment to permit the punishment of flag desecration.

The flag desecration example suggests that Congress may be especially tempted to try to reverse the Supreme Court by statutory means when the Court has handed down a constitutional decision that is less than crystal clear in its meaning. Some members of Congress sensed such an opening when the Supreme Court, in its decision in *Roe* v. *Wade*, declined to decide the question of when life begins. In 1981 Senator Jesse Helms and Congressman Henry Hyde proposed a "Human Life Statute." The first section of the bill provided that "Congress hereby declares that for the purpose of enforcing the obligation of the States under the fourteenth amendment not to deprive persons of life without due process of law, human life shall be deemed to exist from conception." A Senate subcommittee approved the bill by a 3–2 vote, but no subsequent congressional action was taken.[45]

The foregoing examples indicate that Congress and other legislative bodies have a variety of options for reversing a Supreme Court decision with which they disagree. Opportunities for legislative action are particularly clear when the Court has construed a statute rather than identified a constitutional defect in the statute. Even when the Court's decision is based on the Constitution, however, there may be possibilities for legislative reversal or at least circumvention of the Court's decision.[46]

You will notice that none of the foregoing options involves tampering with the jurisdiction of the Supreme Court or other federal courts. That specialized legislative option, available only to Congress, constitutes a further potential mechanism for exerting external political pressure not only on the Supreme Court, but on the federal courts in general.

Congressional Control of Federal Jurisdiction

In Chapters 2 and 3 we learned that Congress possesses one particularly potent weapon of political retaliation against the federal courts, including the Supreme Court. Congress can restrict or even eliminate—by ordinary legislation passed by ordinary majorities—not only the appellate jurisdiction of the Supreme Court but also the original jurisdiction of the lower federal courts. The latter power derives from Congress's power, under Article III of the Constitution, to "ordain and establish" the lower federal courts. The theory is that the power to create the lower federal courts necessarily includes the lesser power to define their jurisdiction.

Congressional power to restrict or eliminate the appellate jurisdiction of the Supreme Court also derives from the language of Article III of the Constitution. Under Article III, Congress is authorized to make "Exceptions" to the appellate jurisdiction of the Supreme Court. The Exceptions Clause arguably provides a constitutional basis for enactment by Congress of ordinary legislation withholding from the Supreme Court jurisdiction to decide specific kinds of cases.

DEPRIVING THE LOWER FEDERAL COURTS OF ORIGINAL JURISDICTION Congress has redefined the original jurisdiction of the lower federal courts on numerous occasions. For the most part, however, congressional action has consisted of the gradual expansion of federal jurisdiction. Congress declined to confer upon federal courts jurisdiction over cases involving federal questions — that is, cases arising under the Constitution and laws of the United States — until 1875. Since that time, however, the federal courts have exercised jurisdiction over federal question cases without interruption.

In 1976 Congress did restrict the jurisdiction of three-judge district courts, and its motives for doing so were at least partly political. Conservative members of Congress felt that three-judge courts represented an all-too-convenient forum for lawsuits challenging the constitutional validity of state laws. The 1976 legislation, however, is one of the rare instances in which Congress has actually restricted the jurisdiction of the lower federal courts for political reasons.

DEPRIVING THE SUPREME COURT OF APPELLATE JURISDICTION Actual examples of congressional legislation restricting the appellate jurisdiction of the Supreme Court are also rare. In fact, Congress has withdrawn jurisdiction from the Supreme Court on only one occasion. During the turmoil of the Reconstruction period following the Civil War, Radical Republicans in Congress feared that a case that was on its way to the Supreme Court — *Ex parte McCardle* — might be used by the Court to declare important pieces of Reconstruction legislation unconstitutional. The Radical Republicans hastily enacted legislation that withdrew from the Supreme Court jurisdiction to review the appeal.

The congressional action came late in the game, for the Supreme Court had already heard oral argument in the appeal! Faced with a specific statute depriving it of jurisdiction, however, the Court conceded it could not proceed. "Strictly speaking," Chief Justice Salmon Chase said in his opinion, the appellate jurisdiction of the Supreme Court is "conferred by the Constitution." But it is also conferred, he said "with such exceptions and under such regulations as Congress shall make."[47] In view of the legislation explicitly depriving the Court of jurisdiction, Chase concluded, the Court "cannot proceed to pronounce judgment in this case."[48]

There has been considerable debate since the Court's decision in *McCardle* about whether it would be constitutional for Congress to enact similar legislation today. The issue is not whether Congress possesses the basic power to make exceptions to the appellate jurisdiction of the Supreme Court, but whether there are any limits on that power, and if so, what they are.[49]

One argument that is made is that, even though Congress can make exceptions to the Court's appellate jurisdiction, it would be unconstitutional for Congress to deprive the Court of jurisdiction in *particular kinds* of cases, for example, those involving school prayer or abortion. In part because of doubts about the legitimacy of prohibiting courts from deciding particular kinds of cases, recent efforts to restrict the jurisdiction of the Supreme Court (and/or the lower federal courts) have not fared very well in Congress. In 1979 Senator Helms introduced legislation that would have deprived the Supreme Court of appellate jurisdiction and the U.S. District Courts of original jurisdiction to decide school prayer cases.[50] The legislation passed the Senate, but not the House, and subsequent attempts to pass jurisdiction-limiting legislation have failed.[51]

Senator Helms (along with Congressman Hyde) has also introduced legislation to prevent the lower federal courts from deciding abortion cases. Section 2 of the Helms–Hyde "Human Life Statute" (Section 1 of which is described above) would have deprived the lower federal courts of jurisdiction over any case involving a state law or municipal ordinance that prohibits abortion. In 1981 the legislation was considered by a Senate subcommittee but proceeded no further in the legislative process.[52]

In recent years, a substantial amount of legislation has been introduced in Congress to curtail the jurisdiction of the Supreme Court or the lower federal courts, but most of it has not received serious consideration. In 1981 and 1982 some thirty bills to strip the federal courts of jurisdiction were introduced in Congress. None of them was passed by either house, however, and most of them did not move beyond the committee stage.[53] A recent attempt to restrict the Supreme Court's jurisdiction—a bill to deprive the Court of jurisdiction over flag desecration cases—was defeated by a vote of 90–10 in the Senate.[54]

Now that the Supreme Court itself has become substantially more conservative than it was just a few years ago, the pressure in Congress to pass legislation to strip the Court of jurisdiction in certain kinds of cases—for example, those involving prayer, abortion, criminal procedure, or busing—has subsided. Even during the period when the Court was the object of substantial congressional hostility for its liberal decisions, however, Congress was notably unwilling to actually move against the Court by enacting legislation to limit its jurisdiction.

Reversing the Supreme Court by Amending the Constitution

The most unambiguous way for the political branches to reverse a Supreme Court decision is to amend the Constitution. The Court has the final word on the meaning of the Constitution and on questions of alleged conflict between the Constitution and ordinary law. However, the Court's interpretation of the meaning of the Constitution can be directly challenged by changing the text of the Constitution through the amendment process.

Amending the Constitution, of course, is not easy. The first step, according to Article V of the Constitution, is for Congress to propose an amendment by a two-thirds vote in both the House and the Senate.[55] Following that, the amendment must be submitted to the states, where it has to be ratified by the legislatures of three-fourths of the states.[56]

Four of the twenty-six amendments to the Constitution were proposed for the express purpose of reversing decisions of the Supreme Court. The Eleventh Amendment (1795) reversed the Court's decision in *Chisholm* v. *Georgia* (1793), which had interpreted Article III to permit the federal courts to accept jurisdiction in suits against a state by citizens of another state. The Fourteenth Amendment (1868) conferred citizenship on "[a]ll persons born or naturalized in the United States," including former slaves, thereby reversing the Court's holding in *Dred Scott* v. *Sandford* (1857) that slaves, and indeed all persons of African descent, were not citizens. The Sixteenth Amendment (1913) authorized Congress to enact an income tax, thereby reversing the Court's decision in *Pollock* v. *Farmers' Loan and Trust Co.* (1895), which had overturned a federal income tax law. Finally, the Twenty-sixth Amendment (1971) conferred the right to vote in state elections on eighteen year olds, thereby reversing the Court's decision in *Oregon* v. *Mitchell* (1970), which had held that Congress lacked the power under the Constitution to accomplish that result by statutory means.

In recent years, the principal advocates of constitutional amendments to reverse Supreme Court decisions have been political conservatives. However, they have not been notably successful in achieving their objectives. In 1983 the Senate debated constitutional language that would have returned the abortion decision to the states—by stipulating that "A right to abortion is not secured by the Constitution"—but the amendment fell eighteen votes short of the necessary two-thirds majority.[57] In 1984 the Senate debated an amendment to allow voluntary prayer in public schools. The final vote in the Senate was 56 to 44, eleven votes shy of the necessary two-thirds.[58]

The most recent congressional attempt to reverse the Supreme Court occurred in 1990. Congress debated an amendment stipulating that "Congress and the states shall have the power to prohibit the physical desecration of the flag of the United States." The amendment was in response to the Supreme Court's decisions in *Texas* v. *Johnson* (1989)—striking down a state flag desecration law—and *United States* v. *Eichman* (1990)—striking down a congressional flag desecration statute. Public opinion polls showed that 60 to 70 percent of the population supported a constitutional amendment to permit the punishment of flag burning.[59] When the amendment came to a vote on the floor of the House, however, it was defeated 254–177; that is, it was thirty-four votes short of the necessary two-thirds. The vote in the Senate (51–48) fell fifteen votes short of the necessary two-thirds majority.[60]

Conclusion

The various judicial and nonjudicial institutions with which the Supreme Court shares political power in the American democracy possess a formidable array of Court-curbing weapons. Some of them are essentially informal; that is, they are not explicitly prescribed by the Constitution. Political leaders can publicly criticize the Court. The American public can express its opposition to the Court in opinion polls. Local communities can resist implementation of the Court's decisions. In all these ways, the Court may feel the "heat" from its political environment.

At the national level, Congress and the president also possess an array of more formal options for curbing the Court. All are part of the theory of checks and balances on which the American constitutional system is based. The silence of the Constitution permits Congress or the president to propose legislation altering the size of the Court or the size of the majority within the Court needed to reach certain kinds of decisions. In addition, the explicit language of the Constitution authorizes Congress to remove individual justices from office by convicting them of impeachable offenses.

The Supreme Court must also be respectful of the preferences of both Congress and the president because the Court is very often dependent on Congress or the president — or both — for enforcement of its decisions. Presidential or congressional failure to actively assist the Court in enforcing its judgments may represent an unsavory instance of the process of checks and balances. There is no doubt, however, that, in practice, the noncooperation of the political branches can seriously weaken the force of the Supreme Court's policy pronouncements.

Finally, Congress and the president possess various clearly defined constitutional powers that can be used to restrain or reverse the Court. Congress is empowered to make exceptions to the appellate jurisdiction of the Supreme Court (and to define the original jurisdiction of the lower federal courts). In addition, Congress and other law-making bodies, such as state legislatures, have an array of statutory options for circumventing or reversing the Court's constitutional and nonconstitutional decisions. Congress can pass and send to the states a constitutional amendment explicitly reversing any decision in which the Court, in the view of Congress, has erroneously interpreted the meaning of the Constitution.

It is therefore clear that various political actors — including the president, the Congress, the lower courts, state legislatures, and the American people — possess a long list of options by which they can attempt to restrain or reverse the Supreme Court. What is perhaps as remarkable as the number and diversity of these options, however, is the infrequency with which they have been used successfully. The Court has been reversed by constitutional amendment only four times in history, and none of the recent attempts to reverse the Court's "liberal" decisions on issues such as abortion, busing, school prayer, and flag desecration has garnered the necessary two-thirds majority in either House of Congress. The Court has been deprived of its appellate jurisdiction only once in history, and none of the recent attempts to restrict the Court's jurisdiction has made much headway in Congress, let alone been passed by both the House and the Senate. Congress has had more luck reversing Supreme Court decisions based on statutory construction, rather than judicial review, but even here the congressional record seems relatively unimpressive.

No doubt the cumulative effect of anti-Court pronouncements and actions in recent years has had some effect on the thinking of individual members of the Court. As measured by evidence of concrete success, however, it is difficult to conclude that *any* of the mechanisms of external control of the Supreme Court has been particularly effective. This suggests that applying "external" political pressure to the Supreme Court may not be the most promising way to influence the Court. We turn, therefore, to an alternative strategy for bringing the Court into line with majoritarian preferences, namely, reconstituting the Court through the appointment process.

Notes

1. Speech of March 9, 1937. Senate Report No. 711, 75th Cong., 1st Sess. Reprinted in Elder Witt (ed.), *Congressional Quarterly's Guide to the U.S. Supreme Court* (1990), pp. 961–63.

2. *New York Times*, October 22, 1971, p. 24.

3. James F. Simon, *In His Own Image: The Supreme Court in Richard Nixon's America* (1973).

4. Edwin Meese III, "The Attorney General's View of the Supreme Court: Toward a Jurisprudence of Original Intention," 45 *Pub. Admin. Rev.* 701, 704 (November 1985). For additional discussion of the role of "original intent" in constitutional interpretation, see Chapter 14.

5. Edwin Meese III, "The Law of the Constitution," 61 *Tul. L. Rev.* 979 (1987). For responses to the Meese argument, see Symposium, "Perspectives on the Authoritativeness of Supreme Court Decisions," 61 *Tul. L. Rev.* 977–1085 (1987).

6. Bob Woodward and Scott Armstrong, *The Brethren: Inside the Supreme Court* (1979), pp. 238–40.

7. For examples of public attacks on the Supreme Court in earlier decades, see John R. Schmidhauser and Larry L. Berg, *The Supreme Court and Congress: Conflict and Interaction, 1945–1968* (1972); Robert Scigliano, *The Supreme Court and the Presidency* (1971); Walter F. Murphy, *Congress and the Court* (1962); and C. Herman Pritchett, *Congress Versus the Supreme Court* (1961).

8. In 1989, in a nationwide poll commissioned by the *Washington Post*, only 9 percent of Americans named Rehnquist when asked to identify the chief justice, and more than two-thirds could not name a single member of the Court. *Washington Post*, June 23, 1989, p. A21.

9. Studies of public support for the Supreme Court are reviewed in Gregory A. Caldeira, "Courts and Public Opinion," in John B. Gates and Charles A. Johnson (eds.), *The American Courts: A Critical Assessment* (1991), pp. 303–34. See also Gregory A. Caldeira and James L. Gibson, "The Etiology of Public Support for the Supreme Court," 36 *Am. J. Pol. Sci.* 635 (1992); James L. Gibson and Gregory A. Caldeira, "Blacks and the United States Supreme Court: Models of Diffuse Support," *J. of Pol.* (forthcoming); Gregory A. Caldeira, "Neither the Purse Nor the Sword: The

Dynamics of Public Confidence in the United States Supreme Court," 80 *Am. Pol. Sci. Rev.* 1209 (1986); David Adamany and Joel B. Grossman, "Support for the Supreme Court as a National Policymaker," 5 *Law and Policy Q.* 405 (1983); Roger Handberg and William S. Maddox, "Public Support for the Supreme Court in the 1970s," 10 *Am. Pol. Q.* 333 (1982); and Joseph Tanenhaus and Walter F. Murphy, "Patterns of Public Support for the Supreme Court: A Panel Study," 43 *J. of Pol.* 24 (1981).

10. *Gregg* v. *Georgia*, 428 U.S. 153, 179–82 (1976).

11. For a thorough discussion of the relationship of public opinion to Supreme Court decision making, see Thomas R. Marshall, *Public Opinion and the Supreme Court* (1989). Chapter 3 of this book focuses on the justices' uses of public opinion in their decision making.

12. Id. at 78–80.

13. The relationship between public opinion and Supreme Court decision making is explored in detail in Chapter 15.

14. Note that a separate and very interesting question is whether Supreme Court decisions exert an influence on public opinion. For discussions of this issue, see Marshall, *Public Opinion and the Supreme Court*, Ch. 6; James L. Gibson, "Understandings of Justice: Institutional Legitimacy, Procedural Justice, and Political Tolerance," 23 *Law and Soc. Rev.* 469 (1989); Charles H. Franklin and Liane C. Kosaki, "Republican Schoolmaster: The U.S. Supreme Court, Public Opinion, and Abortion," 83 *Am Pol. Sci. Rev.* 751 (1989); Benjamin I. Page and Glenn R. Dempsey, "What Moves Public Opinion?" 81 *Am. Pol. Sci. Rev.* 23 (1987); and Larry Baas and Dan Thomas, "The Supreme Court and Policy Legitimation: Experimental Tests," 12 *Am. Pol. Q.* 335 (1984).

15. Several studies have examined the relationship between public opinion and *lower court* decision making. See, for example, George W. Pruet, Jr., and Henry R. Glick, "Social Environment, Public Opinion, and Judicial Policymaking: A Search for Judicial Representation," 14 *Am. Pol. Q.* 5 (1986); Charles Silver and Robert Y. Shapiro, "Public Opinion and the Federal Judiciary: Crime, Punishment, and Demographic Constraints," 3 *Population Res. and Policy Rev.* 255 (1984); James L. Gibson, "Environmental Constraints on the Behavior of Judges: A Representational Model of Judicial Decision Making," 14 *Law & Soc. Rev.* 343 (1980); James H. Kuklinski and John E. Stanga, "Political Participation and Government Responsiveness: The Behavior of California Superior Courts," 73 *Am. Pol. Sci. Rev.* 1090 (1979); and Beverly Blair Cook, "Public Opinion and Federal Judicial Policy," 21 *Am. J. Pol. Sci.* 567 (1977).

16. For examples of the pressure and intimidation with which southern judges were confronted, see Jack Peltason, *Fifty-Eight Lonely Men: Southern Federal Judges and School Desegregation*; Richard G. Richardson and Kenneth N. Vines, *The Politics of Federal Courts* (1970); and Robert F. Kennedy, Jr., *Judge Frank M. Johnson, Jr.: A Biography* (1978). The influence of local conditions on judicial decision making in civil rights cases is also explored in Michael W. Giles and Thomas G. Walker, "Judicial Policy-Making and Southern School Segregation," 37 *J. of Pol.* 917 (1975); and Kenneth N. Vines, "Federal District Judges and Race Relations Cases in the South," 26 *J. of Pol.* 338 (1964).

17. Woodward and Armstrong, *The Brethren*, pp. 238–40.

18. See, generally, Gerald N. Rosenberg, *The Hollow Hope: Can Courts Bring about Social Change?* (1991); Charles A. Johnson and Bradley C. Canon, *Judicial Policies: Implementation and Impact* (1984); and Jesse H. Choper, "Consequences of

Supreme Court Decisions Upholding Individual Constitutional Rights," 83 *Mich. L. Rev.* 1 (1984).

19. See, for example, Rosenberg, *The Hollow Hope*, Ch. 3; Matthew D. McCubbins and Thomas Schwartz, "Congress, the Courts, and Public Policy: Consequences of the One Man, One Vote Rule," 32 *Am. J. Pol. Sci.* 388 (1988); Douglas G. Feig, "Expenditures in the American States: The Impact of Court-Ordered Reapportionment," 6 *Am. Pol. Q.* 309 (1978); Eric M. Uslaner, "Comparative State Policy Formation, Interparty Competition, and Malapportionment," 40 *J. of Pol.* 409 (1978); Ward E.Y. Elliott, *The Rise of Guardian Democracy* (1974); and Robert G. Dixon, *Democratic Representation: Reapportionment in Law and Politics* (1968).

20. See, for example, Rosenberg, *The Hollow Hope*, Ch. 1; Charles S. Bullock III and Charles M. Lamb (eds.), *Implementation of Civil Rights Policy* (1984); Stephen Wasby, Anthony D'Amato, and Rosemary Metrailer, *Desegregation from Brown to Alexander: An Exploration of Supreme Court Strategies* (1977); Harrell R. Rodgers, Jr., and Charles S. Bullock III, *Coercion to Compliance* (1976); and Harrell R. Rodgers, Jr., and Charles S. Bullock III, *Law and Social Change: Civil Rights Laws and their Consequences* (1972).

21. See, for example, Rosenberg, *The Hollow Hope*, Ch. 3; Myron W. Orfield, Jr., "The Exclusionary Rule and Deterrence: An Empirical Study of Chicago Narcotics Officers," 54 *U. Chi. L. Rev.* 1016 (1987); Stephen J. Schulhofer, "Reconsidering *Miranda*," 54 *U. Chi. L. Rev.* 435 (1987); Patrick A. Malone, "'You Have a Right to Remain Silent': *Miranda* after Twenty Years," 55 *The American Scholar* 367 (Summer 1986); Liva Baker, *Miranda: Crime, Law, and Politics* (1983); Peter F. Nardulli, "The Societal Cost of the Exclusionary Rule: An Empirical Assessment," *Am. Bar Found. Res. J.* 585 (Summer 1983); Thomas Y. Davies, "A Hard Look at What We Know (and Still Need to Learn) about the 'Costs' of the Exclusionary Rule: The NIJ Study and Other Studies of 'Lost' Arrests," *Am. Bar Found. Res. J.* 611 (Summer 1983); and Stephen Wasby, *Small Town Police and the Supreme Court* (1976).

22. See, for example, Rosenberg, *The Hollow Hope*, Ch. 2.

23. See, for example, Frank J. Sorauf, *The Wall of Separation: The Constitutional Politics of Church and State* (1976); Kenneth M. Dolbeare and Phillip E. Hammond, *The School Prayer Decisions: From Court Policy to Local Practice* (1971); William K. Muir, Jr., *Prayer in the Public Schools: Law and Attitude Change* (1967); and Richard Johnson, *The Dynamics of Compliance* (1967).

24. James Madison, "Federalist No. 51," in Roy P. Fairfield (ed.), *The Federalist Papers*, (1961), p. 160.

25. Charles Alan Wright, *The Law of Federal Courts* (1983), pp. 12–14; and Scigliano, *The Supreme Court and the Presidency*, pp. 51–55.

26. Shelden D. Elliott, "Court-Curbing Proposals in Congress," 33 *Notre Dame Lawyer* 597 (1958); and Maurice S. Culp, "A Survey of the Proposals to Limit or Deny the Power of Judicial Review by the Supreme Court of the United States," 4 *Ind. L. J.* 386 (1929).

27. Dean L. Yarwood and Bradley C. Canon, "On the Supreme Court's Annual Trek to the Capitol," 63 *Judicature* 322 (1980).

28. Charles Warren, *The Supreme Court in United States History* (1947), Vol. 1, p. 293.

29. Woodward and Armstrong, *The Brethren*, pp. 75–79.

30. Impeachment is also the only method by which lower federal court judges can be removed from office. Since 1789, seven judges have been convicted of impeach-

able offenses. The two most recent convictions (Judge Alcee L. Hastings of Florida and Judge Walter L. Nixon of Mississippi) occurred in 1989. See Robert A. Carp and Ronald Stidham, *The Federal Courts* (1991), p. 125. In recent years, impeachment of federal judges has most often been used in situations where a judge has been convicted of federal crimes but has refused to resign from office, thereby ensuring that he will continue to draw his federal salary while serving time in a federal penitentiary! At least two federal judges (Judge Robert Aguilar of California and Judge Robert F. Collins of Louisiana) have recently been convicted of federal criminal offenses. Each faces probable impeachment by the Congress.

31. Alexander Hamilton, "Federalist No. 78," in Fairfield (ed.), *The Federalist Papers*, p. 227.

32. The decision to which Jackson was reacting was *Worcester* v. *Georgia*, 31 U.S. 515 (1832). See Richard P. Longaker, "Andrew Jackson and the Judiciary," 71 *Pol. Sci. Q.* 341 (1956); and Joseph C. Burke, "The Cherokee Cases: A Study in Law, Politics, and Morality," 21 *Stan. L. Rev.* 500 (1969).

33. Alexander Bickel, *The Least Dangerous Branch: The Supreme Court at the Bar of Politics* (1962), pp. 259–61.

34. *Ex parte Merryman*, 17 Fed. Cases 144 (1861). For discussions, see Mark E. Neely, *The Fate of Liberty: Abraham Lincoln and Civil Liberties* (1991); and Scigliano, *The Supreme Court and the Presidency*, pp. 39–44.

35. Earl Warren, *The Memoirs of Earl Warren* (1977), pp. 289–92; and Bernard Schwartz, *Super Chief: Earl Warren and His Supreme Court—A Judicial Biography* (1983), p. 175.

36. Three years earlier, in *Maher* v. *Roe* (1977), the Court by a 6–3 vote had sustained a Connecticut law that barred the use of Medicaid funds to pay for abortions. For additional discussion, see Chapter 10.

37. Edward Keynes, *The Court vs. Congress: Prayer, Busing, and Abortion*, Ch. 8.

38. See Rosenberg, *The Hollow Hope*, Ch. 1.

39. Ronald Stidham and Robert S. Carp, "U.S. Trial Court Reactions to Changes in Civil Rights and Civil Liberties Policies," 12 *Southeastern Pol. Rev.* 7 (1984).

40. Congress and the president are not the only forces outside the Court on which the Court must depend for implementation of its decisions. The reaction of lower court judges and of local elected officials and other community leaders will affect the success of innovative Supreme Court policy pronouncements. For citations to the growing literature on the local impact of Supreme Court decisions, see notes 19–24 supra.

41. See Symposium, "Civil Rights Legislation in the 1990s," 79 *Calif. L. Rev.* 591 (1991).

42. See *Congressional Quarterly Weekly Report*, March 12, 1988, p. 677; March 26, 1988, p. 774.

43. Beth M. Henschen, "Statutory Interpretations of the Supreme Court: Congressional Response," 11 *Am. Pol. Q.* 441 (1983).

44. For other examples of exceptional solicitude for individual rights on the part of Congress and other nonjudicial bodies, see Louis Fisher, *Constitutional Dialogues: Interpretation as Political Process* (1988), pp. 255–59; Jesse H. Choper, *Judicial Review and the National Political Process* (1980), pp. 68–69.

45. Keynes, *The Court vs. Congress*, Ch. 9.

46. The various state legislative responses to *Roe* v. *Wade* are additional examples of statutory attempts to circumvent, if not reverse, a constitutional decision of the

Supreme Court. In the wake of *Roe* v. *Wade*, states passed laws requiring parental or spousal consent for abortions and imposing special restrictions on physicians who perform abortions and on hospitals and clinics in which abortions are performed. See Chapter 10.

47. *Ex parte McCardle*, 74 U.S. (7 Wall.) 506, 512–13 (1869).

48. Id at 515. For detailed discussions of the political and legal ramifications of the *McCardle* decision, see William Lasser, *The Limits of Judicial Power: The Supreme Court in American Politics* (1989), Ch. 3; and William Van Alstyne, "A Critical Guide to Ex parte McCardle," 15 *Ariz. L. Rev.* 229 (1973).

49. Recent contributions to this debate include Akhil Amar, "The Two-Tiered Structure of the Judiciary Act of 1789," 138 *U. Pa. L. Rev.* 1499 (1990); Gerald Gunther, "Congressional Power to Curtail Federal Court Jurisdiction: An Opinionated Guide to the Ongoing Debate," 36 *Stan. L. Rev.* 201 (1984); Symposium, "Congressional Limits on Federal Court Jurisdiction," 27 *Vill. L. Rev.* 893 (1982); Lawrence G. Sager, "Constitutional Limitations on Congress' Authority to Regulate the Jurisdiction of the Federal Courts," 95 *Harv. L. Rev.* 17 (1981); and Lawrence H. Tribe, "Jurisdictional Gerrymandering: Zoning Disfavored Rights Out of the Federal Courts," 16 *Harv. Civil Rights-Civil Liberties L. Rev.* 129 (1981).

50. Keynes, *The Court vs. Congress*, Ch. 7.

51. For additional discussion, see Chapter 8 supra.

52. Keynes, *The Court vs. Congress*, Ch. 9.

53. Max Baucus and Kenneth R. Kay, "The Court Stripping Bills: Their Impact on the Constitution, the Courts, and Congress," 27 *Vill. L. Rev.* 988 (1982).

54. Lawrence Baum, *The Supreme Court* (1992), p. 234.

55. The Supreme Court held in the National Prohibition Cases in 1920 that the constitutional requirement of "two-thirds of both Houses" means two-thirds of those present and voting, not two-thirds of the entire membership.

56. Article V also provides that amendments may be proposed by a convention called by the Congress "on the Application of the Legislatures of two-thirds of the several States." This method of proposing constitutional amendments has never been employed. In 1964, however, thirty-one (out of the required thirty-four) state legislatures petitioned Congress to call a convention to overturn the Supreme Court's decision in *Reynolds* v. *Sims* (1964), which required that state legislative districts must be equal in population. In the 1970s, thirty-three states—one less than needed— petitioned Congress to call a convention to propose an amendment to require that the federal budget be kept in balance. The amendment process is discussed in C. Herman Pritchett, *Constitutional Law of the Federal System* (1984), Ch. 2.

57. Keynes, *The Court vs. Congress*, Ch. 9. For additional discussion, see Chapter 10 supra.

58. Keynes, *The Court vs. Congress*, Ch. 7. For additional discussion, see Chapter 8 supra.

59. See, for example, George Gallup, Jr., and Dr. Frank Newport, "Americans Back Bush on Flag-burning Amendment," *The Gallup Poll Monthly*, June 1990, p. 2; and *Congressional Quarterly Weekly Report*, June 16, 1990, p. 1877.

60. *Congressional Quarterly Weekly Report*, June 23, 1990, p. 1962; June 30, 1990, p. 2063.

C H A P T E R   1 3

Internal Restraints on the
Supreme Court:
The Appointment Process
and Its Consequences

In 1936, in *United States* v. *Butler,* the Supreme Court struck down the Agricultural Adjustment Act of 1933. The act was a key piece of New Deal legislation, and the *Butler* decision was a good example of the conservative activism of the Supreme Court which contributed to the showdown, in 1937, between President Roosevelt and the Court. The outcome of that showdown, as we have seen, was that the Supreme Court ceded primary responsibility for policy making on economic issues to the legislative and executive branches of government.

When the *Butler* case was handed down, it included a celebrated dissent by Justice Stone. In his dissent, Stone declared that "while unconstitutional exercise of power by the executive and legislative branches of government is subject to judicial restraint, the only check upon our own exercise of power is our own sense of self-restraint."[1] Stone's remarks suggest that he, personally, was skeptical of the value of external restraints as a control on the decision-making behavior of the Supreme Court. They also suggest that an important key to understanding the Court—and perhaps to influencing its behavior—may lie in the internal composition of the Court itself.

This chapter focuses on the appointment process and its impact on Supreme Court decision making. The assumption underlying our discussion is that reconstitution of the Court through the appointment process may represent the most effective way to keep the Court in line with the preferences of a majority of the American people. We begin by describing the appointment process and the characteristics of individuals who are appointed to the Supreme Court. In Section II, we examine the relationship between justices' values and their voting behavior. Finally, in Section III, we look at the appointment process in historical perspective and discuss whether the president's power to appoint Supreme Court justices is a viable strategy by which the political system can exert "internal influence" on Supreme Court decision making.

220

The Appointment Process:
How It Works and Who Gets Chosen

The Constitution prescribes that the president "shall nominate, and by and with the Advice and Consent of the Senate, shall appoint . . . Judges of the supreme Court." As this constitutional language suggests, the process by which individuals are appointed to the Supreme Court is not very complicated. The basic steps include (1) nomination by the president, (2) confirmation hearings before the Senate Judiciary Committee, (3) confirmation by a majority vote in the Senate, and (4) appointment to the Supreme Court. In this section we examine how the appointment process works and the characteristics of those who are selected to serve on the Court.

The President's Role in the Appointment Process

The Constitution explicitly confers on the president the power to nominate Supreme Court justices. The president's choice of a nominee will be made in consultation with members of the White House staff, the attorney general, and other presidential confidants and advisors. In some cases, the nominee may be someone the president already knows personally. In other cases, the president will meet the nominee for the first time during the appointment process itself.

At least in recent years, all presidents have undoubtedly maintained a ready list of potential nominees. Some Supreme Court resignations are announced in advance. Most resignations, however, occur with little or no warning, and of course the sudden death of a justice is always a possibility. Any president who wishes to move forward quickly with a nomination must identify a list of possible nominees well in advance of an actual vacancy on the Court.

Even if the president has a short list of possible nominees, however, there will still be some delay before a name can be announced. Ordinarily, there will be at least some disagreement within the administration about which of several candidates would make the best choice. In addition, there may be some last-minute investigation of a nominee's background and credentials. Finally, of course, the nominee will need to be contacted and interviewed by the president or at least by the president's staff. Some recent nominations have gone awry because damaging revelations about a candidate came to light following the president's formal announcement. To minimize this possibility, nominees are now routinely interviewed and asked a series of direct questions about their background.

The one feature of the appointment process that will probably not cause much delay is gaining the assent of the nominee. In the earliest years of the Republic, some individuals declined to serve on the Court because appointment to the Court was not yet regarded as particularly prestigious. Even in modern times, a few individuals have declined to be nominated or have agreed to serve with reluctance. Most of those who receive a presidential telephone call asking them if they wish to be nominated to the Supreme Court, however, are likely to say "yes" without much hesitation!

Other Participants in the Appointment Process

As soon as the president announces his choice of a nominee, and sometimes even before the announcement itself, a host of other groups and individuals become involved in the appointment process. At one time in American history, appointing a justice to the Supreme Court might have been a relatively cozy affair involving only the president and the Senate. Today that is no longer true.[2]

One prominent participant in the appointment process in recent years has been the American Bar Association (ABA). The ABA is the leading national organization of lawyers in the United States, and for some time it has believed it should play a key role in the process of selecting federal judges — including Supreme Court justices. In 1946 it moved to formalize its role by creating a Committee on the Federal Judiciary, the purpose of which is to evaluate nominees for the federal bench. Since 1956 the Committee has sought to provide evaluations of Supreme Court nominees.[3]

In fact, relations between the White House and ABA have not always been very cordial. Some presidents have allowed the ABA to prescreen prospective nominees. From the president's point of view, of course, this arrangement has the drawback of limiting the president's options in making a selection. Other presidents have insisted that the ABA make its judgments about a candidate's qualifications only after the nominee has been announced to the public. President Nixon actually altered his relationship with the ABA in the middle of his presidency. The ABA was allowed to prescreen his initial nominees to the Supreme Court, but not his later ones. President Reagan did not allow the ABA to prescreen any of his nominees. The ABA therefore plays an important role in the selection process. The exact nature of that role, however, will be dictated in part by presidential preferences.[4]

Once a nominee is announced, interest groups mobilize to show support for or opposition to the president's choice. In recent years, the appointment process has become more politicized, and the participation of interest groups has increased substantially. Many politically active citizens believe that what is at stake in recent Supreme Court nominations is nothing less than the future of policies such as affirmative action and decisions such as *Roe* v. *Wade*. As a result, they have pulled out all the stops in their efforts to see that particular nominees are either confirmed or defeated.[5]

Interest groups were especially prominent in the confirmation process that eventually resulted in the defeat of Robert Bork to fill the vacancy created by Justice Powell's retirement in 1987. The Bork nomination was regarded as a critical watershed in the development of the Court, because Bork, who was perceived as being rigidly conservative, would be replacing Powell, who was perceived as a moderate. The crucial character of the Bork nomination generated enormous activity on the part of interest groups.[6]

Senate Confirmation

The confirmation process in the Senate begins only days after the president's announcement of a nomination. The nominee will pay courtesy calls on members of the Senate in an attempt to allay particular doubts and give senators an opportunity to gauge his or her personal attributes.

Pursuant to the rules of the Senate, the Senate Judiciary Committee will hold hearings on the nomination, usually a few weeks after it has been announced. Confirmation hearings are now televised and may last several days. Depending on the level of controversy surrounding the nomination, the hearings may involve a significant amount of tension and combative interchange. The culmination of the hearings will be a vote by the Committee to recommend or not recommend to the Senate that the nominee be confirmed.

The nomination of Clarence Thomas in 1991 was surrounded by an unprecedented amount of controversy. Following his initial appearance before the Senate Judiciary Committee, Thomas returned to answer charges that he had sexually harassed Anita Hill, a law professor who at the time of the alleged harassment (in the early 1980s) had been working for Thomas at the Equal Employment Opportunity Commission and the Department of Education. At the second round of hearings, Hill publicly repeated her charges of sexual harassment and Thomas denied that the events she described had ever occurred. Almost everyone who took part in or watched the hearings — which included a substantial proportion of the American people — came to the conclusion that one or the other of the principals was lying. The hearings themselves ended in a standoff, however, and Thomas was subsequently confirmed by the Senate by the exceptionally close vote of 52–48.[7]

The last step in the confirmation process is a debate and vote in the Senate itself. Senators who support and oppose the nominee will address the Senate and rehearse the arguments for and against confirmation that have surfaced since the nomination was made. Eventually, the Senate will vote. A majority of those present and voting is sufficient to confirm the nomination. Shortly after confirmation, the appointee will join the Court and begin hearing cases.

The Historical Record of Senate Action

Between 1789 and 1991 (with the nomination of Clarence Thomas to replace Thurgood Marshall), American presidents made 146 nominations to the Supreme Court.[8] Four persons were nominated and confirmed twice; all four were associate justices who subsequently became chief justice. Charles Evans Hughes served as associate justice from 1910 to 1916, then resigned from the

Court to run (unsuccessfully) for president, and was subsequently nominated and confirmed as chief justice in 1930. Three other individuals—Edward White (in 1910), Harlan Stone (in 1941), and William Rehnquist (in 1986)—were elevated from associate justice to chief justice while on the Court.

The Senate ordinarily confirms a president's nominee but retains—and occasionally exercises—its constitutional prerogative to reject the president's choice.[9] Since 1789, twelve nominations, or a little less than one in ten, have been rejected by a formal vote in the Senate. An additional sixteen nominations have been rejected by the Senate without a formal vote, either because the Senate postponed or took no action on the nomination or because the nominee withdrew his name. Altogether, then, twenty-eight nominations, or about one-fifth of the total, have failed to gain Senate confirmation.[10]

The most recent nominee to be formally rejected by the Senate was Robert Bork. As noted earlier, President Reagan nominated Bork in 1987 to fill the vacancy created by Justice Powell's resignation. Bork was perceived by liberals as someone who would take an ultraconservative position on constitutional issues and would substantially strengthen the emerging conservative majority on the Court. When the Bork nomination came to a vote in the Senate, in October 1987, it was defeated by a margin of 42 to 58.[11]

In the wake of Bork's defeat, Reagan announced the nomination of Douglas Ginsberg. Within a matter of days, however, a variety of unfavorable revelations forced Ginsberg to withdraw his name from contention. Given its brief lifespan, the Ginsberg nomination may not even be classified as a formal nomination by Court historians.[12]

Bork's defeat was the first since two of President Nixon's nominees had failed to be confirmed in 1969–1970. In 1969 Nixon nominated Clement Haynsworth to fill the vacancy created by the resignation of Justice Fortas, but the nomination was rejected by the Senate (by a vote of 45–55). Nixon then nominated G. Harrold Carswell, but he too was rejected by the Senate (by a vote of 45–51) in 1970. Finally, Nixon nominated Harry Blackmun, whom the Senate confirmed (by a vote of 94–0) on May 12, 1970.[13]

The vacancy that Nixon had such difficulty filling was itself the product of a struggle between the president and the Senate. In 1968 President Johnson had nominated Abe Fortas, then an associate justice, to succeed Earl Warren as chief justice. When the Fortas nomination reached the Senate floor, however, it faced significant opposition. Eventually, a Senate vote to terminate a filibuster against the nomination failed to attract the necessary two-thirds majority, and Fortas withdrew his name. Earl Warren then agreed to continue as chief justice (and was succeeded, in 1969, by Warren Burger). Fortas himself remained on the Court as an associate justice, but his troubles were far from over. Damaging revelations about his off-the-Court financial relationships were published in the spring of 1969. On May 14, 1969, under threat of impeachment, Fortas resigned from the Court, thereby creating the vacancy for which President Nixon made his two ill-fated nominations.[14]

The Senate's Role in the Appointment Process

Not all nominees succeed, therefore, in surmounting the hurdle of Senate confirmation. Indeed, in recent years the Senate has become more aggressive in exercising its constitutional prerogative to advise and consent to Supreme Court nominees. Prior to 1968, the Senate had failed to confirm only one nominee in the twentieth century. Since 1968, however, the Senate has rejected four nominees — Fortas, Haynsworth, Carswell, and Bork.

The Senate's higher profile in the appointment process has generated a lively debate about what role it *should* play in determining the composition of the Supreme Court. Not surprisingly, presidents argue that under the Constitution the chief executive should retain primary responsibility for selecting Supreme Court justices and for molding the ideological orientation of the Court as an institution. Not surprisingly, among those who voice support for this position are senators who agree with the president about what sorts of people should be appointed to the Court.

On the other side of the debate are senators (and others) who argue that the Senate should have a co-equal role with the president in selecting Supreme Court justices. They note that the Constitution prescribes a formal role for the Senate in the appointment process. They also emphasize that the Supreme Court is a policy-making body and that therefore the Senate should play an active role in evaluating not only the qualifications, but also the policy preferences, of the president's nominees. Not surprisingly, the senators who are most likely to use this argument are those who disagree with the president's taste in nominees and would like to be in a position to substitute names of their own.[15]

As we have seen, the Senate has begun to play a stronger role in the appointment process. The evidence also suggests, however, that the president continues to hold most of the cards in the appointment process and can easily win confirmation of any nominee who is well qualified and not exceptionally controversial.

The Characteristics of Supreme Court Nominees

Somewhat surprisingly, neither the Constitution nor federal law prescribes any minimum qualifications for Supreme Court justices. Unlike the president — who, under the Constitution, must be thirty-five years old, a natural born citizen, and a resident of the United States for at least fourteen years — a Supreme Court nominee could violate any or all of these requirements and still be eligible to serve on the Court. This is not to say, of course, that the choice of Supreme Court nominees is not constrained by a powerful set of norms and expectations. Realistically, a rather narrow spectrum of the population is eligible to be appointed to the Court. However, the criteria that inform the selection process derive not from the Constitution or the law but from unwritten rules embedded in the fabric of American political culture.

Social Origins of Supreme Court Justices

Between 1789 and 1991 (with the confirmation of Clarence Thomas), 106 individuals have served on the Supreme Court. Not surprisingly, a large proportion — perhaps 85 to 90 percent — have come from families that were economically secure and enjoyed high social status. Only a "handful" of justices, according to one scholar, "were of essentially humble origin."[16] Among those justices, of course, are some of the Court's most prominent members, including William Douglas, Arthur Goldberg, and Thurgood Marshall, and Chief Justices Earl Warren and Warren Burger. The typical appointee, however, is someone from a high status background.

Other features of the background of Supreme Court justices distinguish them, as a group, from the general population. About two-thirds of the justices have come from politically active families, and about one-third have been related by blood or marriage to individuals who themselves had careers in the judiciary. The ability of families to transmit particular values and advantages is clearly evident in the disproportionate number of justices who come from families with a tradition of political activity and/or judicial service.[17]

Race, Sex, and Religion

Needless to say, racial minorities and women have been relatively scarce on the Supreme Court. The first black justice, Thurgood Marshall, was appointed in 1967, and the first female justice, Sandra Day O'Connor, was appointed in 1981. Almost certainly, future presidents will make an effort to perpetuate the representation of women and blacks on the Court. At the same time, the enormous diversity of the American population precludes the possibility that each of the multitude of racial and ethnic minorities will enjoy regular representation on the Court, which consists, after all, of only nine members.

The religious affiliation of Supreme Court nominees is no longer a particularly important issue in the appointment process. Historically, there have been five Jewish and six Catholic justices, while most of the remaining justices have been Protestants of one denomination or another. At one time, a nominee's religious affiliation was considered significant, in part because it was believed that the Court should "represent" the population as a whole. In recent years, however, the principal criteria for judging whether particular institutions adequately represent the population as a whole have been race, ethnicity, and gender, and religion has receded in importance. In addition, of course, a Supreme Court that included at least one person from each religious group in the United States would have to contain decidedly more than nine members!

Education and Legal Training

Supreme Court justices as a group have been more likely than the average individual to have attended prestigious colleges and universities, and all members of the Court have acquired a legal education. From the point of view of the Constitution and the law, legal expertise is not a prerequisite of Supreme Court service, but in practice, no justice has ever been appointed who did not have legal training.

In the nineteenth century and into the early twentieth century, lawyers and judges often acquired their legal education by apprenticeship. In the twentieth century, law schools became the dominant source—and today they are essentially the exclusive source—of legal education. The last Supreme Court justice to be trained by apprenticeship was James F. Byrnes, whom President Roosevelt nominated in 1941. Since that time, all justices have been educated in law schools.

In recent years, a handful of schools, including Harvard, Stanford, Yale, and Northwestern, have produced a disproportionate number of justices. The current Court consists of four Harvard graduates (Blackmun, Scalia, Kennedy, and Souter), two Stanford graduates (Rehnquist and O'Connor), two Yale graduates (White and Thomas) and one Northwestern graduate (Stevens).

Political Activity and Partisanship

A substantial proportion of justices were deeply involved in government and politics prior to their appointment to the Supreme Court. Some, such as Justice Black and Chief Justice Warren, had held high elective office. Others, for example, Justice White and Chief Justice Rehnquist, had held high administrative positions in the federal government. Almost all Supreme Court appointees have been politically active in some sense or other. Good examples are Justice Powell (who was active in school affairs in Virginia and was at one time president of the American Bar Association), Justice O'Connor (who was elected to and eventually became majority leader of the Arizona State Senate), and Justice Fortas (who practiced law in Washington, D.C., and participated in myriad ways in Democratic politics at the federal level).

Given the intensely political backgrounds of many Supreme Court justices, it is perhaps not surprising to learn that about 90 percent of appointees to the Court have come from the same political party as the appointing president. Of course, there have been some notable cross-party appointments. Among them were Benjamin Cardozo (a Democrat appointed by President Hoover in 1932), Harlan Stone (a Republican elevated from associate justice to chief justice by President Roosevelt in 1941), William Brennan (a Democrat appointed by President Eisenhower in 1956), and Lewis Powell (a Democrat appointed by President Nixon in 1971).

Prior Judicial Experience

One question that is often asked about Supreme Court appointees is whether they have had prior *judicial* experience, as distinct from merely *legal* experience. About 50 percent of all appointees have served as judges prior to being appointed to the Supreme Court, but only about 25 percent have had "extensive judicial careers."[18] Justice Frankfurter, who was a law professor and had no judicial experience, maintained that "the correlation between prior judicial experience and fitness for the Supreme Court is zero."[19] The accuracy of his observation is borne out by the large number of respected justices who had little or no judicial experience prior to their appointment to the Supreme Court. Among them are John Marshall, who is almost universally considered to be the greatest of all Supreme Court justices, as well as Charles Evans Hughes, Louis Brandeis, Harlan F. Stone, Hugo Black, William Douglas, Robert Jackson, Earl Warren, Byron White, Lewis Powell, and William Rehnquist.

The trend in recent years has been to appoint justices who did have at least some prior judicial experience. This trend may reflect the fact that presidents believe prior judicial experience represents an important professional qualification. A more cynical but perhaps more realistic explanation, however, is that prior judicial experience allows presidents to get a firmer fix on the political and judicial attitudes of potential nominees. In any case, every appointee since 1975 has had state or federal judicial experience, including John Paul Stevens (U.S. Court of Appeals for the Seventh Circuit), Sandra Day O'Connor (Arizona Court of Appeals), Antonin Scalia (U.S. Court of Appeals for the District of Columbia), Anthony Kennedy (U.S. Court of Appeals for the Ninth Circuit), David Souter (New Hampshire Supreme Court), and Clarence Thomas (U.S. Court of Appeals for the District of Columbia).

Conclusion

The process of appointing a justice to the United States Supreme Court is relatively straightforward but also intensely political. The potential appointee is nominated by the president, scrutinized and then confirmed by the Senate, and, finally, appointed to the Court. Once on the Court, a justice serves until he or she dies, resigns, or is impeached.

The individuals who have served on the Supreme Court since 1789 have not been typical of the population as a whole. Supreme Court justices are more likely than the average American to come from high-status, politically active families, to be related by blood or marriage to others in the legal profession, and to possess degrees from prestigious colleges and universities. All Supreme Court justices have acquired legal training, and those appointed in recent years have tended to be graduates of the most prestigious law schools. With three exceptions, all Supreme Court justices have been white males.

Most Supreme Court justices—about 90 percent—have been members of the same political party as the president who appointed them. Virtually all Supreme Court appointees have had distinguished careers in politics or law, or both, prior to coming to the Supreme Court. About half of all appointees have had prior experience as judges, and, since 1975, Supreme Court justices have been drawn exclusively from the ranks of persons with lower court experience.

One explanation for the tendency of presidents to select justices who have been active in politics or who have served on lower courts is that presidents do not wish to be unpleasantly surprised by the voting behavior of persons they appoint for life to the Supreme Court. An individual's record of public service provides the president with a basis for predicting how that individual will decide particular constitutional and legal issues. This suggests the importance of examining whether judicial voting behavior is, in fact, predictable, a question to which we turn in the next section.

Justices' Values and Judicial Behavior

In the ideal, a Supreme Court justice is someone who is probing, objective, dispassionate, open-minded, conscientious, and fair. For such a justice, each case is absolutely unique and should be decided on its own merits, with careful reference to the facts of the case, the state of the law, the relevant judicial precedents, and the text of the Constitution. The justice's personal values or policy preferences should not influence how the justice votes, and the result in each case should appeal to virtually everyone in the community, including those who are parties to the case, as a "just result."

Does this idealistic conception accurately describe the behavior of justices of the Supreme Court? Undoubtedly, many justices embody at least some of these ideal characteristics. There is also no doubt, however, that some distance exists between the idealistic conception of judicial behavior and the reality of Supreme Court decision making. Our focus in this section is on the voting behavior of the justices and the factors on which it is based.

Voting Behavior among Supreme Court Justices

A number of options may be used to identify voting patterns among Supreme Court justices. Most of them start from the assumption that constitutional issues, like other issues in the political arena, can be examined with reference to the traditional liberal-conservative spectrum. In most cases, and certainly in most civil liberties cases, a victory for one side in the litigation can be classified as a liberal result, while a victory for the other side can be classified as a conservative result. Voting patterns among Supreme Court justices are explored by determining how individual justices voted over time in particular categories of cases.

One useful perspective on voting patterns among Supreme Court justices is provided by information compiled every year by the editors of the *Harvard Law Review*. The *Review* publishes statistics on the percentage of time that individual justices agreed with one another in full-opinion cases during the previous term of the Court. Statistics for the 1989 term of the Court are presented in Table 13.1.

It is clear from the table that there are distinct voting patterns among Supreme Court justices and that some pairs of justices are more compatible with one another than other pairs. Chief Justice Rehnquist agreed with Associate Justices White, O'Connor, Scalia, and Kennedy more than 80 percent of the time during the 1989 term. However, he agreed with Justices Brennan and Marshall less than 40 percent of the time, and with Justices Blackmun and Stevens only slightly more often. Justices Brennan and Marshall, on the other hand, found themselves on the same side of nearly 95 percent of cases decided by the Court, and each, in turn, agreed with Justices Blackmun and Stevens about two-thirds of the time.

The conclusion that there are distinctive voting patterns among Supreme Court justices is bolstered by evidence of how the Court divided in its 5-to-4 decisions during the 1989 term. There were thirty-nine such decisions, and in eighteen, or nearly half of the total, the five-person majority consisted of the same five justices—Rehnquist, White, O'Connor, Scalia, and Kennedy. In seven additional cases, however, Justice White joined with Justices Brennan, Marshall, Blackmun, and Stevens to form a five-person "liberal" majority.[20] With the addition of Justice Souter (in 1990) and Justice Thomas (in 1991),

TABLE 13.1

Voting Alignments among Supreme Court Justices, 1989 Term

	Justices								
	Rehnquist	Brennan	White	Marshall	Blackmun	Stevens	O'Connor	Scalia	Kennedy
Kennedy	83	44	74	41	56	46	83	84	—
Scalia	81	38	71	37	50	45	80	—	
O'Connor	82	42	75	39	57	47	—		
Stevens	48	66	53	64	61	—			
Blackmun	55	73	62	70	—				
Marshall	37	94	46	—					
White	82	46	—						
Brennan	38	—							
Rehnquist	—								

Note: This table reports the percentage of the time that one justice voted with another in full-opinion decisions (in both civil liberties and non-civil liberties cases) during the 1989 term. The table includes both unanimous and nonunanimous decisions.

SOURCE: "The Supreme Court, 1989 Term (Part IV: The Statistics)," 104 *Harv. L. Rev.* 360 (November 1990).

the conservative majority on the Court has increased, and it will be difficult to put together a liberal majority on very many, if any, of the civil liberties cases that reach the Court.

We must be careful, of course, not to exaggerate the degree to which voting on the Supreme Court follows rigid ideological lines. Even though agreement between liberals and conservatives on the Court is rare, it is not nonexistent, even in civil liberties cases. One of the cases decided during the 1989 term was *United States* v. *Eichman*, in which the Court, by a 5-to-4 majority, struck down the congressional statute prohibiting flag desecration. The majority consisted of Justices Brennan, Marshall, Blackmun, Scalia, and Kennedy. Agreement among these five justices on civil liberties issues is not very common. As the *Eichman* decision proves, however, it is not unheard of.

Individual Justices' Support for Civil Liberties

An additional perspective on voting patterns among Supreme Court justices is provided by statistics showing the frequency with which individual justices support the "liberal" outcome in civil liberties cases over time. As we noted in Chapter 4, researchers have found measurable trends in support for liberal versus conservative outcomes in civil liberties cases on the part of the Court as an institution. The data collection project which has yielded this information — the Supreme Court Data Base Project — has also collected systematic evidence of voting patterns in civil liberties cases among individual justices.

The results are presented in Table 13.2. The table shows the percentage of liberal votes cast by individual justices in nonunanimous civil liberties cases over time. The table also shows whether there was any change in support for liberal outcomes on the part of individual justices who were members of the Court under both Chief Justice Warren (1953–1969) and Chief Justice Burger (1969–1986).

The table clearly reveals the existence of vast differences in support for liberal outcomes in civil liberties cases. Justice Douglas voted in a liberal direction well over 90 percent of the time in both the Warren and Burger courts. Not far behind — voting in a liberal direction at least three-fourths of the time — were Chief Justice Warren and Associate Justices Brennan, Marshall, Goldberg, and Fortas, as well as Justice Black (but only during the Warren Court). Evidence of the depth of the liberal-conservative split on the Warren Court is found in the fact that after Justice Black, the next most liberal justice was Justice White, who supported liberal outcomes only 44 percent of the time. Not one member of the Warren Court voted in a liberal direction "moderately often," that is, between 45 and 74 percent of the time.

The table also indicates that at least some justices may alter their stance on civil liberties issues as their career on the Court develops. Justice White was somewhat less supportive of liberal outcomes during the Burger Court than during the Warren Court. Justice Black, the table shows, was consider-

TABLE 13.2

Justices' Support for Liberal Outcomes in Nonunanimous Civil Liberties
Cases during the Warren and Burger Courts

	Warren Court *(1953–1969)*			*Burger Court* *(1969–1986)*	
Justice	Liberal Decisions (%)	(n)	Justice	Liberal Decisions (%)	(n)
Douglas	96.1	(583)	Douglas	94.1	(374)
Goldberg	87.3	(102)			
Marshall	83.5	(79)	Marshall	88.5	(1078)
Fortas	81.1	(159)			
Warren	77.6	(576)			
Brennan	76.0	(509)	Brennan	85.5	(1086)
Black	74.7	(582)	Black	43.9	(107)
			Stevens	61.4	(676)
White	44.2	(278)	White	33.7	(1103)
Stewart	39.6	(424)	Stewart	43.6	(782)
			Blackmun	39.5	(1056)
Jackson	38.9	(18)			
Frankfurter	37.1	(278)			
			Powell	31.2	(940)
Whittaker	26.1	(184)			
Clark	24.7	(485)			
			O'Connor	24.5	(318)
Harlan	22.1	(551)	Harlan	27.6	(105)
Burton	21.4	(159)			
			Burger	17.6	(1099)
Minton	17.5	(63)			
Reed	12.2	(74)			
			Rehnquist	5.6	(959)

Note: A "liberal outcome" is defined as a victory for (1) a person accused or convicted of a crime, (2) a civil liberties or civil rights claimant, (3) an indigent litigant, (4) an Indian litigant, (5) someone alleging that government has violated his or her right to due process of law, or (6) someone alleging that government has violated his or her right of privacy.

SOURCE: Jeffrey A. Segal and Harold J. Spaeth, "Decisional Trends in the Warren and Burger Courts: Results from the Supreme Court Data Base Project," 73 *Judicature* 103, 106 (1989).

ably less supportive of liberal outcomes as his tenure on the Court lengthened.[21]

Of course, the opposite trend—from being relatively conservative to being relatively liberal—is also possible. The justice in recent years who exemplifies this possibility is Blackmun. The *Harvard Law Review* data on agreement among pairs of justices (see Table 13.1 above) reveals that over the years Justice Blackmun has gravitated to a point of greater agreement with the liberal than with the conservative members of the Court. In his early years, Blackmun agreed with Chief Justice Burger much more often than he did with

Justice Brennan. In the 1985 term, however, these "levels of agreement" were reversed. Blackmun agreed with Burger about half the time but agreed with Brennan in 80 percent of cases. In the 1986–1988 terms, Brennan and Blackmun continued to agree in nearly 80 percent of the Court's cases.[22]

The foregoing statistics suggest several tentative conclusions. First, there are detectable voting patterns among Supreme Court justices, and those patterns are strongly related to the ideological content of cases the Court is asked (and chooses) to decide. Second, however, not all justices on the Court are rigidly liberal or rigidly conservative in their voting patterns. Some justices are better classified as moderates or swing votes, because they sometimes vote in a liberal direction and sometimes in a conservative one. Third, at least some justices may gradually alter their position on civil liberties issues over the course of their career on the Court. Finally, individual cases may create "strange bedfellows" among the justices, producing an outcome in which even the most liberal and most conservative justices find themselves on the same side of an issue.[23]

Thus, various factors — including the presence of moderate justices, gradual changes in the orientation of individual justices, and the formation of unusual alliances in particular cases — may blur the ideological clarity of voting patterns on the Supreme Court. At the same time, the patterns themselves are rather strong and quite persistent. This raises the question of what "causes" justices to behave in relatively predictable ways.[24]

Origins of Judicial Voting Behavior

Researchers have had only moderate success in pinning down the sources or causes of the voting behavior of Supreme Court justices. There are a variety of impediments to establishing a connection between justices' characteristics and how they vote on constitutional issues. Together these impediments leave us with less than a clear picture of why justices behave as they do.

Personal Values and Voting Behavior

The most proximate source of voting behavior, of course, will be a justice's personal values or policy preferences. If a justice holds liberal or conservative views on various social and political issues, he or she will be likely to vote in accordance with those views once appointed to the Supreme Court. The linkage between personal values and voting behavior may be difficult to establish, however, because of the difficulty of obtaining independent measures of justices' values, that is, measures that predate their appointment to the Court. In the past, Senate hearings on a justice's confirmation were not necessarily very lengthy or probing. During recent years, although Senate hearings have become elaborate affairs, justices have become quite adept at deflecting questions about their personal values and their future voting behavior. It is considered improper for a justice to allow his or her personal values to intrude on the process of deciding cases. Therefore, it is exceedingly unwise for a nominee to enable senators to establish a connection between, for instance, the nominee's views on abortion and the nominee's intentions should the Court be presented with an opportunity to overrule *Roe* v. *Wade*. In short, the search for a connection between justices' values and their voting behavior has tended to frustrate both senators and social scientists.[25]

Judicial Role Values and Voting Behavior

An additional category of values that may influence a justice's voting behavior are what are sometimes known as "judicial role values." These are values that a justice may hold, for instance, about the propriety of dissenting from Court decisions (regardless of the decision itself) or about the legitimacy of judicial activism versus judicial restraint (regardless of the issue before the Court). Given the obvious importance of policy preferences in influencing judicial behavior, the interesting question is whether a justice's view of the proper role of a judge will ever override his or her view of the proper outcome of a case from a policy point of view.

Certain situations pose this dilemma with great clarity. Imagine, for instance, that a justice believes in judicial restraint but also believes that the fetus enjoys a "right to life" under the Constitution. For such a justice, deciding a case in which a state has passed a law outlawing abortion is easy, because there is no conflict between a posture of judicial restraint and support for an anti-abortion result. If, on the other hand, a state enacts legislation explicitly authorizing abortion, the justice will face a dilemma. Should he or she exercise judicial restraint and allow the legislation to stand, or should he take an activist position and vote to overturn the legislation on the ground that it interferes with the constitutionally protected right to life?

An additional example of the tension between role values and policy preferences is provided by the issue of affirmative action. By almost any measure, Justice Brennan would be classified as a judicial activist, and he has always been in favor of judicial intervention in situations of alleged discrimination against blacks, women, and ethnic minorities. The dilemma for Justice Brennan, therefore, is how to approach cases involving alleged discrimination against white males. The consistent position for a justice who was wholly committed to judicial activism would be to overturn preferential treatment because it conflicts with the principle that the Constitution is color blind and cannot tolerate discrimination based on race. This outcome, however, conflicts with the belief that blacks and others have been the victims of societal discrimination and should benefit from affirmative action programs, even at the expense of innocent whites. In the *Bakke* case, Brennan solved this dilemma by arguing that the Court should be slightly less activist in evaluating racial classifications that discriminate against whites than those that discriminate against blacks.[26]

Brennan's partial abandonment of a position of judicial activism in affirmative action cases is an indication that a justice's role values are likely to take second place to his or her policy preferences when a conflict between the two arises. Judicial scholars — to say nothing of the justices themselves — continue to debate the relationship between role values and policy preferences as a source of judicial behavior. The most plausible conclusion, however, as expressed by one leading student of the Court, is that "history suggests that positions on activism and restraint have served chiefly as justifications of policy choices rather than determining those choices themselves."[27]

Party Affiliation and Voting Behavior

A connection may also exist between the political party affiliation of Supreme Court appointees and their voting behavior while on the Court. Indeed, such a connection would seem to be almost self-evident. President Franklin D. Roosevelt made mostly Democratic appointments and in addition chose individuals who were economic liberals and were generally supportive of individual rights. Republican presidents from Nixon to Bush have, for the most part, chosen members of their own party and have looked for individuals who would be disposed to vote for rather than against government on issues involving freedom of speech, equal protection, criminal procedure, and privacy. Thus, it would be surprising *not* to find at least some connection between party affiliation and voting behavior.

Unfortunately, given the small number of people on the Court and the changing composition of American political parties, it has been difficult for researchers to establish a firm connection between party affiliation and voting behavior among Supreme Court justices. In addition, of course, one obvious strategy for making successful appointments to the Supreme Court is for the president to cross party lines, but not ideological lines, in selecting a nominee. A Democratic president who chooses a liberal Republican or a Republican president who chooses a conservative Democrat will substantially improve the prospects for confirmation by providing two separate groups of senators with a reason to vote for the nominee. Even the occasional use of this strategy, however, will undermine any hypothesized connection between party affiliation (i.e., being a Democrat) and voting behavior (i.e., voting in a liberal direction).[28]

The Impact of Race, Sex, and Social Origins on Voting Behavior

A final possible source of voting behavior among Supreme Court justices may be characteristics such as their race, sex, or social origins. The theory is that certain groups — for example, blacks, women, or persons of humble origin — are relatively likely to cast liberal votes in constitutional cases. The theory runs into immediate trouble, however, when faced with examples such as Chief Justices Warren and Burger (both of whom had humble origins, but one of whom was liberal and one of whom was conservative) and Justices Thurgood Marshall and Clarence Thomas (both of whom are black and from humble origins, but one of whom was very liberal and one of whom, evidently, is very conservative).

Some scholars have claimed that the background characteristics of Supreme Court justices are good predictors of voting behavior.[29] Others have disputed the strength or lasting accuracy of these findings.[30] For now, it appears we must be cautious about predicting how justices will vote on constitutional issues based purely on information about their backgrounds or characteristics.

Conclusion

We have all been taught that a judge should approach each case without preconceptions and should make decisions based purely on the law and the facts. It is not that we expect judges to be people who have no personal values or policy preferences; but we do expect judges to put aside those values and preferences when deciding cases. Judges are supposed to be conscientious, fearless, and objective and should reach decisions based on the merits of the opposing claims in light of the governing principles of statutory and constitutional law.

This ideal conception of what judges do is not completely erroneous, but at least in the case of Supreme Court justices it requires substantial revision in order to conform to reality. Supreme Court justices are chosen in part because of their intellectual qualifications and in part because of their long-held views on social, economic, political, and constitutional issues. Once on the Court, most justices behave accordingly. They bring to the Court considerable intellectual energy and professional competence. They also approach each case with an array of personal values and policy preferences that predate their appointment to the Court, that have been developed over a lifetime of often intense professional activity and public service, and that cannot fail to exert a substantial influence on how the justice perceives and decides particular cases.

The impact of policy preferences on voting behavior produces distinctive and persistent voting patterns among the justices. The evidence suggests that many justices are committed to either relatively liberal or relatively conservative political values before they reach the Supreme Court and that those values continue to influence their decision making during the years they serve on the Court. There are, of course, exceptions. Some justices are judicial moderates and do not align themselves consistently with either the liberal or the conservative wing of the Court. Moreover, the views of some justices undergo a substantial transformation during their years on the Court. Finally, some cases produce unusual coalitions of justices. On balance, however, the evidence suggests that Supreme Court decisions are explicable in terms of the "left-right" continuum that we commonly use to evaluate political issues and that personal values and policy preferences are largely responsible for determining how individual justices react to specific cases.

The weight of the evidence suggests, therefore, that presidents who are inclined to do so can remake the Supreme Court in their image through the appointment process. A president who carefully selects well-qualified but ideologically compatible nominees may be able to mold the Supreme Court into an institution that decides constitutional issues in conformity with presidential preferences long after the president himself has left office. To determine whether this represents a viable strategy for exerting "internal control" of Supreme Court decision making, let us turn to the historical record.

The Appointment Process in Historical Perspective

Since 1789 a total of 106 individuals have served on the Supreme Court. All were appointed by presidents who were determined, to some degree or other, to leave their imprint on the Court. The question we address in this section is the degree to which presidents have succeeded in shaping the Supreme Court to their liking and the degree to which, in doing so, they have been able to make the Supreme Court responsive to the will of the majority.[31]

The President and the Supreme Court in the Early Years

President Washington, of course, was the first and only president to have an opportunity to appoint the entire Supreme Court at one time. He appointed staunch Federalists to the Court, as did his successor, John Adams. Indeed, it was Adams who appointed John Marshall as chief justice, in 1801, and launched the Court on an extended period of Federalist decision making that lasted up to and beyond Marshall's death in 1835.

Washington and Adams wanted nominees, writes one Supreme Court scholar, "who would support the broad exercise of power by the national government . . . and who would limit the power of the states to interfere with . . . national purposes."[32] Washington and Adams were singularly successful in achieving this objective, for "no Federalist dissent was ever recorded against the great Federalist decisions of the first forty years of the Republic."[33] In addition, even the justices appointed by Jefferson and Madison developed a sympathy, once on the Court, for Federalist principles, and they almost never dissented from the Court's Federalist decisions.[34]

In this latter phenomenon — justices appointed by Jefferson and Madison who voted for Federalist outcomes in constitutional cases — we see an early example of the difficulty that presidents may face in guaranteeing that their values are reflected in Supreme Court decisions. Once on the Court, a president's appointees may fall under the sway of incumbent justices or may alter their views on constitutional issues. The president's attempt to perpetuate his values and those of the constituents he represents may come to naught.

The Civil War and the Supreme Court

President Lincoln faced a number of problems when he took office, including a Supreme Court that was not altogether supportive of his approach to the slavery issue. During the course of his presidency, Lincoln appointed five justices to the Court, including Chief Justice Salmon Chase, who replaced Roger Taney, with whom Lincoln had tangled on several occasions before and during the War. The justices whom Lincoln appointed supported him on critical issues during the war, but after the war—and after Lincoln's death—they joined with other members of the Court to declare some of the actions that Lincoln had taken during the war to be unconstitutional.[35]

A dramatic example of the importance of the appointment power occurred during the administration of President Grant (1868–1876). In 1870, by a vote of 4 to 3, the Court in *Hepburn* v. *Griswold* invalidated a congressional statute, passed to help finance the Civil War, that authorized private individuals to use paper money as legal tender for the purpose of discharging debts. On the very day the Court handed down its decision—and, according to some, in part because he was aware in advance of how the Court would vote—President Grant nominated two individuals to fill vacancies on the Court (William Strong and Joseph Bradley) who were known to support the Republican policy of permitting paper money to be used as legal tender.[36] Fifteen months later, in a pair of cases known as the Legal Tender Cases, the Court overruled itself and, by a vote of 5 to 4, upheld the congressional legislation.

President Roosevelt, the New Deal, and the Supreme Court

President Franklin Roosevelt had no opportunities to appoint anyone to the Supreme Court during his first term in office. Between 1937 and 1943, however, he made up for lost time, appointing eight new justices and elevating Harlan Fiske Stone to chief justice. Well before he made his later appointments, Roosevelt had secured control of the Court and could depend on the Court to uphold New Deal legislation. According to Robert Scigliano, Roosevelt's appointees did not agree among themselves on "subsidiary questions of economic regulation." That hardly mattered, however, because "[n]ot one of Roosevelt's justices ever took a position in a case against the New Deal or against a state tax or business regulation on the ground that the state enactment was not permitted by the due process clause of the Fourteenth Amendment. By 1941, with seven Roosevelt justices on the Court, Roosevelt's domestic objectives were, for all practical purposes, fully achieved."[37]

The reaction of Roosevelt's appointees to the new civil liberties cases that were coming to the Court was more complicated. In *Minersville School District* v. *Gobitis*, decided in 1940, all five of Roosevelt's early appointees (Black, Reed, Frankfurter, Douglas, and Murphy) voted to uphold the flag salute requirement. As we saw in Chapter 5, however, by 1942 three of those justices—Black, Douglas, and Murphy—had concluded that *Gobitis* was "wrongly decided." When the Court reexamined the flag salute issue in *West Virginia State Board of Education* v. *Barnette*, in 1943, only Frankfurter and Reed (along with Hoover appointee Owen Roberts) voted to uphold the power of the school board to expel students for refusing to salute the flag.

Congress, the Supreme Court, and the Child Labor Issue

The reaction of the "Roosevelt Court" to one important issue of congressional regulatory power illustrates why it may be more efficacious to control the Supreme Court from the inside than to employ external methods to try to restrain the Court. In 1918, in *Hammer* v. *Dagenhart*, the Supreme Court invalidated a congressional statute restricting the movement in interstate commerce of goods made by child labor. The *Dagenhart* decision was an example of the economic conservatism of the Supreme Court and of the Court's hostility to the expansion of congressional regulatory power over economic affairs.

In response to *Dagenhart* — and to *Bailey* v. *Drexel Furniture Co.* (1922), a second Supreme Court decision overturning congressional legislation aimed at regulating child labor — Congress in 1924 passed and sent to the states a child labor amendment. The purpose of the amendment was to reverse the Court's decisions and to permit Congress to prohibit child labor. By the late 1930s, however, the amendment had been ratified by only twenty-eight of the thirty-six states necessary to meet the Constitution's requirement of approval by "the Legislatures of three-fourths of the several States."

In the meantime, however, the New Deal Congress passed new legislation — the Fair Labor Standards Act of 1938 — which outlawed interstate commerce in products made by child labor. In 1941, in *United States* v. *Darby Lumber Co.*, the "Roosevelt Court" unanimously overruled *Dagenhart* and upheld the legislation. The obvious lesson was that, once the Supreme Court's opposition to child labor legislation had been neutralized through the appointment process, Congress could achieve its long-sought goal of outlawing child labor with comparative ease.[38]

Truman, Eisenhower, Kennedy, and Johnson

President Roosevelt had a special need to try to remake the Supreme Court as quickly as possible into a body that would give constitutional approval to his legislative policies. Some of his successors in office have been less obsessed with the Court's composition. President Truman's four appointees — Sherman Minton, Harold Burton, Tom Clark, and Fred Vinson — were noted for their personal loyalty to Truman rather than their expertise on constitutional issues. "[W]ith the possible exception of Justice Clark," one scholar has written, "Truman's Justices were perhaps the least distinguished group of appointments made by any President in this century."[39] At the same time, Truman's desire to reward his friends did not require him to sacrifice ideological goals. Truman, this same scholar has written, "cared about three things: support for government regulatory authority, sympathy for the civil rights of blacks, and a stern appreciation of the needs of internal security during the Cold War. He got what he wanted."[40]

President Eisenhower, a moderate Republican president, made five appointments to the Court. With three of them—John Harlan, Charles Whittaker, and Potter Stewart—he was not, presumably, displeased. The other two, however, were a different story. Eisenhower nominated Earl Warren to become chief justice in 1953 and William Brennan to become associate justice in 1956. Warren and Brennan were key members of the liberal bloc of justices that coalesced in the early 1960s. When Eisenhower was asked, after leaving office, whether he had made any mistakes while president, he is reported to have replied: "Yes, two, and they are both sitting on the Supreme Court."[41]

President Kennedy was in office only three years but made two appointments to the Court. Justice White, who is now the senior associate justice on the Court, has generally been viewed as taking a moderate to conservative position on constitutional issues. Justice Goldberg, who was on the Court for only three years (from 1962 to 1965), was a solid member of the Court's liberal bloc of justices.

President Johnson made two appointments to the Court during his five years in office. In 1965 he appointed Abe Fortas to replace Goldberg, and in 1967 he elevated Thurgood Marshall to the Supreme Court from the U.S. Court of Appeals for the District of Columbia (a position to which Marshall had been appointed, in 1962, by President Kennedy). Johnson attempted to appoint Fortas to the position of chief justice in 1968, but, as we have seen, Fortas's name was withdrawn when the Senate failed to end a filibuster against the nomination.

President Nixon and the Origins of Today's Conservative Court

President Nixon was publicly committed to altering the Supreme Court's stance on various constitutional issues. He made a particular issue of wanting to reverse the Court's strong record of support for the procedural rights of criminal defendants. During both the 1968 campaign and his presidency, he announced that he would search for justices who would be tough on criminals and take a "law and order" position on issues of defendants' rights. In pursuit of this goal, he appointed Warren Burger to the position of chief justice and added three new justices—Blackmun, Powell, and Rehnquist—to the Court.

Nixon achieved his goal of curtailing the Supreme Court's support for criminal defendants. A study by two scholars of the voting record of Nixon's appointees concluded that Nixon was "markedly successful in choosing nominees . . . whose voting behavior [in criminal procedure cases] reflected policy views that were in agreement with his own."[42]

Nixon was much less successful, however, in exploiting the appointment process to achieve his policy goals in other areas. In his choice of Warren Burger to become chief justice, one commentator has written, "President Nixon found himself a chief justice who was tough on crooks, but then alas he turned out to be tough on presidents, too, and soft on abortion."[43] The conclusion that Burger was "soft on abortion" refers to the fact that Burger — along with Blackmun and Powell, two other Nixon appointees — was part of the seven-justice majority that held in *Roe* v. *Wade* that state laws prohibiting abortion are unconstitutional. The conclusion that Burger was "tough on presidents" is based on the fact that Burger authored the opinion of the Court in *United States* v. *Nixon* (1974). The Court's decision ordered Nixon to release secretly recorded White House tapes, and when the tapes implicated Nixon in the conspiracy to cover up the Watergate break-in, the president was forced to resign from office.

The Republican Party, the White House, and the Supreme Court Since 1969

President Nixon's Supreme Court appointments were the first of a succession of justices appointed by Republican presidents. President Ford became president when Nixon resigned in 1974. In 1975 he appointed Justice Stevens to fill the vacancy left by the resignation of Justice Douglas. Douglas had been appointed by President Roosevelt and had served on the Court for thirty-six years, longer than any other justice in history.

President Reagan's appointments to the Court began with Justice O'Connor, whom he appointed in 1981. In 1986 William Rehnquist became chief justice, replacing Chief Justice Burger, and Antonin Scalia took Rehnquist's place as associate justice. President Reagan's final appointment was Justice Anthony Kennedy, who joined the Court in 1988.

President Bush's nomination of David Souter was confirmed by the Senate in 1990. Souter replaced Justice Brennan, who retired in 1990 after thirty-four years on the Court. The most recent appointment to the Court was Bush's choice of Clarence Thomas to replace Thurgood Marshall, who retired in 1991.

Jimmy Carter is the only Democrat to occupy the White House since 1969, and no vacancies occurred during his presidency (1977 – 1981). The vagaries of the appointment process since 1969 have therefore produced a Court that includes only one justice — Justice White — who was appointed by a Democratic president.

The Overall Record of Presidential Success

All presidents, when presented with an opportunity to appoint someone to the Supreme Court, have been aware that the person they appoint will serve for life. Under the circumstances, all presidents have been concerned, to some degree or other, with choosing justices with whom they will feel comfortable. "There is nothing shocking in the fact," one scholar has written, "that Presidents generally appoint persons they believe share, by-and-large, their own views on important constitutional questions."[44] Some presidents have been more concerned than others about picking nominees who will display personal loyalty or will vote precisely as the president would wish on issues that might come before the Court. No president, it is safe to say, has been oblivious to these considerations.

Scholars who have examined the question have concluded that presidents are successful about 75 percent of the time in selecting justices who decide cases, once they are on the Court, as the president would wish them to.[45] There are, of course, notorious "failures" from this point of view. Two of Eisenhower's choices — Warren and Brennan — and one of Nixon's choices — Blackmun — come to mind. On the whole, however, presidents have been rather successful in choosing justices who reflect their views.

What is perhaps even more important, however, is that presidents can raise their "success rate" in choosing compatible nominees to nearly 100 percent if they take a few simple precautions. Notably, they should exercise care in choosing nominees, selecting nominees with an established record of judicial service on a lower court, and making ideological fidelity a principal criterion in the selection process. It is highly unlikely, Lawrence Tribe has concluded, that

> a determined President who takes the trouble to pick his Justices with care [and] who selects them with an eye to their demonstrated views on subjects of concern to him . . . will simply guess wrong and end up nominating a liberal in conservative garb or a conservative in liberal dress. Such rude surprises have occurred, but they are few, and a President with any skill and a little luck can usually avoid them — and can, with fair success, build the Court of his dreams.[46]

The Appointment Process and Political Control of the Supreme Court

The evidence is fairly clear, therefore, that a president who is determined to do so can make appointments to the Supreme Court who will fulfil the president's policy goals. Supreme Court appointees serve for life. If they are chosen with careful attention to their views on constitutional issues, they can perpetuate the policy preferences of the president who appointed them long after the president himself has left office.

Ultimately, however, our concern is not with whether presidents can appoint individual justices who will fulfil the president's policy agenda but whether the appointment process is a viable method for maintaining majoritarian control of Supreme Court decision making. The latter question raises at least two issues that are bypassed by the former. The first issue is whether the appointment process can remake the Supreme Court with sufficient speed to keep the Court in tune with majoritarian preferences. The second is whether the president, in making Supreme Court appointments, is in fact a faithful representative of the will of the majority.

Assuming for the moment that the president does represent the will of the majority, it is clear that the appointment process is at best a painstaking method of remaking the Court. On average, a vacancy on the Supreme Court occurs once every twenty-two months. At that rate, it takes over sixteen years, or four presidential terms, to replace all nine members of the Court.

The present system is the equivalent, in that sense, of making th
Court an elective body but allowing citizens to replace the justices, a
only a little more often than six times in each century.

Of course, if there is a sustained period of dominance by one political
party or the other — as there was in the case of the Democratic party between
1932 and 1952 or the Republican party between 1968 and the present — it is
possible for the political majority represented by the president to gradually
remake the Court. The irony, however, is that once that process has been fully
accomplished — indeed, precisely *because* it has been fully accomplished —
any *new* majority that emerges in American politics will be looking at a period
of many years before *its* preferences can achieve adequate representation
within the confines of the Court. From this perspective, the appointment
process is clearly not a particularly prompt or efficient mechanism for keeping
the Supreme Court in touch with the will of the majority.

In addition, of course, we must be careful not to assume that the president is an adequate representative of the will of the majority for purposes of
reconstituting the Supreme Court. It is true that the president is the only
elected official who is chosen by a national constituency. It is also true,
however, that only about half of all eligible voters cast ballots in any given
presidential election. Moreover, no single presidential candidate can perfectly
represent the preferences of the American people on every constitutional issue
that may face the Supreme Court. To the extent that the preferences of the
president diverge from those of the American people, the appointment process is not a foolproof method of allowing the will of the majority to exert an
internal influence on the direction of Supreme Court decision making.

Thus, the appointment process has severe drawbacks as a method of
maintaining majoritarian control of the Supreme Court. On balance, however,
it seems fair to conclude that as a method of political control it is preferable
to the various external restraints we discussed in Chapter 12. It is unthinkable
that a liberal justice such as Thurgood Marshall or William Brennan would
ever modify his settled views in response to the threat of impeachment or
other external pressures on the Court. Nor is it likely that William Rehnquist
or Antonin Scalia will ever announce his conversion to a liberal Democratic
view of the world. The replacement of a justice who thinks one way by a
justice who thinks another way can have a substantial impact on Supreme
Court decision making. The replacement of several justices can have a profound effect. In the absence of such an internal transformation in the composition of the Court, however, it is not realistic to expect the Court to
substantially change its approach to constitutional issues.[47]

Conclusion

The process of appointing Supreme Court justices involves several actors,
including the president, the Senate, interest groups, and the American public.
The president is empowered by the Constitution to nominate new justices.

The Senate holds hearings and votes to confirm or not to confirm the president's choice. Interest groups testify for or against the nominee during the Senate hearings. The American public is "consulted" in public opinion polls conducted during the confirmation process. If the nominee is confirmed by a majority vote in the Senate, he or she takes a seat on the Supreme Court and begins deciding cases.

The Senate usually, but not invariably, confirms the president's nominee. Many justices are confirmed by a unanimous vote or by acclamation. Since 1968, however, four nominations — those of Fortas (to become chief justice) and Haynsworth, Carswell, and Bork (to become associate justices) — have been defeated by the Senate. Moreover, President Reagan's nomination of William Rehnquist to become chief justice (in 1986) and President Bush's nomination of Clarence Thomas to become associate justice (in 1991) resulted in relatively close votes in the senate.

Persons appointed to the Supreme Court since 1789 have not been typical of the population as a whole. Relatively few justices have come from humble origins. Of the 106 individuals who have served on the Court, only two have been black and only one has been a woman. All Supreme Court justices have had legal training, and about one quarter have had substantial judicial experience prior to being appointed to the Court.

Voting behavior among Supreme Court justices may be explained in part in terms of the distinction between liberal and conservative solutions to political problems. Many justices — some more than others — are consistently likely to vote in a liberal or a conservative direction in constitutional cases. Although there are exceptions, on balance the liberal-conservative spectrum by which political issues in general are analyzed is helpful in comprehending and predicting the voting behavior of Supreme Court justices.

The personal values and policy preferences of Supreme Court nominees have been developed over a lifetime of public service and professional activity. Presidents rely on this information in deciding whom to nominate. All presidents have shown at least some concern for the policy preferences of those they choose to nominate. Some presidents, notably Lincoln, Roosevelt, Nixon, Reagan, and Bush, have been particularly determined to use the appointment process to control or reshape the Court.

Overall, presidents have been successful about 75 percent of the time in selecting justices who continue, during their tenure on the Court, to reflect the president's views. A president who is careful in selecting justices and makes ideological compatibility a principal criterion for selection can practically guarantee that his nominees will decide cases more or less as the president would wish.

Even though presidents can usually succeed in selecting ideologically compatible nominees, however, the appointment process is an imperfect mechanism for translating the will of the majority into Supreme Court decisions. First, the Court can be reconstituted only one justice at a time. Thus, a president or political party must remain in office for an extended period in order to effect a substantial change in the Court's orientation. Second, presidents do not always represent the will of the majority on constitutional issues. To the extent that the president does not represent the views of a majority of the American people, the appointment process is an imperfect mechanism for securing majoritarian control of Supreme Court decision making.

Despite its drawbacks, the appointment process appears to be a more efficacious way to control the Supreme Court than the various external controls we discussed in Chapter 12. There is considerable wisdom in Justice Stone's observation, quoted at the beginning of the chapter, that "the only check upon [a justice's] exercise of power is [his or her] own sense of self-restraint." That being the case, no mechanism for exerting political control over the Supreme Court will ever be quite as effective as replacing departing justices with others who hold different views on constitutional issues.

Notes

1. *United States* v. *Butler*, 297 U.S. 1, 79 (Stone, J., dissenting).

2. See Symposium, "Confirmation Controversy: The Selection of a Supreme Court Justice," 84 *Nw. Univ. L. Rev.* 832 (1990).

3. The role of the ABA is explored in Joel B. Grossman, *Lawyers and Judges: The ABA and the Politics of Judicial Selection* (1965).

4. For additional discussion of the role of the ABA in recent nominations, see Robert A. Carp and Ronald Stidham, *The Federal Courts* (1991), pp. 104–6; and Lawrence Baum, *The Supreme Court* (1992), pp. 32–33.

5. Martin Shapiro, "Interest Groups and Supreme Court Appointments," 84 *Nw. Univ. L. Rev.* 935 (1990).

6. Ethan Bronner, *The Battle for Justice: How the Bork Nomination Shook America* (1989); and Robert H. Bork, *The Tempting of America: The Political Seduction of the Law* (1990).

7. Timothy M. Phelps and Helen Winternitz, *Capitol Games: Clarence Thomas, Anita Hill, and the Story of a Supreme Court Nomination* (1992).

8. Elder Witt (ed.), *Congressional Quarterly's Guide to the U.S. Supreme Court* (1990), pp. 995–98.

9. For a discussion of the factors affecting the likelihood of confirmation by the Senate, see Jeffrey A. Segal, "Senate Confirmation of Supreme Court Justices: Partisan and Institutional Politics," 49 *J. of Pol.* 998 (1987). For a detailed examination of the appointment of Pierce Butler to the Supreme Court in 1922, see David J. Danelski, *A Supreme Court Justice Is Appointed* (1964).

10. Three of the individuals who were not confirmed by the Senate were subsequently renominated and confirmed. Among them was Roger Brooke Taney, who became chief justice, succeeding John Marshall, in 1836.

11. Reagan's 1986 nomination of William Rehnquist to become chief justice was also exceptionally controversial. The Senate debate lasted five days, and when it was over, Rehnquist was confirmed by a vote of 65–33.

12. One authoritative source — Witt (ed.), *Congressional Quarterly's Guide to the U.S. Supreme Court* — declines to consider the Ginsberg nomination a formal nomination. See id. at 652.

13. The Haynsworth and Carswell nominations are chronicled in Richard Harris, *Decision* (1971).

14. See Laura Kalmen, *Abe Fortas: A Biography* (1990); and Bruce Allen Murphy, *Fortas: The Rise and Ruin of a Supreme Court Justice* (1988).

15. The argument for an increased role for the Senate in the appointment process is developed in Lawrence Tribe, *God Save This Honorable Court: How the Choice of Supreme Court Justices Shapes Our History* (1985).

16. John R. Schmidhauser, *Judges and Justices: The Federal Appellate Judiciary* (1979), p. 49.

17. Id. at 49–58.

18. Id. at 93.

19. Felix Frankfurter, "The Supreme Court in the Mirror of Justices," 105 *U. Pa. L. Rev.* 781, 795 (1957).

20. *Harvard Law Review*, November 1990, p. 362.

21. See S. Sidney Ulmer, "The Longitudinal Behavior of Hugo LaFayette Black: Parabolic Support for Civil Liberties," 1 *Fla. St. L. Rev.* 131 (1973). See also S. Sidney Ulmer, "Parabolic Support for Civil Liberty Claims: The Case of William O. Douglas," 41 *J. of Pol.* 634 (1979).

22. For a discussion of Blackmun's evolving position on constitutional issues, see Note, "The Changing Social Vision of Justice Blackmun," 96 *Harv. L. Rev.* 717 (1983).

23. There are other ways of examining patterns of voting behavior on the Supreme Court. One is to look at dissent rates, that is, the proportion of the time that particular justices dissent from liberal versus conservative decisions of the Court. See Jeffrey A. Segal and Harold J. Spaeth, "Decisional Trends in the Warren and Burger Courts: Results from the Supreme Court Data Base Project," 73 *Judicature* 103 (1989). Another is to prepare a "scalogram" showing how justices voted in a set of cases — for instance, all cases decided during a particular term of the Court. See Baum, *The Supreme Court*, pp. 140–41.

24. Note that it is possible to examine the justices' voting patterns in cases other than civil liberties cases. For discussions of the justices' voting behavior in "economic" cases, see Timothy M. Hagle and Harold J. Spaeth, "The Emergence of a New Ideology: The Business Decisions of the Burger Court," 54 *J. of Pol.* 120 (1992); Segal and Spaeth, "Decisional Trends in the Warren and Burger Courts"; Craig R. Ducat and Robert L. Dudley, "Dimensions Underlying Economic Policymaking in the Early and Later Burger Courts," 49 *J. of Pol.* 521 (1987); and Robert L. Dudley and Craig R. Ducat, "The Burger Court and Economic Liberalism," 39 *Western Pol. Q.* 236 (1986).

25. For a recent study that does rely on independent measures of justices' values and that finds a strong connection between those values and voting behavior, see Jeffrey A. Segal and Albert D. Cover, "Ideological Values and the Votes of U.S. Supreme Court Justices," 83 *Am. Pol. Sci. Rev.* 557 (1989).

26. *Regents of University of California* v. *Bakke*, 438 U.S. at 324–79 (1978) (Brennan, J., concurring in the judgment in part and dissenting in part).

27. Baum, *The Supreme Court*, p. 148.

28. The task of uncovering relationships between party affiliation and voting behavior is much easier in the case of lower court judges. See Carp and Stidham, *The Federal Courts*, pp. 142–47.

29. C. Neal Tate and Roger Handberg, "Time Binding and Theory Building in Personal Attribute Models of Supreme Court Voting Behavior, 1916–1988," 35 *Am. J. Pol. Sci.* 460 (1991); and C. Neal Tate, "Personal Attribute Models of the Voting Behavior of U.S. Supreme Court Justices: Liberalism in Civil Liberties and Economics Decisions, 1946–1978," 75 *Am. Pol. Sci. Rev.* 355 (1981).

30. S. Sidney Ulmer, "Are Social Background Models Time-Bound?" 80 *Am. Pol. Sci. Rev.* 957 (1986).

31. For additional discussion, see Henry J. Abraham, *Justices and Presidents: A Political History of Appointments to the Supreme Court* (1985).

32. Robert Scigliano, *The Supreme Court and the Presidency* (1971), p. 126.

33. Id.

34. Id. at 127. See also Tribe, *God Save This Honorable Court*, p. 56.

35. *Ex parte Milligan* (1866) (overturning Lincoln's wartime use of military commissions to try civilians). See Allan Nevins, "The Case of the Copperhead Conspirator," in John A. Garraty (ed.), *Quarrels That Have Shaped the Constitution* (1987), pp. 101–18.

36. Charles Fairman, "Mr. Justice Bradley's Appointment to the Supreme Court and the Legal Tender Cases," 54 *Harv. L. Rev.* 1128 (1941); and Sidney Ratner, "Was the Supreme Court Packed by President Grant?" 50 *Pol. Sci. Q.* 343 (1935).

37. Scigliano, *The Supreme Court and the Presidency*, p. 137.

38. See Frank J. Sorauf, "Winning in the Courts: Interest Groups and Constitutional Change," in *This Constitution: Our Enduring Legacy* (1986), pp. 221–34.

39. Tribe, *God Save This Honorable Court*, pp. 68–69.

40. Id. at 69.

41. Abraham, *Justices and Presidents*, p. 263. Eisenhower's pained observation nicely captures the risk that presidents take in making lifetime appointments to the Supreme Court. Unfortunately, there is some question whether the quote itself is accurate. See Alyssa Sepinwall, "The Making of a Presidential Myth," *Wall Street Journal*, September 4, 1990, p. A15.

42. David W. Rohde and Harold J. Spaeth, *Supreme Court Decision Making* (1976), p. 110.

43. Martin Shapiro, "Fathers and Sons: The Court, the Commentators, and the Search for Values," in Vincent Blasi (ed.), *The Burger Court: The Counter-Revolution That Wasn't* (1983), p. 237.

44. Scigliano, *The Supreme Court and the Presidency*, p. 148.

45. See id. at 146; Rohde and Spaeth, *Supreme Court Decision Making*, pp. 107–8.

46. Tribe, *God Save This Honorable Court*, p. 76. See also Jeffrey Segal, "Supreme Court Support for the Solicitor General: The Effects of Presidential Appointments," 43 *Western Pol. Q.* 137 (1990).

47. For additional discussion of the impact of membership change on Supreme Court decision making, see Lawrence Baum, "Membership Change and Collective Voting Change in the United States Supreme Court," 54 *J. of Pol.* 3 (1992).

CHAPTER 14

Normative Justifications
of Judicial Review

In the previous two chapters, we examined a variety of both external and internal restraints on the Supreme Court. We saw that Supreme Court decisions may be reversed, although not always very easily, by the political branches of government. We also saw that the Court may be reconstituted through the appointment process and may in time come to reflect a substantially altered set of political preferences. Clearly, the Supreme Court is an integral part of the political system. Moreover, the existence of strong connections between the Court and its political environment helps to resolve the tension between judicial review and majoritarian democracy. To the extent that the Court responds to pressures emanating from the political environment in which it operates, the tension between judicial review and majoritarian democracy is reduced.

The discussion in the previous two chapters was based on an assumption, however, that not everyone would share. That assumption is that the essence of American democracy is majority rule by elected representatives and that all policy makers in a democratic political system should be accountable to the public through the electoral process. In this chapter, we will abandon that assumption. We will argue that it may be entirely proper for an unelected Supreme Court to play a countermajoritarian role in the political system. In short, we will stop "apologizing" for the fact that the Supreme Court does not conform to majoritarian principles and will explore the possibilities of constructing an affirmative justification of judicial review.

The chapter is divided into three sections. In Section I, we sketch a traditional and relatively uncontroversial affirmative defense of judicial review. We also note, however, that for many judges and scholars this defense is incomplete unless it includes an important corollary, and that *if* this corollary is accepted, it becomes difficult to justify many of the most important decisions of the modern Supreme Court. In Section II, we explore two

al normative theories of the role of the Court in American democracy. ch is derived from the traditional justification of judicial review but
purports to justify a broader array of countermajoritarian Supreme Court
decisions. Finally, in Section III, we examine several rather expansive theories
of judicial review. These theories have been developed in part to supply a
normative justification for some of the most controversial decisions of the
modern Supreme Court.

Judicial Review in a Constitutional Democracy

Most normative justifications of judicial review begin precisely where John
Marshall did in his decision in *Marbury* v. *Madison* in 1803. You will recall
from our discussion of *Marbury* in Chapter 1 that Marshall heavily empha-
sized the fact that the United States is governed by a *written* Constitution.
What Marshall did in *Marbury*, in effect, was to parlay the fact that the
United States is governed by a written Constitution into a conclusion that the
Supreme Court possesses the power to assess the constitutional validity of
ordinary legislation.

Judicial Review under a Written Constitution

We can break down Marshall's argument into the following five steps: First,
Marshall says, the decision to embody fundamental principles of government
in a written Constitution "is the basis on which the whole American fabric has
been erected." Second, an intrinsic feature of a political system based on a
written Constitution is that the Constitution is not on the same level as
ordinary law but is "paramount law." Third, one of the purposes of the
Constitution is to "establish certain limits not to be transcended" by the
departments of government, including the legislative branch. Fourth, the job
of enforcing the Constitution is "the province and duty of the judicial department." Fifth, courts are obligated, upon discovering that an ordinary law is
repugnant to the Constitution, to declare the law unconstitutional, that is, to
exercise the power of judicial review.

As we proceed further into this chapter, we will see that Marshall's
argument is not without its flaws. For the moment, however, we may
accept it at face value as a classic statement of the proposition that judicial
review is basically legitimate in a political system governed by a written
constitution.

The next step in constructing a normative justification of judicial review
is to examine the Constitution itself. When we do, we see immediately that it
contains several features that were designed to impose limits on the power of
both popular and legislative majorities. First, the Constitution defines a "re-

publican form of government," that is, a representative democracy in which policy decisions are made not by the people themselves but by those whom the people elect to represent them. Second, the Constitution divides and distributes power in a variety of ways. In particular, it mandates (1) separation of powers, in which the legislative, executive, and judicial branches of government are differentiated from one another, and (2) federalism, in which power is divided between the national and state levels of government. Third, the Constitution includes various specific prohibitions on government. The most famous are in the Bill of Rights, but others — such as the prohibition of suspension of the writ of habeas corpus and the prohibition of any bill of attainder or ex post facto law — are located in the Constitution itself.

Democratic Stability and the Constitution: The Framers' View

In the minds of the framers, the ultimate purpose of the various prescriptions and proscriptions in the Constitution was to guarantee democratic stability and preserve individual rights. The case for the benefits of a republican form of government was made by James Madison in "Federalist No. 10." The effect of "the delegation of the government . . . to a small number of citizens elected by the rest," he said, would be "to refine and enlarge the public views, by passing them through the medium of a chosen body of citizens, whose wisdom may best discern the true interest of their country, and whose patriotism and love of justice will be least likely to sacrifice it to temporary or partial considerations."[1]

Madison was equally emphatic that creation of a system of checks and balances — including federalism and separation of powers — was essential, as he said in "Federalist No. 51," "to the preservation of liberty."[2] In the political system envisioned by the framers, he said, "the power surrendered by the people is first divided between two distinct governments, and then the portion allotted to each subdivided among distinct and separate departments. Hence a double security arises to the rights of the people. The different governments will control each other, at the same time that each will be controlled by itself."[3]

Finally, Madison became convinced as part of the ratification process that it would be expedient to add a Bill of Rights to the Constitution. In presenting his version of the Bill of Rights to the first Congress, in 1789, he said that "it will be proper in itself, and highly politic, for the tranquility of the public mind, and the stability of the Government, that [the Constitution be amended to include] a declaration of the rights of the people." The principal reasons for adopting a Bill of Rights, Madison argued, were, first, to guard against "the abuse of the powers of the General Government," and second (and in Madison's mind even more importantly), to guard against "the body of the people, operating by the majority against the minority."[4]

Judicial Review and the Madisonian Conception of American Democracy

The affirmative argument for judicial review is premised on this Madisonian conception of democratic government. Madison and other framers supported the establishment of a representative democracy based on principles of popular sovereignty and majority rule. At the same time, they insisted on the need for constitutional limits on governmental power and constitutional guarantees of individual rights. In the end, therefore, the democracy they envisioned was *not* exclusively majoritarian in its features. Rather, it was a constitutional democracy, that is, a democracy premised on the need to maintain a delicate balance *between* majority rule and minority rights.

Madison and the other framers were well aware that the concept of constitutional democracy would be difficult to translate into working reality. There is an obvious tension between allowing elected majorities to make governmental decisions but simultaneously guaranteeing that none of those decisions will impinge on the constitutional rights of individual citizens and minority groups. Nevertheless, Madison and the other framers were convinced that this compromise held the greatest promise for ensuring the long-term stability of American government.

Constitutional Democracy and the Role of the Courts

Thus far in our development of the affirmative defense of judicial review, we have conveniently ignored one serious problem. The problem is how to justify giving to the judiciary, in particular, the power to enforce the constitutional balance between majority rule and minority rights. It is not difficult to accept the proposition that the Constitution is "paramount law." It is also not difficult to accept that one implication of the supremacy of the Constitution is that government must operate under constitutionally prescribed restraints. It does not follow automatically from any of this, however, that judges are the only public officials or even the best public officials to police the boundaries between constitutional restrictions and governmental power. Constitutional democracy may be a good idea—even a brilliant idea. Judicial supremacy, however, is another question entirely.

John Marshall purported to answer the question of who is responsible for enforcing the supremacy of the Constitution in his opinion in *Marbury* v. *Madison*. Not everyone, however, is impressed with his reasoning. The bulk of Marshall's opinion is devoted to establishing that the Constitution is supreme and that this has unavoidable implications for the validity of ordinary law that conflicts with the Constitution. Marshall does a forceful and competent job of elucidating the implications of living in a society that is governed by a written constitution. Most commentators do not take exception, therefore, to Marshall's abstract conclusion that "an act of the legislature repugnant to the constitution is void."

When Marshall comes to the question of who should be responsible for detecting and resolving conflicts between the Constitution and ordinary law, however, his opinion takes on an arbitrary quality. In what is perhaps the most famous sentence in the whole opinion, Marshall asserts that "It is, emphatically, the province and duty of the judicial department, to say what the law is." If there is a conflict between the Constitution and ordinary law, Marshall says, it is the job of the courts to resolve the conflict and to do so by giving effect to the supremacy of the Constitution. "This," he says, "is the very essence of judicial duty."

Marshall's assertion that judges are responsible for enforcing the supremacy of the Constitution is stated with confidence and was, as we saw in Chapter 1, a stroke of political genius. The assertion itself, however, encounters at least three major difficulties. First, as we have noted, the Constitution is absolutely silent on the question of how its supremacy should be enforced. Second, constitutional decision making is not a mechanical act, but one that involves human judgment. A law declared unconstitutional by a court was passed by legislators who obviously did not think, when they passed the law, that they were violating the Constitution. It therefore becomes clear that the process of constitutional adjudication is one that involves conflicting *interpretations* of the meaning of the Constitution. It also involves a variety of participants, some of whom may be judges but all of whom are fallible human beings. Third, as we have also noted, judges are not politically accountable. Therefore, they occupy an exceptional and even doubtful status in the American system of democratic self-government.

Judicial Review in a Constitutional Democracy

What the affirmative defense of judicial review does, in effect, is to take this third difficulty — the fact that judges are not politically accountable — and turn it into an advantage! The virtue of a constitutional democracy, the argument goes, is that it incorporates *both* majoritarian and countermajoritarian features. The countermajoritarian features of American democracy cannot, however, enforce themselves. Constitutional limits on governmental action and constitutional guarantees of individual rights will be meaningless in the absence of a concrete institutional mechanism to keep the majority in check. What better institution to play this role, the argument concludes, than the judiciary, which is, by design, not directly accountable to the will of the majority?

The special strength of this affirmative defense of judicial review is that it directly confronts the allegation that judicial review is "undemocratic." It starts from the irrefutable premise that the political system designed by Madison and the other framers is not a pure example of majoritarian democracy. Rather, it is a constitutional democracy. Such a system not only *can include* but *must include* an institutional mechanism for controlling popular and legislative majorities. In the American system, that mechanism consists of unelected, life-tenured judges armed with the power to enforce constitutional restraints on governmental power.

The Evolution of Affirmative Justifications of Judicial Review

The Supreme Court has operated on the assumption that judicial review represents a positive component of the American system of constitutional democracy since John Marshall's decision in *Marbury*. Over time, however, the Court has refined the content of its defense of countermajoritarian judicial review. Prior to the 1930s, the Court frequently invoked the Due Process Clause and other provisions of the Constitution to protect the economic and property rights of business corporations and wealthy segments of the population. Since the 1930s, however, the Court has agreed to concentrate on protecting the civil liberties of individuals and minority groups and to leave the resolution of other types of policy issues to the executive and legislative branches of government.

The modern view of the role of the Court in American democracy was given classic expression, as we saw in Chapter 5, in Justice Jackson's opinion in the *Barnette* case. "The very purpose of a Bill of Rights," Jackson argued, "was to withdraw certain subjects from the vicissitudes of political controversy, to place them beyond the reach of majorities and officials and to establish them as legal principles to be applied by the courts." Jackson's remarks, along with those contained in Footnote Four to the *Carolene Products* case, capture the Court's determination to play an active countermajoritarian role in the policy-making process. They also implicitly concede, however, that the Court will focus its energies on civil liberties issues rather than on the full range of contemporary issues of public policy.

Modern constitutional commentary is saturated with restatements of Justice Jackson's defense of judicial review. A good example is found in the scholarship of law professor Jesse H. Choper. "[T]he overriding virtue of and justification for vesting the [Supreme] Court with [the] awesome power [of judicial review]," Choper has written, "is to guard against governmental infringement of individual liberties secured by the Constitution."[5] Moreover, Choper argues, the task of safeguarding individual rights should be assigned to the Supreme Court—and not to some other governmental institution—precisely because the Supreme Court "is insulated from political responsibility and unbeholden to self-absorbed and excited majoritarianism. The Court's aloofness from the political system and the Justices' lack of dependence for maintenance in office on the popularity of a particular ruling promise an objectivity that elected representatives are not—and should not be—as capable of achieving."[6]

The Framers' View of the Judicial Role

Like so much else that is central to the theory and practice of American democracy, the view that courts are the most suitable institutions to enforce the supremacy of the Constitution can be traced, in part, to James Madison.[7] On June 8, 1789, in his speech to the House of Representatives urging the adoption of a Bill of Rights, Madison argued that if the proposed amendments are incorporated into the Constitution, "independent tribunals of justice will consider themselves in a peculiar manner the guardians of those rights; they will be an impenetrable bulwark against every assumption of power in the Legislative or Executive [branch]; they will be naturally led to resist every encroachment upon rights expressly stipulated for in the Constitution by the declaration of rights."[8]

Alexander Hamilton was also influential in shaping the early debate about the legitimacy of judicial review. The Constitution itself, of course, says nothing about the subject. In Hamilton's contributions to the *Federalist Papers*, however, we find a clear indication that at least one of the framers did anticipate that courts would exercise the power of judicial review. "By a limited Constitution," he said in "Federalist No. 78," "I understand one which contains certain specified exceptions to the legislative authority. . . . [These limitations] can be preserved in practice no other way than through the medium of courts of justice, whose duty it must be to declare all acts contrary to the manifest tenor of the Constitution void. Without this, all the reservations of particular rights or privileges would amount to nothing."[9]

Hamilton went on to argue that if courts were going to serve as "bulwarks of a limited Constitution against legislative encroachments," then the Constitution in turn must guarantee the independence of the judiciary. It was therefore one of the important strengths of the proposed Constitution, in Hamilton's view, that it stipulated that judges would hold their offices during "good Behaviour" and in this fashion guaranteed "permanent tenure of judicial offices."[10]

Judicial Review and the Constitution: An Important Corollary

Today, almost no one questions that courts should exercise the power of judicial review of legislation. Moreover, most people are comfortable with the affirmative defense of judicial review which we have developed, that is, that the Constitution is in part a countermajoritarian document and that courts are best suited to enforce its countermajoritarian provisions.

For many of those who either sit on the Supreme Court or comment on its decisions, however, the traditional justification of judicial review is unacceptable unless it incorporates an important corollary. That corollary is that if the courts *are* going to exercise countermajoritarian decision-making power under the Constitution, it is essential that they adhere closely to the *text* of the Constitution in reaching their decisions.

The rationale for insisting that judges adhere to the text of the Constitution is twofold. First, it guarantees that judicial decisions will be an expression of values embodied in the Constitution rather than values that are personally attractive to the judge who is deciding the case. Second, it guarantees that countermajoritarian judicial decisions will be anchored in a document that embodies the will of the people, that is, the will of those Americans who drafted and ratified the Constitution and its subsequent amendments.

An obvious difficulty with the requirement that judges must base their decisions strictly on the text of the Constitution, however, is that many provisions of the Constitution are notoriously vague. As a result, some of those who support the basic idea that judges should adhere closely to the text of the Constitution have taken the further step of insisting that the meaning of the text should be determined with reference to the "intent of the framers."

Judicial Review and the Intent of the Framers

The question of whether and how closely the Supreme Court should adhere to the intent of the framers acquired substantial public visibility in 1985, when it became the centerpiece of a series of public speeches by President Reagan's attorney general, Edwin Meese. Meese argued for what he called a "jurisprudence of original intention." "Those who framed [the principles embodied in the Constitution]," Meese said, "meant something by them. And the meanings can be found, understood, and applied." Meese argued that it was only by closely adhering to the text and original meaning of the Constitution that unelected judges could legitimately presume to exercise the power of judicial review in a democratic society. "The power to declare acts of Congress and laws of the states null and void," Meese said, "is truly awesome. This power must be used when the Constitution clearly speaks. It should not be used when the Constitution does not."[11]

The attorney general's speeches brought the debate over original intent into public view, but the debate itself had been simmering among legal scholars for many years. By far the most prominent advocate of a theory of original intent was Robert Bork, President Reagan's unsuccessful 1987 nominee to the Supreme Court. In a 1971 article, Bork, then a law professor, provided a classic exposition of the theory of original intent.[12]

Bork began by sketching the Madisonian prescriptions that are common ground among all those who contemplate the role of the Supreme Court in American democracy. "A Madisonian system," Bork said, "is not completely democratic, if by 'democratic' we mean completely majoritarian." On most issues of public policy, "majorities are entitled to rule for no better reason than they are majorities." On some issues, however, majority rule must give way to minority rights. Moreover, the areas that are placed off limits to majority control are precisely those that are identified in the countermajoritarian provisions of the Constitution, including the Bill of Rights. Under the

Madisonian conception of American democracy, as Bork put it, "[s]ociety consents to be ruled undemocratically within defined areas by certain enduring principles believed to be stated in, and placed beyond the reach of majorities by, the Constitution."[13]

The second step in Bork's argument for original intent is also one that forms an integral part of all contemporary theories of judicial review. The Supreme Court, Bork says, is the governmental institution that is authorized to resolve the tension between majority rule and minority rights in specific cases. When the Court exercises the power of judicial review, it is defining, in Bork's words, the "respective spheres" of "majority freedom," on the one hand, and "minority freedom," on the other.[14]

At this point, however, the "corollary" of which we spoke a moment ago becomes all important. For Bork, and for others who support an "originalist theory" of constitutional interpretation, the power to resolve the tension between majority rule and minority rights imposes, as Bork says, "severe requirements upon the Court."[15] In particular, judges must not decide cases based on nonexistent provisions of the Constitution. Nor must they impute to existing provisions of the Constitution meanings that cannot properly be derived from the language or original understanding of those provisions. In Bork's view, a judicial decision that is not based on the text or original meaning of the Constitution is presumably based on the judge's personal values, but these, by definition, are not a legitimate basis for the exercise of countermajoritarian judicial review. In short, the proper role of the courts in a democratic society requires that courts "must accept any value choice the legislature makes unless it clearly runs contrary to a choice made in the framing of the Constitution."[16]

Difficulties with Original Intent

There is obvious force in arguing that judges should adhere to the intent of the framers. The argument is based on the premise that, unless modern judges base their decisions on the intent of the framers, they are violating the fundamental precept that the Constitution itself is the only legitimate source of limitations on majority rule. The argument for original intent is not without its defects, however, nor is there any dearth of scholarship aimed at pointing out what those defects are.[17]

Arguments attacking the merits of an originalist theory of constitutional interpretation can be divided into two broad categories. One set of arguments questions whether it is *possible* to ascertain the intent of the framers. A second set questions whether it is *desirable* to require judges to adhere to that intent.

The reasons why it may be difficult to achieve a sound understanding of the original meaning of the Constitution are fairly obvious. First, the historical record may be too sparse or too contradictory to support any definitive conclusions about how particular provisions of the Constitution were under-

stood by those who wrote them or read them. Second, the people w
participated in drafting or ratifying the Constitution (or subsequent amendments such as the Bill of Rights and the Civil War amendments) numbered in
the thousands or millions. Moreover, they constituted a thoroughly diverse
group. It is therefore problematic to speak at all of *the* original understanding
of the Constitution. Presumably, the Constitution was understood in different ways by different groups of people.

Even supposing it is possible to ascertain the original meaning of the
Constitution, however, the question remains whether it is desirable to insist
that judges adhere to that meaning in making their decisions in specific cases.
Broadly speaking, judges and scholars who are skeptical of the merits of
original intent — "nonoriginalists," as they are often described — raise two
issues. First, they note that neither those who wrote the Constitution nor
those who ratified it were very representative of the population as a whole.
Significant segments of the population, including blacks, women, and people
without property, were formally excluded from the political process. Nonoriginalists argue that those who advocate a theory of original intent do so in
part because they insist that unelected judges should not have the power to
contradict the preferences of a current majority unless they can base their
decisions squarely on principles that were enshrined in the Constitution by an
earlier extraordinary majority of Americans. However, if the principles
enshrined in the Constitution reflect the values of a narrow and unrepresenta-
tive elite, rather than a broad spectrum of the American population, it
becomes unclear why the original understanding of those principles should be
the sole touchstone for contemporary judicial decisions.

The second reason for rejecting originalism as a desirable theory of
constitutional interpretation, nonoriginalists argue, is that the Constitution
must change with the times. Justice Brennan was an outspoken advocate of
allowing judges to give new and updated meanings to constitutional language.
"Current judges read the Constitution," he said, "in the only way we can: as
twentieth century Americans. We look to the history of the time of framing
and to the intervening history of interpretation. But the ultimate question
must be: What do the words of the text mean in our time? For the genius of
the Constitution rests not in any static meaning it might have had in a world
that is dead and gone, but in the adaptibility of its great principles to cope
with current problems and current needs."[18]

Implications of the Debate
over Original Intent

The gulf between originalist and nonoriginalist theories of constitutional
interpretation is not necessarily unbridgeable. All constitutional commentators, including Justice Brennan, acknowledge the importance of the text and
original meaning of the Constitution. At the same time, proponents of original
intent, including Robert Bork, concede that it may be difficult to ascertain the

srovisions of the Constitution and that in any case constitu-
on should focus on the principles embodied in those provi-
on their narrow historical meaning. Thus, the debate over
eed not divide judges and scholars into two mutually exclu-
oreclose the possibility of synthesizing a common theory of
nterpretation.

At the same time, the debate over original intent has serious implications
for contemporary constitutional decision making. It is widely acknowledged,
for instance, that while the Fourteenth Amendment *was* intended to end
various forms of legal discrimination against blacks, it was *not* meant to
prohibit racial segregation of public schools or other public facilities. From an
originalist perspective, therefore, the legitimacy of the Supreme Court's decision in *Brown* v. *Board of Education* becomes problematic.[19] It is also universally acknowleged that the right of privacy is not explicitly mentioned in the
Constitution. To anyone who insists that judicial decisions should be based
on the text or original meaning of the Constitution, therefore, Supreme Court
decisions such as *Griswold* v. *Connecticut* and *Roe* v. *Wade* are clearcut
examples of the injection of justices' personal values into the decision-making
process.[20]

Thus, the debate over original intent has a direct impact on the scope of
contemporary judicial review. The Supreme Court is authorized to enforce
the supremacy of the Constitution and in doing so is entitled to reach
countermajoritarian decisions. In the minds of many judges and scholars,
however, unless those decisions are firmly anchored in the text or original
meaning of the Constitution, they constitute an abuse of judicial power.
Moreover, a theory of constitutional interpretation that requires that judges
adhere closely to the text or original meaning of the Constitution leads
inexorably to the conclusion that several important decisions of the modern
Supreme Court represent illegitimate examples of the Court's recognized
power of judicial review.

Conclusion

James Madison and other framers of the Constitution did not envision a
political system based purely on majoritarian principles. On the contrary, they
believed that the power of the majority should be forced to yield, on occasion, to the rights of the minority. They embodied their ambitious attempt to
balance majority rule and minority rights in the text of the Constitution. The
resulting political system — the American political system — is perhaps best
described as a *constitutional democracy.*

The core of an affirmative defense of judicial review is based on the fact
that the United States is governed by a written Constitution. The Constitution
is the "supreme Law of the Land." In addition, it imposes limits on governmental power and guarantees individual rights. It follows that a state or

federal statute that is repugnant to the Constitution must yield to the superior principles embodied in the written Constitution.

The institution with primary responsibility for enforcing the supremacy of the Constitution, including its limitations on governmental power and majority rule, is the Supreme Court. Constitutional commentators widely agree that the politically unaccountable Supreme Court is best suited among the various institutions of American government to enforce the counter-majoritarian provisions of the written Constitution. Support for vesting the Supreme Court with the power to enforce the Constitution was expressed by key figures in the founding period — including Alexander Hamilton, James Madison, and John Marshall — and it remains a prominent theme in the writings of modern constitutional commentators.

The Supreme Court's assumption and exercise of the power of judicial review, however, has generated an important contemporary debate. Some judges and scholars — proponents of an originalist theory of constitutional interpretation — argue that judicial review is illegitimate unless it is based on the original meaning of the Constitution. Nonoriginalists counter, however, that discovering the original meaning of the Constitution may be impossible and that, in any case, it is undesirable to allow the original meaning of the Constitution to constrain contemporary constitutional decision making.

One important implication of the debate over original intent is that many decisions of the modern Supreme Court cannot, in fact, be justified in terms of the text or original meaning of the Constitution. The questionable legitimacy of many of the Court's most important recent decisions has prompted some judges and scholars to develop normative justifications of judicial review that go beyond those that can be derived directly from provisions of the written Constitution. It is to these more expansive theories of judicial review that we now turn.

Judicial Review and Democratic Politics

We saw in the previous section that a basic normative justification of judicial review can be derived from the fact that the U.S. Constitution is a written document that is designed not only to ensure majoritarian democracy but also to guarantee individual rights. Many constitutional commentators have recognized, however, that the traditional justification of judicial review may not adequately explain many of the Supreme Court's most important recent decisions. They have therefore expanded the scope of normative justifications of judicial review to include two additional arguments. The first is that judicial review is essential to the protection of the procedural norms of democratic politics. The second is that judicial review is essential to the protection of the fundamental rights of particular minorities.

Judicial Review and the
Procedural Norms of Democracy

Most definitions of democracy, including the one that we examined in the introductory chapter, are essentially "procedural" in character. They do not specify *who* should be elected or *what* policies government should enact into law. Instead, they specify *how* the electoral process should be structured and *how* the legislative process should operate once elected representatives have been chosen. In short, they do not prescribe the substantive outcomes that the political process is expected to produce. Rather, they stipulate the rules of the game of the process itself.

Some normative justifications of judicial review focus on the rules of the game of democratic politics. As discussed in Chapter 1, democratic theorists argue that the essence of democracy is popular control of government through periodic elections. Moreover, almost all democratic theorists argue that a political system is not truly democratic unless certain conditions are met. Those conditions are usually grouped under the general headings of "political equality" and "political freedom." They include the requirement that all adult citizens should possess the right to vote; that all interested candidates should be free to form political organizations and compete for political office; that voters should have access to various sources of information; and that voters and candidates alike should be guaranteed complete freedom of speech and freedom of the press.

A procedural defense of judicial review assigns to courts a special role in safeguarding the rules of the game of democratic politics. In particular, it calls on the courts to protect freedom of speech and freedom of the press, to overturn governmental restrictions on the right to vote, to safeguard the right of citizens to join organizations, and to protect the right of organizations to function freely in the political arena. In addition, it assigns to courts the job of making sure that candidates and parties are able to gain access to the ballot. Finally, it calls on the courts to ensure that everyone's vote is counted equally. In sum, a procedural defense of judicial review argues that courts should play an active role in opening the channels of political communication and safeguarding the integrity of the democratic process.

One obvious strength of a procedural justification of judicial review, as you may have noticed already, is that it effectively neutralizes the charge that judicial review is an undemocratic feature of American politics. A procedural justification of judicial review positions the courts to play an active role in guaranteeing that the democratic process operates in a fashion that is open, efficient, and fair. Thus, judicial review becomes a handmaiden of majoritarian democracy, not its enemy. It may still be true that particular judicial decisions are countermajoritarian — that is, they overturn legislation enacted by a duly elected legislative majority. But the premise of procedural justifications of judicial review is that legislation which restricts the political process is itself undemocratic. In overturning such legislation, therefore, the courts are

oring the integrity of the democratic process and guaranteeing that it will
duce genuinely majoritarian outcomes.

The Supreme Court and
Procedural Democracy

Supreme Court justices have on many occasions spoken eloquently of the role
of the courts in protecting the procedural norms of American democracy.
Chief Justice Hughes offered a particularly succinct statement of the procedural rationale for judicial review in the 1937 case of *De Jonge* v. *Oregon.* The
case involved legislation aimed at the Communist party and other organizations accused of advocating the overthrow of the government by force. De
Jonge had attended a meeting of the Communist party and was subsequently
convicted of the crime of "criminal syndicalism." The Court overturned his
conviction, and in his opinion for the Court, Chief Justice Hughes captured
the essence of a procedural defense of judicial review. "The greater the
importance of safeguarding the community from incitements to the overthrow of our institutions by force and violence," Hughes wrote, "the more
imperative the need to preserve inviolate the constitutional rights of free
speech, free press and free assembly in order to maintain the opportunity for
free political discussion, to the end that government may be responsive to the
will of the people and that changes, if desired, may be obtained by peaceful
means. Therein lies the security of the Republic, the very foundation of
constitutional government."[21]

In recent decades, the Supreme Court has in fact devoted a major portion
of its time to cases involving alleged legislative or executive interference with
key components of the democratic process.[22] The Court's decisions in cases
involving freedom of speech and the press — including *Yates* v. *United States*
(1957), which we discussed in Chapter 7 — are now sufficiently numerous to
justify the publication of separate law school casebooks devoted exclusively
to this body of jurisprudence.[23] Closely related to the Court's free speech
decisions have been those involving alleged interference with freedom of
association. Over the years, the Court has reviewed and usually (though not
always) overturned restrictions on organizations such as the NAACP,[24] the
Communist party,[25] and the Socialist Workers party.[26] Finally, a substantial
body of Supreme Court caselaw deals with access to the ballot,[27] the right to
vote,[28] and other aspects of the electoral process.[29]

Another body of caselaw — the Supreme Court's reapportionment
decisions — may be seen as an attempt by the Court to realize the principle of
political equality that figures so prominently in most definitions of majoritarian democracy. Despite substantial shifts in population — usually from rural
areas to cities — many states as of 1960 had not redrawn the boundaries of
their electoral districts. The result was that rural districts were overrepresented in Congress and state legislatures; that is, they had as many elected
representatives as districts with far larger populations. In a series of decisions

that commenced with *Baker* v. *Carr* in 1962, the Supreme Court developed and applied the constitutional standard of "one person, one vote."[30] The rationale for the Court's reapportionment decisions was explained by Chief Justice Warren in his opinion for the Court in *Reynolds* v. *Sims* in 1964.[31] "As long as ours is a representative form of government," Warren said,

> and our legislatures are those instruments of government elected directly by and directly representative of the people, the right to elect legislators in a free and unimpaired fashion is a bedrock of our political system. . . . [W]e conclude that the Equal Protection Clause guarantees the opportunity for equal participation by all voters in the election of state legislators. Diluting the weight of votes because of place of residence impairs basic constitutional rights. . . . Our constitutional system amply provides for the protection of minorities by means other than giving them majority control of state legislatures.[32]

The final sentence in the foregoing passage suggests that Chief Justice Warren was aware that the Court's reapportionment decisions were particularly defensible in terms of democratic theory. The standard justification of judicial review, as discussed in the first part of this chapter, is that courts should protect minority rights in an otherwise majoritarian political system. In the reapportionment cases, however, the majority, not the minority, had been deprived of its rights! By insisting that all legislative districts be equal in population, the Court was engaged directly in the process of perfecting the majoritarian model of democratic politics.

We should also note that procedural justifications of judicial review often include one final, but somewhat distinct, component. The arguments we have examined thus far have sought to justify judicial review as essential to preserving procedural norms of majoritarian democracy. An additional procedural responsibility of the Court, however, grows out of the concept of due process of law. In American law, *due process* is ordinarily a short-hand term for the panoply of constitutional rights to which criminal defendants are entitled. Among them are the Fourth Amendment prohibition of unreasonable searches and seizures, the Fifth Amendment prohibition of self-incrimination, and the Sixth Amendment guarantees of the right to a jury trial and the right to counsel. Although the Court's decisions in these areas of the law are often extremely controversial, there is little or no controversy about the fact that cases raising issues of due process of law fall squarely within the decision-making authority of the Supreme Court and other courts.[33]

Judicial Review and the Fundamental Rights of Minorities

The procedural justification of judicial review which we have outlined above seeks to justify countermajoritarian Supreme Court decisions on behalf of groups and individuals who wish to engage in activities such as speaking, publishing, campaigning, and voting. Frequently, however, groups or individuals are deprived of rights that they consider fundamental but that are not directly related to the democratic process. The question then arises as to whether the Supreme Court should protect fundamental rights *other* than those that contribute directly to the smooth functioning of the majoritarian political process.

Supreme Court decision making to protect the "fundamental rights" of minorities is enormously controversial. The reason is that most of the fundamental rights that minorities seek to vindicate by resort to the courts are not explicitly guaranteed by the Constitution. To protect those rights, therefore, the Supreme Court must go beyond the text or original intent of the Constitution itself. Once it does so, however, it opens itself to the charge that it is engaging in countermajoritarian judicial review without having any clear constitutional foundation for its actions.

Of course, judicial protection of *some* of the fundamental rights of *some* minorities is not controversial. The Fifteenth Amendment, for instance, prohibits states from discriminating against racial minorities in the electoral process. The Amendment stipulates that "The right of citizens of the United States to vote shall not be denied or abridged by the United States or by any State on account of race, color, or previous condition of servitude." The Nineteenth Amendment also placed the voting rights of women on a specific constitutional footing. "The right of citizens of the United States to vote," it says, "shall not be denied or abridged by the United States or by any State on account of sex."

Judicial decision making based on the Fifteenth and Nineteenth amendments is not controversial, because in each case the Constitution itself has delineated both the types of minorities and the types of rights that are entitled to protection. The hard questions arise, however, when the Court attempts to articulate a normative justification of judicial review in behalf of other minorities and other rights.

The Equal Protection Clause in Constitutional Law

The place to which everyone turns for an answer is the Equal Protection Clause of the Fourteenth Amendment. The Clause stipulates that "No state shall . . . deny to any person within its jurisdiction the equal protection of the laws." The Fourteenth Amendment was added to the Constitution in the wake of the Civil War. Since that time, the Equal Protection Clause has become an exceptionally fertile source of contemporary constitutional cases.

On the face of it, since the Constitution contains an explicit guarantee of "equal protection of the laws," judicial review of legislation and other governmental action that discriminates against particular minorities would seem to represent a legitimate and uncontroversial example of Supreme Court decision making. From the point of view of the constitutional theories we have been discussing, however, nothing could be further from the truth.

The problem arises because the Equal Protection Clause is singularly difficult to imbue with a specific meaning. Broadly speaking, two approaches to the problem are possible. One is to read the Clause itself and to discern its meaning from the language in which it is written. The other is to delve into the political history surrounding the adoption of the Clause to derive its meaning from the intent of those who framed it. Unfortunately, each of these options has serious drawbacks.

The difficulty with the first option is that a literal reading of the language of the Equal Protection Clause would position the Supreme Court to re-decide most, if not all, issues addressed by legislative bodies. Virtually all legislation classifies people; that is, it treats or affects some people differently from others. If the Supreme Court accepted the literal invitation of the Equal Protection Clause, it would spend all its time deciding whether particular laws as applied to particular groups or individuals did or did not deny them the equal protection of the laws. If that were to happen, however, the Supreme Court would become, in the apt phrase of those who resist the idea of such an expansion of judicial power, a "super-legislature."

Not surprisingly, the open-ended meaning of the text of the Equal Protection Clause has led to a search for some way to interpret the Clause which will support an appropriate level of judicial activism but will prevent the Supreme Court from becoming a super-legislature. One possibility is to base the decision to engage in judicial review on the original meaning of the Clause. As it turns out, however, the original meaning of the Equal Protection Clause may in fact have been quite limited. As we noted above, those who drafted the Amendment intended it to protect newly freed slaves from particular kinds of discriminatory treatment. The Clause probably was not intended, however, to prohibit racial segregation—as opposed to unequal or discrimi-natory treatment under the law—nor was it intended to guarantee equal protection to groups other than the newly freed slaves. Any justification of judicial review based strictly on the original meaning of the Equal Protection Clause, therefore, will not support a very wide variety of judicial decisions. Using the Clause to invalidate alleged discrimination against women, for instance, will be controversial. So will using the Clause to invalidate alleged discrimination against other nonracial groups, including children, the aged, homosexuals, aliens, or the poor.

Ascertaining the true meaning of the Equal Protection Clause therefore has serious implications for contemporary constitutional decision making. The meaning one chooses will impinge directly on the question of the role of the Supreme Court in American democracy. If the Equal Protection Clause is taken literally, the possibilities for judicial review are practically unlimited. If the Clause means no more today than it did when it was written, however, its usefulness as a basis for deciding constitutional cases is severely reduced.

The search for the true meaning of the open-ended constitutional guaran-tee of equal protection of the laws has generated an enormous outpouring of judicial decisions and scholarly comment. Among the Court's many en-counters with the Equal Protection Clause is the *Bakke* case which we discussed in Chapter 11. It is not easy to make confident predictions about the future of Supreme Court decision making. One thing we can predict with complete assurance, however, is that the Supreme Court has not seen the end of the difficult and controversial task of giving meaning to one of the Constitution's most enigmatic provisions.[34]

Equal Protection and Representative Democracy

One legal scholar, John Hart Ely, has developed a theory of constitutional interpretation that attempts to link the exercise of judicial review under the Equal Protection Clause to a theory of judicial review—such as the one we discussed earlier in this section—which is based on the Court's special responsibility for safeguarding the procedural norms of democracy.[35] Ely argues that "what are sometimes characterized as two conflicting American ideals—the protection of popular government on the one hand, and the protection of minorities from denials of equal concern and respect on the other—in fact can be understood as arising from a common duty of representation." He then goes on to elaborate what he calls a "participation-oriented, representation-reinforcing approach to judicial review."[36]

One component of Ely's theory is a restatement of the procedural defense of judicial review which we have discussed above. "Virtually everyone agrees," Ely says, "that the courts should be heavily involved in reviewing impediments to free speech, publication, and political association. . . . [R]ights like these, whether or not they are explicitly mentioned [in the Constitution], must nonetheless be protected, strenuously so, because they are critical to the functioning of an open and effective democratic process."[37]

The second component of Ely's theory attempts to justify judicial protection of minority rights under the Equal Protection Clause, but only in factual situations that implicate the core values of a representative democracy. Ely argues that it is possible to identify occasions when minorities have been deprived of a fair opportunity to participate in the political process, even though they have not been deprived of the right to vote or suffered any other clearcut deprivation of their constitutional rights. He concludes, therefore, that one of the key responsibilities of the courts must be to identify and correct those situations in which "representatives beholden to an effective majority are systematically disadvantaging some minority out of simple hostility to or prejudiced refusal to recognize commonalities of interest, and thereby denying that minority the protection afforded other groups by a representative system."[38]

Normative Justifications of Judicial Review and Footnote Four of the Carolene Products Case

You may have noticed that our discussion thus far in this chapter has closely tracked a particular statement of the proper role of the courts in a democratic society. In 1938, in the famous Footnote Four to his opinion in *United States*

v. *Carolene Products Co.*, Justice Stone delineated three categories of cases in which the Supreme Court and other courts might, he said, be expected to play an especially active role. Footnote Four is significant in part because it articulated not only what we have called the traditional justification of judicial review, but also the two theories of judicial review that can be most easily derived from that justification.

Stone asserted in paragraph one of Footnote Four that courts should be especially vigilant in examining the constitutional validity of legislation that "appears on its face to be within a specific prohibition of the Constitution." This view of the role of the courts essentially restates the traditional defense of judicial review. As long ago as the founding period, Madison and Hamilton had argued that the United States is a constitutional democracy, not merely a majoritarian democracy, and that courts should play a key role in defending minority rights against majority tyranny. In *Marbury* v. *Madison* in 1803, Chief Justice John Marshall injected the Supreme Court into the heart of the political process with his decision that enforcement of the supremacy of the Constitution in cases of alleged conflict between the Constitution and ordinary law was "the very essence of judicial duty."

In paragraph two of Footnote Four, Stone suggested that courts had a special role to play in evaluating legislation "which restricts those political processes which can ordinarily be expected to bring about repeal of undesirable legislation." The language of paragraph two is a succinct statement of the argument that courts should play an active role in protecting the procedural norms of democracy and guaranteeing the integrity of the majoritarian political process.

Finally, in paragraph three, Stone suggested that courts might have a special responsibility for protecting an additional array of unspecified minority rights. The underlying justification for such a judicial role, Stone said, was that "prejudice against discrete and insular minorities may be a special condition, which tends seriously to curtail the operation of those political processes ordinarily to be relied upon to protect minorities." The language of paragraph three intimates the possibility of additional kinds of judicial intervention in the majoritarian political process and clearly prefigures the contemporary debate over the proper scope of judicial protection of the fundamental rights of minorities.

Conclusion

Judges and scholars have developed two normative justifications of judicial review that go beyond the traditional view that courts should enforce constitutionally prescribed limitations on governmental power. One justification assigns to courts an active role in protecting the procedural norms of democracy. According to this theory, the purpose of judicial review is to facilitate the emergence of popular majorities and to guarantee that the will of the majority will prevail in both the electoral and the legislative process.

Judges and scholars have also developed a variety of theories that attempt to legitimate judicial protection of the nonprocedural but "fundamental" rights of minorities. It has proved to be singularly difficult, however, to achieve a consensus on the true meaning of the constitutional provision — the Equal Protection Clause of the Fourteenth Amendment — on which such review is based. As a result, disagreements over the proper scope of judicial review to vindicate the fundamental rights of minorities are particularly intense and will persist for some time to come.

Thus far in this chapter we have discussed three different normative justifications of judicial review. The *traditional justification* authorizes courts to enforce specific provisions of the written Constitution. The *procedural justification* authorizes courts to play an active role in protecting the procedural norms of democracy. Finally, the *fundamental rights justification* authorizes courts to protect selected rights of particular minorities under the Equal Protection Clause. Each of these justifications is capable of generating great controversy among judges and scholars. Nevertheless, each of them is based, however precariously, on the text of the Constitution. It is when judges stray beyond the "four corners" of the Constitution itself that the process of constructing a normative justification of judicial review becomes truly demanding.

Judicial Review and the Unwritten Constitution

What should a Supreme Court justice do when a situation arises which calls for judicial intervention but which is *not* explicitly addressed by the Constitution? Someone who believes that judges should base their decisions exclusively on the text or original understanding of the Constitution will answer, without hesitation, "Nothing at all!" For other judges and commentators, however, the absence of specific constitutional language does not represent an absolute barrier to judicial intervention in the policy process. Many judges and commentators are comfortable with the idea that judges should be able to look beyond the confines of the text or original understanding of the Constitution for answers to important contemporary policy disputes. For them, the essential task is to construct a theory of constitutional interpretation that will justify a resort by judges to "extraconstitutional" sources of judicial authority.

Griswold v. *Connecticut* and the Modern Debate over Constitutional Interpretation

The Supreme Court's 1965 decision in *Griswold* v. *Connecticut* was an important catalyst of the modern debate about the limits of judicial discretion to enforce unwritten constitutional rights. The facts in *Griswold* forced individual justices to take a position on whether it was appropriate to look beyond the Constitution itself for guidance in resolving contemporary social issues.

You will recall from our discussion of *Griswold* in Chapter 10 that it was common ground among the justices that the Constitution does not contain an explicit guarantee of the right of privacy. At the same time, all members of the Court were perturbed to learn that it was illegal under Connecticut law for a married couple to use contraceptives. The issue that divided the Court, therefore, was not whether the law was unwise — all nine justices agreed that it was — but whether the Supreme Court possessed the power, in the absence of a specfic constitutional guarantee of the right of privacy, to declare the law invalid.

The constitutional dilemma presented by the *Griswold* case provoked a broad spectrum of reactions from the justices. Justice Douglas, you will recall, wrote the opinion of the Court. He acknowledged that the right of privacy is not mentioned in either the Constitution or the Bill of Rights. He nevertheless argued that "specific guarantees in the Bill of Rights have penumbras, formed by emanations from those guarantees that help give them life and substance."[39] He also argued that the right of privacy, at least as it applies to the institution of marriage, is "older than the Bill of Rights."[40] He thus concluded that "the right of privacy which presses for recognition here is a legitimate one."[41]

The Douglas opinion in *Griswold* is a bold assertion that the Supreme Court may exercise the power of judicial review in a specific case even though it cannot base its decision on a particular provision of the Constitution. Justice Douglas purported to find a basis for the Court's exercise of judicial review in the "penumbras" of specific provisions of the Constitution, rather than the provisions themselves, and in a right of privacy which is "older," as he put it, than the Constitution itself.

Justices Black and Stewart, as we noted in Chapter 10, were vehemently opposed to Douglas's approach to the case. "I like my privacy as well as the next one," Justice Black wrote in his dissenting opinion, "but I am nevertheless compelled to admit that government has a right to invade it unless prohibited by some specific constitutional provision."[42] The Connecticut statute, Justice Stewart dissented, "is an uncommonly silly law. . . . But we are not asked in this case to say whether we think this law is unwise, or even asinine. We are asked to hold that it violates the United States Constitution. And that I cannot do."[43]

Constitutional Policy Making and the Modern Supreme Court

The *Griswold* case was not the first in which the Supreme Court took a controversial position on a civil liberties issue. In cases such as *Barnette, Brown, Schempp,* and *Gideon* — all of which were decided before the *Griswold* case — the Court had established its reputation as a principal defender of

individual rights. It was *Griswold*, however, that raised th
legitimacy of extraconstitutional policy making by the judicia
larly stark form. The Court's decision triggered an intensive
judges and scholars for a satisfactory justification of judicial de
beyond the text of the Constitution.

The modern debate over the propriety and limits of extraconstitutional
policy making by the judiciary has been in high gear for about thirty years.
Most commentators trace the origins of the debate to the Supreme Court's
decision in *Griswold* and to the publication, in 1962, of Alexander Bickel's
book *The Least Dangerous Branch*. By now, the contributions to the debate
itself are so numerous that we cannot possibly note them all, let alone explore
them in any detail. To conclude our discussion of normative justifications of
judicial review, however, it may be valuable to allude briefly to two representative theories of extraconstitutional judicial decision making.[44]

Natural Rights and Judicial Review

In a 1975 law review article, Thomas Grey raised the possibility that principles
of "natural law" might serve as an appropriate basis for Supreme Court
decisions in constitutional cases.[45] Grey argued that most of the important
constitutional decisions of the modern Supreme Court cannot be traced to
any of the relatively specific provisions of the Constitution or to the original
understanding of the relatively vague provisions of the Constitution, such as
the Due Process Clause and the Equal Protection Clause, on which so many
contemporary decisions are based. However, Grey is (or was, at the time)
unbothered by this fact, because he was comfortable with the idea that courts
should function "as the expounder of basic national ideals of individual
liberty and fair treatment, even when the content of these ideals is not
expressed as a matter of positive law in the written Constitution."[46]

In his article Grey undertakes to respond to what he (and others) call the
interpretive model of judicial decision making. This model insists that the
only role of judges is to "interpret" (rather than "rewrite") the Constitution,
and that judicial decisions that cannot be traced to the text or original
understanding of the Constitution represent an illegitimate exercise of judicial
power in a democratic society. In Grey's view, a purely interpretive model of
judicial decision making is unacceptable. He thus resolves to offer an affirmative justification for a "noninterpretive" model of judicial decision making.

Grey contends that an affirmative justification of noninterpretive judicial
review can be found in the framers' understanding of natural law and its
relationship to the written Constitution. "For the generation that framed the
Constitution," Grey argues,

> the concept of a "higher law" . . . was widely shared and deeply felt. An
> essential element of American constitutionalism was the reduction to written
> form—and hence to positive law—of some of the principles of natural rights.
> But at the same time, it was generally recognized that written constitutions could

not completely codify the higher law. Thus in the framing of the original American constitutions it was widely accepted that there remained unwritten but still binding principles of higher law. . . . As it came to be accepted that the judiciary had the power to enforce the commands of the written Constitution when these conflicted with ordinary law, it was also widely assumed that judges would enforce as constitutional restraints the unwritten natural rights as well.[47]

Noninterpretive Review in Human Rights Cases

Another important contribution to the contemporary debate about the role of the courts in a political democracy is Michael Perry's justification of noninterpretive review in human rights cases.[48] Perry, like Grey, begins by distinguishing between interpretive and noninterpretive review. The Supreme Court engages in interpretive review, Perry says, when it assesses the validity of legislation "by reference to one of the value judgments of which the Constitution consists." Noninterpretive review, by contrast, occurs when the Supreme Court "makes the determination of constitutionality by reference to a value judgment other than one constitutionalized by the framers."[49]

Perry traces the modern debate over Supreme Court decision making to the claim by interpretivist theorists, including Robert Bork, that "all noninterpretive review is illegitimate; that the Court may enforce against electorally accountable policymakers [such as elected representatives] only norms constitutionalized by the framers."[50] The implications of this claim are extremely serious, Perry notes, because virtually all of the Supreme Court's modern human rights decisions—including *Brown* v. *Board of Education* and *Roe* v. *Wade*—"cannot fairly be understood as the products of anything but noninterpretive review, and therefore cannot be deemed legitimate unless the noninterpretive review that generated them can be justified."[51] As a result, Perry concludes, "[t]he central question of contemporary constitutional theory is . . . whether it is legitimate for the Supreme Court to oppose itself to the other branches and agencies of government on the basis of value judgments *beyond* those constitutionalized by the framers."[52]

The premise of Perry's argument that noninterpretive judicial review in human rights cases is legitimate is that the American people have always had a "religious" understanding of themselves. By this he means that Americans believe they have a special responsibility to exercise moral leadership in the world. "They persist," Perry says, "in seeing themselves as a beacon to the world . . . *especially in regard to human rights.*"[53]

In the twentieth century, Perry notes, Americans have encountered several difficult human rights issues, including issues of "distributive justice and the role of government, freedom of political dissent, racism and sexism, the death penalty, and human sexuality." For better or worse, however, our "electorally accountable policymaking institutions," according to Perry, "are not well suited to deal with such issues in a way that is faithful to the notion of moral evolution or, therefore, to our religious understanding of ourselves.

Those institutions, when finally they confront such issues at all, tend simply to rely on established moral conventions and to refuse to see in such issues occasions for moral reevaluation and possible moral growth."[54]

The basic function of noninterpretive judicial review, Perry argues, is to enable us, "as a people, to keep faith with . . . our religious understanding of ourselves as a people committed to struggle incessantly to see beyond, and then to live beyond, the imperfections of whatever happens at the moment to be the established moral conventions."[55] It is possible, Perry believes, that there *are* right answers to political-moral problems. Assuming that is the case, "the politically insulated federal judiciary is more likely . . . to move us in the direction of a right answer . . . than is the political process left to its own devices."[56]

Conclusion

In both its composition and its operation, the Supreme Court as an institution violates several fundamental principles of democratic self-government. Supreme Court justices are appointed, not elected, and they serve for life. Moreover, they possess the power to overturn legislation passed by duly elected legislative representatives of the people. The exceptional features of the Supreme Court as an institution have led to the plausible charge that judicial review represents an "undemocratic" feature of American government.

A variety of theories have been developed to provide an affirmative justification for the Supreme Court's power of judicial review of legislation. The purpose of these theories is not to excuse or downplay the Court's role in the political process. Rather, it is to establish that the Supreme Court is fully entitled to play an active and at times countermajoritarian role in the policy-making process.

The traditional and most conventional justification of judicial review is derived from the fact that the United States is governed by a written Constitution. This justification argues that one of the essential purposes of the Constitution is to place limits on governmental power and to protect individual rights. It also argues that the Supreme Court and other courts, because they are not politically accountable, are the most suitable institutions to enforce the supremacy of the countermajoritarian provisions of the Constitution.

For many judges and scholars, however, the traditional justification of judicial review is incomplete unless it includes an important corollary. Such judges and scholars are proponents of an "interpretive" or "originalist" theory of judicial decision making. They concede that judges are entitled to enforce the countermajoritarian provisions of the Constitution. They also argue, however, that in doing so judges must base their decisions exclusively on the text or original understanding of the Constitution itself.

Some judges and scholars have developed theories of judicial review that are derived from the traditional theory and that draw upon the strengths of interpretive or originalist theories of judicial review, but that serve to justify additional categories of countermajoritarian judicial review. Theories of judicial review have been developed which emphasize the critical role of the courts in protecting the procedural norms of democracy and the procedural requirements of the criminal justice system. Other theories of judicial review have been developed which emphasize the critical role of the courts in protecting the fundamental rights of minority groups.

It remains doubtful, however, whether many of the most important decisions of the modern Supreme Court can be justified under the traditional theory of judicial review or any of its offshoots. As a result, judges and scholars have developed a variety of avowedly "noninterpretive" or "nonoriginalist" theories of judicial review. Some have argued that principles of natural law may serve as a legitimate foundation for judicial decisions. Others have contended that judicial review plays an indispensable role in stimulating the search for right answers to political and moral questions.

The Supreme Court's exercise of the power of judicial review has provoked a vast array of normative justifications. They run the gamut from interpretive and originalist versions of the traditional theory of judicial review, through justifications that focus on procedural democracy and the fundamental rights of minorities, to theories of judicial review that explicitly endorse the propriety of allowing judges to rely on extraconstitutional sources of support for their policy judgments. Underlying all of these theories of judicial review are two concerns. The first is that judges are not elected. The second is that judicial decisions represent countermajoritarian policy judgments in a majoritarian democracy.

The first concern could be alleviated by altering the method by which judges are chosen. The Constitution could be amended, for instance, to require that federal judges, including Supreme Court judges, must run for election at periodic intervals. In the absence of such a structural change, however, little can be done to refute the proposition that because judges are not elected, they occupy an abnormal position in the American system of democratic self-government.

The second concern that underlies contemporary theories of judicial review — the assertion that judicial review is an example of countermajoritarian decision making in a majoritarian democracy — is more problematic. There is a question whether the concern itself is empirically valid. We turn, in the next chapter, to an exploration of this issue.

<hr>

Notes

1. James Madison, "Federalist No. 10," in Roy P. Fairfield (ed.), *The Federalist Papers* (1961), p. 21.

2. Madison, "Federalist No. 51," in id. at 159.

3. Id. at 161.

4. I *Annals of Congress* 434–39 (June 8, 1789).

5. Jesse H. Choper, *Judicial Review and the National Political Process* (1980), p. 64.

6. Id. at 68.

7. See, generally, Robert J. Morgan, *James Madison on the Constitution and the Bill of Rights* (1988); and Wilfred E. Rumble, "James Madison on the Value of Bills of Rights," in J. Roland Pennock and John W. Chapman (eds.), *Constitutionalism* (1979), pp. 122–62.

8. I *Annals of Congress* 439 (June 8, 1789).

9. Alexander Hamilton, "Federalist No. 78," in Fairfield (ed.), *The Federalist Papers*, p. 228.

10. Id. at 230.

11. Edwin Meese III, "Construing the Constitution," 19 *U. Cal. Davis L. Rev.* 22, 25–29 (1985). See also Meese, "The Attorney General's View of the Supreme Court: Toward a Jurisprudence of Original Intention," 45 *Pub. Admin. Rev.* 701 (1985).

12. Robert H. Bork, "Neutral Principles and Some First Amendment Problems," 47 *Ind. L. J.* 1 (1971).

13. Id. at 2–3.

14. Id. at 3.

15. Id.

16. Id. at 10–11. Bork expands and defends his theory of original intent in *The Tempting of America: The Political Seduction of the Law* (1990), Chs. 6–8. Other forceful assertions of the importance of original intent are found in off-the-court remarks of two sitting justices. See Antonin Scalia, "Originalism: The Lesser Evil," 57 *U. Cin. L. Rev.* 849 (1989); and William H. Rehnquist, "The Notion of a Living Constitution," 54 *Texas L. Rev.* 693 (1976).

17. The scholarly debate over original intent has generated an extensive literature. Contributions include Daniel A. Farber, "The Originalism Debate: A Guide for the Perplexed," 49 *Ohio St. L. J.* 1085 (1989); Leonard W. Levy, *Original Intent and the Framers' Constitution* (1988); Richard S. Kay, "Adherence to the Original Intentions in Constitutional Adjudication: Three Objections and Responses," 82 *Nw. U. L. Rev.* 226 (1988); H. Jefferson Powell, "The Original Understanding of Original Intent," 98 *Harv. L. Rev.* 885 (1985); Robert W. Bennett, "Objectivity in Constitutional Law," 132 *U. Pa. L. Rev.* 445 (1984); Henry P. Monaghan, "Our Perfect Constitution," 56 *N.Y.U. L. Rev.* 353 (1981); Paul Brest, "The Misconceived Quest for the Original Understanding," 60 *B.U. L. Rev.* 204 (1980); and Thomas C. Grey, "Do We Have an Unwritten Constitution?" 27 *Stan. L. Rev.* 703 (1975).

18. William Brennan, "The Constitution of the United States: Contemporary Ratification," 27 *S. Tex. L. Rev.* 433, 438 (1986).

19. See Raoul Berger, *Government by Judiciary: The Transformation of the Fourteenth Amendment* (1977), pp. 117–33.

20. Bork regards *Griswold* v. *Connecticut* as a particularly glaring example of illegitimate decision making on the part of the Supreme Court. See Bork, *The Tempting of America*, pp. 95–100.

21. *De Jonge* v. *Oregon*, 299 U.S. 353, 365 (1937). For additional citations to Supreme Court discussions of the procedural defense of judicial review, see Thomas R. Marshall, *Public Opinion and the Supreme Court* (1989), pp. 37–46.

22. See, Paul L. Murphy, *The Shaping of the First Amendment, 1791 to the Present* (1992); John H. Garvey and Frederick Schauer, *The First Amendment: A*

Reader (1992); Harry Kalven, Jr., *A Worthy Tradition: Freedom of Speech in America* (1988).

23. Steven H. Shiffrin and Jesse H. Choper (eds.), *The First Amendment* (1991); and William W. Van Alstyne (ed.), *First Amendment: Cases and Materials* (1991).

24. *NAACP* v. *Button* (1963) (holding that the NAACP is constitutionally protected from prosecution for alleged violation of a state law against improper solicitation of legal business); and *NAACP* v. *Alabama* (1958) (upholding the right of the NAACP to refuse to disclose its membership lists to state officials).

25. *Scales* v. *United States* (1961) (upholding a conviction under the Smith Act for membership in the Communist party); *Noto* v. *United States* (1961) (overturning a conviction under the Smith Act for membership in the Communist party).

26. *Brown* v. *Socialist Workers* (1982) (holding that the Socialist Workers Party, because it had historically been subjected to harassment by government officials, was exempt from a state law requiring disclosure of campaign contributors).

27. *Anderson* v. *Celebrezze* (1983) (holding that an early filing deadline for independent candidates for president violates the constitutional rights of candidates and voters); *Bullock* v. *Carter* (1972) (overturning substantial filing fees required of candidates seeking to appear on the ballot); and *Williams* v. *Rhodes* (1968) (overturning a state law requiring independent parties to secure a large number of petition signatures in order to be placed on the ballot).

28. *Dunn* v. *Blumstein* (1972) (overturning a durational residence requirement for eligibility to vote in state elections); *Harper* v. *Virginia Bd. of Elections* (1966) (overturning a "poll tax" on the right to vote in state elections); *Terry* v. *Adams* (1953), and *Smith* v. *Allwright* (1944) (applying the Fifteenth Amendment to racially discriminatory party primaries in Texas).

29. *Buckley* v. *Valeo* (1976) (reviewing federal legislation governing the collection and expenditure of campaign funds); *Katzenbach* v. *Morgan* (1966) (upholding the constitutional validity of the federal Voting Rights Act of 1965).

30. The phrase is from Justice Douglas's opinion in *Gray* v. *Sanders*, 372 U.S. 368, 381 (1963).

31. 377 U.S. 533 (1964).

32. Id. at 562, 566 (1964).

33. The Supreme Court's decisions delineating the procedural rights of criminal defendants are numerous and are ordinarily reprinted in separate casebooks. See, for example, Jerold H. Israel, Yale Kamisar, and Wayne R. LaFave (eds.), *Criminal Procedure and the Constitution* (1992).

34. Students seeking an initial overview of the Supreme Court's equal protection decisions can consult C. Herman Pritchett, *Constitutional Civil Liberties* (1984), Chs. 10 and 12, or Lawrence H. Tribe, *American Constitutional Law* (1988), Ch. 16. The text of actual decisions can be found in edited form in all modern civil liberties casebooks.

35. John Hart Ely, *Democracy and Distrust: A Theory of Judicial Review* (1980).

36. Id. at 86–87.

37. Id. at 105.

38. Id. at 103. Ely's theory of constitutional interpretation has been roundly criticized. In this respect, however, Ely is not alone. In recent years, the debate among judges and scholars about the proper role of the Supreme Court in American democracy has been intense. For discussions of Ely's contributions to constitutional theory, see, for example, Symposium, "Constitutional Adjudication and Democratic Theory,"

56 *N.Y.U. L. Rev.* 259 (1981); Symposium, "Judicial Review Versus Democracy," 42 *Ohio St. L. J.* 1 (1981); Lawrence H. Tribe, "The Puzzling Persistence of Process-based Constitutional Theories," 89 *Yale L. J.* 1063 (1980); and Mark Tushnet, "Darkness on the Edge of Town: The Contributions of John Hart Ely to Constitutional Theory," 89 *Yale L. J.* 1037 (1980).

39. *Griswold* v. *Connecticut*, 381 U.S. 479, 484 (1965).

40. Id. at 486.

41. Id. at 485.

42. Id. at 510 (Black, J., dissenting).

43. Id. at 527 (Stewart, J., dissenting).

44. For a comprehensive sample of excerpts from contemporary constitutional theory, see John H. Garvey and T. Alexander Aleinkoff (eds.), *Modern Constitutional Theory: A Reader* 2nd ed. (1991). Among the most recent book-length contributions to the debate are Michael J. Perry, *The Constitution in the Courts* (forthcoming, 1994); Robert A. Burt, *The Constitution in Conflict* (1992); Harry H. Wellington, *Interpreting the Constitution* (1991); Bruce Ackerman, *We the People: Volume One — Foundations* (1991); Leslie Friedman Goldstein, *In Defense of the Text: Democracy and Constitutional Theory* (1991); Robert F. Nagel, *Constitutional Cultures: The Mentality and Consequences of Judicial Review* (1989); Sanford Levinson, *Constitutional Faith* (1988); and Mark V. Tushnet, *Red, White, and Blue: A Critical Analysis of Constitutional Law* (1988).

45. Thomas C. Grey, "Do We Have an Unwritten Constitution?" 27 *Stan. L. Rev.* 703 (1975).

46. Id. at 706.

47. Id. at 715–16. For additional discussion of the role of natural rights in contemporary constitutional interpretation, see Thomas C. Grey, "Origins of the Unwritten Constitution: Fundamental Law in American Revolutionary Thought," 30 *Stan. L. Rev.* 843 (1978); and Suzanna Sherry, "The Founders' Unwritten Constitution," 54 *U. Chi. L. Rev.* 1127 (1987).

48. Michael J. Perry, *The Constitution, the Courts, and Human Rights: An Inquiry into the Legitimacy of Constitutional Policymaking by the Judiciary* (1982).

49. Id. at 10–11.

50. Id. at 65.

51. Id. at 11.

52. Id. at 75. Emphasis in the original.

53. Id. at 98. Emphasis in the original.

54. Id. at 100.

55. Id. at 101.

56. Id. at 102.

CHAPTER 15

The Supreme Court and Public Opinion: The Countermajoritarian Problem in Empirical Perspective

T he Supreme Court is a judicial institution, but it should be very clear by now that the Court is no ordinary judicial institution. To begin with, it occupies a unique position at the pinnacle of a complex system of state and federal courts. In addition, it regularly confronts important and controversial issues of American public policy. Finally, both its composition and its operation are profoundly affected by the swirling currents of American politics. In short, the Supreme Court is a judicial institution with substantial policy-making responsibilities and with substantial ties, both incoming and outgoing, to the political environment in which it operates.

Because the Supreme Court is a political as well as judicial institution, and because it regularly engages in the formulation of public policy, the focus of this book has been on the Court's role in the American system of democratic politics. Today, almost everyone would concede that law and politics are interrelated and that the Supreme Court decisions are policy pronouncements in much the same sense as decisions emanating from Congress or the presidency. Conceding that the Supreme Court *is* a policy-making body, however, leaves unanswered the further interesting question of whether the policy-making power of the Supreme Court can be reconciled with fundamental principles of democratic self-government.

In the previous three chapters, we have explored various ways of reducing or eliminating the conflict between judicial review and majoritarian democracy. In Chapters 12 and 13, we noted that the Supreme Court is an integral part of the political system and that its decision-making behavior is subject to a variety of both external and internal restraints. In Chapter 14, we explored various possibilities for constructing an affirmative or normative justification of countermajoritarian judicial review.

In this chapter, we take an entirely different approach to evaluating the role of the Supreme Court in American democracy. We begin by rethinking what we mean by the allegation that Supreme Court decision making is "undemocratic." This discussion suggests the importance of examining empirical evidence on the distribution of public opinion in the United States. In Section II, we examine this evidence and discuss its implications. Our ultimate goal is to offer a fresh perspective on the longstanding allegation that judicial review is an undemocratic feature of the political process.

The Undemocratic Character of Judicial Review

As we saw in Chapter 1, it is often alleged that judicial review is an "undemocratic" feature of the American political process. There are probably two main reasons for this allegation. The first reason is that the judges who exercise the power of judicial review are not elected and therefore are not politically accountable. If by democracy we mean a political system in which all policy-making officials are accountable to the people through the mechanism of periodic elections, then judicial review, by definition, is an undemocratic feature of the political process.

The previous chapter presented a response to this line of argument, one based on the language of the Constitution. The Constitution stipulates that federal judges shall hold their offices "during good Behaviour" and cannot be removed from office except by the process of impeachment. Thus, the Constitution itself prescribes that Supreme Court justices will be exempt from periodic electoral scrutiny.

The argument that judicial review is undemocratic because federal judges are not elected can therefore be met by arguing that the Constitution itself prescribes that federal judges shall enjoy substantial immunity from political pressures. At this point, however, those who believe that judicial review is an undemocratic feature of the political process can introduce a second, and separate, argument. Judicial review is undemocratic, it can be argued, not only because judges are not elected, but also because judicial decisions overturning legislation are examples of countermajoritarian policy making by the judiciary.

The Countermajoritarian Basis for Questioning Judicial Review

The assumption that Supreme Court decisions are examples of countermajoritarian policy making is almost certainly the most common basis for questioning the legitimacy of judicial review. Judicial review involves the invalidation by unelected judges of decisions reached by elected legislative majorities. Clearly, judicial review violates the fundamental principle that democracy consists of majority rule by elected representatives. Equally clearly, judicial review is, in this sense, undemocratic.

We saw in Chapter 14, of course, that the traditional justification of judicial review is in effect a direct response to the allegation that judicial review is undemocratic because it is countermajoritarian. The traditional justification is based on the premise that the U.S. Constitution is a written document which is the supreme law of the land and which imposes limits on popular and legislative majorities. Those limits are enforced by courts. Countermajoritarian judicial decision making is therefore a legitimate ingredient of the American system of constitutional democracy.

It is important to note, however, that the need to offer an affirmative or normative justification of judicial review only arises because one has conceded a critical factual point. Persons who develop an affirmative justification of judicial review ordinarily concede, for purposes of argument, that judicial decisions overturning legislation are in fact examples of countermajoritarian policy making. They then go on to argue that such decisions are nevertheless justified by principles embodied in the American Constitution.

Suppose, however, that judicial review is *not* in fact an example of countermajoritarian policy making. If that is the case, then it becomes untenable to argue that judicial review is undemocratic — or at least to argue that judicial review is undemocratic because it is countermajoritarian. In addition, there is less urgency about constructing an affirmative justification of judicial review.

Is Judicial Review Countermajoritarian?

The allegation that judicial review is countermajoritarian is almost invariably based on the assumption that Supreme Court decisions overturning legislation are examples of policy decisions contradicting the preferences of a majority of elected legislative representatives. Alexander Bickel's characterization of the problem is a good example. "The root difficulty," he wrote in 1962, "is that judicial review is a counter-majoritarian force in our system. . . . [W]hen the Supreme Court declares unconstitutional a legislative act or the action of an elected executive, it thwarts the will of representatives of the actual people of the here and now; it exercises control, not in behalf of the prevailing majority, but against it. That . . . is the reason the charge can be made that judicial review is undemocratic."[1]

The assumption that Supreme Court decisions overturning legislation are examples of countermajoritarian policy making is plausible. Judicial review, by definition, involves the invalidation by judges of statutes that have been passed by a majority of elected legislative representatives. Upon examination, however, the assumption that judicial review is an example of countermajoritarian policy making turns out to have a number of important weaknesses.

First, we must identify the precise legislative majority whose preferences the Supreme Court is contradicting. A Supreme Court decision overturning a particular statute contradicts the expressed preferences of a majority of the legislators who voted for the statute in the first place. Technically, however, that is the *only* legislative majority that the Supreme Court is necessarily contradicting when it overturns a particular statute. The Court's decision is countermajoritarian vis-à-vis the legislative majority that enacted the statute. Whether it is countermajoritarian vis-à-vis any *other* legislative majority, however, is an open question.

Second, we must resolve whether the preferences of legislative majorities are the only *types* of majorities whose preferences are relevant. A Supreme Court decision overturning a law may be countermajoritarian vis-à-vis the legislative majority that passed the law. Whether the Court's decision is countermajoritarian vis-à-vis any other group of people, however, remains to be determined.

Social Change and Opinion Change

It is theoretically possible, for instance, that legislation passed by a majority of elected legislators does not represent the preferences of a majority of the American public or even a majority of voting citizens. When such a conflict exists — that is, if a particular law does not enjoy the support of the American people — it is not at all clear that a Supreme Court decision striking down the law should be classified as an example of countermajoritarian policy making by the judiciary.

In practice, a conflict between the policy preferences of the public and those embodied in law may arise most frequently as a result of social change. Even if the public and their elected representatives were in agreement at the time a particular law was passed, public preferences may change with time. After a period of years, a law that once enjoyed the support of a majority of the public may no longer enjoy such support, even though the law itself is still on the books. If the Supreme Court overturns a law that originally enjoyed the support of a popular majority but has subsequently lost that support, it is unclear whether it makes sense to characterize the Court's decision as a genuine example of countermajoritarian judicial decision making. The Court's decision overturning the law has vindicated the preferences of a current majority of the American people. To call such a decision countermajoritarian is to focus exclusively on the law itself and to ignore the fact that the current preferences of a majority of the American people no longer coincide with the content of the law.

When Majorities Disagree: A Hypothetical Example

It may be helpful to provide a hypothetical example of the situation we are describing. Suppose, for instance, that Congress, with the support of a majority of the American people, were to pass a law prohibiting abortion. Suppose, however, that over a period of years, popular support for the law eroded to the point where the law no longer enjoyed majority support. If the Court were to strike down the law, its decision would be countermajoritarian vis-à-vis the congressional majority that passed the law *and* vis-à-vis the policy preferences of the American people at the time the law was passed. The Court's decision would *not* be countermajoritarian, however, vis-à-vis a current majority of the American people.

Theoretically, of course, once a particular law loses the support of a majority of the American people, the law itself should be repealed. In practice, however, such a law may remain on the books for several reasons. Legislative bodies are ordinarily overwhelmed with work and cannot reevaluate the content of statutes at regular intervals. Legislative inertia may therefore prevent the repeal of an unpopular law. In addition, intense pressure from the particular interests that benefit from the law may prevent the legislature from repealing the law. Certainly, American politics today presents ample evidence that elected legislators are at least as concerned about special interests as they are about the preferences of the general public.

In the case of abortion, to return for a moment to our hypothetical example, Congress would likely have difficulty repealing an anti-abortion statute once it was enacted, even if, as we have hypothesized, the distribution of public opinion had changed. Organized pressure from pro-life groups and the generally high level of controversy that surrounds the abortion issue would probably be sufficient to dissuade Congress from repealing the law.

In short, it is theoretically possible, and even quite probable, for a law to remain on the books, even though it no longer has the support of a popular majority. How, then, should we regard a Supreme Court decision striking down the law? Certainly, a strong argument can be made that the Court's exercise of its power of judicial review in such circumstances should not be classified as a genuine example of countermajoritarian policy making.

The most extreme situation, of course, is one in which the Supreme Court strikes down a law that no longer enjoys the support of *either* a popular majority *or* a legislative majority. It seems particularly unlikely, of course, that such a law would need to be challenged in court, because by definition the law is unpopular both with the public and with its elected representatives. Even then, however, legislative inertia or special interests could prevent the repeal of the law. In striking down the law, the Supreme Court would be vindicating the current preferences of both a legislative majority and a popular majority. The Court, in other words, would be making a direct contribution to the operation of majoritarian democracy in the United States. In such circumstances, to accuse the Court of engaging in countermajoritarian policy making would seem to be singularly inaccurate and unfair.

State Statutes and National Policy Preferences

In our discussions thus far, we have referred in a general way to legislative majorities, on the one hand, and to popular majorities, on the other. We have hypothesized a situation in which the policy preferences embodied in an existing law conflict with those of a current majority of the American people. We have argued that a Supreme Court decision overturning such a law should not necessarily be classified as an example of countermajoritarian judicial policy making.

In the case of judicial review of state laws, an additional ambiguity lurks in the allegation that Supreme Court decisions overturning legislation are examples of countermajoritarian judicial policy making. The point that must be made about judicial review of state laws is an important one, and it goes directly to the question of the role of the Supreme Court in American democracy.

As we saw in Chapter 4, Supreme Court decisions that overturn state laws are about ten times as common as Supreme Court decisions that overturn federal laws. Moreover, the Court's decisions in state cases have traditionally been at least as controversial as its decisions in federal cases. Finally, the Court's oversight of the constitutional validity of state laws is often portrayed as an indispensable feature of the American system of constitutional democracy.[2]

When the Supreme Court overturns a state law, the Court is contradicting the policy preferences of the legislative majority that passed the law. As we have already discussed, however, it does not necessarily follow that the Court's decision contradicts the policy preferences of a current majority of legislators or a past or present majority of members of the public. In some cases, however, it will be clear that both a current state legislative majority and a current state popular majority support the law declared unconstitutional by the Court. In such circumstances, the Court's decision could be fairly characterized as a genuine example of countermajoritarian policy making.

In the case of judicial review of state laws, however, we must consider an additional perspective. The Supreme Court is a national court; moreover, it is responsible for enforcing our national Constitution. It can be argued, therefore, that to determine whether the Court's decision in a particular case is countermajoritarian, the preferences of the American people are more relevant than those of either a state legislative majority or a state popular majority. A Supreme Court decision overturning a state law may contradict the preferences of both elected state legislators *and* the citizens of the state. It is entirely possible, however, that a nationwide majority of Americans support the Court's decision. When that is the case, we must once again face the difficult question of whether it is appropriate to characterize the Court's decision as a genuine example of countermajoritarian judicial policy making.

As we will see in the next section, discrepancies often exist between the policy preferences of state citizens (or citizens of a particular region of the country) and those of Americans as a whole. Since the Supreme Court is a national court with principal responsibility for enforcing our national Constitution, we must ask whether a Supreme Court decision that overturns a state law is a genuine example of countermajoritarian judicial policy making if the

Court's decision in fact enjoys the support of a nationwide majority of Americans.

Mass Attitudes and Elite Attitudes

Finally, we should note one additional ambiguity that may lurk in the allegation that Supreme Court decisions overturning legislation are examples of countermajoritarian judicial policy making. When opinion surveys are conducted in the United States, the views of various "subsets" of respondents are commonly examined. The opinions of women may be contrasted with those of men, for instance, or the views of blacks with those of whites.

One question that is frequently explored in surveys of attitudes toward issues of public policy is whether the views of citizens who are particularly well-educated differ from those of citizens in general. In addition, research based on opinion surveys has sometimes explored the question of whether there is anything exceptional about the views of citizens who are particularly active in the political process—citizens, for instance, who hold local elective office or are leaders or members of local community organizations.

As we will see in the next section, a discrepancy often exists between the views of well-educated and/or politically active citizens and the views of citizens in general. We will also see that these discrepancies frequently occur on issues of the sort that come before the Supreme Court. A particular Supreme Court decision, for instance, may be supported by a majority of well-educated or politically active Americans—that is, citizens classified by social scientists as "elites" or "political elites"—but be opposed by Americans in general. When that is the case it is once again clear that, at the very least, the Court's decision is not a pure or unadulterated example of countermajoritarian judicial policy making.

Conclusion

The allegation that judicial review is an undemocratic feature of American politics is usually based on the fact that federal judges are not elected or on the assumption that Supreme Court decisions overturning legislation are examples of countermajoritarian judicial policy making. However, normative responses may be made to each of these lines of argument. The Constitution itself prescribes that federal judges shall be appointed for life, that is, until they are removed from office by impeachment. In addition, the "traditional justification of judicial review," as we have called it, offers an affirmative or normative defense of countermajoritarian judicial decision making.

The allegation that judicial review is undemocratic because it is countermajoritarian can also be questioned on factual grounds. The Supreme Court's exercise of its power of judicial review of legislation is clearly an act of countermajoritarian policy making vis-à-vis the legislative majority that passed the law. Whether the Court in overturning a law is contradicting the preferences of any other majority, however, is an open question.

The policy position embodied in the law may not have been supported by a majority of the public at the time the law was passed. It is also possible that public preferences or legislative preferences (or both) have changed since the law was passed. In any of these cases, the Supreme Court in striking down the law will be vindicating the preferences of one majority even as it contradicts the preferences of another. It therefore becomes problematic to describe the Court's decision, without qualification, as an example of countermajoritarian judicial policy making.

In the case of Supreme Court decisions overturning state laws, it is important that the policy preferences of a national majority of Americans be taken into account. The Supreme Court is responsible for enforcing the U.S. Constitution. When one of the Court's decisions is supported by a national majority of Americans — even though it may be opposed by a local, state, or regional majority — it is clear that the Court's decision is not a pure example of countermajoritarian judicial policy making.

Finally, specific groups within the population may hold differing views on policy issues decided by the Supreme Court. The policy preferences of well-educated and/or politically active citizens — who are sometimes described by researchers as elites or political elites — are often different from those of citizens in general. A particular Supreme Court decision may be opposed by a majority of the public but may be endorsed by a majority of well-educated or politically active citizens. The opposite result is also possible. In either case, we cannot describe the Court's decision as an example of countermajoritarian judicial policy making without first specifying which particular majority the Court, by its decision, is contradicting.

The Supreme Court and Public Opinion

In his concurring opinion in *Dennis* v. *United States* (1951), Justice Frankfurter argued that "[c]ourts are not representative bodies. They are not designed to be a good reflex of a democratic society."[3] Frankfurter was correct that the federal courts are not *designed* to be a good reflex of majority opinion. It is not nearly so clear, however, that courts are not "representative bodies," that is, that their decisions cannot or do not reflect the preferences of a majority of the American people.

In this section, we examine empirical evidence regarding the distribution of American public opinion on a variety of issues decided by the Supreme Court. We will see that the Supreme Court is not out of step with the American public nearly as often as one might expect. This finding calls into question the wisdom of persisting to characterize Supreme Court decision making as a prime example of countermajoritarian policy making in American democracy.

The Supreme Court and Public Opinion: An Overview

The most comprehensive study of the relationship between public opinion and Supreme Court decision making has been undertaken by Thomas Marshall.[4] Marshall attempted to locate all possible instances in which the American people had been polled on an issue decided by the Supreme Court. The Court's decision could be in a state case or a federal case, and it could be a decision upholding or overturning a law. For the period between 1935 and 1986, Marshall was able to identify 146 "matches" or comparisons between polling items and Supreme Court decisions.

When he analyzed his sample of 146 matches, Marshall discovered agreement between the Supreme Court and public opinion about 62 percent of the time. In a little more than three-fifths of the cases that comprised his sample, therefore, the Supreme Court and a majority of the American public were in agreement on an issue of public policy.

On the basis of these results, it is difficult to conclude that the Supreme Court is essentially a countermajoritarian policy-making institution. Of course, we do not have systematic evidence of the extent of agreement between the public and the Court. The overwhelming majority of Supreme Court decisions, including some of the Court's most controversial decisions, are not the subject of nationwide opinion polls. Based on the available evidence, however, it seems impossible to conclude that Supreme Court decisions are particularly likely to be examples of countermajoritarian policy making.

Comparative Policy Making: Who Best Reflects the Will of the Majority?

Marshall's results are especially interesting in view of the results of other recent studies of the relationship between public opinion and public policy. In 1979, Alan Monroe compared the content of national public policy with the results of national opinion surveys conducted between 1960 and 1974.[5] He discovered that public opinion and public policy were consistent in 64 percent of the 222 cases he examined. He also discovered that consistency between opinion and policy was approximately the same on issues specifically involving civil rights and civil liberties — on issues, that is, that are likely to be decided by courts as opposed to other decision-making institutions — as it was on policy issues as a whole.[6]

In another recent study, Benjamin Page and Robert Shapiro examined the relationship between opinion change and policy change in the United States.[7] The authors focused on 231 instances in which national opinion polls (conducted betweeen 1935 and 1979) had detected a "significant change" (defined as 6 percentage points or more) in the policy preferences of the American people. The authors then examined whether public policy had changed, and in what direction, in the wake of these opinion changes. The authors discovered that policy change was congruent with opinion change 66 percent of the time. They also discovered that levels of congruence between opinion change and policy change were approximately equal regardless of whether Congress, the presidency, or the Supreme Court was responsible for making the policy in question.

The results of various studies of public opinion and public policy suggest that the Supreme Court is not especially likely to decide issues in a way that conflicts with the preferences of a majority of the American people. In American politics, public policy reflects the will of the majority about three-fifths to two-thirds of the time. Moreover, the Supreme Court appears to reflect the will of the majority approximately as often as policy-making institutions, such as Congress, which were explicitly designed to further the goals of majoritarian democracy.

The fact that Supreme Court decisions reflect the will of the majority approximately as often as Congress or the president suggests the value of looking more closely at the relationship between Supreme Court decisions and public opinion on selected issues of public policy. Such an examination yields important insights into the role of the Supreme Court in American democracy.

The Supreme Court and Freedom of Speech

A substantial number of Supreme Court decisions in both state and federal cases have involved questions of freedom of speech for unpopular groups. The Court's 1957 decision in *Yates* v. *United States*, which we examined in Chapter 7, is a good example. *Yates* arose when members of the Communist party were convicted of violating the Smith Act. In their appeal to the Supreme Court, they argued that the Smith Act abridged their First Amendment rights of freedom of speech and freedom of association. In *Yates*, the Supreme Court narrowly construed the Smith Act and effectively ended its usefulness as a weapon in the fight against alleged Communist subversion.

Decisions such as *Yates* are ordinarily thought to be good examples of the Supreme Court's capacity for countermajoritarian policy making. An examination of trends in public opinion on free speech issues, however, suggests that the picture is a bit more complicated than this.

Opinion Trends on Speech Issues

In the early 1950s sociologist Samuel Stouffer conducted a path-breaking study of Americans' tolerance of unpopular groups.[8] The study consisted of a survey of a national cross-section of ordinary citizens as well as a selected sample of "community leaders," that is, local elected officials and other community leaders. Among the questions respondents were asked was whether they believed that an admitted Communist should be "allowed to make a speech" in their community.[9]

In 1992 Page and Shapiro published a study of trends in American public opinion on a wide variety of policy issues.[10] The authors examined the trend of public opinion in 1,128 cases of "repeated questions," that is, survey questions that had been posed to a national sample of Americans on two or more occasions over a period of time. One question on which they focused was Stouffer's query about the free speech rights of admitted Communists.

The trend of public opinion on this issue is pictured in Figure 15.1. In 1954, when Americans were first asked whether they would allow an admitted Communist to speak in their community, only 28 percent responded "Yes." By 1973, however, public support for free speech rights for Communists had risen to 61 percent. By 1989–1990, about two-thirds of Americans —66 percent—were willing to allow a Communist to make a speech in their community.[11] This rise of nearly 40 percentage points in the proportion of Americans expressing support for the free speech rights of admitted Communists was among the largest changes in public opinion found by Page and Shapiro. The Stouffer question was one of only twenty cases (out of a total of 1,128) in which the American public's views on an issue of public policy changed by more than 30 percentage points.[12]

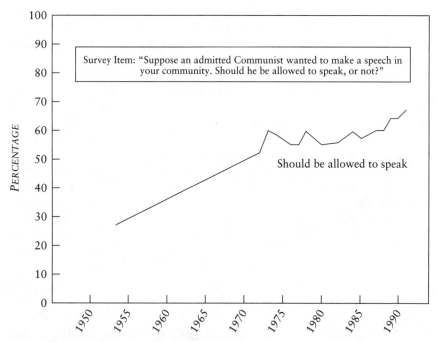

FIGURE 15.1 Public Support for Speech Rights of Admitted Communists

SOURCES: *Richard G. Niemi et al.*, Trends in Public Opinion: A Compendium of Survey Data *(Westport, Conn.: Greenwood Press, 1989); National Opinion Research Center, General Social Surveys, 1972–1991; Cumulative Codebook (Chicago, NORC, 1991).*

The empirical data suggest, therefore, that the Supreme Court in *Yates* and other cases involving free speech for unpopular groups was essentially in step with significant and long-term trends in American public opinion. Americans were becoming more willing to allow unpopular groups such as the Communist party to engage in activities such as speaking in public. The Court's decisions protecting the Communist party and other groups apparently reflected a liberalization in the attitudes of the American public.

From this perspective, it is not so clear that Supreme Court decisions in free speech cases are necessarily good examples of countermajoritarian judicial policy making. Public support for allowing Communists to speak in public was increasing during the forty-year period beginning in the 1950s. At the time they were handed down, particular Supreme Court decisions protecting the free speech rights of the Communist party might have contradicted the preferences of a majority of the American public. Given the trend of public opinion, however, it is not certain that this was the case.[13]

Elite Support for Freedom of Speech

The picture is further complicated when we note that, on issues involving the fundamental rights of unpopular groups, the views of the general public often differ from those of a subset of the population consisting of politically active and/or well-educated citizens. In 1954, as we have mentioned, Stouffer found that only 28 percent of the general public would allow an admitted Communist to speak. Among his sample of "community leaders," however, support for the free speech rights of an admitted Communist stood at 51 percent.[14] In 1973, the Stouffer study was replicated (in order to determine whether public or elite opinion had changed).[15] The updated study found that 78 percent of community leaders were now willing to allow a Communist to speak in their community.[16]

Most surveys have produced similar results; that is, they have found higher levels of support for the fundamental rights of unpopular groups among politically active and/or well-educated citizens than among the population as a whole. Thus, particular Supreme Court decisions protecting the rights of unpopular groups may be opposed by a majority of ordinary citizens but at the same time be supported by a majority of "elite" citizens. When that is the case, we must be particularly careful to specify exactly what we mean by the assertion that the Court's decision is an example of countermajoritarian judicial decision making.[17]

The Supreme Court and Freedom of Speech: A Mixed Verdict

Supreme Court decisions protecting the speech rights of unpopular groups do not, therefore, appear to be clearcut examples of countermajoritarian judicial policy making. By at least two measures — the long-term trend of American public opinion and the distribution (and trend) of opinion among community leaders—many Supreme Court decisions protecting the speech rights of unpopular groups apparently reflected the views of an existing or an emerging majority of the population. In this respect, even though many of the Court's decisions have been classic examples of judicial activism—that is, they have overturned statutes enacted by a majority of elected legislative representatives—the decisions themselves may have enjoyed the support of a majority of the American people or at least a majority of politically active and/or well-educated Americans.

It is tempting, therefore, to conclude that Supreme Court decisions in free speech case are not, after all, very good examples of countermajoritarian judicial policy making. Before we go that far, however, we must note at least three additional pieces of information. First, since the 1950s the general public, as we have seen, has shown a gradual increase in support for the free speech rights of Communists. In the late 1950s and early 1960s, however, this trend was barely underway. When the Supreme Court decided in *Yates* and other cases that the government was violating the constitutional rights of members of the Communist party, it is unlikely that tolerance of Communists had spread to a majority of the population. Thus, even though the Court's decisions reflected the trend of public opinion, the decisions themselves were still examples of countermajoritarian judicial policy making and the Court was, in effect, in the vanguard of social change.

Second, the particular trend on which we have focused concerns public support for the rights of Communists. Public support stood below 30 percent in the early 1950s and rose to above 65 percent in the late 1980s. It is possible, however, that public support for the free speech rights of *other* groups has not changed nearly as much or that new groups have *displaced* the Communist party as the chief object of American intolerance. Recent studies have shown that when Americans are presented with a variety of unpopular groups, and are allowed to choose the group they like the least, many Americans will choose groups other than the Communist party. The studies also suggest that when Americans are asked whether they would support the free speech rights of the group they have chosen as their "least-liked group," whatever that group may be, levels of intolerance remain quite high.[18]

Finally, we should remember what happened when the Supreme Court decided, in *Texas* v. *Johnson* (1989), that the First Amendment protects someone who burns an American flag as an act of protest. Polls taken in the wake of the Court's decision showed that more than 80 percent of Americans believed that flag burning should be illegal.[19] Congress responded to this lopsided division of public opinion by passing the Flag Protection Act of 1989. In 1990, however, the Court in *United States* v. *Eichman* overturned the congressional statute. The Court's decision was clearly countermajoritarian in the two most common usages of the term: it contradicted the preferences of a current majority of the U.S. Congress, and it contradicted the preferences of a current majority of the American people. It is possible, of course, that the Court's decision was supported by a majority of some subgroups of politically active and/or well-educated citizens (although certainly not members of Congress). By almost every other measure, however, the Court's flag burning decision was an act of countermajoritarian judicial policy making.

Perhaps only one safe conclusion may be drawn from the foregoing survey of empirical evidence relating to public opinion and Supreme Court decisions on free speech issues. That conclusion is that anyone who asserts that Supreme Court decisions on free speech issues are clearcut examples of countermajoritarian policy making should be careful to check the facts. Some Supreme Court decisions — for instance, the flag burning decisions — do seem to qualify. As a general proposition, however, the distinct trend of public opinion during that past forty years has been in the direction of greater support for the free speech rights of at least selected unpopular groups. That being the case, many Supreme Court decisions overturning legislation may have been supported (rather than opposed) by a current majority of the American people.

The Supreme Court and Race Relations

A similar conclusion may apply to the Court's decisions in the area of race relations. Supreme Court decisions in cases involving the civil rights and civil liberties of racial minorities are widely regarded as classic examples of countermajoritarian judicial decision making. The Supreme Court's 1954 decision in *Brown* v. *Board of Education* is a particularly well-known example of a judicial decision protecting minority rights and therefore (presumably) contradicting the will of the majority. From an empirical perspective, however, it is not clear that the *Brown* decision was in fact an example of countermajoritarian judicial policy making. Neither is it clear that the Supreme Court is prepared to contradict the preferences of a majority of the American people on the full range of complicated issues involving race relations.

Figure 15.2 shows the trend of nationwide public opinion on a variety of issues affecting race relations. On two of those issues — laws against interracial marriage and laws requiring racial segregation of public schools — public opinion has moved gradually and strongly in the direction of greater support for racial equality. However, when the public is asked to react to two relatively "aggressive" solutions to racial problems — busing to achieve integration and the use of affirmative action to overcome racial inequality — its enthusiasm for racial justice begins to evaporate.

In 1942 white Americans were asked for the first time whether they thought "white students and Negro students should go to the same schools or to separate schools." (These polls involved only white respondents.) A minority of 31 percent answered "Same schools." The next time the question was asked was in 1956, two years after the *Brown* decision. By that time, 49 percent of white Americans approved of whites and blacks attending the same schools. Since 1956 public support for integration has continued to climb, and in 1985 an overwhelming majority of 92 percent of white Americans

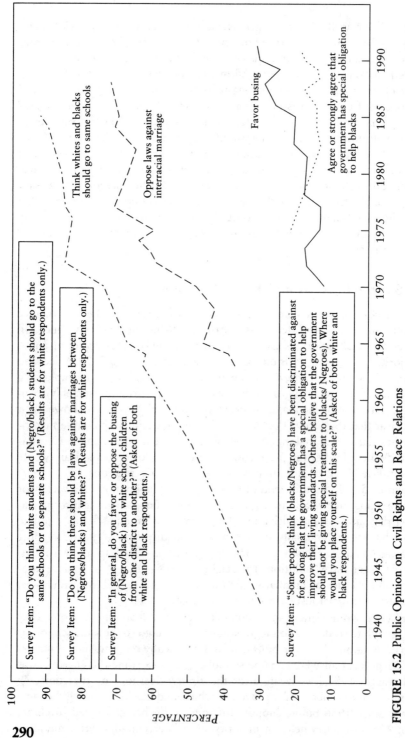

Survey Item: "Do you think white students and (Negro/black) students should go to the same schools or to separate schools?" (Results are for white respondents only.)

Survey Item: "Do you think there should be laws against marriages between (Negroes/blacks) and whites?" (Results are for white respondents only.)

Survey Item: "In general, do you favor or oppose the busing of (Negro/black) and white school children from one district to another?" (Asked of both white and black respondents.)

Survey Item: "Some people think (blacks/Negroes) have been discriminated against for so long that the government has a special obligation to help improve their living standards. Others believe that the government should not be giving special treatment to (blacks/ Negroes). Where would you place yourself on this scale?" (Asked of both white and black respondents.)

Think whites and blacks should go to same schools

Oppose laws against interracial marriage

Favor busing

Agree or strongly agree that government has special obligation to help blacks

FIGURE 15.2 Public Opinion on Civil Rights and Race Relations

SOURCES: *Richard G. Niemi et al.,* Trends in Public Opinion: A Compendium of Survey Data *(Westport, Conn.: Greenwood Press, 1989); National Opinion Research Center,* General Social Surveys, 1972–1991; Cumulative Codebook *(Chicago, NORC, 1991).*

supported the proposition that white and black students should attend the same schools. Page and Shapiro note that "[t]his change of more than sixty percentage points is the largest for any policy preference question of any kind among the thousands we have examined."[20]

Opposition among white Americans to laws against interracial marriage, often called antimiscegenation laws, has shown a similar upward climb. In 1963 only 37 percent of whites expressed opposition to "laws against marriages between blacks and whites." By 1970 opposition to such laws stood at 48 percent, and by 1988, after a continuous but somewhat unsteady rise, white opposition was approaching the 75 percent mark.[21]

The Supreme Court, the American Public, and Racial Issues

The trend of public opinion on school segregation and laws against interracial marriage indicates that American attitudes on race relations have undergone a substantial liberalization in recent decades. The questions to which the public is asked to respond in these polls, however, are relatively hypothetical. Polls on school segregation ask only whether the respondent feels that whites and blacks "should go" to the same schools or separate schools. Polls on antimiscegenation laws do not ask whether the respondent approves or disapproves of interracial marriage, but only whether such marriages should be against the law.

Polling items that ask respondents to react to concrete strategies for solving racial problems elicit a much more ambivalent reaction. In surveys that include both whites and blacks, support for busing to achieve integration has risen — from 14 percent in 1970 to 34 percent in 1991 — but it remains the minority view.[22] As for affirmative action, most polling items, depending on how they are phrased, elicit substantial opposition from blacks and overwhelming opposition from whites.[23]

In light of these complex patterns of public opinion, how are we to assess Supreme Court decisions on race relations? At the very least, the Court's decisions in this area do not appear to merit their current reputation as prime examples of countermajoritarian judicial policy making. In the first place, the Court has shown a marked reluctance to challenge the prevailing consensus against busing and affirmative action. The Supreme Court, as opposed to some lower federal courts, has refrained from taking a strong position in favor of the use of busing as a remedy for school segregation. The Court has also been notably cautious on the issue of affirmative action. As we saw in Chapter 11, the Court's decision in *Regents of the University of California* v. *Bakke* was essentially a carefully crafted political compromise. In its recent decisions, moreover, the Court has stiffened its opposition to affirmative action. It therefore seems to be moving toward an explicit recognition of the preferences of a majority of Americans.

But what about *Brown* v. *Board of Education* itself? *Brown* is easily the most famous Supreme Court decision of the twentieth century. Moreover, its special status derives in part from its reputation as a classic example of countermajoritarian judicial policy making. Is this an accurate assessment?

Certainly there is a substantial basis for concluding that at the time that *Brown* was decided, no other institution of American government was prepared to rule that school segregation must end. The unpleasant reality is that most white southerners, including those who served in Congress avidly supported school segregation and that ending school segregation was not a particularly high priority among politicians representing areas of the country other than the South. Thus, the Court deserves credit for holding that school segregation was unconstitutional and for helping to initiate one of the most important periods of social change in American history.

The data on trends in public opinion also indicate, however, that at the time that *Brown* was decided, the American people were not necessarily opposed to the proposition that segregation of public schools must end. Public support for school desegregation had already begun its slow but steady upward climb. The Court in deciding *Brown* was therefore in step with an emerging, if not yet fully emergent, national majority.

A few years later, in *Loving* v. *Virginia* (1967), the Court held that state antimiscegenation laws were unconstitutional. Like *Brown*, the Court's decision in *Loving* was apparently handed down in the context of the early stirrings of a major liberalization of public attitudes at the national level. Undoubtedly, the Court's decision contradicted the preferences of a majority of southern whites. From a national perspective, however, the Court's decision was not necessarily a clearcut example of countermajoritarian judicial policy making.

Brown and *Loving* illustrate that particular Supreme Court decisions often contain a complex mixture of majoritarian and countermajoritarian elements. The decisions were certainly opposed by a majority of whites in the states to which they applied. Among southern blacks, however, *Brown* and *Loving* almost certainly enjoyed majority support. Among white Americans at the national level, moreover, opinions about school segregation and laws against interracial marriage had begun to change. Public support for the policy positions enunciated by the Court was rising and, at the time the decisions were handed down, was at or near the 50 percent mark. Thus, it is unclear whether the Court's decision in either *Brown* or *Loving* was actually in conflict with the preferences of a majority of the American people.

From the point of view of democratic theory, therefore, the Court's decisions in cases such as *Brown* and *Loving* are by no means unambiguous examples of countermajoritarian judicial policy making. The effect of the decisions was to overturn statutes in several states; thus, they represented sweeping examples of the exercise of judicial review. Moreover, it is undeniable that the decisions made a major contribution to the process of social change. Whether the decisions themselves should be described as classic or unqualified examples of countermajoritarian judicial policy making, however, is not nearly so clear.

The Supreme Court and Abortion

In 1973 the Supreme Court decided, in *Roe* v. *Wade*, that state laws prohibiting abortion were unconstitutional. Like the Court's decisions on school segregation and interracial marriage, the exact significance we attach to *Roe* will depend in part on what we know about contemporaneous trends in American public opinion. In this respect, the *Roe* decision presents an interesting variation on the pattern we have just observed.

Figure 15.3 depicts the trend of public opinion on the issue of abortion between 1965 and 1990. The figure tracks changes in public support for a woman's right to obtain an abortion for three so-called discretionary reasons. Respondents were asked whether they thought it should be possible for a pregnant woman to obtain a legal abortion (1) if she is married and does not want any more children, (2) if she is not married and does not want to marry the man, and (3) if the family has a very low income and cannot afford any more children.[24]

Figure 15.3 shows that public opinion on abortion was changing rapidly in the seven-year period prior to the Court's decision in *Roe* v. *Wade*. In 1965 only 15 to 21 percent of the population supported legal abortion for one or another of the three reasons identified in national surveys. By 1973, however, between 46 and 52 percent of the population expressed support for legal abortion.

Given these trends in public opinion, the political significance of *Roe* v. *Wade* is obviously not easy to describe. The Court's decision effectively overturned restrictive abortion statutes in forty-six states. From this perspective, the decision is definitely an example of countermajoritarian judicial policy making. In the years just prior to the Court's decision, however, public support for legal abortion had been rising rapidly. Moreover, by the time the Court actually decided *Roe*, support for abortion stood very near the 50 percent mark. From the perspective of nationwide public opinion, therefore, *Roe* v. *Wade* was not a countermajoritarian judicial decision. Rather, the decision coincided with the policy preferences of approximately half the American people and was consistent with the direction in which public opinion, just prior to the Court's decision, had been moving.

Race and Abortion:
A Comparative Assessment

As an example of judicial policy making, the Court's decision in *Roe* v. *Wade* bears some resemblance to its decisions in *Brown* and *Loving*. In all three cases, the Court was apparently in step with nationwide trends in public opinion. Moreover, in all three cases, the policy position enunciated by the Court enjoyed the support, at the time of the Court's decision, of approximately half the population.

It is here, however, that any resemblance between *Roe* v. *Wade* and the

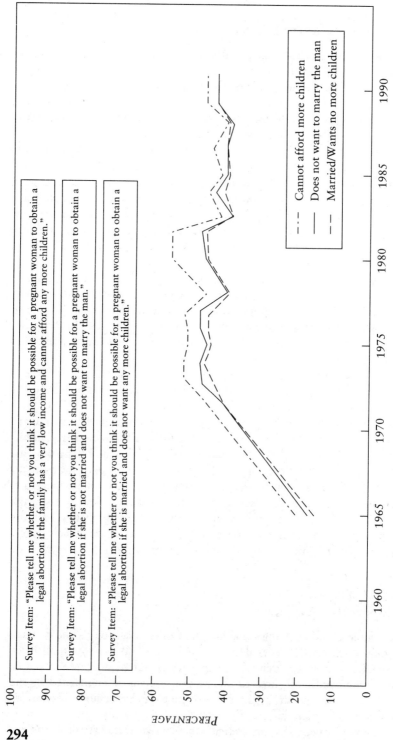

Survey Item: "Please tell me whether or not you think it should be possible for a pregnant woman to obtain a legal abortion if the family has a very low income and cannot afford any more children."

Survey Item: "Please tell me whether or not you think it should be possible for a pregnant woman to obtain a legal abortion if she is not married and does not want to marry the man."

Survey Item: "Please tell me whether or not you think it should be possible for a pregnant woman to obtain a legal abortion if she is married and does not want any more children."

Cannot afford more children
Does not want to marry the man
Married/Wants no more children

FIGURE 15.3 Public Support for Legal Abortion

SOURCES: Richard G. Niemi et al., Trends in Public Opinion: A Compendium of Survey Data (Westport, Conn.: Greenwood Press, 1989); National Opinion Research Center, General Social Surveys, 1972–1991; Cumulative Codebook (Chicago, NORC, 1991).

294

Court's decisions in *Brown* and *Loving* comes to an end. In *Brown* and *Loving*, public support for the Court's position continued to increase in the wake of the Court's decision. By contrast, in *Roe* v. *Wade*, public support for the policy position enunciated by the Court abruptly stopped its upward movement at the time of the Court's decision. In 1990 public support for abortion for one or another of the three discretionary reasons identified in national surveys stood just about where it did in 1973, when the Court decided *Roe*.

The verdict on *Roe* v. *Wade*, therefore, is equivocal. From the perspective of nationwide public opinion, the decision was not an example of counter-majoritarian judicial policy making. Neither, however, was it a decision that clearly conformed to the preferences of a majority of the American people. What is clear, of course, is that the Court in deciding *Roe* was in step with the trend of American public opinion. Just as clearly, however, support for the Court's position leveled off in the wake of the Court's decision. Unlike *Brown* and *Loving*, therefore, the public did not indicate its approval of *Roe* by endorsing the Court's decision in ever-growing numbers. *Roe* is a good example of judicial activism, because it overturned legislation in all but a handful of states and it placed the issue of abortion squarely on the national political agenda. In other respects, however, the decision is singularly difficult to characterize.[25]

Prayer and Contraception: Two Clearer Cases

In each of the areas we have examined — free speech for unpopular groups, race relations, and abortion — it has been difficult to say with certainty whether or not the Supreme Court was engaged in countermajoritarian judicial policy making. Perhaps it is time to allude to some less ambiguous examples! Such examples do exist. The Supreme Court's decisions on prayer in schools and contraception, for instance, are relatively easy to classify.

Figure 15.4 depicts the trend of public opinion on school prayer and contraception. The first public opinion polls on prayer in school were conducted in the wake of the Court's decisions in *Engel* v. *Vitale* (1962) and *School District of Abington Township* v. *Schempp* (1963). They indicated that an overwhelming majority of Americans (approximately 80 percent) believed that "it is all right for the public schools to start each day with a prayer." Public support for school prayer has been declining steadily since that time. As of 1984, however, two-thirds of Americans continued to voice support for the propriety of school prayer.

On the question of contraception — or the question, more accurately, of whether information about contraception should be available — the will of the majority has been clear for many years. As early as 1936, 70 percent of Americans agreed with the proposition that "the distribution of information on birth control [should] be made legal."[26] By the end of the 1950s, 73

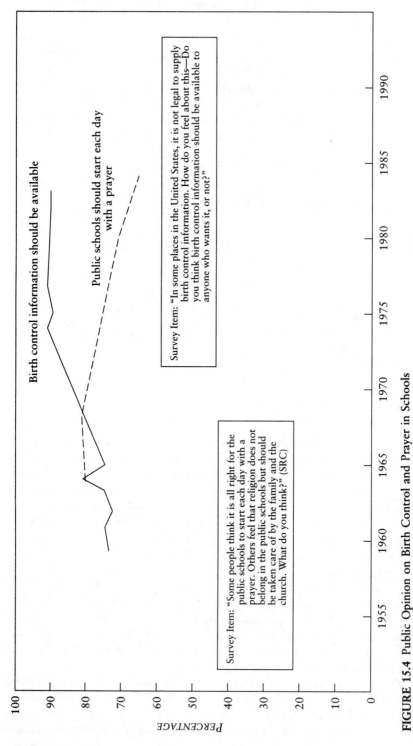

Birth control information should be available

Public schools should start each day
with a prayer

Survey Item: "In some places in the United States, it is not legal to supply birth control information. How do you feel about this—Do you think birth control information should be available to anyone who wants it, or not?"

Survey Item: "Some people think it is all right for the public schools to start each day with a prayer. Others feel that religion does not belong in the public schools but should be taken care of by the family and the church. What do you think?" (SRC)

PERCENTAGE

1955 1960 1965 1970 1975 1980 1985 1990

FIGURE 15.4 Public Opinion on Birth Control and Prayer in Schools

SOURCES: *Richard G. Niemi et al.,* Trends in Public Opinion: A Compendium of Survey Data *(Westport, Conn.: Greenwood Press, 1989); Survey Research Center, American National Election Study (Ann Arbor, Mich.: Inter-University Consortium for Political Research).*

percent of Americans said they thought that birth control information should be available "to anyone who wants it." By the early 1980s, more than 90 percent of Americans took this position.

These polling results indicate that the Supreme Court's school prayer decisions contradicted — and still contradict — the preferences of a nationwide majority of Americans. In this sense, the school prayer decisions are good examples of countermajoritarian judicial policy making. It is possible, of course, that the school prayer decisions are supported by a majority of politically active and/or well-educated citizens. With respect to the general public, however, the Court in deciding that school prayer violates the Establishment Clause was definitely engaged in countermajoritarian judicial policy making.[27]

The Court's decision in *Griswold* v. *Connecticut* (1965), on the other hand, was consistent with the views of a clear majority of the American people. Among the citizens of Connecticut, in 1965, laws against using or disseminating information about contraceptives may have enjoyed majority support. Among Americans as a whole, however, this position had long since ceased to be the majority view, and perhaps it never was. From the point of view of constitutional theory, *Griswold* was and is one of the most controversial decisions ever handed down by the Supreme Court. Ironically, it is also a decision that does not even remotely qualify as a good example of countermajoritarian judicial policy making.

The Supreme Court and Criminal Justice

A final area of Supreme Court decision making that yields interesting insights into the role of the Court in the political process consists of the Court's decisions on issues of criminal justice. This is an area in which trends in public opinion have been pronounced but have not always been in a single direction. It is also an area (as we discussed in Chapters 4 and 9) in which observers of the transition from the Warren Court to the Burger Court detected particularly strong evidence that the liberal judicial activism of the 1960s was rapidly giving way in the 1970s to a more conservative approach to constitutional issues.

Figure 15.5 depicts the trend of public opinion on the issue of capital punishment for murder and on the more general question of whether the courts are dealing "too harshly or not harshly enough with criminals." Surveys show that support for the death penalty among Americans was declining in the 1950s and continued to decline up to the mid-1960s. At this point, however, public opinion changed direction, and by 1990 about 75 percent of the population voiced support for capital punishment for convicted murderers. On the more general question of whether the courts are dealing harshly enough with criminals, there was a rise of 20 to 25 percentage points between the mid-1960s and 1990 in the proportion of Americans who expressed the belief that the courts were "not dealing harshly enough with criminals."

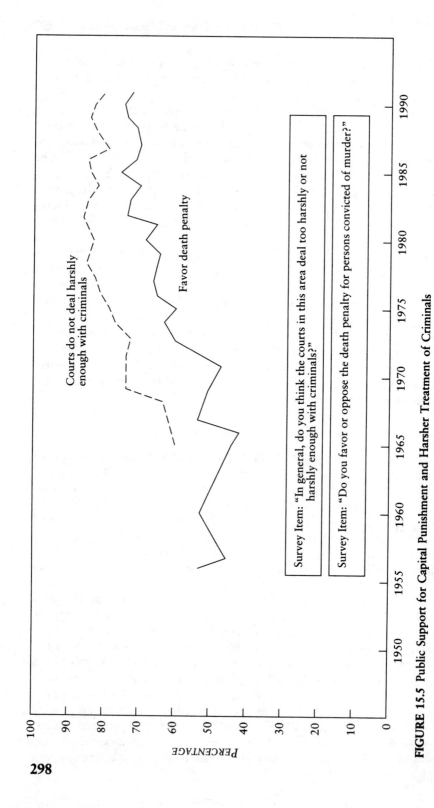

FIGURE 15.5 Public Support for Capital Punishment and Harsher Treatment of Criminals

SOURCES: *Richard G. Niemi et al., Trends in Public Opinion: A Compendium of Survey Data (Westport, Conn.: Greenwood Press, 1989); National Opinion Research Center, General Social Surveys, 1972–1991; Cumulative Codebook (Chicago, NORC, 1991).*

The Supreme Court's two main decisions on the death penalty were handed down in the context of these opinion changes. In 1972, in *Furman* v. *Georgia*, the Court held that the death penalty, as it was then being administered by the states, was unconstitutional. In 1976, however, in *Gregg* v. *Georgia*, the Court upheld newly enacted state death penalty statutes and ruled conclusively that the death penalty was not per se, that is, necessarily, an inappropriate punishment for murder.

If we look at the broad range of issues of criminal justice, it is clear that by the 1980s the Court was doing a rather good job of reflecting public sentiments. In the 1960s many of the Court's most celebrated decisions involved new or expanded protections for criminal defendants. In *Mapp* v. *Ohio* (1961), the Court applied the exclusionary rule to the states. In *Gideon* v. *Wainwright* (1963), the Court held that indigent criminal defendants are entitled to free legal counsel. In *Miranda* v. *Arizona* (1966), the Court held that criminal suspects cannot be questioned unless they have been informed of their rights. The evidence of public attitudes toward issues of criminal justice is not sufficiently systematic to support any firm conclusions about whether the Court's decisions did or did not enjoy majority support. Regardless of public opinion, however, the Court itself was strongly inclined to support the constitutional claims of criminal defendants.

In the 1970s the Court's solicitude for criminal defendants began to weaken, and by the 1980s it collapsed almost completely. The turning point came in 1981. The addition of Justice O'Connor bolstered the conservative majority on the Court, especially on issues of criminal justice, and since that time, with rare exceptions, the Court has ruled in favor of government in constitutional disputes between government and those accused of criminal offenses.

Supreme Court decision making in the area of criminal justice provides strong evidence that Supreme Court decision making is not inherently countermajoritarian and that the Court may at times be quite responsive to majoritarian trends in public opinion. On issues of criminal justice, the views of recent appointees have coincided with the expressed public preference for renewed use of the death penalty and for courts that deal "more harshly" with criminal defendants. The decisions of the Supreme Court as an institution now comport rather closely with what appears to be the will of the majority on issues arising in this key area of constitutional law.

Conclusion: Countermajoritarian Judicial Policy Making in Historical Perspective

In this chapter, we have waded rather deeply into an enormously complicated problem. The allegation that a particular Supreme Court decision is an example of countermajoritarian judicial policy making is not as straightforward as it seems, and we have explored various reasons why this is the case. It may be useful at this point, however, to step back from the details of our analysis and to suggest some broad historical conclusions about the Supreme Court's role in the political process.

The Pre–New Deal Supreme Court

Prior to the constitutional crisis of the 1930s, the Supreme Court was frequently accused of engaging in countermajoritarian judicial policy making. The basis of the allegation was the Supreme Court's frequent use of the Due Process Clause of the Fourteenth Amendment to overturn social welfare and regulatory legislation. Many believed that the legislation overturned by the Court enjoyed the support of not only the legislators who enacted it, but their constituents as well. Thus, it was stated, the conservative economic decisions of the Supreme Court represented an obvious and objectionable intrusion into the majoritarian political process.

Prior to the 1930s public opinion polls did not exist. As a result, there was no "scientific" way to determine the content of the will of the majority. Given the absence of public opinion polls, we will never know for sure which of the Supreme Court's conservative economic decisions, if any, were in fact examples of countermajoritarian judicial policy making.

We do know two things for sure, however, about the pre–New Deal period. First, virtually all of the Court's conservative economic decisions were eventually reversed by Congress or overruled by the reconstituted "Roosevelt Court." Thus, the countermajoritarian pretensions of the pre–New Deal Supreme Court were eventually defeated by the larger and unstoppable currents of the political process. Second, the pre–New Deal Supreme Court rarely decided cases involving civil liberties and tended to decide those civil liberties cases that did appear on its docket in favor of government rather than the individual. In the civil liberties area, therefore, the Supreme Court was not known for its judicial activism, and it rarely behaved in a way that would prompt (or merit) the allegation that it was engaged in countermajoritarian judicial policy making.[28]

The Post–New Deal Supreme Court

In the wake of the constitutional crisis of the 1930s, the reconstituted "Roosevelt Court" devoted much of its attention to cases involving civil liberties. The Court quickly acquired a reputation for judicial activism and as early as the 1940s and 1950s began to compile an impressive record of decisions overturning legislation that allegedly abridged the civil rights and civil liberties of racial minorities, criminal defendants, political dissidents, and other unpopular or underprivileged groups. The Supreme Court's reputation for judicial activism blossomed in the 1960s when the Court, under the leadership of Chief Justice Earl Warren, began handing down substantial numbers of highly controversial civil liberties decisions.

An examination of trends in public opinion in this period, however, suggests that the Supreme Court's reputation for countermajoritarian judicial activism was not entirely deserved. Granted, the Warren Court exercised its power of judicial review more frequently than any previous Court and did so almost exclusively in cases involving civil liberties. Beginning in the 1940s, however, American public opinion began moving in the direction of greater tolerance for dissent, greater support for racial equality, and greater appreciation of women's rights. Because the Court was in step with these broad currents of social change, it was not always necessary for the Court to contradict the will of the majority in order to protect the rights of minorities. The Court in the 1950s and 1960s made important contributions to the process of social change. In addition, it employed its power of judicial review with great frequency. In many of these instances, however, the Court was merely validating an existing or emerging public consensus in favor of greater protection of minority rights.[29]

The Burger Court and Civil Liberties

When Warren Burger became chief justice in 1969, it was widely assumed that the countermajoritarian judicial activism of the Supreme Court would diminish and be replaced by much greater deference on the part of the Court to the preferences of a majority of the American people. In the area of criminal justice, this prediction has largely proved to be correct. Public opinion on issues such as the death penalty and the rights of defendants began to move sharply in a conservative direction in the mid-1960s. Beginning in 1969, Republican presidents took advantage of a succession of opportunities to appoint relatively conservative justices to the Court. By 1981 the Court included a solid majority of justices whose views on issues of criminal justice differed sharply from those of an earlier generation of justices. As a result, the Court began deciding a higher and higher proportion of its criminal procedure cases in favor of government.

On some other issues, however, the Burger Court, like the Warren Court, was able to "have it both ways." That is, it could engage in judicial activism without necessarily contradicting the preferences of a current majority of the American people. Public opinion on certain issues — notably abortion — continued to move in a "liberal" direction in the early 1970s. Thus, when the Court decided *Roe* v. *Wade* in 1973, its decision enjoyed the support of approximately half of the American population. *Roe* v. *Wade* is justly regarded as a striking example of judicial activism. As an example of countermajoritarian judicial policy making, however, *Roe* v. *Wade* is not necessarily an ideal choice.

The Rehnquist Court and the Future of Countermajoritarian Judicial Review

In the 1980s the Supreme Court continued to evolve in a politically conservative direction. William Rehnquist became chief justice in 1986, and Justices Scalia, Kennedy, Souter, and Thomas have subsequently joined the Court. The contemporary Supreme Court, therefore, consists of a solid majority of conservative justices. What does this portend for the future of Supreme Court decision making?

The most uncontroversial prediction, of course, is that the Court's tendency to support the government in criminal procedure cases will continue. The Court may also exercise restraint in other types of cases involving alleged governmental interference with individual rights. Depending on the distribution of public opinion, however, such a posture of restraint may itself represent an example of countermajoritarian judicial policy making. On the assumption that the Court's decision in *Roe* v. *Wade* now enjoys the support of a majority of Americans, for instance, a decision by the Rehnquist Court to uphold legislation restoring criminal penalties on abortion would represent a mixed example of Supreme Court decision making. The decision would reflect the views of legislators who voted for the law but would contradict the preferences of a national majority of Americans.

Conclusion

Judicial review is frequently described as an undemocratic feature of the political process. This allegation is often based on the assumption that Supreme Court decisions overturning legislation are examples of countermajoritarian judicial policy making. Determining whether this is in fact the case, however, is a difficult task.

Supreme Court decisions that overturn legislation contradict the policy preferences of the legislators who voted for the legislation in the first place. It is theoretically possible, however, for a Supreme Court decision overturning legislation to enjoy the support of a past or present popular majority or a current majority of legislative representatives. In addition, a Supreme Court decision that contradicts the preferences of citizens of a particular state or region may enjoy the support of a nationwide majority of Americans. Finally, a Supreme Court decision that is opposed by one subgroup within the population may simultaneously enjoy the support of another subgroup. In all these instances, the assertion that the Court's decision is an example of countermajoritarian judicial policy may be misleading or inaccurate. The assertion cannot be defended unless one is willing to specify the particular group whose policy preferences are being used as a basis for evaluating the Court's decision.

In the half century or so since the invention of the public opinion poll, it has become possible to examine the proposition that particular Supreme Court decisions or areas of Supreme Court decision making are examples of countermajoritarian judicial policy making. In a surprising number of instances, Supreme Court decisions that are alleged to contradict the preferences of a majority of the American people do not in fact enjoy this distinction. In particular, the judicial activism of the Warren Court must be reassessed in light of evidence of substantial and long-term trends in American public opinion. Americans in recent decades have shown an increasing willingness to voice support for the rights of minority groups. That being the case, Supreme Court decisions overturning legislation that was alleged to restrict those rights cannot be classified as a pure example of countermajoritarian judicial policy making.

Notes

1. Alexander Bickel, *The Least Dangerous Branch: The Supreme Court at the Bar of Politics* (1962), pp. 16–17.

2. Oliver Wendell Holmes served as associate justice of the Supreme Court from 1902 to 1932. His observations on law and society are quoted more frequently than those of almost any other member of the Court. "I do not think the United States would come to an end," he said in a speech delivered to a law school audience in 1913, "if we lost our power to declare an Act of Congress void. I do think the Union would be imperiled if we could not make that declaration as to the laws of the several States." See Oliver W. Holmes, *Collected Legal Papers* (1920), pp. 295–96.

3. 341 U.S. 494, 525 (1951) (Frankfurter, J., concurring in the affirmance of the judgment).

4. Thomas R. Marshall, *Public Opinion and the Supreme Court* (1989).

5. Alan D. Monroe, "Consistency between Public Preferences and National Policy Decisions," 7 *Am. Pol. Q.* 3 (1979).

6. Consistency between opinion and policy on issues involving civil rights and civil liberties was 67 percent, compared to 64 percent for policy issues as a whole.

7. Benjamin I. Page and Robert Y. Shapiro, "Effects of Public Opinion on Policy," 77 *Am. Pol. Sci. Rev.* 175 (1983).

8. Samuel A. Stouffer, *Communism, Conformity, and Civil Liberties* (1955).

9. Id. at pp. 39–42.

10. Benjamin I. Page and Robert Y. Shapiro, *The Rational Public: Fifty Years of Trends in Americans' Policy Preferences* (1992).

11. Id. at pp. 81–90.

12. Id. at p. 51.

13. It is also worth reiterating, as we pointed out in Chapter 7, that Congress accepted the Supreme Court's narrowed interpretation of the Smith Act, at least implicitly, by failing to reenact the statute.

14. Stouffer, *Communism, Conformity, and Civil Liberties*, p. 41.

15. Clyde Z. Nunn, Harry J. Crockett, Jr., and J. Allen Williams, Jr., *Tolerance for Nonconformity* (1978).

16. Id. at pp. 41–42.

17. There is a large body of research on "mass-elite" differences in support for civil liberties. See, for example, Michal Shamir, "Political Intolerance among Masses and Elites in Israel: A Reevaluation of the Elitist Theory of Democracy," 53 *J. of Pol.* 1018 (1991); Paul M. Sniderman et al., "The Fallacy of Democratic Elitism: Elite Competition and Commitment to Civil Liberties, 21 *Brit. J. Pol. Sci.* 349 (1991); David G. Barnum and John L. Sullivan, "The Elusive Foundations of Political Freedom in Britain and the United States," 52 *J. of Pol.* 719 (1990); James L. Gibson, "Political Intolerance and Political Repression during the McCarthy Red Scare," 82 *Am. Pol. Sci. Rev.* 511 (1988); James L. Gibson and Richard D. Bingham, *Civil Liberties and Nazis: The Skokie Free Speech Controversy* (1985); and Herbert McClosky and Alida Brill, *Dimensions of Tolerance: What Americans Believe about Civil Liberties* (1983).

18. John L. Sullivan, James Piereson, and George E. Marcus, *Political Tolerance and American Democracy* (1982).

19. *Congressional Quarterly Weekly Report*, June 16, 1990, p. 1880. See also Page and Shapiro, *The Rational Public*, p. 112.

20. Page and Shapiro, *The Rational Public*, p. 69.

21. For further discussion, see id. at p. 71.

22. See id. at 72–73. See also Donald Philip Green and Jonathan A. Cowden, "Who Protests: Self-Interest and White Opposition to Busing," 54 *J. of Pol.* 471 (1992).

23. In addition to the data reported in Figure 15.2, see, for example, *Time Magazine*, May 27, 1991, reporting that 72 percent of whites (compared to 36 percent of blacks) believe that existing government efforts to help blacks get better job opportunities are either "adequate" or "go too far," and that 77 percent of whites (compared to 49 percent of blacks) believe that affirmative actions programs for blacks discriminate against whites either "sometimes" or "a lot." See also Page and Shapiro, *The Rational Public*, pp. 72–4.

24. National surveys also examined public support for abortion for three so-called nondiscretionary reasons: (1) if there is a strong chance of a serious defect in the baby, (2) if the woman's health is seriously endangered by the pregnancy, and (3) if the woman became pregnant as a result of rape. Public approval of abortion for these reasons has always been much higher than public approval of abortion for any of the three discretionary reasons. For additional discussion of opinion trends on abortion, see Chapter 10 supra.

25. An additional issue on which the Supreme Court was clearly in step with the trend of American public opinion is the general issue of equal rights for women. Polls dating back to the 1930s show that at the time only about one-fifth of the population approved of "a married woman earning money in business or industry if she has a husband capable of supporting her." By the early 1970s public approval of a woman working outside the home had risen to between 60 and 70 percent, and by 1990 it had surpassed 80 percent. See Page and Shapiro, *The Rational Public*, pp. 100–4. In 1971, when public support for equal rights for women had risen above the 50-percent mark (as measured by this particular polling question), the Supreme Court in *Reed* v. *Reed* held, for the first time, that a statute allegedly discriminating against women violated the Equal Protection Clause of the Fourteenth Amendment. The Court's decision in *Reed* was apparently consistent with both the trend and the distribution of American public opinion. The Court's decision in *Reed*, like the Court's decisions on speech, race, and abortion, is not, therefore, a particularly good example of countermajoritarian judicial policy making.

26. These results, not shown in Figure 15.4, are reported in Page and Shapiro, *The Rational Public*, pp. 104–5.

27. For discussions of mass-elite differences in support for school prayer, see John C. Green and James L. Guth, "The Missing Link: Political Activists and Support for School Prayer," 53 *Pub. Op. Q.* 41 (1989); and McClosky and Brill, *Dimensions of Tolerance*, Ch. 3.

28. The classic exposition of this conclusion is Robert A. Dahl, "Decision-Making in a Democracy: The Supreme Court as a National Policy-Maker," 6 *J. of Pub. Law* 279 (1957).

29. For additional discussion, see David G. Barnum, "The Supreme Court and Public Opinion: Judicial Decision Making in the Post–New Deal Period," 47 *J. of Pol.* 652 (1985).

CHAPTER 16

Conclusion:
The Supreme Court and
American Democracy

W e suggested in the Preface that the Supreme Court occupies a curious place in the American constitutional order. On the one hand, the Court is responsible for deciding a wide variety of sensitive issues of public policy. On the other hand, Supreme Court justices are insulated from the key mechanism — the contested election — by which governmental officials are ordinarily held accountable to the American people. The unusual status of the Supreme Court has led to allegations that the Court is an undemocratic policy-making institution and that judicial review is an undemocratic feature of the political process. Clearly, the Supreme Court's special status requires both explanation and justification.

Broadly speaking, four arguments can be offered to attempt to reconcile the Supreme Court's power of judicial review with fundamental principles of democratic self-government. First, one can argue that the Supreme Court is subject to a variety of external restraints and that these restraints constitute an effective mechanism of majoritarian control of Supreme Court decision making. Second, one can argue that the appointment process represents an effective mechanism of internal control of Supreme Court decision making. Third, one can argue that the United States is a constitutional democracy, and the Supreme Court has an affirmative obligation to enforce the countermajoritarian provisions of the Constitution. Finally, one can argue that the Supreme Court's reputation for countermajoritarian judicial activism is exaggerated and that, in practice, the Court rarely contradicts the preferences of a majority of the American people.

In the previous four chapters, we examined each of these arguments in detail. It is now time to consider them as a group and to come to some conclusions about the role of the Supreme Court in American democracy.

External Restraints on the Supreme Court

In Chapter 12 we looked at external restraints on the Supreme Court. We discussed various informal mechanisms for applying pressure on the Court, including public criticism of the Court and grassroots resistance to the Court's decisions. We also discussed various formal mechanisms for restraining the Court. Among the most prominent are the president's power to decline to enforce Supreme Court rulings and Congress's power to impeach Supreme Court justices, to make exceptions to the Supreme Court's appellate jurisdiction, and to propose constitutional amendments.

Perhaps the most striking aspect of the various mechanisms for applying external pressure on the Court is how frequently they have been tried but how rarely they have succeeded. No justice has ever been removed from office, and only one justice — Samuel Chase in 1804 — was impeached by the House. Nor have congressional efforts to limit the Court's appellate jurisdiction been any more successful. In 1869 Congress did prevent the Court from deciding the appeal in *Ex parte McCardle*, but all other congressional attempts to limit the Court's jurisdiction have failed.[1] Finally, none of the Congress's recent attempts to reverse the Court's decisions by constitutional amendment has succeeded. Some amendments have gained majority support: for example, simple majorities voted for prayer amendments in both houses in 1966 and 1971 and in the Senate in 1984, and simple majorities voted for a flag burning amendment in both houses in 1990. In no case, however, has a proposed amendment been approved by the necessary two-thirds majority of either, let alone both, houses of Congress.[2]

There are several possible explanations for Congress's lack of success in challenging the Court. First, Congress faces a genuine dilemma in trying to decide which mechanism to use to challenge the Court. In a mathematical sense, the easiest method of curbing the Court is for Congress to invoke its power to make exceptions to the Court's appellate jurisdiction. Members of Congress, however, have always been a little uneasy about using this power to prevent the Court from deciding particular cases or particular categories of cases. A less questionable method of challenging the Court, of course, is to pass a constitutional amendment. The problem with this strategy is that it requires the assent of two-thirds of both houses of Congress, and achieving this level of agreement in Congress on a controversial issue of public policy is extremely difficult. From the perspective of Congress, therefore, neither of the two principal methods of applying external pressure on the Supreme Court is ideal.

The distribution of political and ideological forces in American politics may also help to explain why Congress has not been notably successful in challenging the Supreme Court. In recent decades, the lion's share of constitutional controversy has swirled around a handful of key issues, especially abortion, prayer in schools, school desegregation, and the constitutional rights of criminal defendants. From the 1950s to the 1970s the Court's position on these issues was liberal or progressive, and thus attacks on the

Court came primarily from the right, that is, from conservative groups and their representatives in Congress. Some scholars have argued that the Court and its decisions were effectively protected by the alliance the Court had forged with the executive branch of government.[3] Others have argued that the Court's success should be ascribed to the presence in Congress of sufficient numbers of elected representatives who were sympathetic to the Court's liberal rulings to prevent them from being reversed.[4] Either way, the Court was able to weather a succession of conservative attacks on both its decisions and its decision-making prerogatives.

A related explanation of congressional reluctance to challenge the Court is based on the discrepancy between the values of ordinary citizens and those held by particular subgroups in the population. Many of the Court's most controversial decisions have expanded the constitutional rights of racial and ethnic minorities and of unpopular groups such as criminal defendants and political dissidents. The general public has expressed disapproval of some (though not all) of these decisions. As we saw in Chapter 15, however, better educated and/or politically active citizens may be more inclined than citizens in general to take a liberal or tolerant position on the issues raised by these cases. Members of Congress, of course, are relatively well educated, and there is no doubt whatever that they are politically active! Because of its composition, Congress as an institution may have been more sympathetic to the Court's decisions on key issues of constitutional law than were the citizens whom Congress represents.[5]

The lack of congressional success in challenging the Supreme Court is therefore open to different interpretations. The historical record itself, however, is clear. Apart from isolated instances, Congress has not successfully invoked any of the various weapons at its disposal for imposing external restraints on the Court.

The Supreme Court and the Tides of History

In view of the unimpressive record of congressional success in challenging the Supreme Court, it is somewhat curious that so many observers have concluded that majoritarian forces almost always prevail when the Court and its political environment clash. In 1957, for instance, political scientist Robert Dahl argued that "the policy views dominant on the Court are never for long out of line with the policy views dominant among the lawmaking majorities in the United States."[6] A few years later, constitutional historian Robert McCloskey wrote that "[i]n truth the Supreme Court has seldom, if ever, flatly and for very long resisted a really unmistakable wave of public sentiment."[7]

Perhaps the most emphatic assertion that the Court is responsive to majoritarian political pressures was offered by Associate Justice Robert Jackson. Speaking to the American Bar Association in 1953, Jackson said:

> [L]et us not deceive ourselves; long-sustained public opinion does influence the process of constitutional interpretation. Each new member of the ever-changing

of our courts brings to his task the assumptions and accustomed
. of a later period. The practical play of the forces of politics is such that
,udicial power has often delayed but never permanently defeated the persistent
will of a substantial majority.[8]

Jackson's remarks emphasize that the Supreme Court is but one component of a complex political system. They also remind us that one explanation
for the Court's acceptance of majoritarian norms has nothing to do with
external pressures that Congress or other political actors can apply to the
Court. "Each new member of the ever-changing personnel of our courts,"
Jackson said, "brings to his task the assumptions and accustomed thought of
a later period." Jackson's observation suggests that it is the appointment
process, rather than the arsenal of external restraints on the Supreme Court,
that is primarily responsible for keeping the Court in touch with the political
system of which it is a part.

The Appointment Process and
Supreme Court Decision Making

On average, presidents appoint someone to the Supreme Court every twenty-
two to twenty-three months. Many observers have concluded that the appointment process is the principal mechanism by which the Supreme Court is
kept abreast of majoritarian preferences in American society. Robert Dahl
concluded, for instance, that

> National politics in the United States . . . is dominated by relatively cohesive
> alliances that endure for long periods of time. . . . Except for short-lived transi-
> tional periods when the old alliance is disintegrating and [a] new one is struggling
> to take control of political institutions, the Supreme Court is inevitably a part of
> the dominant national alliance. As an element in the political leadership of the
> dominant alliance, the Court of course supports the major policies of the
> alliance.[9]

There is no real mystery about how the appointment process serves to
keep the Supreme Court in line with the will of the majority. The country
goes to the polls every four years to elect a president, and the president is
empowered to nominate prospective Supreme Court justices. A principal
factor in the president's decision, especially in recent years, has been the
nominee's values and perhaps the nominee's views on specific issues. Once
on the Supreme Court, the nominee's votes in particular cases will reflect,
to a considerable extent, the values that brought the nominee to the
president's attention in the first place. The process by which the will of
the majority is translated into Supreme Court decisions in particular cases is
tortuous and indirect. It nevertheless constitutes a discernible mechanism by
which the majority can influence the course of Supreme Court decision
making.

The Supreme Court
as a Representative Institution

The influence of the appointment process on Supreme Court decision making has prompted some observers to argue that the Supreme Court is, in effect, a representative institution. In their 1976 book on the Court, for instance, David Rohde and Harold Spaeth concluded that "the justices collectively mirror the value systems of most Americans. . . . In this sense, the Court is a representative body, even though the justices serve for life and are accountable to no one, save their own consciences."[10]

There is much truth in the observation that the appointment process renders the Supreme Court, in effect, a representative institution. Moreover, the appointment process is almost certainly more effective than the various external restraints we examined (in Chapter 12 and elsewhere) in keeping the Court in line with majoritarian preferences. At the same time, as we noted in Chapter 13, the appointment process is not an ideal mechanism for translating the will of the majority into Supreme Court decisions. First, at least some justices will surprise the president who appointed them and diverge from the president's expectations in deciding cases. Second, even though the president is elected by the American people, there is no guarantee that he will faithfully reflect the preferences of a majority of the American people on every issue that comes before the Supreme Court. Finally, the appointment process is not an expeditious method of altering the direction of Supreme Court decision making. It cannot succeed in substantially revamping the priorities of the Court unless there is a sustained period of political dominance by one party or the other.

The efficacy of the appointment process as a mechanism for translating the will of the majority into Supreme Court decisions is therefore unclear. The close connection between justices' values and their decisions means that the appointment process can produce changes in the Court's political orientation. At the same time, the appointment process is an imprecise and time-consuming mechanism for translating the majority will into Supreme Court decisions.

It may be, however, that the search for ways of subjecting the Supreme Court to majoritarian control is fundamentally misguided. Perhaps the Supreme Court's essential role in American democracy is not to reflect the will of the majority but to reach countermajoritarian policy decisions. If that is the case, the key issue is not how the Court can be pressured or reconstituted to better reflect the will of the majority, but how to construct a sound affirmative justification of countermajoritarian judicial policy making.

Normative Justifications of Judicial Review

Chapter 14 was devoted to exploring a range of normative justifications of judicial review. We looked first at what we called the traditional justification. This justification dates from John Marshall's decision in *Marbury* v. *Madison* and is heavily dependent on the fact that the U.S. Constitution is a written document. The traditional justification provides an affirmative defense of countermajoritarian judicial review, but for many analysts, as we noted, it also contains built-in limitations on the range of issues the Supreme Court is authorized to decide and the types of reasons the Court is authorized to use to justify its decisions.

Next we looked at affirmative justifications of judicial review, which focus on the role of the Supreme Court in protecting the procedural norms of democracy and the fundamental rights of selected minorities. In most cases, these theories serve to justify categories of Supreme Court decisions that cannot be subsumed very comfortably under the traditional justification of judicial review.

Finally, we examined constitutional theories that attempt to provide a coherent defense of Supreme Court decisions lying at the outer boundaries of the Court's traditional role. The modern Supreme Court — particularly under the leadership of Chief Justice Earl Warren — was frequently accused of engaging in improper judicial activism. The constitutional theories we examined toward the end of Chapter 14 are designed to justify a broad range of Supreme Court decisions, including some that have at best a tenuous basis in the specific language of the Constitution.

As a group, of course, normative justifications of judicial review serve a qualitatively different purpose than theories that emphasize the degree to which the Supreme Court is constrained, either externally or internally, by the will of the majority. The premise of theories that focus on external or internal restraints on Supreme Court decision making is that the United States is essentially a self-governing majoritarian democracy and that no institution should be allowed to stray very far from obedience to the preferences of a majority of the American people. The premise of normative justifications of judicial review is that the United States is a constitutional democracy and that countermajoritarian judicial policy making is among the Supreme Court's legitimate, indeed essential, responsibilities.

Theories that emphasize majoritarian constraints on Supreme Court decision making do have one thing in common, however, with theories that purport to provide a normative justification of countermajoritarian judicial review. Both assume that Supreme Court decisions overturning legislation are in fact examples of countermajoritarian judicial policy making. That assumption, however, is not necessarily accurate.

The Supreme Court and Public Opinion

In Chapter 15 we examined the distribution of public opinion on a variety of issues that have come before the modern Supreme Court. We discovered that the Court has not defied the will of the majority quite as often as either its supporters or its detractors sometimes allege. On issues such as school busing and the rights of defendants, for instance, the Court has tended to side with

the preferences of a majority of the American people. Moreover, th
Court's reputation as a countermajoritarian policy maker is not gre.
hanced even when we take account of the very decisions that are usually
as examples of the Court's activism. On key issues that reached the Cou.
between the mid-1950s and the mid-1970s — for example, school desegregation, access to birth control information, abortion, and the speech rights of
political dissidents — the clear trend of public opinion was in the direction of
greater support for the rights of minorities. Because the public itself was
increasingly inclined to support the expansion of minority rights, the Court's
decisions in these areas do not qualify as clearcut examples of countermajoritarian judicial policy making.

If we adopt a broader historical perspective, moreover, it is almost impossible to argue that the Supreme Court as an institution is necessarily committed to protecting the fundamental rights of unpopular or disadvantaged
groups. The countermajoritarian reputation of the pre–New Deal Supreme
Court was based on its willingness to protect business from governmental
regulation, not on its willingness to protect the civil rights and civil liberties of
powerless minorities. Only after the constitutional crisis of the 1930s did the
Court turn its attention on a consistent basis to issues arising under the Bill of
Rights and related provisions of the Constitution.

As for the future, of course, it is highly unlikely that the Supreme Court
will soon return to the patterns of judicial activism that characterized the
period between the mid-1950s and the mid-1970s. On the contrary, most
observers predict that it will be a long time before the Court shows any
renewed enthusiasm for expanding the constitutional rights of the sorts of
groups — racial minorities, political dissidents, and criminal defendants — that
turned to the Court in large numbers during the heyday of the Court's
reputation as a guardian of minority rights. In addition, of course, most
observers predict that at least some of the key precedents of recent decades
will be weakened or overruled.

When Supreme Court decision making is examined in the context of the
broad sweep of American history, therefore, the Court cannot easily be
portrayed as an institution intrinsically committed to protecting the constitutional rights of unpopular groups and powerless minorities. No doubt, the
Court has often come to the defense of such groups in the past and will
continue to do so in the future. What remains uncertain is whether the Court
is necessarily a more staunch or dependable friend of such groups than any of
the other institutions of American government.

Conclusion

The Supreme Court plays a vital role in American democracy. It is the highest
court in the American judicial system and one of three co-equal branches of
the national government. It has primary, though not exclusive, responsibility
for interpreting the U.S. Constitution and for defining the scope and content

As a principal guardian of the meaning of the Constitu-
⸱quently called on to assess the validity of statutes passed
⸱rities.

312 decisions on constitutional issues, and in other kinds of cases
⸱amples of public policy. Like the other institutions of American
⸱, the Supreme Court, when it decides cases, is engaged in formu-
⸱enforcing rules and procedures that citizens must obey and around
⸱ney must structure their lives.

The Supreme Court, however, is quite distinct from other policy-making
institutions of American government. Specifically, Supreme Court justices are
not elected, nor are they in any other way directly accountable to the American people. The Court's unusual position in the American system of democratic self-government accentuates the controversy that often surrounds its
policy decisions, particularly its countermajoritarian policy decisions.

There are abundant reasons for concluding, however, that the Supreme
Court is not hopelessly beyond majoritarian control and that judicial review is
not hopelessly inconsistent with the fundamental principles of American
democracy. The political system provides for a number of external restraints
on Supreme Court decision making. These restraints are not necessarily easy
to invoke, but they are a constant reminder to the Supreme Court of its
vulnerability and of its status as one component of a complicated system of
political checks and balances.

The American Constitution also empowers the political branches — in
particular, the president and the Senate — to select members of the Supreme
Court. The appointment process is a painstaking method of altering the
ideological orientation of the Court. On balance, however, it is probably the
most effective mechanism for translating majoritarian preferences into Supreme Court decisions.

The fact that the United States is governed by a written Constitution
offers a third alternative for reconciling the Supreme Court's power of judicial
review with fundamental principles of majoritarian democracy. From the
earliest days of the Republic, the Supreme Court's power to enforce the
countermajoritarian provisions of the Constitution has been widely acknowledged. Since the 1930s, the Court has played a prominent role in defining and
protecting the rights of particular groups, including racial and ethnic minorities, criminal defendants, political dissidents, and other relatively powerless
minority groups.

Finally, the Supreme Court probably does not make excessive use of its
acknowledged power to contradict the will of the majority. Viewed in the
context of trends in American public opinion, many Supreme Court decisions
overturning legislation are not particularly clearcut examples of countermajoritarian judicial policy making.

Despite its unusual characteristics, therefore, the Supreme Court is a vital
and integral part of the complex system of democratic self-government under
which we live. It fulfills an essential governmental function by assuming

primary responsibility for enforcing the countermajoritarian provisions of the Constitution. At the same time, the Court is constrained in a variety of ways by the political environment in which it operates.

Deciding whether the Supreme Court plays an appropriate role in American democracy is not an easy task. The issues we have raised and the material we have examined should provide a solid foundation for reaching conclusions. Whether the role the Court plays in American democracy is fully satisfactory, however, is a question I leave, in the end, to the discretion of the reader.

Notes

1. In recent years, only two attempts to limit the Court's jurisdiction have made any headway. Legislation to deprive the Court of appellate jurisdiction over legislative apportionment cases passed the House, but not the Senate, in 1964, and legislation to deprive the Court of appellate jurisdiction over school prayer cases passed the Senate, but not the House, in 1979. No other recent attempt to limit the Court's jurisdiction has come to a vote on the floor of either house of Congress.

2. In 1971 Congress did lower the voting age to eighteen by passing the Twenty-sixth Amendment. Technically, the purpose of the amendment was to reverse *Oregon v. Mitchell* (1970), in which the Supreme Court had held that Congress's attempt to lower the voting age in state elections through ordinary legislation was unconstitutional. The Twenty-sixth Amendment is usually regarded as one of four examples of congressional reversal of Supreme Court decisions through the amendment process. The issue addressed by this amendment, however, was not particularly controversial. In fact, the amendment was submitted to the states on March 23, 1971, three months after the Court's decision in *Mitchell*, and by June 30, 1971, the amendment had been ratified. On far more controversial issues such as busing, abortion, and prayer in schools, Congress in recent years has not succeeded in reversing the Court through the amendment process.

3. Mark Silverstein and Benjamin Ginsberg, "The Supreme Court and the New Politics of Judicial Power," 102 *Pol. Sci. Q.* 371 (1987).

4. David Adamany and Joel B. Grossman, "Support for the Supreme Court as a National Policymaker," 5 *Law and Policy Q.* 405 (1983).

5. For elaboration, see David G. Barnum and John L. Sullivan, "The Elusive Foundations of Political Freedom in Britain and the United States," 52 *J. of Pol.* 719 (1990). See also David G. Barnum, John L. Sullivan, and Maurice Sunkin, "Constitutional and Cultural Underpinnings of Political Freedom in Britain and the United States," 12 *Oxford J. of Legal Studies* 362 (1992).

6. Robert A. Dahl, "Decision-Making in a Democracy: The Supreme Court as a National Policy-Maker," 6 *J. of Pub. Law* 279, 285 (1957).

7. Robert G. McCloskey, *The American Supreme Court* (1960), p. 23.

8. Robert H. Jackson, "Maintaining Our Freedoms: The Role of the Judiciary," 19 *Vital Speeches* 759, 761 (1953).

9. Dahl, "Decision-Making in a Democracy," p. 293.

10. David W. Rohde and Harold J. Spaeth, *Supreme Court Decision Making* (1976), p. 145. In a recent study, Gregory A. Caldeira and John R. Wright offer a

different perspective on the representative character of Supreme Court decision making. They conclude that the Court "is quite responsive to the demands and preferences of organized interests when choosing its plenary docket. In this regard, the Supreme Court is very much a representative institution. . . . We view the Court's openness to outside demands when choosing its plenary docket as not only necessary for a smoothly functioning representative polity but also as a natural consequence of rational political decision making." See Caldeira and Wright, "Organized Interests and Agenda Setting in the U.S. Supreme Court," 82 *Am. Pol. Sci. Rev.* 1109, 1122 (1988).

APPENDIX A

History of
Supreme Court Appointments

Justice	Date of Confirmation	Replaced	Senate Vote[a]	Years on Court
	George Washington (1789–1797)			
John Jay[b]	9/26/1789			6
John Rutledge	9/26/1789			1
William Cushing	9/26/1789			21
James Wilson	9/26/1789			9
John Blair	9/26/1789			6
James Iredell	2/10/1790			9
Thomas Johnson	11/7/1791	Rutledge		1
William Paterson	3/4/1793	Johnson		13
John Rutledge[c]	12/15/1795	Jay	(10–14)[d]	
Samuel Chase	1/27/1796	Blair		15
Oliver Ellsworth	3/4/1796	Jay	(21–1)	4
	John Adams (1797–1801)			
Bushrod Washington	12/20/1798	Wilson		31
Alfred Moore	12/10/1799	Iredell		4
John Marshall	1/27/1801	Ellsworth		34
	Thomas Jefferson (1801–1809)			
William Johnson	3/24/1804	Moore		30
H. B. Livingston	12/17/1806	Paterson		16
Thomas Todd	3/3/1807	New seat		19
	James Madison (1809–1817)			
Joseph Story	11/18/1811	Cushing		34
Gabriel Duvall	11/18/1811	Chase		23
	James Monroe (1817–1825)			
Smith Thompson	12/19/1823	Livingston		20

Justice	Date of Confirmation	Replaced	Senate Vote[a]	Years on Court
	John Quincy Adams (1825–1829)			
Robert Trimble	5/9/1826	Todd		2
	Andrew Jackson (1829–1837)			
John McLean	3/7/1829	Trimble		32
Henry Baldwin	1/6/1830	Washington	(41–2)	14
James M. Wayne	1/9/1835	Johnson		32
Roger B. Taney	3/15/1836	Marshall	(29–15)	28
Philip P. Barbour	3/15/1836	Duvall	(30–11)	5
John Catron	3/8/1837	New seat	(28–15)	28
	Martin Van Buren (1837–1841)			
John McKinley	9/25/1837	New seat		15
Peter V. Daniel	3/2/1841	Barbour	(22–5)	19
	John Tyler (1841–1845)			
Samuel Nelson	2/14/1845	Thompson		27
	James K. Polk (1845–1849)			
Levi Woodbury	1/3/1846	Story		5
Robert C. Grier	8/4/1846	Baldwin		23
	Millard Fillmore (1850–1853)			
Benjamin R. Curtis	12/29/1851	Woodbury		5
	Franklin Pierce (1853–1857)			
John A. Campbell	3/25/1853	McKinley		8
	James Buchanan (1857–1861)			
Nathan Clifford	1/12/1858	Curtis	(26–23)	23
	Abraham Lincoln (1861–1865)			
Noah H. Swayne	1/24/1862	McLean	(38–1)	19
Samuel F. Miller	7/16/1862	Daniel		28
David Davis	12/8/1862	Campbell		14
Stephen J. Field	3/10/1863	New seat		34
Salmon P. Chase	12/6/1864	Taney		8
	Ulysses S. Grant (1869–1877)			
William Strong	2/18/1870	Grier		10
Joseph P. Bradley	3/21/1870	New seat	(46–9)	21
Ward Hunt	12/11/1872	Nelson		9
Morrison R. Waite	1/21/1874	Chase	(63–0)	14
	Rutherford B. Hayes (1877–1881)			
John M. Harlan	11/29/1877	Davis		34
William B. Woods	12/21/1880	Strong	(39–8)	6
	James A. Garfield (1881)			
Stanley Matthews	5/12/1881	Swayne	(24–23)	7

Justice	Date of Confirmation	Replaced	Senate Vote[a]	Years on Court
Chester A. Arthur (1881–1885)				
Horace Gray	12/20/1881	Clifford	(51–5)	20
Samuel Blatchford	3/27/1882	Hunt		11
Grover Cleveland (1885–1889)				
Lucius Q. C. Lamar	1/16/1888	Woods	(32–28)	5
Melville W. Fuller	7/20/1888	Waite	(41–20)	22
Benjamin Harrison (1889–1893)				
David J. Brewer	12/18/1889	Matthews	(53–11)	20
Henry B. Brown	12/29/1890	Miller		15
George Shiras, Jr.	7/26/1892	Bradley		10
Howell E. Jackson	2/18/1893	Lamar		2
Grover Cleveland (1893–1897)				
Edward D. White	2/19/1894	Blatchford		17
Rufus W. Peckham	12/9/1895	Jackson		13
William McKinley (1897–1901)				
Joseph McKenna	1/21/1898	Field		26
Theodore Roosevelt (1901–1909)				
Oliver W. Holmes	12/4/1902	Gray		29
William R. Day	2/23/1903	Shiras		19
William H. Moody	12/12/1906	Brown		3
William Howard Taft (1909–1913)				
Horace H. Lurton	12/20/1909	Peckham		4
Charles E. Hughes	5/2/1910	Brewer		6
Edward D. White[c]	12/12/1910	Fuller		10
Willis Van Devanter	12/15/1910	White		26
Joseph R. Lamar	12/15/1910	Moody		5
Mahlon Pitney	3/13/1912	Harlan	(50–26)	10
Woodrow Wilson (1913–1921)				
James C. McReynolds	8/29/1914	Lurton	(44–6)	26
Louis D. Brandeis	6/1/1916	Lamar	(47–22)	22
John H. Clarke	7/24/1916	Hughes		6
Warren G. Harding (1921–1923)				
William H. Taft	6/30/1921	White		8
George Sutherland	9/5/1922	Clarke		15
Pierce Butler	12/21/1922	Day	(61–8)	17
Edward T. Sanford	1/29/1923	Pitney		7
Calvin Coolidge (1923–1929)				
Harlan F. Stone	2/5/1925	McKenna	(71–6)	16
Herbert Hoover (1929–1933)				
Charles E. Hughes[c]	2/13/1930	Taft	(52–26)	11

Justice	Date of Confirmation	Replaced	Senate Vote[a]	Years on Court
Herbert Hoover (1929–1933) *Continued*				
Owen J. Roberts	5/20/1930	Sanford		15
Benjamin Cardozo	2/24/1932	Holmes		6
Franklin D. Roosevelt (1933–1945)				
Hugo L. Black	8/17/1937	Van Devanter	(63–16)	34
Stanley F. Reed	1/25/1938	Sutherland		19
Felix Frankfurter	1/17/1939	Cardozo		23
William O. Douglas	4/4/1939	Brandeis	(62–4)	36
Frank Murphy	1/15/1940	Butler		9
Harlan F. Stone[c]	6/27/1941	Hughes		5
James F. Byrnes	6/12/1941	McReynolds		1
Robert H. Jackson	7/7/1941	Stone		13
Wiley B. Rutledge	2/8/1943	Byrnes		6
Harry S. Truman (1945–1953)				
Harold H. Burton	9/19/1945	Roberts		13
Fred M. Vinson	6/20/1946	Stone		7
Tom C. Clark	8/18/1949	Murphy	(73–8)	18
Sherman Minton	10/4/1949	Rutledge	(48–16)	7
Dwight D. Eisenhower (1953–1961)				
Earl Warren	3/1/1954	Vinson		15
John M. Harlan	3/16/1955	Jackson	(71–11)	16
William J. Brennan	3/19/1957	Minton		34
Charles Whittaker	3/19/1957	Reed		5
Potter Stewart	5/5/1959	Burton	(70–17)	22
John F. Kennedy (1961–1963)				
Byron R. White	4/11/1962	Whittaker		
Arthur J. Goldberg	9/25/1962	Frankfurter		3
Lyndon B. Johnson (1963–1969)				
Abe Fortas	8/11/1965	Goldberg		4
Thurgood Marshall	8/30/1967	Clark	(69–11)	34
Richard M. Nixon (1969–1974)				
Warren Burger	6/9/1969	Warren	(74–3)	17
Harry A. Blackmun	5/12/1970	Fortas	(94–0)	
Lewis F. Powell	12/6/1971	Black	(89–1)	16
William H. Rehnquist	12/10/1971	Harlan	(68–26)	15
Gerald R. Ford (1974–1977)				
John Paul Stevens	12/17/1975	Douglas	(98–0)	
Ronald Reagan (1981–1989)				
Sandra Day O'Connor	9/21/1981	Stewart	(99–0)	
William H. Rehnquist[c]	9/17/1986	Burger	(65–33)	
Antonin Scalia	9/17/1986	Rehnquist	(98–0)	
Anthony M. Kennedy	2/3/1988	Powell	(97–0)	

Justice	Date of Confirmation	Replaced	Senate Vote[a]	Years on Court
	George Bush (1989–1993)			
David Souter	10/2/1990	Brennan	(90–9)	
Clarence Thomas	10/15/1991	Marshall	(52–48)	

[a]In many cases, the vote in the Senate was a voice vote or was otherwise unrecorded.

[b]Boldface type denotes the chief justice.

[c]Denotes previous service on the Court.

[d]John Rutledge was nominated to succeed John Jay as chief justice while the Senate was in recess. He presided over the Court during its August 1795 term but was rejected by the Senate by a vote of 10–14 in December 1795.

sources: Elder Witt (ed.), *Congressional Quarterly's Guide to the U.S. Supreme Court* (1990); *Congressional Quarterly Weekly Report.*

Unsuccessful Twentieth-Century Nominations

Nominee	President	To Replace	Date of Nomination	Senate Vote
John J. Parker	Hoover	Sanford	3/21/30	(39–41)
Abe Fortas[a]	Johnson	Warren	6/26/68	Withdrawn
Homer Thornberry	Johnson	Fortas	6/26/68	No Action[b]
Clement Haynesworth	Nixon	Fortas	8/18/69	(45–55)
G. Harrold Carswell	Nixon	Fortas	1/19/70	(45–51)
Robert H. Bork	Reagan	Powell	7/1/87	(42–58)
Douglas Ginsburg	Reagan	Powell	10/29/87	Withdrawn[c]

[a]Denotes previous service on the Court.

[b]Homer Thornberry was nominated for the vacancy that would have occurred if Abe Fortas had been confirmed as chief justice. When the Fortas nomination was withdrawn, Earl Warren remained chief justice and Abe Fortas remained an associate justice. Thus, the vacancy for which Thornberry had been nominated no longer existed. Subsequently, Justice Fortas resigned, and, after two unsuccessful attempts to replace him, Harry Blackmun was nominated and confirmed by the Senate.

[c]The Ginsburg nomination was withdrawn before being formally submitted to the Senate.

source: Elder Witt (ed.), *Congressional Quarterly's Guide to the U.S. Supreme Court* (1990).

APPENDIX B

Table of Cases

A Note on How to Find
Judicial Decisions

Judicial decisions are reported by both governmental and private reporting services. The official (i.e., governmental) reports of U.S. Supreme Court decisions are the *U.S. Reports*. *Abrams* v. *United States*, for instance, will be found in 250 U.S. 616 (1919), that is, on page 616 of volume 250 of the *U.S. Reports*. Lawyers and judges will rely on these "citations" in order to locate a particular case or passage.

The first ninety volumes of the *U.S. Reports* (covering the period between 1789 and 1874) acknowledge the individuals who served as official reporters of Supreme Court decisions. When *Marbury* v. *Madison* was decided, William Cranch was the official reporter. The citation to *Marbury* v. *Madison*, therefore, is 5 U.S. (1 Cranch) 137 (1803).

Supreme Court decisions are also reported in a series published by the West Publishing Company known as the *Supreme Court Reporter*. The *Abrams* decision, for instance, may be found in 40 S.Ct. 17 (1919), that is, on page 17 of volume 40 of the *Supreme Court Reporter*. Ordinarily, decisions are available sooner in the *Supreme Court Reporter* than in the *U.S. Reports*. Thus, citations to recent Supreme Court decisions (in the text and in the Table of Cases) may be to the *Supreme Court Reporter*.

A third source of Supreme Court decisions is a series known as the *Lawyers' Edition*. The *Abrams* case, for instance, is reported in 63 L.Ed. 1173 (1919). The *Lawyers' Edition* began renumbering its volumes in 1956. *Yates* v. *United States*, therefore, is reported in 1 L.Ed.2d 1356 (1957), that is, on page 1356 of volume 1 of the *Lawyer's Edition, 2nd Series*.

Decisions of U.S. District Courts are published by the West Publishing Company in a series known as the *Federal Supplement*. The district court decision in *Brown* v. *Board of Education*, for instance, is reported in 98 F.Supp. 797 (D.Kan. 1951), that is, on page 797 of volume 98 of the *Federal Supplement*.

You will notice that some additional information is provided by the citation to the district court decision in *Brown*. Kansas is a state including a single U.S. District Court. The citation indicates that the case was decided by the U.S. District Court for the District of Kansas. The citation for *Barnette* v. *West Virginia State Board of Education*, by contrast, is 47 F.Supp. 251 (S.D.W.Va. 1942). This means that West Virginia includes more than one district court and that *Barnette* was decided by the District Court for the Southern District of West Virginia.

Decisions of the U.S. Courts of Appeals are published by the West Publishing Company in a series known as the *Federal Reporter*. Recent decisions will be reported in the *2nd Series* of the *Federal Reporter*. The court of appeals decision in *Yates* v. *United States*, for instance, is reported in 225 F.2d 146 (9th Cir. 1955). This means that the decision was handed down by the Court of Appeals for the Ninth Circuit and may be found on page 146 of volume 225 of the *Federal Reporter, 2nd Series.*

Decisions of state courts are reported in additional series published by state governments or private companies (including the West Publishing Company). Abbreviations other than those noted above — that is, other than U.S., S.Ct., L.Ed.2d, F.Supp., and F.2d — will be citations to state court decisions.

For additional help in conducting original research on constitutional questions, see Albert P. Melone, *Researching Constitutional Law* (Glenview, Ill.: Scott, Foresman/Little, Brown, 1990).

Glossary

Acquittal. An acquittal in a criminal case occurs when the judge or jury determines that the defendant is "not guilty." The government may not appeal a verdict of acquittal but may appeal rulings on legal issues made by the judge during the course of the trial.

Adversary Process. See *Ex Parte*.

Amicus Curiae. This Latin term means "friend of the court." Interest groups participate in the appellate process by submitting an *amicus* brief to the Supreme Court in which they present their views on a case in which they are interested but not directly involved.

Anti-Federalists. In the 1780s those who were opposed to the adoption of a new Constitution were known as Anti-Federalists.

Appeal Case. Under federal statutes, some cases are classified as appeal cases. Such cases fall within the mandatory appellate jurisdiction of the Supreme Court; that is, they are cases that the Court is obliged to hear and decide. Today, very few cases are classified as appeal cases.

Appellant. The appellant (also called the petitioner) is the party in either a criminal or a civil case who is dissatisfied with the outcome of a case and decides to appeal it to a higher court.

Appellate Docket. The Supreme Court's Appellate Docket is that portion of its overall docket (i.e., filings) that consists of "paid cases." Paid cases are those in which the litigants have paid the required filing fees and provided the Court with all the necessary paperwork (i.e., briefs, transcripts of the trial proceedings, etc.).

Appellate Jurisdiction. The appellate jurisdiction of a court consists of those cases which that court is empowered to hear after they have been decided by at least one lower court.

Appellee. The appellee (also called the respondent) is the party in either a civil or a criminal case who is satisfied with the outcome of a case but must remain involved in the case because the losing party has decided to appeal to a higher court. The appellee or respondent is therefore the party who is defending against an appeal.

Bench Trial. In a criminal case, the defendant may waive his or her right to a jury trial. When that happens, the trial will be conducted by a judge and will be known as a bench trial.

Bill of Attainder. A bill of attainder is legislation that names a particular individual as an outlaw or an enemy of the state and thereby pronounces guilt without trial or conviction. The framers of the Constitution viewed the bill of attainder as an abuse of legislative power and a violation of individual rights and prohibited both Congress and the states from enacting such bills.

Brief. A brief is the collection of written materials that an appellate court receives from each of the parties to a case. Each party's brief will include a statement of its version of the facts in the case and the arguments that the party wishes to make to the appellate court. The brief may also contain additional materials, such as a transcript of the proceedings at the trial level.

Burden of Proof. The outcome of legal disputes may depend in part on allocation of the burden of proof. The party who bears the burden of proof must meet that burden or else lose the case. In criminal cases, the government must establish the guilt of the defendant "beyond a reasonable doubt." This is an example of a legal rule that not only allocates the burden of proof but also defines the magnitude of the burden.

Cert Pool. Since the early 1970s several justices have joined together to create a cert pool consisting of clerks who serve those justices. Petitions for a writ of certiorari which the Court receives are apportioned among these clerks, and each clerk's recommendation about whether the Court should grant certiorari is shared with all the justices who participate in the cert pool.

Certiorari. The petition for a writ of certiorari is the principal mechanism by which cases are appealed from lower courts (both state and federal) to the Supreme Court. The Supreme Court reviews these petitions and decides whether to grant or deny certiorari.

Certiorari Case. A certiorari case is one that falls within the discretionary appellate jurisdiction of the Supreme Court. In 1988 Congress enlarged the proportion of cases that are classified as certiorari cases. Today almost all cases appealed to the Supreme Court are certiorari cases.

Certworthiness. A certworthy case is one that a clerk or justice believes is worthy of plenary consideration.

Circuit. A circuit is a geographical area over which a particular court or set of courts has jurisdiction. In state court systems, trial courts are frequently known as circuit courts, and a particular circuit court will have jurisdiction to decide cases that arise within a specified geographical area, usually a county. In the federal system, the United States is divided into twelve numbered circuits, each of which is served by a separate U.S. Court of Appeals.

Civil Law. Noncriminal legal relations among private parties are governed by the civil law, and noncriminal disputes that arise between private parties, or between private parties and the government, may become civil cases. A typical civil case is one in which one party (e.g., an individual or a business) is suing another party for an alleged injury (e.g., property damage or physical injury arising from an automobile accident, breach of contract). Cases in which an individual is challenging the constitutional validity of a state or federal law (provided he or she has not already been arrested for violating the law) are also classified as civil cases.

Collegial Court. A court consisting of more than a single judge is known as a collegial court. In the federal system, the courts of appeals and the Supreme Court, but not the district courts, are collegial courts.

Color Blind Constitution. The theory that the Constitution is or should be color blind dates from Justice Harlan's dissent in *Plessy* v. *Ferguson* in 1896. A color blind Constitution would be one that prohibited all forms of racial discrimination, that is, positive or negative discrimination against any racial group. In a modern context, opponents of affirmative action are among those who believe that the Constitution is or should be color blind.

Common Law. In British history, the common law was the accumulated body of judicial precedents created by judges as an outgrowth of their decisions in specific cases. Much of the law in the American states in the early years was also common law, but today virtually all criminal offenses are defined by statutes enacted by legislatures and very few common law offenses or common law crimes remain. The common law may play a larger role, however, in governing legal relations among private parties and in determining the outcome of civil disputes.

Concurrence. A concurrence (or concurring opinion) is an opinion by a justice or group of justices expressing agreement with the Supreme Court's decision in a particular case but offering a distinctive set of reasons why the case should be decided the way it was.

Conference. The nine justices of the Supreme Court sometimes refer to themselves as "the Conference." When the Court meets in conference to discuss and decide cases, only the justices themselves are present.

Contempt of Court. Judges possess the power to hold parties to a case in contempt of court for refusing to comply with a judicial order. A judge may also attempt to maintain discipline within his or her courtroom by holding litigants, lawyers, or spectators in contempt of court.

Conviction. A conviction in a criminal case is a decision by the judge or jury that the accused defendant is guilty of the offense with which he or she has been charged. In most jurisdictions, a convicted defendant has an automatic right to at least one appeal to a higher court.

Court Curbing. Various actions within the power of Congress or the president are classified as techniques for curbing the Supreme Court or its members. Prominent among the Court-curbing powers of Congress is its ability to make exceptions to the appellate jurisdiction of the Supreme Court.

Court Packing. The president is often accused of attempting to pack the Supreme Court by nominating justices who hold similar and perhaps extreme ideological views. The most famous episode of Court packing occurred in 1937 when President Roosevelt proposed to enlarge the Court from nine to fifteen members and—it went without saying—to fill the newly created vacancies with justices who would support Roosevelt on the constitutional issues of the day.

Criminal Law. Criminal offenses are defined by state and local legislatures and by Congress. Persons arrested for violating a state or federal law become defendants in criminal cases.

Cue Theory. Cue theory is a body of social scientific literature that attempts to understand the Supreme Court's decisions to accept cases for plenary review by examining the "cues" inherent in particular cases, that is, characteristics of the case that may cause the Court to decide to grant certiorari.

De Facto Segregation. The term *de facto segregation* refers to a situation where schools are racially segregated, not because the law requires blacks and whites to attend separate schools, but because children are required to attend neighborhood schools and the neighborhoods themselves are racially homogeneous.

De Jure Segregation. The term *de jure segregation* refers to the form of racial segregation in effect in the southern and border states prior to the Supreme Court's decision in *Brown* v. *Board of Education* (1954). *Brown* declared that de jure segregation—that is, segregation required by law—was unconstitutional.

Dead List. See *Discuss List*.

Declaratory Judgment. Under state and federal statutes, parties to litigation may seek judicial relief in the form of a declaratory judgment—a declaration by a court of the rights and obligations of the parties. In cases involving a constitutional challenge to state or federal law, relief may take the form of a declaration by the court that the law is unconstitutional.

Defendant. The term *defendant* is used in two main senses. In a criminal case, the person accused of violating the law is known as the defendant. In a civil case, the party who is being sued is known as the defendant. In a constitutional case involving a challenge to the validity of state law—for example, *Brown* v. *Board of Education* (1954)—the state itself, or a subdivision of the state, will be the defendant.

Direct Democracy. A direct democracy (also known as a pure democracy) is one in which individual citizens participate directly in making governmental decisions. Direct democracy is usually contrasted with representative democracy, in which citizens elect representatives who in turn are responsible for making governmental decisions.

Discretionary Jurisdiction. See *Certiorari Case.*

Discuss List. The chief justice is responsible for preparing a discuss list consisting of cases that he feels the Court should consider including on the plenary docket. Cases that are not included on the discuss list are relegated to the *dead list* and are not formally considered by the Court unless added to the discuss list by one of the associate justices.

Dissent. A dissent (or dissenting opinion) is an opinion by a justice or group of justices expressing disagreement with the result in a particular case. By definition, a dissenting opinion expresses the views of a minority of the Court.

Electoral Accountability. In a political system based on principles of electoral accountability, governmental officials face periodic elections and are removed from office unless they receive renewed authorization to govern from the voters.

Equity Decision. The concept of equity originated in the English legal system in the sixteenth century. Today the term *equity decisions* usually refers to cases culminating in the issuance of an injunction. When lawyers say that a court has granted equitable relief, they mean that the court has issued an injunction.

Ex Parte. An ex parte proceeding is one involving only one side to a legal dispute (plus the presiding judge). Ordinarily an ex parte proceeding is held only in an emergency, because such proceedings violate the fundamental principle that legal disputes should be settled by the adversary process, that is, in a proceeding involving the two opposing parties plus a presiding judge.

Ex Post Facto Law. An ex post facto law is one that operates retroactively to prohibit behavior that was legal at the time it occurred. The Constitution prohibits both Congress and the states from passing ex post facto laws.

Exclusionary Rule. The exclusionary rule is also known as the suppression doctrine, or the doctrine of inadmissible evidence. The main effect of the rule today is to require the exclusion or suppression of evidence (i.e., drugs, weapons, stolen property, or a confession) that has been seized or obtained by the police in violation of the requirements of the Fourth Amendment (which prohibits unreasonable searches and seizures) or the Fifth Amendment (which prohibits self-incrimination).

Executive Privilege. In recent years—notably during the Watergate episode of the Nixon Administration—presidents have resisted requests by courts for information or for some other form of cooperation with the judicial process. The doctrine of executive privilege is often invoked to justify such refusals.

Extraordinary Majority. The U.S. Constitution stipulates that some decisions cannot be reached by a simple majority but can only be reached by an extraordinary majority. Passage of a constitutional amendment, for instance, requires a two-thirds majority in both houses of Congress, and ratification of an amendment requires a three-fourths majority of the legislatures of the states.

Federalism. The U.S. Constitution establishes a vertical division of power between the national level of government, on the one hand, and the states, on the other. This division of power is known as Federalism.

Federalists. In the 1780s the name "Federalists" was adopted by those who proposed to strengthen the national government and who favored the adoption of a new Constitution to accomplish this goal.

Filings. See *Jurisdictional Agenda.*

Good Behaviour. Under the U.S. Constitution, Supreme Court justices and other federal judges hold their offices during "good Behaviour." The Constitution prescribes that judges shall be removed from office by the process of impeachment and that impeachable offenses include "Treason, Bribery, or other high Crimes and Misdemeanors." Beyond this, however, the Constitution does not define "good Behaviour."

Grand Jury. See *Jury Trial.*

Habeas Corpus. The writ of habeas corpus is a judicial order with roots in English history. The phrase itself means "you have the body." Application for a writ of habeas corpus is made by someone (or on behalf of someone) who is in police custody or is confined to prison. The writ of habeas corpus is issued by a judge and requires that the police or prison officials produce the individual in court. Today the principal use of the writ of habeas corpus is to enable state prisoners to request review by a federal court of the validity of their convictions.

Impeachment. The Constitution prescribes impeachment as the sole mechanism by which Supreme Court justices (and other federal judges) can be removed from office. Impeachment requires a majority vote in the House of Representatives and a two-thirds vote in the Senate.

In Forma Pauperis. The Supreme Court allows some cases to be appealed *in forma pauperis,* that is, without filing fees and without meeting the Court's requirements concerning the number and format of trial court transcripts, briefs, and other documents. Cases filed *in forma pauperis* are assigned to the Court's Miscellaneous Docket.

Incorporation. Incorporation was a constitutional theory that enjoyed the support of a majority of the Supreme Court during the 1960s (and to some extent in earlier decades). The theory of *selective incorporation* is that particular provisions of the Bill of Rights are incorporated into the Due Process Clause of the Fourteenth Amendment and thereby become restrictions on the states as well as the federal government. The theory of *total incorporation,* which never commanded a majority on the Court, was that the Due Process Clause was meant to incorporate the entire Bill of Rights.

Indictment. See *Jury Trial.*

Injunctions. Courts possess the power to enjoin both private parties and governmental officials. A court may also issue an injunction against legislation, in which case it is enjoining enforcement of the legislation by governmental officials. Injunctions come in different forms, including temporary (or short-term) injunctions, permanent (or long-term) injunctions, and ex parte injunctions (emergency injunctions issued at the request of only one side to a legal controversy, pending a full hearing at which both parties can be present).

Intent of the Framers. See *Original Intent.*

Interpretive Review/Interpretivism. In contemporary constitutional theory, the phrase "interpretive review" is used to describe a theory of constitutional interpretation which argues that judges should adhere closely to the text of the Constitution in reaching decisions in specific cases.

Judicial Relief. Parties to civil cases decided by state and federal courts are entitled to seek various types of judicial relief. The most common types of judicial relief are declaratory judgments, injunctions, and monetary damages.

Judicial Review. In American law, the term *judicial review* is used to describe the power of the Supreme Court (and other courts) to invalidate legislation on constitutional grounds. A court decision based on the Constitution which invalidates the action of an executive official—for example, the president, an administrative official, or a police officer—may also be classified as an example of judicial review, although not as an example of judicial review of legislation.

Jurisdiction. A court's jurisdiction is the definition of the kinds of cases the court has the power to decide. In American law, legislative bodies are usually responsible for defining the jurisdiction of courts, although courts may play a role in defining their own jurisdiction. Primary responsibility for defining the jurisdiction of the federal courts, including the appellate jurisdiction of the Supreme Court, rests with Congress. The term *jurisdiction* is also used to describe a geographical area. For instance, one might say that "the law in this jurisdiction [i.e., this state or county] is very strict."

Jurisdictional Agenda. The Supreme Court's jurisdictional agenda consists of all cases (about five thousand per year) that are appealed from the lower courts. The term *filings* is frequently used to refer to the Court's jurisdictional agenda.

Jury Trial. Under the U.S. Constitution, defendants in most criminal cases are entitled to a jury trial. A jury trial is conducted before a regular or *petit jury*, which will ordinarily consist of twelve persons but may be smaller, for example, six persons. A *grand jury* is larger than a petit jury (i.e., up to twenty-three persons). Its purpose is to determine whether to "indict" a defendant, that is, to return an indictment that orders that the defendant be held to answer (in a trial before a petit jury) for one or more specified offenses.

Litigant/Litigation. Litigation is a word that is used to describe either a specific case or the judicial process in general. The word *litigation* is ordinarily used to describe civil rather than criminal cases, but there are exceptions. Litigants are the parties to a case (i.e., individuals, businesses, governments).

Majority Opinion. When five or more members of the Supreme Court are able to agree on a single opinion, it will be issued as the Court's majority opinion. The opinion will open with the distinctive phrase "Justice Jones delivered the opinion of the Court."

Majority Rule. In a political democracy, decisions reached by majority rule are those that require, at a minimum, 50–percent-plus-one of those who are eligible to vote.

Mandatory Jurisdiction. See *Appeal Case*.

Miscellaneous Docket. The Supreme Court's Miscellaneous Docket is that portion of its overall jurisdictional docket that consists of cases appealed *in forma pauperis*, that is, without filing fees or the paperwork (e.g., trial court transcripts, briefs) which the Court ordinarily requires.

Natural Law/Natural Rights. A theory of natural rights holds that individuals possess rights that predate and supersede either a written Constitution or statutory law. Two contemporary arguments are based on the theory of natural rights: (1) the argument that the Constitution embodies various principles of natural law and (2) the argument that individuals cannot be deprived of their natural rights even though those rights are not explicitly protected by the Constitution.

Noninterpretive Review/Noninterpretivism. In contemporary constitutional theory, the phrase *noninterpretive review* is used to describe a theory of constitutional interpretation which allows judges to look beyond the text of the Constitution in reaching decisions in specific cases.

Obiter Dicta. Arguments made by a judge in an opinion which are not crucial to the judge's decision or holding in the case are called dicta or obiter dicta.

Oral Argument. Cases to which the Supreme Court agrees to give plenary consideration are scheduled for oral argument. Each side is usually granted one half hour for its oral argument.

Original Intent. The theory of original intent or original understanding argues that the Constitution should be interpreted according to the intent of the framers, that is, the intent of those who drafted it.

Original Jurisdiction. The original jurisdiction of a court consists of those cases which that court is empowered to hear before they are heard by any other court.

Overrule. When the Supreme Court decides that one of its own previous decisions was wrong, it will overrule the decision. The term *overrule* is also used to describe a judge's decision during the course of a trial to refuse to sustain an objection raised by one of the lawyers.

Paid Cases. See *Appellate Docket.*

Per Curiam Opinion. Occasionally, the Court will issue a *per curiam* opinion. *Per curiam* opinions are usually brief, and none of the justices is identified as the author of the opinion. Instead, the opinion is issued *per curiam*, that is, from the Court itself.

Petitioner. See *Appellant.*

Plaintiff. The term *plaintiff* is used to describe one of the parties to a civil case, namely, the party who initiates the case by suing the defendant. In some jurisdictions, in criminal cases the state (i.e., government) is known as the plaintiff or party plaintiff.

Plenary Docket. The Supreme Court's plenary docket consists of those cases (about 120 to 150 per year) to which the Court has agreed to give plenary consideration or full treatment.

Plurality Decision. Some decisions of the Supreme Court are plurality decisions. The Court will issue a plurality decision when fewer than five members of the Court are able to agree on the reasons for deciding a particular case in a particular direction. The opinion of one group of justices will be designated as the plurality opinion and will open with the distinctive phrase, "Justice Jones announced the judgment of the Court, and delivered an opinion in which Justices Brown and Smith join."

Popular Sovereignty. A political system based on the theory of popular sovereignty is one in which the people are the ultimate source of governmental power.

Precedent. When the Supreme Court (or any other court) decides a case in a particular way, it establishes a precedent. Lawyers and judges will acknowledge the existence of the precedent in their future briefs and opinions.

Probable Jurisdiction. If the Court decides to give plenary consideration to a case that is classified under federal law as an appeal case, the Court will do so by issuing an order in which it "notes probable jurisdiction" in the case. Noting probable jurisdiction in an appeal case is the equivalent of granting certiorari in a certiorari case.

Prosecutor. The prosecutor represents the government in criminal cases. In federal cases, the prosecutor is the U.S. attorney (or assistant U.S. attorney) for the federal district in which the case is being tried. In state cases, the prosecutor is usually called the district attorney or state's attorney.

Pure Democracy. See *Direct Democracy.*

Representative Democracy. A representative democracy is distinct from a *direct democracy* or a *pure democracy*. In a representative democracy, governmental decisions are made not by the people themselves but by those whom the people elect to serve as their representatives.

Republican Government. The phrase *republican government* is sometimes used as a synonym for representative government or representative democracy. A republican form of government is one in which citizens vote for representatives, who in turn are responsible for making governmental decisions.

Respondent. See *Appellee.*

Rule of Four. The so-called Rule of Four applies to the Supreme Court's decisions whether or not to grant certiorari and (in practice) whether or not to note probable jurisdiction. Four of nine justices are sufficient to grant certiorari or to note probable jurisdiction and thereby place a case on the Court's plenary docket.

Sedition. Sedition (or seditious libel) is a crime with roots in English constitutional history. It is usually defined as the utterance or publication of words that "cast contempt" on governmental institutions or political leaders and thereby bring such institutions or leaders into disrepute among citizens. Historically, prosecutions for sedition have been used to silence criticism of government and governmental leaders. In the United States, versions of the traditional offense of sedition are embodied in laws that punish criminal anarchy, criminal syndicalism, or advocating the overthrow of the government.

Senate Confirmation. Under the U.S. Constitution, those whom the president nominates to serve on the Supreme Court are subject to Senate confirmation before they are officially appointed to the Court. Confirmation requires a majority vote in the Senate.

Separation of Powers. The U.S. Constitution implements the doctrine of separation of powers by allocating governmental power to three different branches of government—the legislative, the executive, and the judicial.

Seriatim Opinions. In some judicial systems, all or most of the members of a collegial court will express their own opinion about how a case should come out. In contrast, the norm in the U.S. Supreme Court is for a group of justices to agree on a majority opinion and to designate one member of the majority to be the author of an opinion representing the views of the majority.

Simple Majority. Most decisions in a democratic political system require the assent of a simple majority, that is, 50-percent-plus-one of those who are eligible to vote.

Special Circumstances Rule. This rule dated from the Supreme Court's decision in *Betts* v. *Brady* (1942). Under the rule, indigent defendants were entitled to free legal counsel in state cases only when the case involved special circumstances. The Supreme Court abandoned the special circumstances rule in its decision in *Gideon* v. *Wainwright* (1963).

Stare Decisis. *Stare decisis* means "let the decision stand." It is a basic principle of most legal systems that an established precedent should govern future cases unless the precedent itself is overruled or unless the future case can be distinguished, that is, decided differently from the precedent because of a meaningful difference in the facts of the two cases.

Statutory Construction. The Supreme Court decides many cases—primarily cases involving federal law—by the technique of statutory construction. This technique involves construing the meaning of a federal law that is vague or ambiguous. The Court may use the technique of statutory construction to avoid having to decide whether the statute itself is valid or invalid under the Constitution.

Subpoena. A subpoena is an order commanding that particular individuals appear in court or that they supply the court with documents or other materials. The Sixth Amendment's reference to the right of an accused person "to have compulsory process for obtaining witnesses in his favor" is an example of the sort of situation in which a subpoena might be issued.

Summary Judgment. The term *summary judgment* usually refers to a decision of the Supreme Court that is reached without the benefit of oral argument and that is not accompanied, when it is handed down, by a written opinion.

Swing Vote. When the Supreme Court is divided along ideological lines, certain justices sometimes acquire a reputation as swing votes. In a particular case, a justice who is a swing vote will be in a key position to influence the outcome of the case, because he or she will be able to create a majority by choosing to join one side or the other of the Court.

Unenumerated Rights. Some judges and scholars have argued that the Ninth Amendment to the Constitution authorizes the courts to protect unenumerated rights, that is, rights (such as the right of privacy) that are not explicitly guaranteed by the Constitution.

Selected Readings

Abraham, Henry J. 1985. *Justices and Presidents: A Political History of Appointments to the Supreme Court.* 2nd ed. New York: Oxford University Press.

Ball, Howard, and Phillip J. Cooper. 1992. *Of Power and Right: Hugo Black, William O. Douglas, and America's Constitutional Revolution.* New York: Oxford University Press.

Barlow, J. Jackson, Leonard W. Levy, and Ken Masugi (eds.). 1988. *The American Founding.* Westport, Conn.: Greenwood Press.

Baum, Lawrence. 1992. *The Supreme Court.* 4th ed. Washington, D.C.: Congressional Quarterly Press.

Bickel, Alexander. 1962. *The Least Dangerous Branch: The Supreme Court at the Bar of Politics.* Indianapolis, Ind.: Bobbs-Merrill.

Blasi, Vincent (ed.). 1983. *The Burger Court: The Counter-Revolution That Wasn't.* New Haven, Conn.: Yale University Press.

Bork, Robert H. 1990. *The Tempting of America: The Political Seduction of the Law.* New York: Free Press.

Braeman, John. 1988. *Before the Civil Rights Revolution: The Old Court and Individual Rights.* Westport, Conn.: Greenwood Press.

Choper, Jesse H. 1980. *Judicial Review and the National Political Process.* Chicago: University of Chicago Press.

Ely, John Hart. 1980. *Democracy and Distrust.* Cambridge, Mass.: Harvard University Press.

Fairfield, Roy P. (ed.). 1961. *The Federalist Papers.* Garden City, N.Y.: Anchor Books.

Farber, Daniel A., and Suzanna Sherry. 1990. *A History of the American Constitution.* St. Paul, Minn.: West Publishing Co.

Fisher, Louis. 1988. *Constitutional Dialogues: Interpretation as Political Process.* Princeton, N.J.: Princeton University Press.

Garraty, John A. (ed.). 1987. *Quarrels That Have Shaped the Constitution.* Revised edition. New York: Harper and Row.

Garvey, John H., and T. Alexander Aleinikoff (eds.). 1991. *Modern Constitutional Theory: A Reader.* 2nd ed. St. Paul, Minn.: West Publishing Co.

333

Goldstein, Leslie Friedman. 1991. *In Defense of the Text: Democracy and Constitutional Theory*. Savage, Md.: Rowman and Littlefield.

Irons, Peter. 1988. *The Courage of Their Convictions: Sixteen Americans Who Fought Their Way to the Supreme Court*. New York: Free Press.

Johnson, Charles A., and Bradley C. Canon. 1984. *Judicial Policies: Implementation and Impact*. Washington, D.C.: Congressional Quarterly Press.

Keynes, Edward. 1989. *The Court vs. Congress: Prayer, Busing, and Abortion*. Durham, N.C.: Duke University Press.

Lamb, Charles M., and Stephen C. Halpern (eds.). 1991. *The Burger Court: Political and Judicial Profiles*. Urbana: University of Illinois Press.

Lasser, William. 1988. *The Limits of Judicial Power: The Supreme Court in American Politics*. Chapel Hill: University of North Carolina Press.

Levy, Leonard W. (ed.). 1987. *Essays on the Making of the Constitution*. 2nd ed. New York: Oxford University Press.

Levy, Leonard W., and Dennis J. Mahoney (eds.). 1987. *The Framing and Ratification of the Constitution*. New York: Macmillan.

Lewis, Anthony. 1964. *Gideon's Trumpet*. New York: Vintage Books.

Marshall, Thomas R. 1989. *Public Opinion and the Supreme Court*. Boston: Unwin Hyman.

McCloskey, Robert G. 1960. *The American Supreme Court*. Cambridge, Mass.: Harvard University Press.

Morgan, Robert J. 1988. *James Madison on the Constitution and the Bill of Rights*. Westport, Conn.: Greenwood Press.

O'Brien, David M. 1990. *Storm Center: The Supreme Court in American Politics*. 2nd ed. New York: W. W. Norton.

Pacelle, Richard L., Jr. 1991. *The Transformation of the Supreme Court's Agenda: From the New Deal to the Reagan Administration*. Boulder, Colo.: Westview Press.

Perry, H. W., Jr. 1991. *Deciding to Decide: Agenda Setting in the United States Supreme Court*. Cambridge, Mass.: Harvard University Press.

Perry, Michael J. 1982. *The Constitution, the Courts, and Human Rights: An Inquiry into the Legitimacy of Constitutional Policymaking by the Judiciary*. New Haven, Conn.: Yale University Press.

Pritchett, C. Herman. 1984. *Constitutional Civil Liberties*. Englewood Cliffs, N.J.: Prentice-Hall.

Pritchett, C. Herman. 1984. *Constitutional Law of the Federal System*. Englewood Cliffs, N.J.: Prentice-Hall.

Rosenberg, Gerald N. 1991. *The Hollow Hope: Can Courts Bring about Social Change?* Chicago: University of Chicago Press.

Snowiss, Sylvia. 1990. *Judicial Review and the Law of the Constitution*. New Haven, Conn.: Yale University Press.

Sosin, J. M. 1989. *The Aristocracy of the Long Robe: The Origins of Judicial Review in America*. Westport, Conn.: Greenwood Press.

Tribe, Lawrence H. 1988. *American Constitutional Law*. 2nd ed. Mineola, N.Y.: Foundation Press.

Tribe, Lawrence H. 1985. *God Save This Honorable Court: How the Choice of Supreme Court Justices Shapes Our History*. New York: Random House.

Wiecek, William M. 1988. *Liberty under Law: The Supreme Court in American Life*. Baltimore: Johns Hopkins University Press.

Witt, Elder (ed.). 1990. *Congressional Quarterly's Guide to the U.S. Supreme Court.* 2nd ed. Washington, D.C.: Congressional Quarterly.

Woodward, Bob, and Scott Armstrong. 1979. *The Brethren: Inside the Supreme Court.* New York: Simon and Schuster.

Index

Fenwick, Lynda Beck, 147
Filings. *See* Jurisdictional Agenda
Fine, Sidney, 120
Finkbine, Sherry, 161
Fino, Susan P., 44
Fisher, Louis, x, 16, 45, 218
Footnote Eleven (Brown v. Board of
    Education), 128
Footnote Four (United States v. Carolene
    Products Co.), 109–110, 128, 253,
    265–266
Ford, Gerald, 89, 204, 241
Fortas, Abe, 66, 103, 88, 155–156, 159,
    224, 225, 227, 231–232, 240, 244
Frampton, George Jr., 101
France, 82
Frankfurter, Felix, 11–12, 71, 114,
    117–118, 125, 126, 137, 228, 238,
    246, 283
Franklin, Charles H., 174, 216
Freund Committee. *See* Study Group on the
    Caseload of the Supreme Court
Freund, Paul A., x, 62
Fried, Charles, 75
Friedman, Leon, 128
Funston, Richard, 93

Galloway, Russell W. Jr., 104
Gallup, George Jr., 219
Garrow, David J., 190
Garvey, John H., 273–274, 275
Gates, John B., 93, 215
Gibson, James L., 72, 216, 303
Gideon, Clarence Earl, 152–157
Giles, Michael W., 216
Ginsberg, Benjamin, 103, 313
Ginsberg, Douglas, 224
Glick, Henry R., 44, 216
Goldberg, Arthur, 66, 88, 156, 164–165,
    226, 231–232, 240
Goldman, Sheldon, 44, 72, 101, 104–105
Goldstein, Leslie Friedman, 275
Goldstein, Robert Justin, 139
Goodman, Frank I., 128
Gottschall, Jon, 72
Goulden, Joseph C., 45
Graham, Fred P., 159
Graham, Hugh Davis, 190
Gramm-Rudman (Deficit Reduction) Act, 8
Grant, Ulysses S., 238
Great Depression, 86, 134
Green, John C., 304
Green, Donald Philip, 304
Greene, Kathanne W., 191

Grey, Thomas C., 269–270, 273, 275
Grossman, Joel B., 45, 216, 245, 313
Gunther, Gerald, 219
Guth, James L., 304

Habeas Corpus, 37, 44, 153–154, 205, 250
Haber, David, 139
Hacker, Andrew, 131
Hadley, Charles D., 71
Hagle, Timothy M., 246
Halpern, Stephen C., 103, 104, 105
Hamilton, Alexander, 1, 16, 204–205, 254,
    258–259, 266
Hammond, Phillip E., 147, 217
Handberg, Roger, 216, 247
Harlan, John M. (I), 177
Harlan, John M. (II), 57, 66, 136–137, 138,
    140, 156, 165, 240
Harris, Richard, 246
Haskins, George L., 102
Hastings, Alcee L., 218
Hatch, Orrin, 170
Haynesworth, Clement, 204, 224, 225, 244
Heck, Edward V., 104–105
Held, David, 16
Hellman, Arthur D., 61, 63–64, 67, 68, 70,
    72
Helms, Jesse, 146, 169, 210, 212
Henkin, Louis, 16
Henschen, Beth M., 218
Hill, Anita, 223
Hirsch, H. N., 120
Hochschild, Jennifer, 131
Hodder-Williams, Richard, x
Holmes, Oliver Wendell, 102–103, 139, 303
Hoover, Herbert, 117, 227, 238
Howard, J. Woodford Jr., 45, 101, 120
Hruska Commission. *See* Commission on
    Revision of the Federal Court
    Appellate System
Hruska, Roman, 62
Hughes, Charles Evans, [Preface], 76, 102,
    223–224, 228, 261
Hughes Court, 97
Human Life Statute, 169–170, 210, 212
Hutchinson, Dennis J., 130
Hyde Amendment, 170, 206
Hyde, Henry, 169, 170, 206, 210, 212

Ideology
    of Supreme Court, 54–55, 57–59,
        65–67, 83, 88–90, 96–99, 102, 158,
        189–190, 297–303

348 / *Index*